"Cultivating a deeper relationship with one's own psyche and with the collective psyche of humanity is an unending journey that can be filled with adventure and fulfillment. Dr. Ortigo offers here a thoughtful and well-developed map and guide for the journey—from preparation through encounter through grounded integration into the activities of daily life. This is a marvelous book!"

—David E. Presti, Professor of Neurobiology, University of California, Berkeley
Author, Mind Beyond Brain: Buddhism, Science and the Paranormal and
Foundational Concepts in Neuroscience: A Brain-Mind Odyssey

"The wisdom, warmth, and maturity of Dr. Ortigo's understanding of the responsible use of psychedelics is reflected on each page of this provocative and insightful book. Dr. Ortigo offers a comprehensive map to ethical and personalized meaning-making while remaining deeply attuned to the myriad ways in which people are different. He succeeds in offering an authentic approach for navigating both the psychedelic experience and everyday life itself, using the timeless language of myth. One that is inclusive of people regardless of sexual orientation, gender, and cultural background. I wholeheartedly recommend this book to anyone that aspires to work with psychedelics. Avid and aspiring psychonauts, professional facilitators, therapists, experts and first-timers: everyone will find plenty of valuable lessons in this compelling read!"

—Daan Keiman, MA; Psychedelic & Buddhist Chapl
Lead Facilitator & Director of Ethics & Advocacy, S
Co-founder, Guild of Guides Netherlands

T0151179

"Few therapists in the field of psychedelic science can hold the complexity of both pragmatic concerns alongside the deep mystery of the psyche the way Dr. Ortigo does here, and with a humble grace that focuses more on generating questions than it does with answering them for you. What might be most impressive about Dr. Ortigo's work is the accessibility, even to newcomers, of his enticing invitation into deeper reflection, self-awareness, and ultimate transformation. Dr. Ortigo offers a crucible for the expert and novice alike as they embark into the journey of self, bringing opposites together in an artful play that many will find illuminating."

—Evan Sola, PsyD, MAPS Phase 3 Study Psychologist & Co-Therapist

"*Beyond the Narrow Life* serves as an atlas for any explorer seeking a greater sense of connectedness to themselves, others, and the universe. Dr. Ortigo deftly synthesizes existentialism, religion and spirituality, technology, and various schools of thought in psychology in order to guide readers toward "the big questions" with clarity. Depending on the motivation and intention of each individual reader, this book supports a range of expeditions from a tour through more mindful awareness to a full-fledged hero's journey. Bon voyage!"

—Chris Stauffer, MD, Oregon Health & Science University, Department of Psychiatry, MAPS Phase 3 Study Co-Investigator & Co-Therapist

"Dr. Ortigo has creatively and effectively synthesized an abundance of essential clinical information and psychological perspectives to offer a unique contribution to the emerging field of psychedelic psychotherapy and human development. This book is well written, compelling, accessible, and user-friendly. It was written to be a "friend" on the path or "way companion" for self-inquiry, psychedelic integration, psychological healing, spiritual liberation, and the cultivation and maturation of one's humanity. Like entering a labyrinth of possibilities with the best of supports and anchors, this innovative resource will likely become a classic in the emerging psychedelic renaissance. Readers can expect to be challenged, uplifted, surprised, and inspired."

—Harvey L. Schwartz, PhD, Clinical Psychologist & Co-founder, Polaris Insight Center; Dialogues with Forgotten Voices and The Alchemy of Wolves and Sheep

"Finally—a book that is equally useful for the lay public and licensed health professionals! This book should be required reading for anyone interested in psychedelics, psychedelic research, training or being a guide/therapist, or when working with anyone interested in using psychedelics in any setting. Dr. Ortigo presents a beautiful synthesis of material through stories, observations, objective data, models and graphs, insights, quotes, humor, and activities that allow the reader to participate, and encourages a deep dive into both pragmatic and philosophical questions."

—Karen Cooper, RN, BSN, MA, Instructional Supervisor, Center for Psychedelic Therapies and Research, California Institute for Integral Studies; Clinical Sub-Investigator, MAPS research studies; Former Lead Guide & Trainer, Usona Institute

"If you are looking for an original perspective on psychedelic integration through the lens of Jungian and existential themes, this book supersedes all expectations. Psychedelics are emerging as modalities for healing and self-exploration, with public interest growing by the day. Dr. Ortigo's approach to helping people find their own answers and ways of exploring profound questions evoked through psychedelic journeys comes through in all chapters. It's one of those books you'll keep coming back to as you go deeper into the mysteries of consciousness and transformation. Highly recommended for clinicians and self-seekers alike."

—Allison Feduccia, PhD, Founder & CEO, Psychedelic.Support; Co-founder, Project New Day

"Whether you are a psychonaut, an underground psychedelic therapist, or just curious about the emerging revolution in mental health care, you'll benefit from this practical, thoughtful guide to laying the groundwork and integration, the bookends of the psychedelic journey."

—Julie Holland, MD
Author, Good Chemistry: The Science of Connection from Soul to Psychedelics; Editor, Ecstasy: The Complete Guide

BEYOND
THE NARROW LIFE

BEYOND
THE NARROW LIFE

✦ ✦ ✦

A Guide for Psychedelic Integration
and Existential Exploration

Kile M. Ortigo, PhD

✦ ✦ ✦

Foreword by William A. Richards, PhD

SYNERGETICPRESS

Published by Synergetic Press, 1 Bluebird Court, Santa Fe, NM 87508
& 24 Old Gloucester St., London, WC1N 3AL England

Library of Congress Cataloging-in-Publication Data is available

Cover illustration by Gustavo Attab
Cover design by Lysander Alston-Kramer and Amanda Müller
Interior illustrations by Lysander Alston-Kramer
Managing Editor: Amanda Müller
Book design by Brad Greene

Printed in Canada by Marquis

TABLE OF CONTENTS

DEDICATION

To my teachers, formal and informal,
No matter how much I've learned, I keep realizing how much more there is to explore. Thank you for sparking my interest at every step.

To my clients,
I'm honored by how each of you continue to grow and put your trust in our work. I marvel at what's possible through healing. You give me hope for our future.

To my family, near and far,
Our paths may at times be quite different, but I know our hearts are connected always.

To the artists, storytellers, and mythmakers of the world,
You bring magic into our lives, and what you create is so much more than for entertainment alone. Keep sharing your messages to those who're willing to listen.

To loved ones I've lost, including my mentors,
You've taught me as much about how to live as how to approach death—with authenticity and love. I only hope to give back what I've been blessed to receive.

In memoriam:
Carol Ortigo
Janice Hocker Rushing
Steve Rao

FOREWORD

William A. Richards, PhD

Beware! This book may resemble others in your collection of contributions to the psychedelic frontier and the exploration of human consciousness, but it is much more than an exposition of intriguing ideas, concepts, and meditative procedures formulated by scholars, researchers and seers, either past or present. It is also not a collection of 'trip reports,' tantalizing the reader with wild, wonderful, and terrifying adventures within the distant corridors of our minds. Within this innocent-looking book there is power, quite incredible and transformative. With your permission, it will meet you exactly where you are. It will then guide you, ever so gently and wisely, in and through challenging terrain and towards increasing breadth of vision and perhaps even towards what we call the dawn of spiritual enlightenment. If you dare to turn another page, Dr. Ortigo will patiently walk beside you in this unfolding journey, never pushing, never criticizing, never taunting you by contrasting your favorite current insecurities and anxieties with the bliss of enlightened masters. When you need to rest a while, he'll sit with you beside the warmth of the campfire and even offer some touches of playfulness and humor.

With the tools of psychedelic substances, when competently and responsibly used, along with meditative procedures, reflection activities, and other interventions that now allow us to venture into the mystery that we are with reasonable safety and efficacy, those of us who have been immersed in the dominant view of ourselves, others, and the world within so-called Western culture, could well be on the verge of a new surge of development within human consciousness. Each of us is "discovering ourselves in the world" during what Buddhists call "one precious human life," realizing that we indeed are experiencing a journey, and one that is time limited. How much do we want to see? How awake would we like to become? What values do we allow to guide us as we move day by day towards that moment of cessation or transition that we call death? What would we like to contribute to those who will inhabit the earth and design the civilizations of the future following our departure? What words and concepts do we choose to attempt to express our discoveries and share them with others from the rich languages of philosophy, science, myth, and religious systems?

The structure that supports and suspends the contents of this book is often comprised of strong yet flexible fibers from existential philosophers and psychologists and also from pioneers in the art of deciphering symbolic or mythological language such as Joseph Campbell and Carl Jung. In terms of the familiar image of the teacher's finger pointing at the moon (or even at distant galaxies) while the students' attention is riveted on comprehending the teacher's finger, Dr. Ortigo embraces us all in our incredible diversity and invites us to look towards—and actually venture into—the unfathomable heights and depths that he himself humbly has been exploring, focusing not on his (or anyone else's) finger but on the frontier within us where science and vast experiential realms we often consider sacred now increasingly are meeting and interacting.

As recommended by Dr. Ortigo, please move through the pages ahead at your own pace, reflecting on whatever you find yourself writing in the suggested workbook reflections, and respectfully noting your own shifts of attitudes and behavior as they may become manifested during the routines of daily living. As enjoined by one of the great scholars of comparative religions, Huston Smith, full engagement with the wise guidance within this book can facilitate the transformation of our "states" of consciousness into "traits" of behavior as these spiritual, mystical, or otherwise profound *experiences* and similar forays into the depths of our minds become integrated into our daily *lives*, rich in meaning and perhaps potently transformative of the societies in which we live. Enjoy!

The times in which we find ourselves are exciting yet also tinged by a sense of foreboding. We have at our fingertips greater access to information, opinions, and ideas than ever before in human history. On a daily basis, we interact with increasingly sophisticated technologies with even more inventions on the horizon. The average human today is exposed to many more cultures and viewpoints than our ancestral relatives. The underbelly of this excitement is growing anxiety about where our world is headed and what the limits of human potential might be. As individuals, we may also ponder how to understand our place in the world when we are just one out of almost eight billion humans trying to find our way.

Exposure to different viewpoints can but does not always lead to greater understanding. The expanding polarization has made it painfully clear that something is not quite right. Yet few people agree on what that is. An optimistic point of view is that we're experiencing necessary growing pains. Our current discord reflects perhaps just a temporary reaction to our increasing awareness of complex problems. Eventually the now-dominant, scarcity-based win-lose mentality will give way to a mindset of shared humanity, open collaboration, and respect for our differences, not erasure of them. Part of our current struggle, in my opinion, is how we're confronting the loss of our big theories and ideas, ancient mythologies, and beliefs in a mysterious but existent Truth. Without these imperfect yet timeless sources of wisdom and perspective, we're left with a cacophony of disconnected systems of thought and opinions.

Whether linked or coincidental, another story is unfolding in parallel. Alongside the excitement and anxiety about the future of humanity and our planet, a strong re-emergence has been building momentum in the so-called psychedelic renaissance. This renaissance involves growing recognition that despite their cultural baggage in the West, psychedelics may act as useful tools in addressing mental health difficulties and general malaise. But anxiety still lurks underneath the more palpable excitement. How do these substances work to promote wellbeing? Who will have access to them? Who should be the gatekeepers (if any should exist at all)? Can we harness or even understand the profound psychospiritual themes elicited by these experiences?

If research continues to affirm the psychological benefits of psychedelic experiences, then we truly face a paradigm shift in the mental health field.[1] As with any paradigm shift, however, there will be unanticipated challenges to address alongside the potential for beneficial transformation. It's worth it, I believe, so that we can break free from what some academics have recognized as the limits of having overly specialized, disconnected, and narrow fields of study.[2] The work ahead of us will be difficult, but then again, it has never been easy to address human suffering.

In my professional exploration and training in legally sanctioned psychedelic-assisted psychotherapy, I have come to embrace an eyes-wide-open interest over a fear-based dismissal of its potential. I write this book, though, as a response to the unknown and the need to do our ethical due diligence. Will psychedelics become legal? Will the psychotherapeutic benefits outweigh the perceived and actual risks? We will know more in time. But no matter how this field evolves, a need exists for frameworks that explore themes that are elicited by psychedelics—both for people who are preparing and/or integrating an experience and for those who do not have access, interest, or the medical clearance to partake in such journeys.

Although more and more psychedelic media is being published, the growing public interest has been met largely with a relative scarcity of theory-driven yet accessible and pragmatic frameworks for understanding psychedelic experiences. I have spent much of my professional career and personal life exploring interdisciplinary theories, applying them in direct clinical care, and researching the effectiveness of treatments for trauma and its sequalae. Through this work, I have realized the importance of distilling the esoteric and abstract to the practical and actionable. If a concept only exists in the 'Ivory Tower' of elite academia, then it is largely meaningless to the rest of us. If an abstract idea has absolutely no bearing on our inner or outer world, then it is perhaps only good for intellectual indulgence.

This aspiration of bridging the esoteric with the grounded is my challenge in writing this book—translating ineffable experiences into words, images, and exercises that can introduce something useful to a diverse range of readers. The writing process has been humbling and exhilarating. As in therapy, and especially for a book like this one, it's critical for me to walk beside you and not ask of you anything I wouldn't or haven't already done myself. My hope is that this book and its activities open doorways that have always been there but have, for whatever reason, remained closed.

Although I'm a clinical psychologist, I have written this book outside of a rigid, sick-vs-healthy medicalized model of the psyche. Fostering psychological growth and wellbeing is something for which we should all strive, regardless of our prior experiences and the presence (or absence) of a diagnosed 'disorder.' This book is not a substitute for therapy. However, it may work well as a companion to therapy.

All that being said, as a licensed professional, I too must and have considered carefully the legal and ethical aspects of this work. At this time, I cannot encourage or condone the use of psychedelics outside of legally sanctioned contexts. In the United States at the time of this book's publication, these contexts include approved research settings, specific jurisdictions under sanctioned conditions (such as outlined in Oregon's recently passed ballot measure[a] and protected use for specific religious and indigenous communities. These settings prioritize safety, ethics, and specialized support.

Over time, safe and effective options for partaking in psychedelic journeys will likely grow substantially. In the meantime, I offer this book in the spirit of harm reduction for people who have already had psychedelic journeys and want to integrate their experience. I've written it as well to be a useful companion book for people waiting for legalization or access to psychedelic care. As the field expands in the future, we will continue to learn even more about the potential role of this and other frameworks for preparation and integration.

A Very Brief Overview of Psychedelics

Throughout much of our known human history, traditional use of psychedelics has often involved ceremonies and rituals of initiation and healing. Initiation rites and healing practices have varied greatly, but several cultures around the world and across time have used non-ordinary states of consciousness, whether elicited by psychedelic substances or intense breathwork, in their rituals. Here, for interested readers, I briefly introduce a few popular psychedelics that are discussed or alluded to within this book's journey. This overview is not exhaustive, but interested readers can find suggestions in Appendix III for additional resources about the history of psychedelics and related substances.

In the last century, the West has experienced two periods of renewed psychedelic awareness and use—the mid-20th century and our current renaissance of the early 21st century. Before these more recent introductions, psychedelics were likely part of less well-known Western history, chiefly through the Eleusinian Mysteries of Ancient Greece and various pre-Christian traditions and proto-Christian religious practices.[3]

The first reemergence of psychedelics in the West was largely due to two separate strings of events that unfolded across several decades: first, Swiss

---

[a] Oregon Measure 109, which was passed on 3 November 2020 by a popular vote.

chemist Albert Hoffman's discovery of LSD[b] in 1938 and accidental dosing in 1943 on the now celebrated but unofficial holiday known as Bicycle Day;[c] and second, American journalist Gordon Wasson's 1957 *Life* magazine article describing his experience in a Mazatec sacred mushroom ceremony facilitated by tribal elder María Sabina.[4] Due to the publicity of the latter, María Sabina suffered enormous harm. She was ostracized by her community, and her son was murdered in retaliation. Wasson, in turn, experienced a profound lifelong regret for publishing his article and inadvertently causing harm to Sabina and her community because of the overwhelming public interest that resulted. Nevertheless, the reintroduction of psychedelic mushrooms and their active ingredients, psilocybin and psilocyn, into Western society has been a major contributor to modern psychedelic communities around the world.

In more recent decades, ayahuasca has become popularized as a powerful psychedelic consumed in indigenous rituals of various South American tribal communities, such as the Shipibo people of Peru and the Shuar people of Ecuador.[5] Ayahuasca is a unique brew of two or more plants—traditionally, the *Banisteriopsis caapi* vine and the *Psychotria viridis* shrub. When combined, the MAO[d] inhibiting effects of the vine's alkaloids allow the active psychedelic compound DMT[e] from the shrub to survive oral digestion and pass through the blood-brain barrier.

In the West, the DMT molecule was first discovered by Canadian chemist Richard Manske in 1931, but it wasn't investigated for its psychotropic effects until Hungarian psychiatrist Stephen Szara did so in 1957.[6] In 2001, American psychiatrist Rick Strassman famously reported its effects in his book, *DMT: The Spirit Molecule*, in which he describes his research findings across several administrations of DMT to over sixty study volunteers.[7] Of particular note, DMT appears to be the only psychedelic compound that occurs naturally in the human body—for reasons still unknown. As a close chemical relative, 5-MeO-DMT[f] occurs in nature as well and can be derived from the dried excretions of the Sonoran Desert toad (*Bufo alvarius*) or from

---

[b] Lycergic acid diethylamide. Also known as acid.
[c] Technically, Bicycle Day is on April 19th, which was three days after Hoffman's accidental dosing on the 16th. The 19th is celebrated because it's the date Hoffman first ingested LSD on purpose. He began feeling its effects when he was riding home on his bicycle—which is definitely not a recommended activity while under the influence of psychedelics (according to modern psychedelic research studies and perhaps common sense).
[d] Monoamine oxidase
[e] N,N-dimethyltryptamine
[f] 5-methoxy-N,N-dimethyltryptamine

various plants, such as the crushed seeds of the *Adenanthera peregrina* tree of the Amazon rainforest.

Other naturally occurring classic psychedelics include ibogaine and mescaline. Ibogaine is derived from the bark of the iboga tree (*Tabernanthe iboga*) in Central Africa and has been used by various Pygmy tribes in the region. Unlike many of the classic psychedelics, ibogaine can have dangerous and even fatal cardiovascular effects. Mescaline comes from various species of cactus such as peyote and San Pedro. Peyote rituals, for example, have an ancient history in some Native American tribes and more recently has been incorporated in the pan-tribal American Indian Church.

Unlike naturally occurring classic psychedelics, LSD shares its origin with an extended family of psychedelic-esque substances created within Western laboratories. Two of these substances are particularly relevant to modern psychedelic research and were creations from chemist Sasha Shulgin's intrepid experimentation: the first, MDMA,[g] sometimes described as an empathogen for its 'heart opening' effects and healing capacities for posttraumatic stress and relational problems,[8] and the second, ketamine, a dissociative anesthetic with surprisingly diverse applications, from emergency sedation and pain relief to the treatment of depression.[9]

A Note on Cultural Humility and Exchange

Each psychedelic substance has a unique and varied cultural history, just as they have both shared and distinct psychoactive effects. As a Western myself, this book is largely informed by Western traditions and perspectives about the human experience. That said, many of these approaches have their roots in indigenous practices and non-Western traditions. To the extent possible, I have cited sources that either directly influenced my thinking or can act as further readings for people who want to take a deeper dive. Although I do not come from an indigenous community, nor have I been trained by indigenous elders, it remains important to acknowledge the indirect but critical influence many indigenous cultures have had on this book and much of our modern research.

The tension between cultural appropriation and respectful adaptation is a central issue when traversing multiple worldviews. Along our path, we face this same tension. As an American male, my cultural lens is interwoven into the fabric of this journey. Each of you reading this book has your own

----

[g] 3,4-Methylenedioxymethamphetamine

cultural heritage, and often multiple. This heritage affects how you approach this material. In psychedelic communities, ethical questions around cross-cultural exchange are incredibly salient and challenging. We might ask ourselves the following questions: Do we 'deserve' to enter a space disconnected from our culture of origin? If so, how do we demonstrate respect and care for such an honor? How might our presence impact other communities in unintended ways? Why do we even feel the need to have these experiences? After undertaking sacred rites, must we leave everything behind and abandon our previous community, culture, and relationships? What are our own cultural traditions around personal or spiritual growth? Can we reclaim them if we've lost contact with our heritage, our origins? Would that also address the ills of our time and our personal wounds or motivations?

These questions, though asked too infrequently, intersect with some core themes of this book's journey. Searching for meaning, belonging, or transformation, if done less consciously or without respect for others, can sometimes spread our pain without providing the antidote to whatever ills us. Healers, in all traditions, must navigate tensions around helping an individual without harming them further or allowing them to harm others. As secular healers, therapists have taken a role historically belonging to spiritual leaders, shamans, and priests. And us therapists face challenges in navigating multiple worlds too—our own wellbeing and that of clients, our ethical principles and the local laws, our knowledge and opinion and the importance of listening without assuming, the world of psychological science and the many worlds of individual experiences, culture, spirituality, and non-scientific forms of knowledge and understanding. There are many ways of 'knowing.' And many mysteries remain regardless of our chosen path. Too often modern therapy can skirt around these deeper mysteries and choose pragmatism over the profound. I often challenge myself by asking how can the profound also be pragmatic, even if imperfectly so?

Like most therapists, I work with clients from various cultural and religious backgrounds different than my own. This work can be incredibly enriching for both parties, but it requires acknowledging differences with awareness, respect, and openness. In crafting this book's journey, I started by asking: What does a multicultural, pan-spiritual yet atheist-inclusive myth-inspired guide look like? Is it even possible? Or, can I and others only adapt and create separate and distinct frameworks within smaller, more narrowly defined boundaries?

'Coexist' bumper stickers are nice, but when competition appears so ingrained, it's no surprise that ideal has historically been far from realized.

In our fragmented and mistrusting world, is it even an option to create something inclusive and flexible but sufficiently meaningful and straight-forward enough to be useful? Without a sense of community, many if not most people living in our disconnected world may remain uninitiated into a broader sense of community, shared humanity, or recognition of our connection to the earth and even the cosmos. In other words, we are disconnected, not because that is the reality but because we have not been shown many believable paths to be more than what we see on the surface.

My overarching approach is to be relatively agnostic about metaphysical conclusions based on psychedelic experiences—or personal opinions, more broadly speaking. I'm not here to convert or convince anyone of anything beyond the impor-tance of mindful exploration and integration. Al-though I am a clinical psychologist, a profession that holds some weight in my culture (depending on who you ask), my interdisciplinary studies and experiences have introduced me to the role of pow-er in any discussion on weighty topics such as those explored in this book. Jeff Guss, a psychiatrist and psychedelic researcher at New York University, introduced me to a paper both delightfully titled and wonderfully perceptive about some tensions we encounter when discussing psychedelics— Andy Letcher's "Mad Thoughts on Mushrooms: Discourse and Power in the Study of Psychedelic Consciousness."[10]

Letcher outlines different frames of reference in the various debates around psychedelics. One key takeaway is that *what* can and can't be said by *whom* in any given context is governed by often unspoken rules and assumptions. He also argues it's impossible to speak across these different frames of reference or to be truly objective. I've summarized

Holders of Truth (Knowledge) and the Dynamics of Power Foucault

	Pathological	Psychological	Prohibition	Recreational	Psychedelic	Entheogenic	Animistic
Focus of Discourse: Psychedelics are or are not…	Poison, physically or neurologically harmful	Medication or facilitators of psychotherapy	Dangerous and illegal drugs that threaten the public	A means to have pleasurable experiences that express personal freedom	Tools for self-exploration, growth, and creativity	Religious sacraments for encountering the 'God within'	Devices for encountering deities, spirits, aliens, etc.
Example Voices of 'Authority' (in the West)	Western Medicine, Medical Doctors, Mental Health Professionals	Psychologists, Psychiatrists, Therapists	Lawyers, Law Enforcement Officials	Everyday People	Independent Explorers of Consciousness, so-called 'Healthy Normals'	Religious or Spiritual Practitioners, Leaders, Scholars	Indigenous 'Shamans,' Spiritual Practitioners

Letcher's frames of reference below as well as the fundamental questions and assumed voices of 'authority.' The three frames of reference this book does speak to are psychological, psychedelic, and entheogenic.

Ultimately, my hope for this book is to provide just one voice to the larger chorus of this new psychedelic renaissance. There are many other voices to be heard—including yours. Together, we can create something truly special. Whereas this book is my humble offering, I, for one, look forward to hearing the beautiful music that results from your deeper reflections and distinctive talents.

Mythology as a Bridge that Transcends Time

In the grand scheme of our existence, it's unclear how psychologically different our modern struggles are compared to that of our distant ancestors. Almost all our past, our deep history, though so brief in the cosmic timescale, is lost. Most of it never was recorded. Much of it that was recorded also has been lost, from the burning of the Great Library of Alexandria to the oral traditions of indigenous cultures irreparably impacted or wiped out by colonization. Part of repairing this loss and harm is to reconnect, as best we can, to what we do know about our own cultural roots while continuing to listen intently to and learn from each other.

Not all knowledge that appears lost is quite as lost as we might fear. I say this in no way to diminish the tragedy of lost heritage and history but to consider the possibility that some wisdom can be found in hidden places—including our everyday experiences of being in the world. As knowledge of psychedelics spreads to people who never before would consider partaking in such experiences, we're faced with the challenge of needing inclusive and robust models for preparation and integration. We lack, however, what indigenous communities have—a shared understanding about what psychedelic experiences may mean to one's life.

This is where myth comes in. Existential psychologist and scholar Rollo May described myth as stories or "narrative patterns that give significance to our existence."[11] Echoing other thinkers, he further asserts that myth speaks to "an eternal truth in contrast to an empirical truth. The latter can change with every morning newspaper, when we read of the latest discoveries in our laboratories. But the myth transcends time."[12] This "eternal truth," whether or not it is indeed unchanging and knowable, is the source of great mysteries and beauty. But how do we receive the insights of myth in our modern world?

Beyond my work in clinical psychology, I've always deeply appreciated how myth-inspired fiction has served not only as a form of entertainment but also as a vehicle for communicating ancient wisdom while addressing our prior gaps of knowledge and insight. Mythology has always been alive. Its life is found through countless revisions that speak to an evolving culture, is tailored for the current ethos and societal problems, and serves a purpose both for the storytellers and the audiences involved in each retelling.

To be clear, I believe myth as much as science has a role to play in this new psychedelic renaissance and beyond. As you'll hear throughout this book, the power of myth involves the transmission of knowledge alongside warnings through the power of stories. As a species, we've appeared to have always had a strong imagination. For over a century now, we've had the technology to translate our stories into 'moving pictures'—film—and to share them around the world. Not all films are mythic in scale or scope, but the diversity of stories and audiences promises more voices can be heard than ever before. We just need to open our minds to hear and interpret their messages.

In the context of numerous, on-going global ecological, sociopolitical, and psychological crises, I can think of no better myth-inspired beginning than that offered by one of the greatest mythological representations in modern film, *The Lord of the Rings* trilogy. In an ethereal yet haunting voiceover, the unseen Elvish Goddess Galadriel whispers as she opens the first film:[13]

The world has changed.
I feel it in the water.
I feel it in the earth.
I smell it in the air.
Much that once was, is lost
For none now live who remember it.
And some things that should not have been forgotten, were lost.
History became legend, legend became myth,
And for two and a half thousand years,
The ring passed out of knowledge.

Unlike the One Ring created by the Dark Lord Sauron, a demonic force hellbent on domination, the Ring of Power for us is a metaphor for anything that holds great promise as well as great risk. Myth in all its forms reminds us that nothing's been said that hasn't been said before, and that's true of this book. But much has been lost in our modern world. And the infinite, contradictory messages we encounter can harm and confuse as much as they can clarify and support the quest for insight.

This book is to connect us to our various pasts, sometimes in subtle ways, and to bring forward questions that persist in our present lives as well as in our future. Above all, I hope it helps you discover your own inner wisdom and truth, however lightly held and ever unfolding it may be. This book may be about psychedelics to an extent, but not only or even primarily. Its material comes too as much from intuition and heart as it does from intellect and knowledge. There are many roads to Rome, or in this case, various realms of human experience, and if you're willing to search, you can find so much more than what's offered in a life narrowly contained within the boundaries of modern societies, ideologies, and our default modes of consciousness.

This journey is not intended to give you all the answers but to support you in uncovering your own insights. They were there all along, but our ordinary responsibilities and concerns can easily distract us. These everyday tasks have a place too, but to shift into greater awareness and a better integrated understanding of ourselves, we must do the work—and not forget the importance of continued practice. This book may contain some 'answers' and yet only ones that reveal more terrain to explore. Just like in a psychedelic journey, what you find depends on your intentions alongside your willingness to embrace the unexpected.

Trust, explore, and find your hidden pearls of wisdom. Know that if you put in the work, the reward is yours. And its benefits may not end with you and your own interests but can resonate throughout your larger sphere of influence. Let there be surprises. And let there be obvious truths. Both are part of integration because both are part of life. It is with utmost respect and care that I have aimed to write this guide. I hope you gleam some insights and find some answers along the way.

EDITORIAL NOTE

The author's use of singular first-person pronouns ('I,' 'my') refers to his voice or experience. Second-person pronouns ('You' 'yours') refers to the reader as an individual. Most importantly, the frequent use of inclusive, first-person plural pronouns ('we' 'our' 'us') is intended as a general perspective of shared humanity, not as indicating a shared philosophical perspective, culture, or experience. In a similar vein, general terms like 'Western,' 'Eastern,' 'modern,' 'religious,' 'spiritual,' etc., are generally intended in their broadest, least absolute form.

As much as possible, this book uses gender neutral language such as the singular 'they' to avoid inaccurate, unnecessary, or distracting gender-specific pronouns or terminology. Occasionally direct quotes have been updated with gender neutral language indicated by the use of brackets. The exception is when doing so would require extensive bracketing that would be appear gratuitous and distracting.

To reduce wordcount and increase readability, the author has at times minimized the use of conditional words like 'may,' 'could,' 'might,' etc., which from the perspective of scientific, philosophical, and psychological scholarship is generally much more accurate than declarative statements of certainty. Most statements that appear to suggest absolute certainty or consistency across time, space, cultures, and individuals are not intended as the author's assertion of Truth.

DISCLAIMER

This book and its activities are provided in the spirit of harm reduction, for educational purposes, and for the use in personal and societal reflection. Its contents are not intended to advocate for the use of psychedelics under any circumstances beyond those offered in legally sanctioned, culturally respectful, and ethically appropriate settings. Neither the author nor the publisher assumes any responsibility for the potential legal, medical, psychological, or social consequences that may arise from personal use of psychedelics and/or related compounds.

CHAPTER 1

A Journey Not Taken Lightly—
Introduction to the Choice

> It's important to live life with the experience, and therefore the knowledge, of its mystery and of your own mystery.... The big question is whether you are going to be able to say a hearty yes to your adventure.
>
> — Joseph Campbell, *The Power of Myth*[1]

Psychedelic journeys can unfold in seemingly infinite ways. After all, the word *psychedelic* means to manifest the mind,[2] and the mind is infinitely mysterious and complex. Psychedelics can reveal previously unimagined realms that inspire awe and wonder. They can also be more harrowing and challenging than expected, especially when undertaken in the wrong context and without the support of skillful guides. Psychedelics, by being powerful, deserve respect. Challenges can arise alongside triumphs. But life itself is this way. It's a journey. Full of choices. The freedom to choose our path is one of the gifts of consciousness. Yet consciousness is a fountain from which we often drink only in small portions. If we choose to take in more, with or without psychedelics, we may become more aware of not only our minds but also our place within the world or even the universe.

This book is about expanding consciousness by exploring profound questions. Its path is theoretically open to all but seldomly realized to its fullest potential. Why? Because regardless of the path chosen, such journeys can be fraught with traps and unexpected risks. Undertaking a path of transformation seems beyond the capacity of many of us trying to survive day-to-day. At first glance, expanding consciousness appears to be a luxury reserved only for the most stable, successful, powerful, and well-functioning. It may be surprising to hear this book includes as many challenges (if not more) for the well-off socialite 'on the top.' Luxury can be a barrier to modesty and deeper awareness. People who've lived through hardship and survived might be better prepared for our current journey. When we meet life's challenges openly and honestly, work through what we need to, and find our inner strength, we've already shown our resilience.

Accessing inner strength, then, is earned, not because it wasn't there before but because it's sometimes buried deep, covered up by distractions and fears.

Saying 'yes' to a path towards greater awareness, and hopefully wholeness, means embracing uncertainty. It requires courage, patience, and a willingness to experience discomfort. Discomfort often precedes growth. It signals the need to adapt and acts as a herald for changes to come. No matter the specifics of what's led you here, in the end, to an extent at least, we're all in the same boat. We all confront similar questions, even if we do so from very different angles. What's thrilling, though, is finding your own answers and meaning. Whatever you discover will be well earned and yours to keep.

This chapter provides the first step. It introduces the path forward and serves as its 'call to adventure.' By the end, you'll have examined your motivations and intentions for embarking on the journey, weighed the pros and cons of doing so, and started earnest preparations for what's to come. Taking this time to reflect and prepare demonstrates the level of respect required to explore the profound, whether aided by psychedelics or by sustained inquiry alone.

The Choice—An Informed Consent

No one can force you to grow, nor should they. Personal growth is a value an individual either holds or does not. And that value, in turn, is either expressed in life or not. At a basic level, your choice to read this book means you have an interest in growing and expanding your awareness, integrating a greater understanding of yourself, and discovering layers of meaning. The power of that interest may be inchoate, but trust that it's an important inner resource you already possess.

Stability and certainty may be values you hold dearly. If they're stronger than all others, then exploring the themes in this book may not be for you. Asking questions about the nature of existence and the structure and content of the self tends to elicit many possible reactions. This process, if undertaken honestly, is by necessity somewhat disruptive. Existential growth often comes from some kind of existential distress. If you've already had an existential crisis, at any age, then you know what that can feel like. Based on my own experiences, I appreciate the intro to Charles Dickens's *A Tale of Two Cities*:

> It was the best of times, it was the worst of times, it was the age of wisdom, it was the age of foolishness, it was the epoch of belief, it was the epoch of incredulity, it was the season of Light, it was the season of Darkness, it was the spring of hope, it was the winter of despair, we had everything before us, we had nothing before us.[3]

In times of crisis and growth, we confront multiple possibilities. An existential journey questions the ground upon which we stand. Were our decisions the best ones we could have made? What of the life we have not lived? A mounting realization of choice, alongside a dissatisfaction with some aspects of life as it is, create the perfect storm of despair and hope, blame and ownership, questions and beliefs, however tentatively held. In a powerful way, though, such a crisis can make you feel more alive than ever before.

Crises are often thrown at us out of nowhere by life's twists and turns. This book isn't that. It's a curated guide through these same questions. You're not alone here. I won't be throwing you into the deep end without a lifejacket. The choice is yours to make, at every step. As a psychologist, I understand the importance of making an informed choice. Once you've chosen to proceed, we'll go over the book's approach and start setting you up for success. You're the master of your own path. Realizing that can give you the strength to face almost anything.

As with any major decision, it's helpful to weigh potential risks and benefits. Do you feel prepared to embark on a journey filled with questions and few tangible answers? Is your life situated so that you can openly and courageously say 'yes' to this adventure? Taking time to reflect on this decision empowers you with personal freedom and agency—key ingredients to success

Exercise 1.1 provides a systematic guide for making this first crucial decision. It has the added benefit of introducing the type of activities you'll be doing if you choose to move forward. Self-reflection is necessary to foster personal growth. This activity will start with your initial intentions for picking up this book. We'll revisit these intentions as they evolve, so don't worry if they aren't as fleshed out as you'd prefer. Most of this form, though, involves reflecting on the potential risks and rewards of doing this deeper work in your life as it is now.

Exercise 1.1

Making the Choice: Weighing the Benefits & Risks of Journeying

Reflection Question	My Response
What are my intentions for taking this journey? Do I have an ultimate goal or outcome in mind?	I want to...
To weigh benefits and risks, you can think both in general terms and in regard to specific domains. Note any thoughts related to each area that seems relevant.	
What benefits might I gain from undergoing this journey?	**I might benefit by...**
Mood and ability to cope with my emotions	
Physical wellbeing	
Professional responsibilities and work life	
Relationships with loved ones (family, partner, friends, children, etc.)	
Spiritual life	
Other personally relevant domain:	
What risks might I be taking by undergoing this journey?	**I might risk...**
Mood and ability to cope with my emotions	
Physical wellbeing	
Professional responsibilities and work life	
Relationships with loved ones (family, partner, friends, children, etc.)	

Spiritual life	
Other personally relevant domain:	
What does my intuition (my 'gut instinct') tell me to do?	**My intuition tells me…**

Weighing the benefits and risks and factoring in my intuition, I choose at this time to say…		
☐ Yes to the journey! ⬇	☐ No, for now ⇩	☐ Maybe, I need more time to decide ⇩
Awesome! You've made a well-considered decision and chose to follow us down the rabbit hole. Continue reading.	That's totally cool. You're showing insight into what's important to you now and what you need. Spend more time reflecting, if that's helpful, or consider getting support. When you're ready, you can always return.	

If you're still reading, then I offer my sincere congratulations on making a thoughtful choice to proceed. This first decision will continue to resonate throughout your journey. Whenever in doubt, revisit your answers, update them, and adjust your pace as needed. Now that you've said 'yes' to the *call to adventure*, we're ready to preview what lies ahead.

The Path of the Journey— How a Mythological Framework Charts the Way

Creating a robust framework for the human journey is an impossible task for any individual. Luckily for us, countless people have contributed to this eternal project. We humans are elaborate storytellers. From the oral myths of ancient times to the modern films we enjoy at the local theater, we've always appreciated a good story. Beneath the surface, though, these stories hold meaning beyond entertainment.

According to legendary mythologist Joseph Campbell, one broader narrative rises above the rest and weaves together important lessons and warnings about the human experience. He calls this version of the never-ending story the *monomyth* or *hero's journey*.[4] It represents an overarching framework for understanding what it means to be human, trials and triumphs alike. Variations of the monomyth are found in numerous cultures spanning recorded history. In its broadest form, the journey begins with a person heeding a *call to adventure*—which you've heard in some form prior to picking up this book. And by now, you've answered this call with a 'yes.'

Campbell fleshed out his mythological framework in his book *The Hero with a Thousand Faces*.[5] Even if you've never heard of him, you'll know the story if you've watched popular film series like *Star Wars, Harry Potter, The Lord of the Rings*, or *The Matrix*. Almost every Marvel movie also shares elements of this overarching narrative. Although details differ in each telling, a general structure of the monomyth involves a protagonist working through the phases of Departure, Initiation, and Return.[6] The monomyth is not a fairy tale for kids. It's a story about overcoming challenges, avoiding pitfalls and temptations, and reaching a higher level of consciousness not only for personal growth but also for the good of one's community.

With this book, we too will follow the broader narrative of the hero's journey. Our next step is to cross the first threshold into another realm. The major task is preparing not only to find but to embrace the insights that emerge. As with any journey, your exact path may vary, but some key destinations are often shared along the way. These destinations for us are called waypoints and correspond to nine chapters. Each chapter represents a critical area for reflection, paired with concrete activities to aid your explorations. I've split these chapters into three story arcs that parallel the path of the mythic hero. Though not by accident, these arcs also conveniently parallel the three phases of psychedelic therapy—*Preparation, Psychedelic Experience*, and *Integration*.

Our path, then, follows three major arcs, each consisting of three chapters. These major arcs are: 1) Expanding Awareness, 2) Confronting Existential Trials, and 3) Integrating the Self. In myth, allies are critical to success and come in many forms. So too for us. Most fundamental is how the book itself serves as a guide.[7] Each arc introduces an additional metaphorical ally in the form of an attitude or quality that can support your explorations of the overarching theme.

That's a lot to digest. As a summary, Box 1.1 connects these arcs with the phases of the monomyth and psychedelic therapy. The rest of this chapter will preview the themes contained within each arc. Don't worry about the details just yet. We'll get there in time, and I'll remind you where we're at throughout each stage. The following preview simply acts like a teaser for a movie you've already decided to watch. You wouldn't want too many spoilers up front, right? It's good to be surprised—even if it's because you forgot what you already knew.

Box 1.1

Parallels Spanning the Monomyth, Psychedelic Therapy, and This Book's Journey

Monomyth	Psychedelic Therapy	This Book's Journey
Departure	Preparation	Expanding Awareness
Initiation	Psychedelic Experience	Confronting Existential Trials
Return	Integration	Integrating the Self

Arc 1—Expanding Awareness

Any departure requires some preparation. A crucial part of our preparation is fostering expanded awareness. In traditional models of psychology, awareness is often equated to consciousness of experience or oneself. Expanding consciousness can involve cultivating mindfulness and gaining greater insight into one's personality or typical behavior or emotional patterns. Deeper insight requires acknowledging the *unconscious*—that is, our individual collection of implicit yet influential motivations, hang-ups, and beliefs. In our psychedelic-informed journey, however, awareness of one's personal unconscious is only the tip of the iceberg. In fact, an iceberg is one of the most common metaphors to describe the human psyche. As Figure 1.1 shows, the most surface-level visible part of ourselves is the *persona*—what we readily display to others. Below that is the *ego*—what helps us organize and make sense of ourselves and deal with external 'reality.' Submerged in the water is the *personal unconscious*. Aspects of the ego reside here too. A major division exists between the conscious and unconscious—what's exposed, seen by ourselves and others, and what's lurking beyond our awareness and the secrets we keep.

From a psychedelic lens, even this modification may be too small. If we expand the image further, we might propose something more like Figure 1.2. By broadening our viewpoint even a little, we may uncover structures so different, foreign, and unseen that they shatter our conceptualization of an orderly, unified, and contained mind. Here could lie many elements of the *collective unconscious,* what's not specific to the individual but to all of humanity. Beyond that, unknown, non-human content and processes could live. This idea might seem incredulous. It certainly once did to me. Yet, understanding the psyche, in all its complexity, ends in becoming humbled. We apply organizational structures and principles to simplify and understand what may be incomprehensible to our conscious mammalian brains.

Even so, we're but one small part of a cosmos full of mystery. Expanding awareness must include that which isn't even human—in other words, pretty much the entire universe. Alongside the contents of the human psyche will be a complementary exploration of the mysteries of the cosmos itself and the non-human nature of reality—as we know it at least. Acknowledging

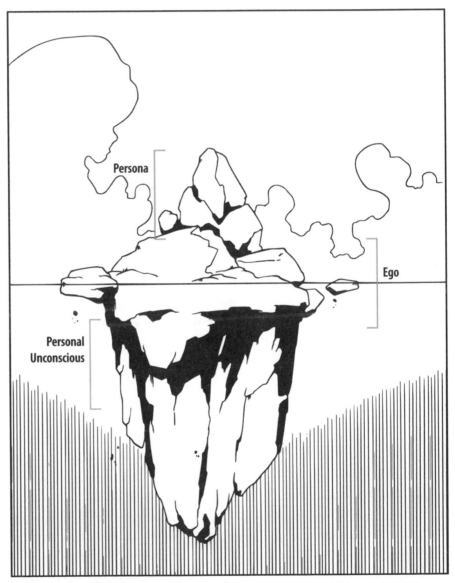

Figure 1.1 Basic iceberg model of the psyche—the conscious and the unconscious

The Mysterious Unknown

Figure 1.2 Speculative psychedelic model of the psyche—the conscious, the unconscious, and the mysterious unknown

mysteries and the boundaries of knowledge isn't saved for the mystical. It's basic science. Science, arguably in its most unadulterated form, is a philosophical approach to gaining knowledge through systematic empiricism, experimental design, mathematical analysis, and logical inferences. Its corresponding method requires formulating and testing hypotheses based on theoretical models and building upon already accepted, if not fully confirmed, knowledge.

What that means in a nutshell is science exists because we understand the limits of the human mind. And that there are more unknowns than knowns, more questions and ideas than firm answers. In reality, as science collects data and evidence to address our basic questions, it adds exponentially more questions—some not even considered beforehand. That's either scary or exciting! Unlike non-scientific viewpoints, though, science does not speak confidently about, or at all, to what cannot be tested or falsified.[8] Those domains, unfortunately, are probably the majority of what constitutes our deepest questions.

During a humorous but informative on-stage interview, the popular astrophysicist Neil deGrasse Tyson was asked, "In your career as a scientist, if there is one question you wish to address…what would that science question be?" After a brief pause, he responded:

> I wonder if, in fact, the human intellect is sufficient to actually decode the full operations of this universe in which we live…. I lose sleep on that question each night…. My cop-out answer is I think often about the questions we do not yet know to ask because [of] discoveries yet to come, but when they arrive, will put us in a new vista, a new place to stand enabling us to see questions undreamt of and unimagined before we got there. So, when I again lay awake at night, I ponder what kinds of questions lay beyond our reach…. And, by definition, I can't because we haven't gotten there yet, but that doesn't mean I shouldn't dream of that frontier.[9]

It's from this place of humble yet informed curiosity that we embark on our voyage. We'll start with what we 'know' about the universe encapsulating us, before we expand to the unknowns within each individual—all the while realizing 'unknowable' may not reflect an honest appraisal. The answers may exist but be beyond what our human minds can ever truly understand.

To sum up, our first arc peers behind the veil of our everyday lives and tries to open our minds to other possibilities. The attitude we foster here is curiosity. The experiences that hopefully result are ones of wonder and awe.

These experiences prepare us for facing the more personal and sometimes heavier content in our second arc.

Arc 2—Confronting Existential Trials

If you're still with me, the good news is that our second arc focuses on very human-centric concerns. Each is framed as a trial of initiation. Each trial involves an existential domain of inner conflict and fear simply inherited by being human. When applied to our individual lives, an existential perspective can be a stark contrast to many assumptions we might make about life—for example, that everyone has a soul mate, a most fulfilling lifepath, or destiny. Questioning these assumptions may sound disheartening. Without certainty, then are our lives without meaning? A nihilist might end with that conclusion. But buried in this perspective is a lot of room for personal agency and power that will unfold throughout this book. As within a psychedelic experience, what manifests can be unexpected and beyond logic. At the same time, something in these experiences are significant to people who've had them. Something similar can occur when we openly confront life's greatest questions. Accordingly, then, our second arc looks deeper into the void. Armed with curiosity and an expanded awareness, you can pass each existential trial, and in doing so, you might discover deeper parts of yourself and hidden strengths. These strengths won't deny your humanity but will embrace your authenticity.

Arc 3—Integrating the Self

Confronting existential trials is central to our mythic quest. But we can't stop there. The final leg of our journey is about integrating insights and moving past a narrow, ego-dominated understanding of ourselves, others, and the world. As referenced earlier, the ego is a key structure of the mind. Its core functions keep us safe and manage the often unrealistic desires and impulsive parts of ourselves we fear we cannot, or should not, let loose upon the world. From this viewpoint, it appears the ego is a good thing, and it's certainly a necessary component of mental health and wellbeing. So, why would we want to sideline one of our most important allies? Well, the brief answer is that the ego can get so good at its job that our conscious selves become too rigid and too conventional—too 'functional' at the expense of a more flexible, complete, and integrated self. In this arc, we'll not seek to destroy the ego. Just loosen its reigns and question some of its motivations and assumed solutions to the problems of our unconscious and to the demands of society.

Last but not least—or not even last if we're being nonlinear—is the symbolic and creative components of the larger human journey. What comes before is at least partially dominated by the verbal and intellectual. It's contained within the confines of a book, after all. Throughout, though, you'll be learning from a variety of other self-expressive, sensory, and emotional activities. Our ending is no ending at all, but a launching pad for continued engagement within your corner of existence. Its goal is to provide guidance and clues for answering the question, "So, where do I go from here?" and to embrace continuing explorations, practices, and creativity to realize the range of possibilities that may lie ahead.

The Process of the Journey—How to Use this Book

You now have a broad if not puzzling preview of some themes along our path. If you remain on board, you might be asking, "How on Earth are we going to do this?" Good. That question relates to the process for using this book. There are certainly many options. However, if I could give some concrete recommendations, they'd be as follows.

Tip 1—Find your own pace. This journey is not a race nor a competition. There's not even a clear, one-size-fits-all endpoint. Some chapters and concepts may be more challenging for you than others. That's not only okay, it's actually an encouraging sign. Remember, growth isn't always easy. Still, you're the best judge as to whether you're coping well with any challenges that may arise. A back-and-forth flow exists between *exploration,* which allows us to discover new insights, and *integration,* which requires time and effort at putting those insights into practice. If you need more time at certain places, give yourself permission to do so. Taking time doesn't mean stopping your journey. Maintaining momentum, though, is important. When needed, pause to reaffirm any of your self-care and coping practices, and reach out to supportive people in your life. Strong emotions may surface, but they shouldn't overwhelm your ability to function. If anything starts to cause problems, then slow down, do something fun (and mindless!), and come back when you have built up your inner resources. You don't need to give up just to slow down.

Tip 2—Practice activities and go beyond simply reading chapters. It's important to balance intellectual learning with learning through experience. Reading a book alone cannot make you grow and expand. That happens through applying what you've learned and experiencing new ways of relating to yourself, others, and the world. There's a parallel with psychedelics. A transcendent experience alone doesn't necessarily lead to integrating the insights into one's life. The activities and reflections for each chapter are crucial for the integration process, so I suggest trying them out and seeing what happens.

Tip 3—Avoid making quick decisions. Common, sage advice for people after having a psychedelic experience is to hold off on making major life decisions upon returning to their everyday life. That's for everyone, no matter how positive and meaningful a journey may have been. Why? Making rash decisions can have unforeseen consequences. Remember all those life domains you considered earlier? Your emotional and physical wellbeing, work and finances, relationships, spirituality, etc. Keep those factors in mind as you move forward. Many upcoming reflections will, by necessity, raise questions in several—if not all—of those life domains. Sometimes, you'll reaffirm what you know. At other times, you may raise doubts. Know that a thought or feeling can exist without requiring a response. Except for sudden life-or-death situations, moving quickly from an emotion or idea to action is rarely the best approach, even if in the end, you still choose to make a change. Pausing before action is a sign of self-discipline, which supports your long-term wellbeing. Remember, this book is a journey, not a final destination. If you've realized you need to leave a toxic job or relationship, that's great and may be the direction to go in. But, giving yourself time lets you examine the decision from multiple angles, and thus confirm it's the right move to make. It also allows you to prepare for any stress a change might entail. Whether prompted by a psychedelic journey or this book, taking time to make major decisions improves your likelihood of success.

Tip 4—Share the journey with others. You might want to talk to your closest friends or family members about the journey on which you're embarking. Your existing relationships are powerful tools for growth. Self-reflection is not a purely private endeavor. It can catapult to new levels by authentic conversations with mature, insightful people you trust and respect. That doesn't mean taking their perspective and adopting it as your own. But having genuine connections and discussions with trusted others can flesh out and give life to your ideas and feelings. No one needs to convert or be converted; only to feel supported, loved, and challenged. One option is to complete this book together. Each person can read the material, practice the exercises, and then check in with each other before moving onto the next chapter. Having a travel partner can do wonders for maintaining motivation and deepening your insights.

Tip 5—Consider starting (or continuing) psychotherapy. Therapy isn't the only tool, but it's a great one for personal development. Not all therapists will be trained or knowledgeable in all areas explored in this book. That's fine, and even beneficial if you're able to maintain your own exploration of answers when someone else, even a therapist, shares a different perspective. The role of therapy here may be to make sure you maintain balance, avoid going too far or too fast down the rabbit hole, or have someone who's 'on your side,' reliably available if you should need them. Confronting profound questions about yourself and your place in the cosmos and our modern world can evoke contents of your mind that laid just beneath the surface. It can be uncomfortable but also incredibly fruitful. If you're not already in therapy, then the following signs might signal you'd benefit from additional support:

- Increased anxiety or fear related to any topic addressed (particularly ones like death, loneliness, meaninglessness).

- Depressed mood, hopelessness, trouble falling or staying asleep, increased or decreased appetite or weight, decreased libido, diminished energy levels, and/or lack of enjoyment in most areas of life (including things you used to enjoy)[10]

- Increased stress or dissatisfaction in your career or relationships. Some distress is normal and even an impetus for reading a book like this one. Sometimes, though, stress may be too high to manage alone. I don't mean simply to tolerate and push through. I mean being willing to acknowledge distress, actively cope, and make wise decisions that balance your emotional needs and larger goals.

Tip 6—Use trial-and-error. As with my clients, I encourage a trial-and-error approach. Do what works for you. If you're enjoying a certain topic, feel free to continue exploring it. That may mean spending extra time doing all recommended activities or practicing certain ones even after moving onto other chapters. Repeat what you want to repeat. If after reviewing a chapter, you think its content is less relevant or meaningful for you at this time, you can spend less time with it. But first, maybe ask why it seems unimportant. No matter your answer, you can always return and do a deeper dive when it makes more sense. As you find material that resonates, you can be creative and generate your own exercises that expand upon your insights. All these options assist in individualizing your journey, which in many ways is the most critical task.

Tip 7—Have fun! In life, adventure, pleasure, enjoyment, and humor provide nourishment. At times, I'll offer moments of levity. I hope doing so can balance the reverence of this book's heavy material with occasional lightheartedness. These moments aren't to show disrespect. Maybe they land, maybe they don't. But finding your own humor is most important. Psychedelics can be playful even when they invoke deep reflections. Continue to do the things you enjoy in life. Eat your favorite dishes, go on hikes, watch movies, read fiction, and play video games. Working within these depths requires knowing when to come up for air. I won't know exactly when you need to inject more humor and joy into your life while undergoing this journey, but I trust you know when you need a break. Remember to relax, let loose, be silly, and laugh.

Tip 8—Engage with modern myth. You might consider watching films and television shows or reading books that are personally meaningful, resonate with your cultural worldview or heritage, and/or explore relevant psychological or mythical themes. You might choose ones that hold the spark of childhood magic or new stories that appeal to your modern sensibilities, perspectives, or concerns. I'll occasionally reference specific myths and films, but since this journey is yours first and foremost, personalize it by exploring media tailored to your tastes.

The Features of the Journey—
What to Expect from Each Chapter

Tackling the greatest questions about life can be daunting. Even the most practiced and intrepid psychonauts can have some fear before entering a psychedelic state. Some level of unease is normal. And perhaps honest because one never knows what could happen. That's the thrill and the risk. The possibilities are maybe infinite. Not having a guide, shaman, or therapist to support you during a psychedelic journey, though, amplifies the risks.

Lucky for us, using a book has one benefit over taking a psychedelic. As you've already experienced, I can preview the contents of our journey and give you a heads up about any potential problems you may confront. Another benefit is that I can provide a more consistent structure. That structure involves not only the larger three-arc journey, which weaves the themes together to build a narrative, but also the features shared by each chapter within each arc. As we disassemble and reassemble the ground underneath us, having some consistent structure increases a sense of safety. Box 1.2 reviews the shared features and structure of each chapter.

Box 1.2
Shared Features of Each Chapter

Quote & Introduction
A relevant or inspiring quote followed by a preview, rationale, or teaser to introduce the chapter's major theme and tie it to ones that came before

Self-Reflections Check-In
A pause before diving deeper into the current chapter's theme, offering time to reflect on the unfolding impact of the previous chapter's content and the activities you chose to practice afterwards

Core Chapter Content
A series of explorations that chart key concepts, ideas, and frameworks relevant to the chapter's theme, including how it relates to both psychedelic and human experience more broadly, occasionally interspersed with simple exercises that personalize your explorations of the theme

Application in Everyday Life
A box of suggestions for how you might apply or explore further insights related to the chapter's theme in everyday life with concrete examples to illustrate

Psychedelic Journey Report
An anonymous, genuine account of a person's psychedelic experience, de-identified but illustrative of how the chapter's theme can emerge in psychedelic states and/or how afterwards a person might create meaning from and integrate the experience in their life

Grounding Words—A Brief Summary
A quick survey of major topics covered in the chapter and things hopefully accomplished simply by reading and thinking about the material. Sometimes the summary hints at possible implications for later chapters

Your Assignment, Your Choice
A key component of this book is how it offers a curated menu of recommended activities or resources to personalize your experience and explorations. Each destination contains four options for gaining additional insights related to its main theme

Travel Journal

Each chapter ends with a journal prompt with 3-4 reflection questions tied to the chapter's theme, which allow you to document your personal journey. You may respond in various ways: with simple prose, poetry, drawings, or other creative expressions, and with a stream-of-consciousness or through more careful, systematic reflection—all options guided by personal inspiration, proclivities, intentions, or goals. Your Travel Journal can also become a daily journaling practice that chronicles your work in this book, your life occurring in parallel, and a place to record your dreams

Meditation

A script with brief instructions for practicing a focused meditation, usually lasting 10-15 minutes, and related to a core concept within the chapter; these meditations consistently comprise one of the four options available in each chapter's recommended assignments

By keeping the basic structure consistent, I hope you feel more secure in exploring each topic. Having this consistency provides a basic idea of what to expect, a metaphorical railing to hold onto as you bravely look towards the unknown.

Initial Preparations—Self-Care Plan

As noted earlier, every journey requires preparation. To support your success, I recommend creating a personalized self-care or safety plan. Exercise 1.2 will guide you in constructing one. Although it provides the structure, the contents of the plan should be highly personalized and incorporate your already-existing insights about what makes you feel healthy physically and psychologically. When in doubt, enlist the help of others—your therapist, if you have one, and your friends, partner, or close family members. Accessing social support is a key ingredient to any self-care plan.

Exercise 1.2

Creating a Journey Self-Care Plan

My Journey Self-Care Plan

To keep myself sufficiently grounded, clearheaded, and healthy, I benefit from the following:

PHYSICAL HEALTH CHECKLIST	MENTAL HEALTH CHECKLIST	SOCIAL SUPPORT CHECKLIST
• Adequate sleep _____ hrs/night	• Pleasure, fun, and hobbies such as: _____	• Regular contact with close friends
• Sufficient nutrition	• Meditation or mindfulness practice	• Practices of kindness, giving and receiving
• Physical activity (yoga, hiking, weight-lifting, running, team sports, etc.)	• Limited use of substances or addictive behaviors (phones, tv, etc.)	• Good communication with my family (partner, parents, children, etc.)
• Other: _____	• Other: _____	• Other: _____
• Other: _____	• Other: _____	• Other: _____
• Other: _____	• Other: _____	• Other: _____

The following will let me know I need to slow down, get extra support, or recommit to my plan:

MY BODY	MY THOUGHTS	MY BEHAVIOR
• Being tired	• Negative thoughts about myself	• Isolating myself from others
• Loosing appetite or weight	• Negative thoughts about other people	• Being irritable and impatient with others
• Acute or worsened physical pain	• Negative thoughts about the world	• Calling out of work more than usual
• Skipping doctor's appointments (checkups, dental, vision, etc.)	• Thoughts that are all-or-none or black-and-white	• Drinking more alcohol or smoking more than usual (or is healthy)
• A diffuse, general feeling of being 'not well'	• Repetitive thoughts or obsessions	• Not doing things I usually enjoy, like: _____
• Changes in blood pressure and/or heart rate	• Thoughts of hopelessness or being powerless	_____

- Other: _____   • Other: _____   • Other: _____

  _____   _____   _____

- Other: _____   • Other: _____   • Other: _____

  _____   _____   _____

- Other: _____   • Other: _____   • Other: _____

  _____   _____   _____

In response to any problems I might observe, I will:

- Reach out to talk to my close friends, family, or community including:

  _____

  _____

- Start or recommit to professional support, as in psychotherapy, psychiatry for medications, and/or faith leaders in my community. Professionals that come to mind include:

  _____

  _____

- Revisit and adjustment my safety plan

- Slow down the pace of my journey and reading

- Call the 24-hour crisis hotline at 1-800-273-8255

- Try out the online chat options at SuicidePreventionLifeline.org

- Other:

  _____

  _____

When in doubt, I know all I need to do is pause, breath, and center myself in the present moment. If helpful, I can write down and remind myself of a healing mantra or positive, wise, uplifting statement. My mantra, for now, is:

_____

_____

Grounding Words—A Brief Summary

As discussed earlier, no matter how deep and esoteric we go, we'll have a touchstone in each chapter's summary. Today, you took your first major step. You learned a bit about the universal yet highly personal journey of asking questions about the cosmos, consciousness, and the human experience. You also learned that doing so was a choice, just like any other, but one not to be taken lightly. Heeding this warning, you reflected on your ultimate goal as you understand it now, weighed the possible pros and cons, including the potential impact on important areas of your life, and then made a decision to move forward. After making this choice, you learned more about the overarching narrative, some key themes, and core features of the impending journey. You also reviewed tips for using this book and maintaining your safety and health. And then, you arrived here.

Your Travel Journal

Now, let's start off your independent practice with a relatively simple task—your first Travel Journal entry. Prompts like the following will be a consistent feature of each chapter, so now's a perfect time to introduce them. You can use the space provided, or respond in a separate notebook dedicated to documenting your journey. If you're willing, I recommend adopting a daily journaling practice to deepen reflections and insights. This journal is a great place to record any dreams you have along the way too. Sharing their origins with myth and psychedelic experiences, dreams can help you explore the unconscious. Either way, when you're ready, write down in full prose, bullet points, symbolic drawings, or some combo as your answer to this first journal prompt. We begin your Travel Journal with a simple yet fundamental question. There's no right or wrong. This journal is yours and yours alone.

Travel Journal

Who am I?

The First Arc: Expanding Awareness to Prepare for the Unknown

> Depend upon it, there is mythology now as there was in the time of Homer, only we do not perceive it, because we ourselves live in the very shadow of it, and because we all shrink from the full meridian light of truth.
>
> —Max Müller[1]

The *call to adventure* often involves a sign that exists beyond our everyday understanding of ourselves and the world. It acts as a launching pad for deepening awareness. The call can come in many forms—some exciting, some frightening, and some outright strange.

What led you to this book? Maybe you heard about the psychedelic renaissance and became determined to find out more. Maybe you heard about their potential to heal some pain or trauma you've faced. Or, you were called by your own altered state of consciousness—whether it came from a psychedelic, a breathwork-induced trance, or a spontaneous shift into an otherworldly feeling. Strange, powerful dreams can also signal an adventure awaits somewhere within.

Being here means you've heeded that call, and you're ready to cross the first threshold. This start to the journey is exhilarating. Campbell described this phase as the *Departure*.[2] A classic illustration in film is Dorothy opening the door of her broken house to reveal the land of Oz shining in brilliant colors.[3] For the parallel in psychedelic therapy, the Departure phase best corresponds to *Preparation*. By agreeing to undertake this book's journey, you've committed to a period of preparation too. Much of the prior chapter provided the basic groundwork for this preparation. You've already taken a critical leap of faith, one that will prepare you for what comes next—chiefly, the trials of initiation.

When hearing a *call to adventure*, not everyone will say 'yes'—not just to this book or others like it, but to the full journey of life. One example may be the business executive who's devoted their entire life to acquiring assets while striving for higher levels of power and influence. This person may notice some unease in the few quiet moments they allow themselves to have—or cannot avoid. But instead of slowing down, they respond by becoming busier, re-committing to material success, and filling their life with distractions, from the glamorous to the commonplace.

The path ahead of us is the road less traveled. This first arc's theme is expanding awareness. Although preparation sounds less thrilling, what lies ahead is anything but mundane. Expanding awareness means understanding the layers of mystery that both surround us and are within. I'll refer to each chapter as a waypoint, meaning it's one destination of the overarching journey. The waypoints comprising this arc are as follows:

Chapter	Journey Destination	Theme
Ch 2	Waypoint I	Cosmic Awareness: Vastness of Space and Time
Ch 3	Waypoint II	Self-Awareness: Layers of the Conscious and Unconscious Mind
Ch 4	Waypoint III	Experiential Awareness: Four Modes of Experiencing

Each surveys a domain of our existence that we at least partially ignore or misunderstand. These gaps are never completely filled, but that's not the point. The goal is to expand beyond your default level of awareness—that is, your starting place.

Meeting Your First Ally

As teased in the last chapter, each arc introduces a new ally, representing an attitude or quality that supports your endeavors. In this arc, your ally is *Curiosity*. To use it, simply pay attention to anything that sparks curiosity. These moments can occur as you're reading the chapter, completing embedded exercises, or doing suggested activities on your own. Whenever it shows up, curiosity acts as an ally in two ways. First, it provides clues for personalizing your experience. What triggers curiosity is different for everyone, so following your natural interests will guide you to a distinctive path. Second, curiosity provides energy in the form of motivation. You can use this energy to venture into specific areas much deeper than what's done in this book. A curious attitude might even lead to the more intense experience of awe. Awe naturally emerges when we confront profound mysteries. Awe may be even more important than assumed at first glance. Even the ancient wisdom text *Tao Te Ching* suggests, "When [people] lack a sense of awe, there will be disaster."[4] Trust your curiosity to guide you to places of significance. And trust any moments of awe as signals that you're on the right track.

To enliven this metaphorical ally further, you can take a moment to visualize either a person in your life or a fictional character who embodies curiosity. Choose someone you'd trust to accompany you on an adventure, not because of their physical qualities but because of their willingness to explore, try new things, express excitement, and remain open to possibilities. Fill in the details within your imagination including what they look like and why they exemplify this attitude. When you could use a bit more support or encouragement, imagine this person or character providing you a boost of energy.

Besides recalling their image as needed, you might also want to select a physical token that can trigger a connection to this person or attitude. A stone, small figure, keychain, ring, and so forth are a few options. During psychedelic experiences, similar tokens can be a resource or a gateway for connecting with the journeyer's intentions or inner strengths. But, even without psychedelics, these physical representations can be useful tools.

Intention Setting

When you weighed the risks and benefits of going down this path, you jotted down some initial motivations for looking at this book in the first place. Now's a good time to transform these motivations into more elaborated intentions. These intentions will be revisited and updated before transitioning to each new arc. The prompt below is specific to this first arc, so consider how your broader intentions might fit. If you'd like to track your intentions for the overarching journey too, record them underneath your specific ones about expanding your awareness.

> **As I embark on this journey to expand awareness, my intentions are to...**

Awesome. You're now truly ready. I'm excited for you, and hope you feel excitement too. Go forth and explore. Discover insights as you prepare for all the mysteries that lie ahead.

CHAPTER 2

Cosmic Awareness—
Vastness of Space & Time

> For we are the local embodiment of a Cosmos grown to self-awareness. We have begun to contemplate our origins: starstuff pondering the stars; organized assemblages of ten billion billion billion atoms considering the evolution of atoms; tracing the long journey by which, here at least, consciousness arose. Our loyalties are to the species and the planet. *We* speak for Earth. Our obligation to survive is owed not just to ourselves but also to that Cosmos, ancient and vast, from which we spring.
>
> —Carl Sagan, *Cosmos*[1]

Journey Waypoint I

Here we are—at the true beginning of our journey together. And where shall we start? I suppose the easy stuff. The basics of what we know from modern physics and astronomy about the cosmos. Fear not. There'll be no differential equations embedded here. Nevertheless, explorations of existential and psychedelic themes must, I believe, begin from the perspective of what we know and do not know about the nature of reality and the universe. Most mental health professionals spend their time contemplating psychological wellbeing and problems in living life, usually some mix of work, school, love, and play. This focus on human concerns is so fundamental to understanding mental health it's a given—an *a priori* assumption of most psychological frameworks and treatment models.

That's why we're not starting with the human. We are but an infinitesimal, if not incredibly significant (says the human), part of a much greater whole. Awareness, though, does require us—or at least some kind of consciousness. Awareness is either the same thing as consciousness or an inherent quality of it. Having any kind of awareness requires two things: (1) something that's aware (the *observer*) and (2) something that's the focus of awareness (the *observed*). Observer and observed, thus, are intertwined not only with each other but also the very concept of awareness.

Although awareness, consciousness, or whatever we want to call it, is crucial to our task at hand, we're looking outwards before we look within. We're starting our journey by focusing on what our consciousness, paired with the tools of science, has allowed us to understand about the universe in which we live. For the sake of simplicity, I'll refer to this grander perspective as *cosmic awareness*—an expanded sense of the vastness and mysteries of space and time as we know it. This form of awareness is distinct from others we'll find in this arc for a few reasons. Chief among these, though, is how it deemphasizes us. At the same time, we—in this case, everyone who thinks about these sorts of things—are a crucial piece of the larger frame. By exploring the cosmos, we may also consider what our place might be within it.

Self-Reflections Check-In

What you just read might be a bit too abstract for your liking, so let's take a moment to check in and ground ourselves before we abstract ourselves out of existence. Before you arrived here, you made a choice to embark on a journey and made some initial preparations. At the end of the first chapter, you also made the first entry into your Travel Journal by answering the question, "Who am I?" In the preview for the first arc, you then clarified your intentions. Keep whatever you wrote or created with you at all times. You wouldn't want to lose yourself or your intentions so early after our departure. We've barely even started after all. Check in with yourself now and notice how you're feeling. You can close your eyes if it helps you focus. When you're ready and willing, let's begin the work of this chapter—the first waypoint of this journey.

The Cosmos as We Understand It— Or, the Perspective that Transcends All Others

Many people who've had powerful psychedelic journeys describe experiencing an atypical sense of time and/or space. Psychedelics can transform qualities of the surrounding world through sensory or other mental shifts in perspective. One person may continuously see the leaves of a plant wither and die then be reborn. Another perceives these leaves as normal but becomes mesmerized by their natural movement in the wind and realizes the plant is imbued with the mystery of life, just as it is. Even with closed eyes, people may voyage inside their own minds to what appear to be far out planets, stars, or quasars. Time collapses. The passage of minutes and hours seem like an eternity, a blink of an eye, or somehow both. Similar changes to consciousness can occur outside psychedelic journeys. Have you ever experienced an altered sense of time or space? What happened? How did you feel during and after the experience?

Researchers have documented a limitless array of these otherworldly experiences triggered with or without psychedelics.[2] What's impressive is modern science has uncovered many bizarre phenomena that, if we didn't know better, could be described as psychedelic mumbo-jumbo. But they're not. They're what the smartest of us, alongside tools of mathematics, simulations, and creatively designed experiments, are delving into as the rest of the human population goes about our daily lives.

In my daily life as a psychologist, I've realized one gift of therapy is a shift in perspective. These shifts mean getting outside our typical point of view and default understanding—sometimes by taking another person's viewpoint, sometimes by looking at the bigger picture. When all else fails, or when someone already 'gets it' and remains stuck, I suggest one last thing: What we're about to do here. All things considered, there's no bigger picture or perspective than that of the entire cosmos.

Cosmology, quantum mechanics, and math may not be your thing. That's okay. At the same time, I suggest you bear with me as we try to grasp a basic understanding of what these scientific perspectives can give us. Despite the limitations of our all-too-human minds, science has allowed us to expand our collective awareness far beyond what our ancestors thought was possible. Whether you already have scientific proclivities or believe you're incapable of understanding even the basics, contemplating the cosmos is an option for everyone. The numbers and theories I mention are relevant, but they're secondary to our goal of expanding awareness.[3] Hopefully, you'll discover a sense of curiosity along the way—or better yet, a feeling of awe. As in psychedelic experiences, if we're open, then the mysteries we can find are truly endless.

To spark our curiosity and begin our explorations, it's best to start with the basics—the dimensions of space and time. Unfortunately, words alone fail to describe the completely unfathomable dimensions of our known universe and of the fundamental elements of our world. Despite this Sisyphean challenge, we're going to try to introduce, at minimum, a greater understanding of just how expansive space and time are. Whether we zoom in or zoom out, you might begin appreciating how incredibly narrow our typical, everyday perspective is. To engage your imagination further, we'll pause occasionally and reflect on the questions evoked by your expanding cosmic awareness. Later in the chapter, you'll find suggestions for continuing your explorations, including more audiovisual or experiential options.

Awareness of Space

To start, let's focus on *space*, three-dimensional space to be specific. In our typical view of space, we can mark a position by three coordinates and describe movement relative to the original position in three key directions, or some combo (Figure 2.1).

No big deal. We experience this type of spatial awareness and movement every day. Think about going to and from your bed, heading to work, school, or out to do errands, and then returning home. All the space you occupy, day in and day out, can probably be measured in miles (or kilometers). Your phone or watch probably has a step tracker, so you might have a good idea of how much distance you travel each day, by foot at least. If you want to impress yourself, think about the place farthest away from your home that you've visited. Maybe another country. Maybe another continent. Keep these distances in mind. Or even write them down.

Don't get too impressed, though. Even hermits and homebodies are constantly traveling millions of miles. Just when we think we've grasped spatial awareness, we realize that we're actually ignoring the complex rotations of Earth and its orbit around our sun. That perspective too is limited. Our solar system and our galaxy are constantly in motion.

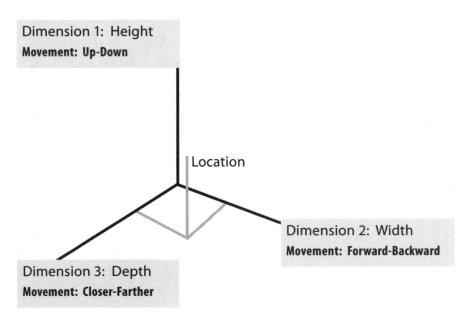

Figure 2.1 Basic three-dimensional space and movement

In working with space here, we won't bother much with the reality of rotations, orbits, and movements of other celestial objects. Understanding spatial distances at the cosmic level is challenging enough without the universe and everything in it constantly being in motion—as in reality! In other words, to streamline our look at space, we'll have to pause time.

Zooming Out—From Local to Interstellar Space

Our Earthly Home. Now that we're all on the same page, let's start our imaginary journey. In your mind's eye (a fancy word for imagination), picture yourself where you are now. Then imagine floating upwards in the sky on a lovely, sunny day. As you rise, you see your house, familiar streets and buildings, and eventually your entire town. As you continue upward, you enter the range of a typical commercial airline flight—a little under 7 miles above the surface (roughly 11 kilometers for our metric-minded travelers). Here you're also above where most of Earth's major observable weather occurs.

The view of your hometown starts to transition to a view of the region of the country it's in. Soon enough you realize you're seeing more than you ever could through an airplane window. Now we approach the edges of our planet's main atmosphere, the thermosphere—somewhere 50-370 miles from the surface (~85-600 km). As a reference point, the International Space Station's orbit is typically around 250 miles (~400 km) above Earth. If we could drive along a vertical highway and ignore the risk of crashing into airplanes and satellite traffic, it'd take less than a four-hour drive at 65 miles-per-hour. That's only a little more than a third of California's coastline.

Arriving here wasn't too hard, so the moon must be nearby, right? No, the moon is on average almost 100 times farther from Earth than the International Space Station—roughly 225-252,000 miles depending on its orbital position. This planetary companion to our home, which we take for granted so easily, is our nearest neighbor, yet it lies more than 9x the distance away from us than the length of our little planet's equator. Despite this distance, its gravity plays a crucial role in Earth's ecosystem—from the tides of the ocean to the tilt of the planet's axis.

Our Home Solar System. Rising farther beyond the Earth and its moon, our view begins to get eclipsed with that of the sun, the massive nuclear fusion power plant that gives energy to our solar system. If it weren't for Earth's protective atmosphere and magnetosphere, we might not be as thankful for the sun's presence. Even at an average 93 million miles away, the energetic force of the sun's ultraviolet rays would kill us and most other forms of life.

Our ozone layer filters some but not all harmful energies that can damage our DNA.

When we imagine such distances in miles, our standard units of measurement, even of the more reasonable metric system, just don't make much intuitive sense. The numbers become abstractions. Instead, let's switch to *astronomical units* (AUs). One AU is approximately 93 million miles (~150 million kilometers)—that is, the average distance from the center of the Earth to the center of the sun. Even with AUs, our human minds struggle to comprehend the immensity of these distances. The size of our solar system too remains a bit of a mystery. Pluto, our much-maligned dwarf planet neighbor, is on average more than 39 AUs from the sun. If Pluto marked the edge of our solar system, we'd have a rough idea of its magnitude. But of course, it's not that easy. The truth is we haven't figured it out yet. We know about dwarf planets farther out than Pluto, such as the rapidly rotating ellipsoidal (flattened egg-shaped) Haumea or the quizzically named Makemake. And then there's Eris, named after the Greek goddess foil to harmony. Eris earned its moniker by sparking tremendous cultural discord after its discovery prompted scientists to downgrade Pluto's planetary designation.

Pluto's demotion might have stung. But we may have another contender out there for the ninth planet. If we peered into the shrouded outer reaches of our solar system, we might discover the mysterious *Planet X,* a cooler name than the alternative 'Planet 9,' which is yet another reminder of Pluto's fall from grace.[4] Planet X is theoretical because it's based on mathematical calculations that account for unusual orbital patterns of distant smaller objects. If initial ideas are correct, it could be ten times the size of Earth and take 10-20,000 years to complete a single solar orbit.[5] It's safe to say countless secrets remain within our own solar system.

Our Galactic Home. If we continue our mental voyage through the stars, we begin to confront distances to which even an AU pales in comparison. Here's where we shift to a *light-year*—the distance light can travel, unhindered in a vacuum, in one Earth year. One light-year is approximately 63,000 AUs. The term may be confusing. A light-year is a measurement of distance, not time. It's an easier-to-understand counterpart to the *parsec* which accounts for simultaneous movements of multiple interstellar objects. See why we needed to pause time?

Our next nearest star—Proxima Centauri—is an estimated distance of more than 4 light-years. By galactic standards of distance, we're close neighbors. Why? Because our Milky Way Galaxy is estimated to be 100,000 light-years in diameter with a thickness of 1,000 light-years. The Milky Way is a barred spiral galaxy, which describes its elongated shape with arms of star systems spiraled about it. The distance from our solar system to the center of the galaxy is somewhere between 24,000 and 29,000 light-years. Our system is but one among 100-400 billion other star systems within the Milky Way Galaxy, each with their own collection of planets, asteroids, and other celestial objects.

Our Universal Home. 'Home' sounds inaccurate when we zoom out to these cosmic scales. Yet, our home it is. Less than a hundred years ago, we thought our galaxy was it. It seemed plenty large enough to encompass all of reality, right? We were wrong yet again. It wasn't until the 1920's when the American astronomer Edwin Hubble provided convincing evidence Andromeda wasn't a nebula, as first thought, but actually an entirely separate galaxy. Our Milky Way greeted its first intergalactic neighbor. Within a few years, more and more galaxies were discovered. Scientists now estimate well over 100 billion galaxies exist. Let that sink in.

Today, we've learned to be humble when guessing the size of the cosmos. The key distinction (dare we say ultimate one) is between the known observable universe and the unknown—even unknowable reaches of the cosmos. Moreover, as far as we can tell, the universe is expanding. The current observable universe has an estimated radius of about 46.5 billion light-years and a diameter almost twice that.[6] And, guess who's in the center of the cosmos? Our very own Milky Way Galaxy!

Let's hold back our excitement. Appearing to be the center of the universe is an artifact of the abstract and seemingly *only* philosophical point made at the outset of this chapter—awareness depends on both the observer and the observed. When expanding our awareness, we confront inherent limitations. Despite the ambition of having a cosmic perspective, we can never truthfully decentralize the observer—ourselves. Our very location in the universe limits what we can see in any given direction, so as our field broadens, it gives the illusion that we're, at least roughly, at the center of the cosmos. That may be a nice illusion for our collective egos, but true awareness means breaking through illusions when we can. When confronting inherent restrictions, even the power of astronomy cannot pierce the veil into the unknown. We can only guess at the actual size of the universe. The cosmos is quite possibly infinite.

If other cosmic observers are out there, they too have an observable universe limited by their location and the boundaries of space and time. Perhaps in the future, we'll discover some new technology that allows us to look beyond this veil. Perhaps not, but from this cosmic perspective, however incomplete it may be, it's hard to consider such human-centric concerns like bad traffic, cold coffee, or even the lifespan of any single person, no matter how famous, as important as we often think they are.

Zooming In—The Infinitesimal Spaces Within

Okay, a deep breath may be in order. If you made it this far, you're doing exceptionally well. Us mere mortals have only recently been privy to this immense knowledge. For now, we can return to Earth, to the present, and to your body. Rest here briefly in our more tangible, contained world in which we live every day. Set aside these cosmic scales of space—and that feeling of being infinitely small in comparison.

Let's begin our journey of zooming in and explore how much space exists within us. Start by looking at your fingertip. What do you see? Maybe the shades of color and the unique pattern of ridges of your fingerprint. No matter how close you look at your finger, we quickly reach the limits of our visual perception. A decent optical microscope can enhance our visual acuity by about 4-400x times. Whatever we observe at this magnification may be a bit more alien if not alarming or disgusting. Human skin is an extensive eco-system of valleys and hills, dirt and sweat, and plenty of dead skin cells—and creepy little mites that colonize our outward layers. Resist the urge to go wash your hands. Unless, of course, you haven't done so today.

As we zoom into the cellular level, our more esthetic and emotional reactions start to dissipate. If we could see all the cells contained within our body, we'd see an endlessly diverse array—but not all of them human. In fact, only about half the cells in our body are truly human.[7] You might find relief in knowing that by mass, non-human cells, which are mostly bacteria, take up far less physical space. However, by mass, the majority still isn't 'human.' It's water. So, what's really *human* about us? Well, DNA's a good guess. Unfortunately, it accounts for only a trivial proportion of our mass—and the vast majority of our DNA isn't specific to our species—or even functional as far as we can tell.[8] We shouldn't underestimate the power of DNA, however. It provides the essential, though not totally sufficient, script for producing life as we know it.

And look what happened. We got distracted by merely human concerns, yet again, when all we supposedly care about right now is the inner dimensions of space. Our human-centric viewpoint is powerful indeed. Let's go with it then and explore one of Earth's most important resources—water. Water is critical to our body's functioning and to life as we know it. Water molecules consist of three atoms—two hydrogen and one oxygen, which leads to its designation, H_2O. Hydrogen is the simplest element here, so let's zoom in there. Outside chemical compounds like water, a complete hydrogen atom contains one proton and one electron.[9] Hydrogen makes up more than half the atoms inside the human body (roughly 63%).[10] An average adult body holds about 4 octillion hydrogen atoms.[a]

Although remarkable, we shouldn't get too carried away about the amount of hydrogen within each human body. Hydrogen exists almost everywhere. It's the most common chemical substance in the universe as we understand it. A human-centric perspective is seductive but narrow. If we return to our current task, however, even this fundamental chemical element of the cosmos—and human bodies if we insist—isn't the end of our inward journey. Hydrogen, the simplest atom, exists on a scale that alone is unfathomable. The size of a hydrogen atom is about 0.1 nanometers in diameter, or 1/10,000,000 of a millimeter. If you look at a ruler, does that scale make sense to your human eye? Even if we could see at this level, we wouldn't see the image most of us learned in school. There's no floating ball rotating around another floating ball. We'd observe something far stranger, perhaps like a cloud—in which our subatomic building blocks behave occasionally like spinning particles and at other times like waves of energy.

Where this so-called particle-wave duality leads us is more akin to a never-ending labyrinth than a straight path towards a clear destination. At subatomic levels, we require a completely different model of physics to grasp the fundamental makeup of all matter as we know it. Enter *quantum mechanics*. Almost everything we hold dear about our seemingly concrete world breaks down here. In the quantum realm, for example, we cannot predict the simultaneous location, speed, and behavior of subatomic particles. Quantum phenomena forces us to speak of probability fields and information while abandoning language that implies precision and certainty. The implications of quantum theory provide the bedrock for ideas as wild as the *multiverse*—the possibility that innumerable other universes exist in parallel to our own.[11]

Ending here might seem like a cliffhanger, a teaser for even more profound mysteries lying within the fabric of space. Nevertheless, our task of zooming

---

[a] In other words, more than 4,000,000,000,000,000,000,000,000,000 hydrogen atoms.

in is meant only to spark curiosity and broaden our everyday awareness. Instead of a deep dive into quantum mechanics and its implications, I'll let you decide whether to venture into these bizarre realms. And endure the complex math and theory involved. If you'd like to go further down the rabbit hole, Box 2.1 provides a few breadcrumbs to help jumpstart your independent voyage.

Box 2.1
Quantum Breadcrumbs for Further Inquiry

Concept or Phenomenon	Brief Description
Heisenberg Uncertainty Principle	Impossibility of knowing a subatomic object's position and momentum simultaneously (not due to measurement error alone).
Nonlocality and Quantum Entanglement	The instantaneous connection between particles, regardless of distance, once they have interacted with one another—which violates the otherwise set cosmic speed limit based on light travel.
Superposition	Ability of quantum particles to be in multiple states or positions at the same time.
Decoherence	The collapse of the probability wave of a quantum object upon interacting with an 'observer' or outside environment, moving from the realm of quantum mechanics to that of classical physics.
String theories	Various proposed grand unifying theories of quantum mechanics and general relativity that assert the fundamental elements of our reality are infinitesimal one-dimensional vibrating 'strings.' These strings exist within normal spacetime and multiple subspace dimensions. Examples include the 10-dimensional superstring theory and the 11-dimensional M-theory—which as described by its originator, Edward Witten, "M stands for magic, mystery, or matrix, according to taste."[12]

The Mysteries of Space—A Curiosity Generator Task

Let's take a break from abstract numbers and theories and do a personalized reflection exercise. We can call this simple task the *Curiosity Generator* because its main goal is exactly that—getting in touch with your personal sense of curiosity. Curiosity uncovers questions as much as it tries to answer them. The questions we have about space and the cosmos are limitless, but more than likely, you have a few specific ones that pique your interest. Interest leads to the path of wonder and awe. Below is a prompt to generate questions that capture the attention of your inner explorer. Take no more than a couple of minutes to come up with at least three. If you have more, then you can always revisit, add to, or refine these questions later.

> **As I explore the mysteries of space, from the cosmic to the subatomic, my biggest questions are:**

Awareness of Time—the 4th Dimension

Three dimensions down. If we ignore string theory, then we only have one more to go. At the start of our journey through space, remember when I said we were going to ignore, for the most part, movement, rotations, and orbits? Basically, I was asking us to freeze time—the fourth dimension of spacetime. Time is something we all experience, for better or worse. As we know it, time is constant. Most of us have watches, either worn or embedded in our smart phones. With or without watches, days come and go. The passage of time is inevitable. Our earliest ancestors understood this fact of life. Time has been represented symbolically in myth and art across cultures.[13] As observed in day-and-night and seasonal cycles, early humans in many cultures understood time as recurrent and nonlinear. That's distinct from our everyday modern Western viewpoint of time as a constant straight line. But is our ordinary linear view of time more accurate?

Cosmic Time Scales

When shifting into a cosmic perspective, our personal experience of time looks like pennies compared to the entire sum of money minted throughout human history. Our current estimation of the age of the universe is that it's 13.8 billion years old.[14] At the time of writing this book, the world-wide average human life expectancy was 72 years.[15] If a single human was magically born at the beginning of the universe (and spacetime as we know it), that person, let's call them Alpha, would need to have lived more than 191 million consecutive lifespans to reach our current point in history.

The first half of their extremely long lifespan wouldn't have been on Earth. Our home planet came onto the scene 4.5 billion years ago—about two-thirds through the universe's entire span of existence.[16] It wasn't the most hospitable of places for life until much later. No one knows when life really began here, but the most concrete and relatively non-controversial evidence points to somewhere between 3.5 to 3.7 billion years ago.[17] Notwithstanding Neanderthals and non-human primates, the arrival of homo sapiens may be of most interest. That didn't happen until about 305,000 years ago.[18] Alpha would have been a very lonely human for the vast majority of their time in the cosmos. That's assuming, of course, Alpha didn't socialize with non-human species. Or, that some other intelligent life didn't accompany Alpha at some point—although intelligence doesn't guarantee good company. Whether found by accident or gifted by Prometheus, the earliest use of fire by a humanoid species dates back to 790,000 years ago—predating our species by almost 500,000 years.[19]

After the arrival of homo sapiens, Alpha would have lived another 4,166 consecutive lives before reaching our current time period. Even if they befriended early humanoids, almost all of Alpha's cosmic lifespan would have consisted of being the only humanoid intelligence in the entire universe. At least as far as we know. We're a very young form of life in a very old Earth and an ancient universe.

Temporal Relativity

Now that we all feel relatively young and knowledgeable, and less alone than Alpha, we can dive into more complex elements of time. Some of you might have bristled when you read, "time is constant." Good. You already knew that's misleading. For the rest of us, strap in again. Time is definitely not constant. And that's not just for people on psychedelics.

Many of us have heard about the *theory of relativity*, as formalized by the brilliant physicist Albert Einstein. Relativity applies to both our macro-level cosmic and micro-level subatomic explorations of space. First off, space and time are inseparable and intricately interconnected. Time is now understood as the fourth dimension of spacetime. Secondly, within a vacuum, the speed of light is a cosmic constant—an intergalactic speed limit apparently impossible to break.[20] To account for this absolute speed limit, Einstein realized that time *must* be relative—objectively relative, not merely subjectively so. For simplicity's sake, we'll consider here only general relativity.[21] General relativity occurs when gravitational fields differ in intensity. The film *Interstellar* demonstrates this effect most dramatically on screen. To avoid spoilers, I'll leave you with a timestamp for the relevant scene, roughly an hour into the film.[22]

For most people, realizing time isn't immutable is a bit destabilizing. One 'fact' of life we were taught, or took for granted, as being steadfast and reliable just isn't so. The effects of relativity are most dramatic, though, in conditions outside the typical human realm. Relativistic effects are so minuscule at the normal conditions we deal with every day that at first, they may appear meaningless. Even so, relativistic effects add up over time and affect our modern technology. We need look no farther than inside our own pockets to realize their impact. GPS satellites experience a weaker gravitational pull than we do on our planet's surface. According to general relativity, time should move slower for us. That's exactly what we observe. Our GPS systems must account for this effect when pinpointing our location and trajectory.

The observed phenomena of relativity involves something called *time dilation*—the relative stretching of time depending on acceleration and gravity. We're not quite done with the implications yet. Because we decided to unfreeze time in order to examine it, we now have to revisit our cosmic zooming out exercise. Remember those distances to the nearest star, to the center of our galaxy, and to our galactic neighbors? Now that we understand time a bit more, we're ready to go a few steps further.

First, and probably most obvious, the stars and any light they emit, observable by human eyes or not, are from a long, long time ago. The cosmic speed limit of light makes sure of that. Second, relativity dictates that depending on what that light had to pass through or around, its path reaching Earth may have been affected by more than physical distance alone—especially with our universe seemingly expanding. Gravity from large objects and spectacular cosmic events, like black holes, affect both the path of light and time itself. Black holes, also known as singularities, are especially mysterious because even light cannot escape their event horizon, the point of no return. When we look up at the stars, even with our naked eyes, we're not only seeing the past. We're seeing countless different time periods. The universe is not a uniformly operating clockwork machine, at least not analogous to the mechanical clocks with which we're familiar. No single, consistent point in time is shared by all the cosmos.

Subjective Time

So much more could be said, but let's set aside abstract theoretical physics. Thinking about time from a human lens isn't quite straightforward either. On a subjective level, time also appears relative. Think back to when you were a child. Do you remember how long a year felt? Those kids in sixth grade probably appeared so much older than you when you were a third grader. Perhaps a school day itself felt like an eternity while the summer break was gone in a flash. As we get older, a year passes at what seems to be an accelerating rate. That's not what happens objectively, but our increasing experience of the years behind us start to impact how we consider the years ahead. Our perspective of how much time has passed is relative to how much time we've lived, or have left to live.[23] On top of that, we tend to remember less of the relatively uneventful days, weeks, and months as we age.

You may be thinking something along the lines of "Youth is wasted on the young." But, having your past experiences, no matter how you judge them, has allowed you to be here now. Somehow, your past has led you to this journey. Moving toward higher levels of awareness inherently requires time—just as the greatest cosmic events throughout history have required enormous amounts of time to unfold. Luckily, we don't have to wait billions of years. The universe that came before us has graciously paved our way.

The Mysteries of Time—A Curiosity Generator Task

It's time—so to speak—for another break. Generate three or more questions as you did before, but instead of three-dimensional space, contemplate the anomalous nature of time. Take no more than two minutes, knowing you can add to this list later.

As I explore the mysteries of time, my biggest questions are:

Fostering Growth through Curiosity about the Cosmos

We just covered a lot of material. But, then again, remember this journey is a self-paced one. I hope, if needed, you were able to stop and take breaks along the way. Even with our ally curiosity, an emerging cosmic awareness can be a lot to take in. The first rule of *The Hitchhiker's Guide to the Galaxy* is: Don't Panic.[24] Now you know why. After all this thinking, and (with a bit of luck) learning too, I'll put on my psychologist hat again, and ask—how do you feel? Are you experiencing yourself as infinitesimally small, immensely large, or somehow both? Or, maybe these words mean nothing now in the face of these cosmic perspectives.

For many people, realizing the vastness of time and space and the deep mysteries of the cosmos can be initially overwhelming. That's because this realization also makes us confront how extremely narrow our everyday human perspective really is—and just how 'small' we really are. After the preliminary shock wears off, folks tend to fall loosely into two camps: 1) people who embrace this perspective and contemplate it regularly, and 2) people who go on about their business, either consciously or unconsciously trying to forget the unfathomable nature of the cosmos. Because you're reading this book and said 'yes' to the adventure, I'm hoping you land in the first camp—the people who embrace curiosity and live in wonder about the sheer magnitude and nature of the universe.

Carl Sagan said it well, "All the elements of the Earth except hydrogen and some helium have been cooked by a kind of stellar alchemy billions of years ago in stars, some of which are today inconspicuous white dwarfs on the other side of the Milky Way Galaxy. The nitrogen in our DNA, the calcium in our teeth, the iron in our blood, the carbon in our apple pies were made in the interiors of collapsing stars. We are made of starstuff."[25] In 1968, from the vantage point of the moon, NASA astronaut William Anders snapped a photo of Earth that has become one of the most famous pictures of all time.[26] And for good reason. The intellectual knowledge that we're on a small blue planet amid a vast cosmos became imbued with new life. Several astronauts have described experiencing what's been called the *overview effect*—a profound sense of awe, humility, and oneness with nature upon seeing our home from an undoubtedly novel perspective.[27]

Whether elicited by intellectual awareness, unusual perspectives, or psychedelics, awe and wonder might occasionally be accompanied by bouts of existential shock even for the most veteran journeyers among us. That's natural too. The word 'awe' is defined as "an overwhelming feeling of reverence, admiration, [or] fear...produced by that which is grand, sublime, [or] extremely powerful."[28] A growing cosmic awareness does not require a one-dimensional view of the cosmos as all wonderful, beautiful, and peaceful. It certainly is not. But, it's also not all terror, desolation, and violence. It's the totality of all that is. The known and the unknown. The wholeness and the void. The creative and destructive forces of nature. This perspective, like the overview effect, can evoke self-transcendent experiences, such as a diminished sense of self or a type of consciousness less focused on our separateness and individual identity.

The cosmos is so vast and so mysterious it goes beyond the limitations of human understanding. It ultimately goes beyond what we can even know with our best scientific tools and methods. In fact, our current cosmological models point to the existence of dark energy and dark matter, which together account for up to 95% of the entire universe.[29] The kicker is we have no clear idea what these exotic constituents of the cosmos actually are. No one's ever directly detected them. The nature of both dark energy and dark matter is one of many remaining mysteries that we may or may not be able to solve. That shouldn't stop us from trying. But realizing the limits of our knowledge and techniques can lead to an informed and honest sense of humility—and certainly awe. Echoing Shakespeare, we might conclude, "There are more things in heaven and earth...than are dreamt of in your [my, or our] philosophy"—or whatever preferred scientific or metaphysical ideas we espouse.[30] Expanding cosmic awareness can make mundane experiences seem miraculous. From this perspective, frustrating experiences like being stuck in traffic become something to appreciate. At times, you may feel a sense of wonder that any of this ordinary life is even possible. Actually, that may be the most sensible reaction of all.

Concrete Suggestions & Journey Report

Moving from the abstract to the tangible, Box 2.2 provides some options for reflecting on this part of our journey in your everyday life. These are merely suggestions. How you might bring cosmic awareness to your life is, in the end, up to you. Feel free to brainstorm and come up with other possibilities based on your personal experience and life circumstances.

You might also wonder how any of this cosmic stuff connects to psychedelics. To help make these connections, this chapter and the ones that follow contain journey reports. Each personal account in this book is authentic but de-identified to protect the journeyer's confidentiality.[31] For now, as some light reading, look at this chapter's Journey Report 2.1. This story comes from a volunteer writing about his first psychedelic experience. What happened fits a few themes explored in this chapter. What it means is for him, and now you, to decide.

Box 2.2
Expanding Cosmic Awareness within Everyday Life

Suggestion	Example
Find an image that evokes contemplations about the cosmos.	You set a picture of your favorite galaxy, planet or other cosmic phenomena as your phone or computer background. Every time you see this image, you briefly connect to a grander cosmic perspective.
Listen to specific songs or pieces of music that you associate with the mysteries of space and time and illicit reflections about the cosmos or the nature of reality.	You create a playlist for your personal reflections on the cosmos, with evocative songs like: "Seven Lights" by Sergey Cheremisinov "Derelicts" by Carbon Based Lifeforms & Ester Nanmark "The Cloud" by Jerry Goldsmith "Ximehua" by Soriah & Ashkelon Sain "Psychic Gibbon" by Younger Brother "Smoked Glass and Chrome" by Ott
Commit to a regular practice of contemplating the cosmos.	Before going to bed each night, you make a habit of looking up at the moon and stars and reflect on your place in the universe.
Expand your memory of a random moment and place in time that you'd normally dismiss as boring or routine.	While taking a morning shower, you pause and focus on the miracle of your very existence. You wonder if you might be able to remember this exact yet mundane experience of showering many years later despite it being nothing special—at least according to your everyday point of view.
Remind yourself periodically of your location in time and space throughout your normal day.	While going about your day, you think about your individual movement in the context of the earth's rotation and orbit around the sun. You then consider an even grander scale, becoming aware of this solar system's movement within the Milky Way Galaxy. And then expand your awareness further by considering our galaxy's location within the local cluster and ultimately within the incomprehensible universe itself, across cosmic scales of space and time.

Grounding Words—A Brief Summary

This chapter introduced you to the first waypoint along your path. You learned or refreshed your memory about what we know about the cosmos. You didn't start this journey with overly simplistic or easy concepts. You jumped into the deep end. You weathered the storm of difficult-to-conceive numbers and distances. You learned about the amazing work of genius human scientists who dedicate their lives to understanding the cosmos—from the most galactic scales of spacetime to the most infinitesimal building blocks of our universe. And despite traveling into the cosmic void, you made it out the other end. What you learned by visiting this waypoint is a perspective that supersedes all others. It will act as both a seed for your growing awareness and a touchstone as you explore the next steps in this journey. Although we'll shift our focus to human concerns, we can remember that any other mysteries you find still exist within this biggest mystery of all.

Your Assignment, Your Choice

When I say 'assignment,' I do so in jest. I could preach all day about what you *should* do. But, as a psychologist, I know that's not only annoying but also ineffective. That said, I do have some ever-so-gently-offered recommendations to personalize your journey. I've organized these exercises into two larger categories—*Reflective-Intellectual* and *Experiential-Emotional*. In reality, these options and paths overlap. In practice, each of us usually prefers one or the other—intellectual understanding or emotional experiencing. After looking at the options, I recommend choosing at least one activity each day that passes before you complete the next chapter. That activity may be the same every day, or you can take a mix-and-match approach. Do as much as you feel inspired to do. If you sincerely engage with these activities, though, you might find yourself going down the rabbit hole a little further than expected. If you do, then you might hear an inner voice saying, "Welcome to the cosmos."

Assignments 2.1
Expanding Your Cosmic Awareness

Reflective-Intellectual	Experiential-Emotional
☐ Task—Watch **Cosmos: A Spacetime Odyssey,**[32] **One Strange Rock,**[33] or a similar documentary about the universe or our planet	☐ Task—Go to a nearby science **museum** and/or **planetarium,** especially if involving a guided survey of the universe
Time—Minimum of first episode	Time—Minimum of 4 hrs
Aim—To see a full audiovisual-representation of the spacetime journey touched upon in this chapter	Aim—To explore your specific scientific interests and/or to experience a planetarium illustration
☐ Task—Read or watch content related to questions emerging from your **Curiosity Generator** responses on the fabric of reality and spacetime	☐ Task—Practice the meditation in **Meditation 2.1 "Exploring the Cosmos"**
Time—No minimum as long as you lose yourself in explorations and learning	Time—Minimum of 2-3x/week, 10-15 min each
Aim—To follow your curiosity and learn more about fascinating theories, their implications, and their scientific basis	Aim—To visualize and use your active imagination in contemplating the mysteries inherent within the universe

After reviewing your options, respond to this chapter's Travel Journal prompt. Note too that your Travel Journal is where you can document your experiences upon completing your chosen activities. As with the first chapter's prompt, express your reflections in whatever ways feel right to you now within these coordinates of physical and psychological space and time. Flowing prose, stream of consciousness, bullet points, doodles, elaborate art. All are welcome.

Travel Journal

What fascinates me most about space, time, and the cosmos?

How does it feel to experience my emerging cosmic awareness?

What might this perspective offer me personally?

JOURNEY REPORT 2.1   Voyage to the Stars

The first time I took mushrooms [psilocybin], I did so with two friends. One was doing it with me (their first time too) and the other was our sitter. He was experienced in psychedelics, all around trustworthy, and present only to make sure we were safe and had support if needed.

I was always curious about psychedelics but never had an opportunity to partake until much later in life. Although I was eager, I had no real idea what to expect and was just a touch anxious.

After eating about four and a half grams of the dried mushrooms, I laid back, put on my eye mask, and listened to a playlist of ethereal and 'tribal' tracks with occasional chanting. Slowly my natural imagination began to sharpen beyond blurred dream-like images and became something completely alien and strange. My mind started expanding and my initial thoughts about my life, family, and friends became like a distant memory. I shot up into space, far into the stars above the earth. I wasn't in our solar system very long, though. I remember orbiting a strange planet, made of metal and dirt, with moving parts like tunnels shifting and writhing. Before I knew it, I was a part of this planet. We were as one.

It's so strange, but I wasn't scared at all. I had no idea what was really happening, but it felt so profound and intriguing. Emotionally, I felt I was in rapture. I was understanding something that I hadn't quite grasped before. I was seeing—no, I was experiencing what it must feel like to be a part of something larger, not really alive but still vital somehow. The phrase 'world machine' sprang to mind out of nowhere. It somehow captured the limitlessly complex interconnections I was witnessing.

Report continues on next page

The trip lasted for about 6 hours, but I traveled to so many planets, witnessed stars form, and even created a few myself with the help of some other cosmic entity. I felt so many wonderful things, I was just amazed that all of this was even possible for me to experience as a human. I'm not sure what was really happening, but I know it made me feel so much more hopeful and connected to the cosmos than I had before. Prior to this experience, I was fascinated by our universe, but the regular stress I had with my job, bills, and minutia of modern life just seemed so insignificant compared to the rapture I had just experienced.

As an agnostic for years, I really was shocked how spiritual it all felt. Yet grounded. I sensed as if everything was connected to some greater whole that was so beyond anything I had felt before. It wasn't human at all, but it was powerful and somehow 'good.' Words can't do it justice. The first words I uttered (feebly, mind you) were, "I never knew how connected everything was." My friends laughed knowingly and kindly smiled as I stared, wide-eyed and speechless. It was like someone else said those words. That journey changed my life. I think about that feeling every day, now several years after that first experience. It's brought alive all my academic and spiritual interests in a way I'll forever treasure.

—Mark, Age 31

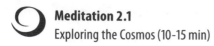

Meditation 2.1
Exploring the Cosmos (10–15 min)

Carefully read this script to get a sense of the contents of this meditation. Then, close your eyes and lead yourself through it. Remember, it's not about getting it 'right.' If you're exploring the cosmos through your imagination, you're doing well.

Find a comfortable, quiet place to sit and relax into your body. Don't worry about where you place your legs, arms, or hands, as long as it's comfortable for you at this moment. Close your eyes and focus on breathing in and breathing out....Ride the waves of your breath until you settle into a relaxing rhythm. In your mind's eye, picture yourself in the room you're in. Fill this image with as much detail as comes naturally....

Instead of staying here, start to imagine rising above your body and into the sky....Continue ascending but look back at the place where your body resides and the surrounding area...Then continue upwards, until you can picture the entire Earth...Notice the colors of the Earth, from the blues and greens...to the white gray of the clouds...and any visible snowcapped mountains.

Gently turn around and look towards the moon, our planet's loyal companion....Search now to find the Sun. When you see it, imagine feeling the warmth of its powerful rays...Continue venturing out to other planets, perhaps Venus or Mars...Maybe one of our mysterious gas giants, Jupiter or Saturn....In the farthest regions, you may imagine the unknown parts of our solar system...Take your time to explore...Observe whatever catches your imagination...

Now, as if unconstrained by normal limits of space and time, fly far beyond our solar system until you gain an expanded view of our Milky Way Galaxy, with its spiraling arms of star systems....Although you no longer see Earth, you know it's there amidst the countless others...

Gather courage, if you need, to explore even farther, seeing other galaxies of endless shapes and sizes....Dust clouds of various colors, beyond the normal pallet of human sight....You witness, too, spectacular cosmic events. Singularities forming from collapsing massive stars....Or grander still, colliding black holes that send gravitational shockwaves across the cosmos. Spend as much time here as you desire, exploring the vastness and wonder of the universe, what's seen and unseen...

When you're ready, begin your trek back to our galaxy…Then to our solar system, our little corner of the universe…before heading back to our home planet. As you approach, you feel the warmth again of the sun and the comfort of seeing Earth….Slowly you descend through the atmosphere…and through the clouds…and find yourself back in your body…

Having returned to your body, ride the waves of each breath in and each breath out. You're here now, in this body of yours, in this place back on Earth….Still with eyes closed, start to imagine the room around you….Fill it with as many details as you can….As you reach the limits of your memory, slowly reopen your eyes. Breathe in the air of this present moment, fully grounded in your awareness of your place in the cosmos.

CHAPTER 3

Self-Awareness—Layers of the Conscious & Unconscious Mind

Our psyche, which is primarily responsible for all the historical changes wrought by the hand of man on the face of this planet, remains an insoluble puzzle and an incomprehensible wonder, an object of abiding perplexity—a feature it shares with all Nature's secrets.

—Carl Jung, *The Undiscovered Self* [1]

Journey Waypoint II

Now with our growing cosmic perspective, we can return to the realm of human concerns. Self-awareness is a suitable companion to cosmic awareness. As you learned, we face fundamental limitations in understanding the cosmos. In a very literal, scientific sense, we can only observe the universe from our little corner of the cosmos—by doing the observing from our home planet and looking outwards. In a parallel fashion, we can only observe ourselves from our own consciousness and our own limited point of view—we are both the observer and the observed. It may sound egotistical, but each of us, as individuals, are the center of our own observable universe. All external sources of information must be filtered by our own minds. Don't worry, though. We humans have some impressive abilities to take multiple perspectives and use our knowledge of ourselves in trying to better understand the minds of others. It's here that we can find the more uplifting qualities of humankind—compassion, empathy, kindness, altruism, and selflessness, just to name a few.

If only we could stop there. The secret is that all the good and bad we see in others, all the selfless and selfish motivations we observe in the outside world, exist somewhere deep (or not so deep) inside of our own minds. Ignoring the parts of ourselves we don't understand, or don't want to know about, may cause harm to ourselves and sometimes others. Still, it's not all dark in the hidden recesses of our mind, and if we explore openly, we might just find some wonders too. As Aristotle believed, "Knowing yourself is the beginning of all wisdom." [2] Thus, the focus of this chapter is another ambitious one, and belongs to this entire book. How can we expand awareness of our deepest selves?

Self-Reflections Check-In

Before diving in further, let's check-in. In our first waypoint along this psychedelic-inspired journey, we visited the stars, tiptoed around the weirdness of the subatomic, and started opening our minds to a perspective beyond our normal human-centric one. It was an ambitious start, but I hope the activities you chose at the end helped personalize your voyage. What were one or two things you took away from the idea of cosmic awareness? What more did you learn or reflect on in the activities you chose? Do you have lingering questions you'd like to continue exploring? With any luck, your responses to the chapter activities and Travel Journal prompts stimulated your curiosity. Your expanding cosmic awareness may continue to resonate with the themes emerging in this chapter and others. Take your time if you want to reflect more, and when you're ready, proceed.

The Mysteries of Consciousness—
Expanding Awareness of the Human Psyche

The nature of consciousness is one of the thorniest and most critical questions about life and existence itself. Many people assume consciousness is confined to complex lifeforms and seated within neurobiological functions of the animal brain. Even if we constrict ourselves to conservative and conventional scientific understandings of consciousness, which are largely framed within materialism, we discover many thought-provoking questions. That consciousness exists at all is amazing in and of itself. Does life inevitably appear throughout the cosmos? Or, is it an exceedingly rare cosmic anomaly? Is consciousness an accident of evolution? Or, is it an unavoidable outcome? The very existence of consciousness is thus inherently mysterious.

Despite some amazing feats of intelligence observed in sea mammals, cephalopods, birds, and non-human primates, we humans appear to have the most complex form of consciousness currently known to science. 'Consciousness' may be too narrow and deceptive a term when describing the human psyche. There's more to our minds than what our conscious thoughts, feelings, and knowledge suggest. From a philosophical standpoint, this perspective is nothing new. Nevertheless, it runs counter to how most of us live our day-to-day lives. Our minds (primarily through the functions of the ego) organize our experiences of the outside world and our moment-to-moment access to thoughts, feelings, and motivations. Consciousness filters out what it deems, for whatever reason, is too extraneous, distracting, or overwhelming. It's a good thing that it does this. Even with the limits of human perception, if we were fully aware of all the information present in our external and internal world simultaneously—and without the ability to turn that awareness off—we'd probably short-circuit. There's just too much going on, especially in our modern era, that stimulates and requires processing.

Fortunately, the healthy human brain condenses our perceptual experiences into a more manageable, conscious subset. This function of the brain is what English author and early Western psychedelic advocate Aldous Huxley called the ego's "reducing valve."[3] It allows us to avoid becoming overwhelmed and helps us manage relatively complex tasks without expending unnecessary mental energy. Managing mental resources allows multitasking—like driving your car to work while listening to an audiobook or podcast. When they work well, these streamlined, more automated aspects of our human mind betray a greater reality of chaos, chance, conflict, and boundless complexity.

Because these realms are by default outside our awareness, we find much to discover for our continuing journey. Expanding awareness in our everyday world involves (1) reflecting on our own consciousness, including uncovering hidden parts of our psyche and personality, and (2) realizing the fullness of experience in each moment, much of which we ignore. This chapter focuses on the first—what we'll simply call *self awareness*. The next chapter will focus on the second—*experiential awareness*.

Expanding self-awareness requires facing complexity. To do that, we must build upon what we already understand, piece by piece. Although conceptual models are always incomplete, they serve to condense and organize ideas, allowing us to process information in piecemeal chunks. They work just like our brains do by default. Without organizing models, we'd be lost. We could just stop here, throw our hands up, and say, "The human mind is endlessly complex and unknowable, so why bother?" That'd be disappointing and defeatist. As we saw with the cosmos, expanding awareness can continue even when we face inherent limitations.

Thus, as adventurous explorers, we charge forward. To aid us on our journey, we'll use a conceptual model that embraces complexity and mystery—that of the well-known, if not occasionally controversial, Swiss psychiatrist Carl Jung.[4] Jung's multifaceted theories warrant a deep discussion. We don't need to understand *everything*, though. We only need to expand beyond our starting place and default level of awareness. This chapter focuses on two vital aspects of self-awareness—layers of human consciousness and key aspects of personality.

Motivations of the Ego—From Defense to Compromise

At the beginning of our journey, we previewed an iceberg model of the psyche—a common metaphor for the mind's conscious and unconscious elements. The iceberg model borrows from Freudian psychoanalysis. Despite common misconceptions, Jung's theory doesn't run counter to many of Freud's ideas. Both espouse the importance of the unconscious. Both argue that distinct but interrelated parts of the mind influence behavior. The ego's implicit motivations to seek pleasure and minimize anxiety—within the constraints of perceived reality—also remain relevant.

Although not our sole focus, psychoanalytic ideas about the ego and its tools contribute a great deal to our goal of expanding self-awareness. Its jargon has seeped into the fabric of our modern culture. Freud's ideas have been used for over a century in several fields outside psychology—including critical analysis of art, literature, and film. Especially at lower doses, psychedelics can conjure thoughts, images, and emotions befitting of psychoanalysis. Despite historically being reactionary and anti-psychoanalytic, modern psychological science has been forced to recognize the existence of the unconscious mind. Regardless, a "'conscious-centric' bias" continues to permeate many areas of psychological research.[5]

Instead of going into Oedipal complexes and cigars, let's stick with two key ideas: defense mechanisms and compromises. Both involve how the mind deals with inner conflict and minimizes conscious distress. Conflicts arise naturally when conscious and unconscious motivations diverge, when different conscious motivations battle with one another, or when either type of motivation is incompatible with external reality. None of us are so simple and consistent that we feel 100% one way about everything. Conscious awareness of inner conflicts and ambivalence can, at times, be maddening—whether it's about mundane choices like what to cook for dinner, or as big as considering a career change. Alas, conscious conflicts are only a small portion of the ones our psyches face.

In general, the ego tries to minimize conscious distress, uncertainty, and conflict. Indeed, the unconscious part of the ego can handle many of these struggles through its arsenal of defense mechanisms. *Defense mechanisms* are the ego's strategies for keeping distressing feelings, ideas, or conflicts from entering our conscious mind.[6] When unsavory impulses do escape and enter conscious awareness, they usually cause some kind of distress, like anxiety, guilt, or shame. Mild-to-moderate distress is normal and manageable for most of us. But sometimes the emotional risk is too much to allow. That's when defense mechanisms kick in to protect us.

Despite what you may hear, defense mechanisms are not all bad. They work to transform unconscious motivations and conflicts into many interesting things, some healthier than others. The absence of defense is, in general, closer to psychosis than enlightenment. The ego is largely our friend. It's doing its best with what it has. Expanding self-awareness isn't about taking a sledgehammer to all our defenses. Some strategies, however, are more effective than others. Figure 3.1 describes common defense mechanisms, organized by their level of sophistication.[7] The ones near the top represent relatively conscious

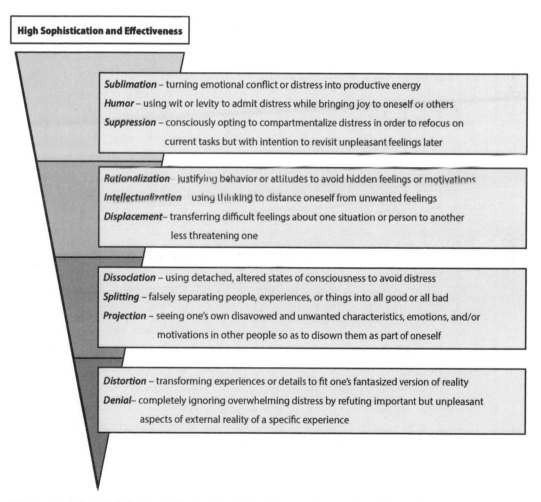

High Sophistication and Effectiveness

Sublimation – turning emotional conflict or distress into productive energy
Humor – using wit or levity to admit distress while bringing joy to oneself or others
Suppression – consciously opting to compartmentalize distress in order to refocus on current tasks but with intention to revisit unpleasant feelings later

Rationalization – justifying behavior or attitudes to avoid hidden feelings or motivations
Intellectualization – using thinking to distance oneself from unwanted feelings
Displacement – transferring difficult feelings about one situation or person to another less threatening one

Dissociation – using detached, altered states of consciousness to avoid distress
Splitting – falsely separating people, experiences, or things into all good or all bad
Projection – seeing one's own disavowed and unwanted characteristics, emotions, and/or motivations in other people so as to disown them as part of oneself

Distortion – transforming experiences or details to fit one's fantasized version of reality
Denial – completely ignoring overwhelming distress by refuting important but unpleasant aspects of external reality of a specific experience

Figure 3.1 Selected defense mechanisms with brief descriptions, ordered by level of psychological sophistication and effectiveness (adapted from Vaillant, 1994)

efforts to face and cope with everyday consensus reality. The lower ones distort reality, sometimes beyond recognition. When we confront the trials of initiation, we'll reflect on how defense mechanisms can show up when facing our deeper existential concerns.

No matter the specific issue involved, the ego often works by forming *compromises* among competing motivations or sides of a conflict—either consciously or unconsciously.[8] Compromises are negotiations between different parts of the psyche. When done well, they promote desirable outcomes. As a healthy example, imagine a person afraid of public speaking. Instead of canceling an upcoming talk, they start their presentation by making a joke about their nervousness, which endears them to the crowd and elicits smiles and light laughter. It's a win-win—and a great illustration for why humor can be such a healthy option.

There you go. We reviewed Freudian ideas without discussing genitalia. I promise that was intentional. But, in all seriousness, being aware of conflicts, defenses, and compromises can greatly inform our efforts moving forward. Throughout our journey, self-awareness means realizing how our habitual ways of coping can sometimes cause more harm than they serve to address.

The Layers of Consciousness

Jung and Freud deeply respected each other, but during a fateful, shared overseas voyage to America, irreparable cracks emerged in their relationship.[9] Fortunately, we're unencumbered by their personal ruptures or dogma. We can treat Jung's model as an important expansion, not a dismissal of Freud's. Many of the very strange yet meaningful experiences people have in moderate-to-high-dose psychedelic journeys don't exactly align with Freudian theory. In contrast, Jung offers us much in understanding not only the depths of the psyche but also the dream-like symbolic visions elicited by psychedelics. Jung believed the psyche grapples with far more than ego-level concerns. From his perspective, the psyche's ultimate motivation is to work through the process of *individuation*—the path towards greater psychological wholeness, harmony, and distinctiveness.[10] We'll talk about individuation more in our journey's final arc. At this point, just know that expanding awareness is very much in line with this higher intention.

The Conscious Self—Persona and Personal Identity

Persona. Among Jung's many intriguing ideas, one of his most straightforward—that of the persona—has survived the test of time relatively unscathed.

Acting like a mask, the *persona* is simply the outwardly expressed parts of ourselves. Our persona is largely informed by cultural expectations of how we should behave given our current situation and social or professional roles.[11] In a 1957 interview, Jung offered an example of a doctor who acts like a doctor and looks like a doctor, complete with "good bedside manners" (we'd hope), and the ascribed authority such a role suggests.[12] The risk is that the doctor "may even identify himself with [his persona] and believe that he is what he appears to be."[13] Personas are necessary for us to interact with the outside world and function in society. They're how we perform for others. But they're never all that we are. It's a shallow, limited life for people who overidentify with their persona.

To a certain extent, we can all fall into that trap. Through social media, our efforts to curate and perform ourselves are often even more exaggerated than in times past.[14] Whether through Instagram, Facebook, Snapchat, or LinkedIn, the parts of ourselves and our experiences that we express are even more carefully selected than our everyday, 'real world' personas. Instead of decrying our new digital reality, we can ponder how digital self-expression might reveal new layers of the persona. Digital personas may, to some extent, be necessary and adaptive, but they're not without risks. Comparing our carefully curated social media persona with someone else's can be fraught with dangers to our mood and self-esteem.[15] Receiving even positive feedback for our persona (like a well-timed, clever tweet) can sometimes lead to paradoxical negative reactions like, "Everyone thinks I'm hilarious and fun now, but they don't know what I'm really like."

Awareness of our public personas includes knowing its opposite: our conscious but private selves. As an explorer of consciousness, you're likely already aware of parts of yourself less shared with the outside world. Moving from the persona into deeper layers of consciousness, then, is a movement you understand. If you've ever kept a personal secret, you get it. If you've shared vulnerable feelings only with your most trusted friends, you get it too. Appropriate boundaries are important to psychological wellbeing, so keeping some things closer to your chest makes sense. But when you feel wildly different on the inside versus outside, you might consider if your persona has run amok. Do you feel unsafe expressing yourself more fully? Or only in specific settings? For all of us, considering ways in which we perform for others can highlight areas of growth. Even a healthy, reflective person can find themselves possessed and overcome by the trappings of the persona and the sociocultural expectations that feed into its creation and maintenance.

Personal Identity. As we push further into the layers of our conscious minds, we find the persona is encompassed within and interacts with a larger sense of self—our *personal identity.*[16] Identity is how we understand ourselves as separate individuals with continuity and 'sameness' over time. The more authentic our persona, the more it expresses genuine aspects of our conscious reactions and personal identity. Identity doesn't appear out of thin air. It's developed over time.[17] The adequate exploration of our options is important. So is committing to a more stable sense of self. A sequence of exploration followed by commitment results in the achievement of a mature identity.[18]

Multifaceted identities are resilient and durable. They can evolve throughout life based on shifting circumstances, abilities, and roles. A teenager whose life revolves around performing well in soccer will naturally emphasize other skills and parts of themselves as they age, perform various jobs, have kids, and retire. At the same time, at least upon reaching adulthood, their racial, ethnic, gender, and sexual identities remain relatively stable (though not always). For many people, identity transitions occur fluidly throughout our lifespan, without much conscious thought. For others, the formation and reformation of identity becomes an ongoing task punctuated by periodic crises. These crises stimulate new explorations that in turn help update one's prior identity. Yet other people may ignore underlying uncertainties about their identity because doing so evokes anxiety, something the ego dislikes. Instead, they may double down, put their nose to the grindstone, and keep busy to avoid feeling their secret doubt.

Regardless of the chosen path, having an identity offers a way to understand ourselves. It's the foundation for the overarching narrative of our life story. Our conscious mind provides this understanding and orchestrates this narrative. Of course, achieving an identity doesn't mean it lasts forever. We often make early choices that we later realize are incomplete. Revisiting questions of identity can be triggered by significant loss, growing doubt and uncertainty, or drastically changed life circumstances. Alternatively, we can choose to explore identity through conscious deliberation and inquiry. Whatever motivated you to engage in this journey, you belong to this intrepid group. Your response to the very first Travel Journal prompt, "Who are you?" likely captured elements of both your persona and identity. And perhaps hints of more.

The Personal Unconscious—Complexes and Parts

If we follow the breadcrumbs to the hidden layers of consciousness, we can cross another threshold and enter the strange realm of the unconscious. Many motivations, defense mechanisms, and phenomena described earlier are contained within the unconscious. Jung saw these elements as part of only its first layer—the *personal unconscious*, that which is specific to us as individuals but outside our awareness. Not being a simple novelty, the unconscious plays a powerful role in influencing our attitudes and behavior. Research has shown that our unconscious motivations only weakly correspond to our conscious ones.[19] As Jung contended:

> A man [sic] likes to believe that he is the master of his soul. But as long as he is unable to control his moods and emotions, or to be conscious of the myriad secret ways in which unconscious factors insinuate themselves into his arrangements and decisions, he is certainly not his own master.[20]

Gaining awareness of our unconscious, therefore, enables us to access greater levels of not only insight but also personal agency. Jung believed the personal unconscious contained *complexes*.[21] A complex is a collection of feelings, thoughts, interpretations, memories, and behavioral patterns that coalesce around an idea or experience. Complexes may intermingle with defense mechanisms and implicit motivations, but they aren't solely focused on these concerns.[22] They're most often activated or triggered by a situation, thought, or experience. But the emotional component is usually most powerful and indicative of something underneath the surface of our mind.

An example might help. Take a moment to think about money. What comes to mind? Any other words or descriptions? Images? Sensations? How about emotions? Personal memories? Money, in theory, is a neutral concept and word. But like most words, various cultural and personal expectations and stereotypes influence what come to mind. Even when we try to combat these stereotypes or outside influences, our minds automatically factor them in, through implicit associations and value judgments.[23] Direct experiences and messages, especially the earliest and most emotionally salient, can create internal programs of our mind. Like personas and identities, complexes aren't inherently negative or unhealthy. They develop for everyone. Even so, self-awareness requires uncovering how our personal complexes influence our subjective experiences, behaviors, and emotional triggers.

An extension of these ideas is found in *internal family systems* therapy, which happens to be especially influential in MDMA-assisted psychotherapy.[24] According to this model, our system of consciousness works as a whole but contains several different parts. The most significant, particularly in the context of trauma, are *protectors* and *exiles*. Protectors include ego-like *managers* that attempt to prevent painful or overwhelming emotions to emerge by using various defense mechanisms. *Firefighters*, on the other hand, are protectors that leap quickly into action when those overwhelming emotions leak into conscious awareness. Because prevention has failed at that point, their primary tactic is a panicked attempt at distraction, resulting in varyingly destructive behaviors, such as impulsive substance use.

Protectors can be aligned in their defensive strategies or in conflict. What they're both trying to avoid, however, is a full awareness of any exile parts. *Exiles* hold intense emotional anguish and unprocessed trauma or grief. For a person to heal, the managers must be willing to let down their guard and let the exiles express their pain. MDMA's therapeutic potential partly lies in how it facilitates increased safety and trust in the co-therapists as well as a person's ability to feel compassion towards their exiled parts. With or without MDMA or classic psychedelics, the internal family systems approach encourages both therapists and clients to ask protector parts for 'permission' to work with the exiles. To reach the unconscious, we often need to be gentle, relaxed, and show some self-constraint. Keep in mind this language of parts, protectors, and exiles is figurative. It's used to illustrate how internal conflicts can make us act in very different ways than we normally do—or would prefer—depending on the situation and the parts that become activated.

The Collective Unconscious—Shared Archetypes

Often the formation of personal complexes and parts involves more universal aspects of the psyche—what Jung called *archetypes*. Archetypes are the primary constituents of Jung's deepest layer of the human psyche—the *collective unconscious*.[25] Even more so than its personal counterpart, the collective unconscious is seldom accessible through direct means. It's the realm of potential themes and associations we inherit simply by being human. Archetypes are forms that provide a larger mold while complexes fill them with personal content. Archetypes are primal and instinctual. Preverbal and symbolic. Dynamic and powerful. As such, they're hard to express with words—like the ineffable nature of psychedelic experiences. Archetypes share this ineffability but can be outlined with examples and metaphors. They're indentations in the ground where, if it were to rain, natural pools would develop into lakes, and streams would become rivers. But the content of the rain and exact path the water follows comes from personal and collective experiences.

For a more concrete illustration, we can consider the mother archetype. Take a few moments and quickly list whatever comes to mind when you think of the word 'mother.' No matter how random it may seem. By doing so, you're practicing *free association*—a critical technique, alongside dream analysis, for gaining greater access to the unconscious.

In your list of associations, you'd likely find elements of your mother complex. You might find your list has words such as 'safe' and 'loving.' You may have thought of opposite words, though, like 'intrusive,' 'overwhelming,' and 'terrible.' It's this duality that reflects how archetypes lack clear-cut content. We inherit the proclivity to organize thoughts, feelings, and other associations around the idea of a mother, but we're not given the exact content of the mother archetype. Many expectations are culture-bound and unfortunately can intersect with sexism. Whereas all cultures have their own variations, the mother archetype itself exists across cultures.

The list of identified archetypes is long and expanding, but Box 3.1 provides some key examples. Since film is one modern vehicle for expressing such collective motifs, I've added characters from *Star Wars* to exemplify how these archetypes are portrayed in this now multi-generational story inspired by the monomyth.[26] For good measure, I've thrown in characters from *The Matrix* films as well. Keep in mind these stories and characters, like archetypes, may be expressed quite differently in other cultures and time periods. Myth, including the monomyth, is bigger than any one person, story, or culture.

Box 3.1

Select Archetypes with Brief Descriptions & Examples from *Star Wars* & *The Matrix*

Archetype	Brief Description	Star Wars Example[27]	The Matrix Example[28]
THE CHILD	A youthful figure who embodies playfulness, inquisitiveness, greater possibilities, hopefulness, or unusual wisdom, although occasionally more vulnerable and naïve than they realize. They may be gifted with special talents or a strong courageous and compassionate heart.	**Young Anakin** Prequel Trilogy— *The Phantom Menace*	**'Spoon' Boy** *The Matrix*
THE HERO	A figure that fights for their community, willing to speak for others, the protagonist in most mythic stories, including the core monomyth.	**Luke Skywalker** Original Trilogy	**Neo** *The Matrix, The Matrix Reloaded, The Matrix Revolutions*

Box continues on next page

THE SHADOW	The disavowed aspects of oneself or community, often portrayed as the enemy but can also represent the ignored or inferior Other, either for the individual protagonist or the culture at large. In its most extreme form, the shadow represents transcendent evil.	**Darth Vader** Original Trilogy **Kylo Ren** Sequel Trilogy **Palpatine** All Trilogies	**Agent Smith** *The Matrix, The Matrix Reloaded, The Matrix Revolutions*
THE ANIMA OR ANIMUS	A figure that represents the unexpressed gender characteristics of the conscious persona, personality, or protagonist, sometimes connected to romantic love, sometimes as an inner voice that offers communications from the unconscious and/or messages of encouragement.[29]	**Princess Leia Organa** Original Trilogy **Fin** Sequel Trilogy	**Trinity** *The Matrix, The Matrix Reloaded, The Matrix Revolutions*
THE WISE ELDER	A community elder or other person of authority who can aid individuals on their journey, provide guidance, and ancient knowledge and wisdom. The elder helps initiate the individual into the tribe, larger community, or secret traditions.[30]	**Obi-Wan Kenobi** Original Trilogy— *A New Hope* **General Leia Organa** Sequel Trilogy— *The Rise of Skywalker*	**Morpheus** *The Matrix, The Matrix Reloaded* **The Oracle** *The Matrix, The Matrix Reloaded, The Matrix Revolutions*
THE TRICKSTER	A figure that transcends multiple worlds or perspectives and can play tricks on the naïve or unaware; their tricks can be malicious, neutral, or good-humored but regardless, their tricks often awaken a once-naïve person to a larger or alternative reality full of promises and perils. Tricksters can be wild cards or consistently benevolent or malevolent.	**Lando Calrissian** [Harmful, later redeemed] Original Trilogy— *The Empire Strikes Back* **Yoda** [Supportive] Original Trilogy— *The Empire Strikes Back*	**Cypher** [Harmful] *The Matrix* **Persephone** [Helpful, but neutral] *The Matrix Reloaded*
THE SELF	The organizing, wholistic personality that encompasses and integrates conscious and unconscious elements, an alternative center of the psyche compared to the conscious ego.	**Rey** Sequel Trilogy— *The Rise of Skywalker* [Ending]	**Neo** *The Matrix Revolutions* [Ending]

Note. These descriptions are naturally incomplete since each archetype can be expressed in numerous and potentially countless forms. Some *Star Wars* and *The Matrix* characters fit multiple archetypes depending on the film and their portrayed relationship with other characters. Yoda plays the part of a well meaning Trickster as well as a Wise Elder. Also, of note, the Self archetype plays a similar role in internal family systems therapy as it's described here.

Religion and mythology are two classic domains for expressing arche-typal themes. Although historically noteworthy, the influence of religion and ancient myth have become diminished. The waning power of specific myths or religions, however, demonstrates an ageless cycle of loss and renewal—itself an archetypal pattern. When old myths become stale or less relevant to a culture's current concerns, new ones arise. Yet, eventually, these newer forms become outdated and must be replaced as well.

Even for those of us disinterested in religion and myth, archetypes find ways to sneak into life. If you've had very powerful or strange dreams, it's pos-sible you've encountered some archetypal material. That's why dream journals are important features of Jungian analysis. Unlike Freud, Jung believed dreams are not simply trying to disguise unconscious desires or fears. They're trying to share something important, albeit symbolically and often in an unusual or puz-zling manner. Dreams typically provide clues to our personal unconscious, but collective and archetypal themes can still emerge. Dreams, psychedelic jour-neys, and other visionary experiences involving deities, aliens, or profoundly mysterious encounters likely are touching upon archetypal phenomena.

Nowadays, though, perhaps our most powerful shared source of arche-typal themes is through creative fiction—the mostly widely available and pop-ular of which are films and TV shows. Besides their entertainment value, the stories they tell provide a vehicle into shared collective unconscious themes, fears, hopes, and mysteries. These stories, especially within more imaginative genres like fantasy and science fiction, have become our modern mythology. If dreams pave the 'royal road' to your personal unconscious, then creative fiction lays out the path to our collective unconscious. That's why this book often references works of fiction. It's not just because they're fun. They offer us insightful messages and clues that otherwise might be lost inside the twist-ing labyrinth of our minds.

Dreams, art, mythology, and film share parallels with psychedelic expe-riences. They can propel us to unseen landscapes of beauty and wonder, yet also potentially evoke profound anxiety and fear. These experiences can raise and explore the most critical questions about human existence and the cosmos. In whatever form they take, messages from the collective uncon-scious represent the legacy of our ancestors, the concerns of our present world, and the possibilities for our future.

The Cosmic (Un)conscious?

Contrary to popular opinion, archetypes and the collective unconscious can be understood from multiple angles, including a material, non-mystical worldview. Jung himself appeared indecisive about their fundamental nature. Other scholars have also vacillated in viewing the collective unconscious as representing a primordial form of mental activity, a cosmic God-like "Mind at Large" (Huxley's position), or simply a genetically or culturally inherited feature of human consciousness.[31] Many people believe the mystical-like states triggered by psychedelics, deep meditation, or intense breathwork confirm, at minimum, the existence of the collective unconscious. Others go further and believe layers exist beyond even the collective unconscious.[32] Are these deeper layers variations of the unconscious or something else entirely?

Such hypothetical and metaphysical realms are ones we're unable to review adequately here. They require far more exposition, speculation, and leaps of faith than the collective unconscious. Nonetheless, these discussions are common in the psychedelic world and thus, bear mentioning. Remember the second, more speculative model of the psyche (Figure 1.2)? Those strange tendrils of the submerged iceberg, what I then called 'the mysterious unknown,' may belong to these realms. If that iceberg-esque image seemed absurd, it's because it was. Such metaphors eventually reach their limit. As an alternative, Figure 3.2 better visualizes ideas from this chapter, including the speculative cosmic dimension.

From a purely descriptive perspective, the experiences of people who've visited these seemingly transcendent realms *are* real. That is, they exist subjectively, and therefore, must be acknowledged. The extent to which they're due to neurochemical reactions (even in non-substance induced states) or contact with something truly transcendent is unknown. Not because we lack possible explanations or ideas but because they're hard to prove or agree upon. The best arguments can involve different underlying suppositions—assumptions we start with but can't prove with unequivocal data or foolproof reasoning. If the cosmos (and by extension, the mind) is fundamentally governed by consistent, predictable laws, then materialistic arguments *could* win. If the cosmos is fundamentally governed by information processing and probability (what some even call mind), then non-material arguments *might* prevail.[33]

Even if one side 'wins,' more controversies await. The rabbit hole twists and turns regardless of the path chosen. As it is for the farthest reaches of the cosmos, the human mind may itself contain more secrets than we can

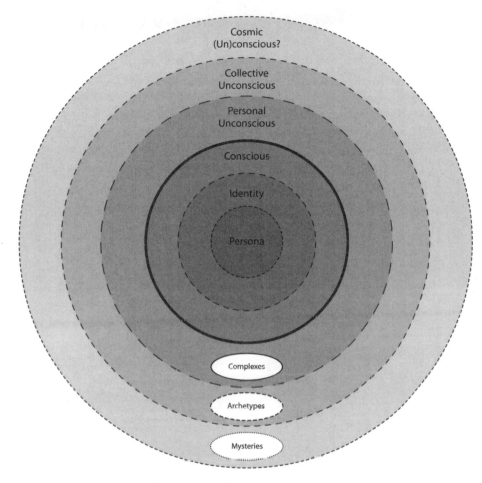

Figure 3.2 Psychedelic-Inclusive Layers of the Psyche

ever understand. We try, though, and maybe that's part of what makes us human. We can follow our sense of wonder and consider possibilities even when answers lead to greater questions and the 'Truth' inevitably remains out of reach.

The Mysteries of Consciousness—
A Curiosity Generator Task

Speaking of wonder, it's time to invoke your own curiosity about consciousness—from the accessible layers of the mind to its deepest unconscious recesses. List at least three questions that pique your interest about topics we've already covered, even if only briefly. Remember these questions don't need to be perfectly formed. They're just starting points, invitations for further exploration. Your inner explorer can lead the way. Take a couple minutes now, knowing you can return later if so inclined.

> **As I explore the conscious and unconscious mind, my biggest questions are:**

Pathways toward Self-Knowledge— Models of Personality

Alright, you've received a heavy dose of psychological theory. That's really just a taste of the potential contents of your own mind. Theory is only helpful if it can be applied to real experiences and lead to greater understanding—or in the highest standard of science, accurate prediction. Unlike cosmic phenomena, awareness of our individual selves can be much more directly obtained, or at least inferred, if we put in the effort. The big problem, however, is we're not always the best source of information about ourselves. That's the result of those shadowy layers of the unconscious. As Alan Watts said, "Trying to define yourself is like trying to bite your own teeth."[34]

Nevertheless, we can cautiously charge forward while keeping this caveat in mind. Our next step in exploring self-awareness involves the concept of personality. *Personality* refers to a person's characteristic psychological, emotional, and behavioral patterns and motivations that are experienced by the individual or observed by others. Numerous theories of personality exist, but most popular personality tests focus on how people describe their own personality—that is, what they're conscious of and can report. Personality, though, is much more than how we identify or describe ourselves—or how anyone else would describe us, for that matter. It can consist of the stories we tell about ourselves, the narratives we create to explain how we think, feel, and behave, and the collection of memories we've formed over time. It's also those parts of ourselves that we cover up, deny, or fail to nurture. In truth, we've already been talking about personality, albeit from a psychodynamic-heavy perspective.[35]

The human personality contains both manifest and latent expressions of the self. Personal growth, a value this book espouses, wouldn't be possible without unrealized potentialities within each of us. To grow, we must start with what we know about ourselves, accept what we don't, and expand our self-awareness past the existing, narrow viewpoints with which we began. Those qualities that aided you in exploring cosmic awareness come in handy here too.

Personality Traits—The Big Five

Trait-based theories of personality focus on how people differ on various, independent dimensions. To balance our highly abstract explorations so far, we can focus on a fairly straightforward trait model: *The Big Five*. Although its whimsical name doesn't suggest it, the Big Five is a modern, research-based model of personality traits.[36] The Big Five traits were originally discovered after cataloging common words we use to describe differences between people's personalities. The assumption is the more important the trait, the more words would exist to describe it.[37] After scouring dictionaries for longer than anyone would find appealing, researchers created a comprehensive list of personality-related words. They then used statistical techniques to organize words by their underlying shared domain. After replicating results in different samples, they revealed five larger domains. Drum roll, please. And here they are:

Extroversion	-versus-	Introversion
Agreeableness	-versus-	Argumentativeness
Conscientiousness	-versus-	Disorganization
Neuroticism	-versus-	Emotional Stability
Openness to Experience	-versus-	Conventionality

An easy mnemonic, no doubt uncovered by inventive Psych 101 students, is OCEAN (Openness-Conscientiousness-Extroversion-Agreeableness-Neuroticism). Figure 3.3 introduces the underlying facets contained within each larger domain. The domains and facets mean pretty much what they sound like—a benefit of using everyday language as the starting place.

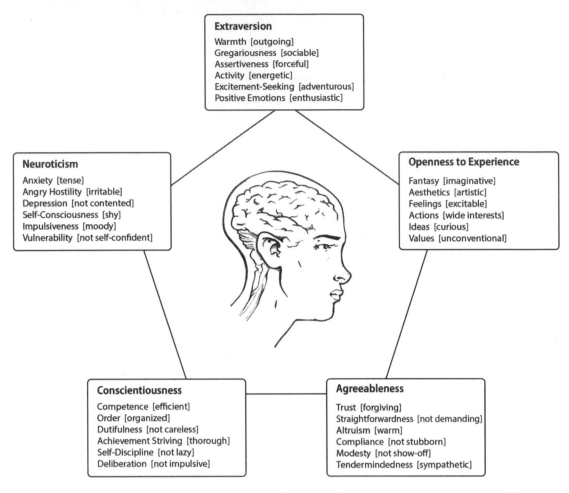

Figure 3.3 Big Five personality factors and facets (with correlated adjective).[a]

At this point in our journey, one domain is especially relevant to our exploration of psychedelic-inspired themes. In full disclosure, it happens to be my favorite: *Openness to Experience*. Openness highlights a person's interests in exploring their inner and outer worlds alongside a willingness to make their own decisions about values, ideas, and ways of knowing. Clearly, this trait describes and connects to our ally curiosity. Openness is related to higher levels of creativity and intellect, which are also relatively stable characteristics.[38]

It's curious then that psychedelics can influence this otherwise stable personality trait. Openness appears to increase when a person has a mystical experience under the influence of psilocybin, the active chemical in 'magic' mushrooms. In one study, the increases lasted for at least a year and were observed in five of six facets: Openness to Fantasy, Aesthetics, Feelings, Ideas, and Values.[39] For people who didn't have a mystical experience, Openness didn't change. MDMA can have a similar effect. Increases in Openness, in fact, partly drive the reduction of PTSD symptoms in MDMA-assisted psychotherapy.[40] These changes are remarkable given that we view personality as mostly stable upon reaching adulthood (if not earlier). Outside undergoing other types of intense psychotherapy, only major events cause lasting effects on personality, but not always in a healthy direction.

As an approach to describing personality, the Big Five is generally accepted. It's been criticized, though, for lacking a sophisticated basis in theory and for relying too heavily on a shaky assumption. What if normal language doesn't fully capture important layers of personality? Describing personality is fine and good, but what really *is* personality to begin with? And how does it interact with situational factors and culture? A variant of the Big Five addresses a few missing pieces.[41] What's most helpful for us is the distinction between basic tendencies and characteristic adaptations. *Basic tendencies* capture built-in and largely genetically influenced patterns of behavior and emotion. *Characteristic adaptations* are adjustments made to adapt to our social and cultural environment. These adaptations also encompass personality changes that can occur after powerful, transformative experiences. With the right setting, mindset, and dose, psychedelics elicit such experiences, which in turn, allow a person to break down previously formed adaptations and create new ones.

All of us have strengths, challenges, and a lot of double-edged swords when it comes to how our personality fits with our environment and the complexity of human relationships. Lucky for us, psychedelics aren't the only pathway to make changes. Any emotionally, intellectually, or spiritually powerful experience can shake up the mind and create new possibilities and opportunities for growth. In the language of neuroscience, these changes might correspond to *neuroplasticity*—how neurons in the brain form new connections and adjust old ones throughout our lifespan.[42] Your journey as undertaken in this book and its activities aim to do just that.

Personality Types—An Alternative Approach

Personality types describe different kinds of people. Speaking in categorical terms offers a nice shorthand, but it can belie a more convoluted reality. Traits that vary along a continuum, like the Big Five, tend to be the name of the game in modern personality research. That being said, the combination of traits and characteristics help us understand ourselves as a whole. That's what personality types might capture better—how different parts of ourselves interact to form the bigger picture of who we are. Unfortunately, effectively researching personality types is inherently challenging and cost prohibitive.[43]

Elaborate typologies and sophisticated theories, with all their nuance and complexity, are hard to capture in a series of True-False or multiple-choice questions. That's especially true when the person answering them must contend with an ego that keeps certain insights out of awareness.[44] Jung's concepts of Intuiting-vs-Sensing and Thinking-vs-Feeling, however, are useful and will be revisited in future chapters.[45] In the meantime, feel free to reflect on what you know about your personality type. One perk of an individual journey is that self-exploration and knowledge don't require we limit ourselves to what's true for the general population. As long as you're gaining genuine insights about yourself, you're on the right track.

Variations of Personality—A Curiosity Generator Task

Now's another good time to pause and access your inner curiosity. Just as before, take a few moments to list three or more questions about personality. These questions may be about your own personality, or about theories and ideas related to the broader topic.

> **As I explore the nature of personality, my biggest questions are:**

Fostering Growth through Self-Curiosity

According to legend, the entrance of the ancient Temple of Delphi was engraved with the Greek maxim 'Know Thyself.'[46] Like many things in life, that's easier said than done. Yet, self-curiosity is the opening to greater self-awareness. While exploring this chapter, you likely asked questions beyond those I posed. That's yet another gift from your ally curiosity. When considering self-awareness, we're better thinking of it as an expanding sense, a continuous process rather than a concrete goal that we can meet or not. The human psyche and personality are complex, multifaceted, and pretty fascinating when we stop to think about it. Each of us has an intricate collection of motivations, tendencies, and variously hidden or expressed inner conflicts and strengths.

When comparing the mysteries of the cosmos and the human mind, the cosmos wins. Our minds are embedded, after all, within the greater cosmos. Sure, that's a bit of a copout. But on average, the human brain has 86 billion neurons compared to over 100 billion galaxies in the observable universe.[47] Still, mysteries are abundant at whatever scale we choose to focus. Neuroscientist Christof Koch playfully summarizes "the central puzzle" of consciousness as being "how a three-pound organ with the consistency of tofu exudes the feeling of life."[48] Like the last chapter's question about feeling very large or small after venturing into the extremes of time and space, we're confronted with the limitations of both knowledge and language.

When contemplating the human psyche, a sense of wonder may not be the typical response. In fact, for many people, thinking about consciousness and personality may seem second-nature or even banal. It's easy to take such things for granted. But that's where the depths of the unconscious can take the lead in reawakening curiosity. Curiosity is a key ingredient to navigating the depths of our own mind. Once we think we've figured everything out, we realize we can dig even further, sparked perhaps by surprising interactions with others or questions spontaneously coming to mind on our daily commute. Curiosity and insight come together as if soulmates destined to find each other—if soulmates exist, that is.

Since we're still early in our journey, there will be times where you do a reflection activity, read about a novel concept, or practice a new skill and come to an 'Aha!' moment. Those moments are great, but they aren't the only ways you know you're venturing into new territory. Insights don't always lead to excitement or confidence. Some are hard, and some painful to admit. But that's how you know you're on a real adventure. Uncovering hidden pain and vulnerability signals that we're all only human in the end. Our deepest personal struggles parallel the deeper struggles of human life.

In difficult moments, a mantra may help you navigate your exploration of more turbulent waters. Psychedelic researcher, scholar, and psychologist Bill

Richards suggests using 'in and through.'[49] It's not just a helpful touchstone for people undergoing psychedelic journeys. It's for anyone trying to live their lives with awareness and honesty. Some insights may force us to make tough choices. If so, go in and through. Unexpected feedback from others may occasionally be hard to hear. Yet again, go in and through. This mantra is a reminder to trust the process of growth. As championed by modern psychedelic researchers, we must trust our *inner healer* to take us where we need to go, even if it sometimes feels painful or scary.[50] The notion of an inner healer isn't new. It's the part of our mind that understands how to mend our wounds and grow from adversity. The inner healer belongs to the archetypal Self. Whatever we call it, this part of our consciousness is an ally and guide in all life's journeys.

Concrete Suggestions & Journey Report

For some concrete ideas about bringing self-awareness to life, see Box 3.2. These are only examples. If you're inspired to do something else to expand self-awareness, then by all means, follow your inspiration. For an illustration of how this topic relates to psychedelics, see Journey Report 3.1. Among other themes, this journey demonstrates how a single psychedelic experience can have multiple phases and areas of exploration. The pleasant initial part of Emilia's journey focused on her relationships with others and desire to connect more deeply. Later, her attention shifted to an intense, unpleasant weight and pressure at different locations in her body. During her psychedelic journey, Emilia was unaware that these locations corresponded to areas of traumatic injury from a motorcycle accident seven years prior to the journey. The strong sensations were symbolic and served to bring her awareness to insufficiently processed memories and emotions about the accident. Although unpleasant, she was able to focus on breathing to minimize her distress and experienced healing long after the journey was over.

Box 3.2

Expanding Self-Awareness within Everyday Life

Suggestion	Example
Reflect on feedback you've received in recent years. Consider whether the feedback message was more about the person giving it or if it touched upon something likely true about yourself.	A long-term friend has been telling you how bad you are at responding to text messages in a timely manner. You've also heard something similar from an ex-partner. You previously brushed this feedback off because you thought it was normal to ignore messages when 'in the middle of something.' But now, upon reflection, you admit that 'something' has usually been watching YouTube videos or playing video games. You decide to reach out to your friend and share an intention to be more responsive—within reason, of course.
Notice patterns about what routinely occupies your conscious mind in quieter moments.	You realize spend a lot of time thinking about your job, even when you're not on the clock. Only when prompted or when something's wrong do you consider your relationships with friends and family members.
Revisit 2-3 favorite fictional characters within film, TV, books, or traditional mythology and consider their personal meaning and relevance.	Choosing your favorites is easy. First, you re-watch your favorite Marvel movie *Captain Marvel* and notice how Carol Danvers must see through deception before awakening to her true nature and unleashing her full potential.[b] Then, you re-read segments of Bram Stoker's *Dracula,* a favorite from high school.[c] You admire Professor Van Helsing for his open-mindedness and possession of esoteric knowledge. You suppose the overlap, which is hard to discern at first, involves the theme of hidden knowledge and unconventional insight.
Reflect on your earliest memory of life.	You remember the birth of your younger sibling and the mix of excitement and confusion you initially felt. You reach out to your sibling and share the memory and laugh together.
Connect to the part of yourself that's motivated you to undergo this journey of self-reflection and discovery.	You reflect on your choice to read this book and say 'yes' to the journey. You wonder if this part of yourself is the cheerleader, the one in charge, or your own inner healer.

---

[b] Boden, 2019

[c] Stoker, 1897/2001. Note this version also includes an excerpt from Freud's essay, "The Uncanny" (originally published in 1919). Features of the uncanny overlap with Jung's shadow and trickster archetypes.

Grounding Words—A Brief Summary

In this chapter, you took your next step in our journey and realized the mysteries of consciousness parallel those of the cosmos. As you pondered the limits of self-knowledge, you began realizing that a lot more of you exists just under the surface of your conscious, ego-controlled awareness. Although the hidden layers of your mind contain unexpressed motivations and desires, its unconscious depths don't end there. The deepest layers of the unconscious contain archetypal forms and patterns shared with people inside and outside of your own culture, extending to all of humanity—if not also with other life. You then explored other aspects of yourself as revealed through models of personality, primarily the Big Five. Whether we talk of traits or types, you, like all others, face limits here too. The degree to which you understand your personality is restrained by your existing awareness of both conscious and unconscious patterns. You didn't give up, though. You embraced the challenges of expanding self-awareness. By doing so, you reaffirmed your ally of curiosity and discovered its connection with higher levels of openness. You strengthen your resolve to uncover parts of yourself harder to understand or acknowledge. You have faith that you can go 'in and through' when difficulties arise. With this trust, you move forward and even feel eager for what's to come. After all, there's so much to explore in what you already know of yourself and what you still have left to uncover.

Your Assignment, Your Choice

Now that you're steeped in several ideas to expand self-awareness, it's time to select your independent assignments. Just like last time, you have two larger categories to choose from—*Reflective-Intellectual* and *Experiential-Emotional*. Even reflecting on how you make the decision may provide useful information about yourself. But no pressure. As before, aim to do at least one activity each day before you proceed to the next chapter. You can mix it up or double-down on the same activity—again, your choice.

Assignments 3.1

Expanding Self-Awareness

Reflective-Intellectual	Experiential-Emotional
☐ Task—Take **personality tests,** such as free ones offered by: [51]	☐ Task—Start **daily journaling** using a stream-of-consciousness approach (write whatever comes to mind, even if random or non-linear, may also include dreams)
Truity.com OpenPsychometrics.org SelfActualizationTests.com	
Recommended—Big Five Personality Test, Open Extended Jungian Type Scales, or for fun, the "Which Character?" Quiz	
Time—Minimum of two tests with time to reflect on results (1 hr)	Time—15-30 min per day, or up to two pages
Aim—To satiate curiosity about how your personality (at least its more conscious elements) compares with others	Aim—To uncover recurring themes, patterns, conflicts, and other contents of your mind
☐ Task—Pick **archetypes** from the list in this chapter, research it, and consider how it manifests in your life or culture	☐ Task—Practice the meditation in **Meditation 3.1 "Exploring the Museum of Your Mind"**
Time—Minimum of 2 archetypes and 3 representations in pop culture, myth, or religion (1 hr)	Time—Minimum of 2-3x/week, ~10 min each practice
Aim—To expand your understanding of various ways archetypes are expressed in culture, myth, dreams, etc.	Aim—To examine the contents and randomness of the mind, giving you clues about your consciousness and the layers within

After reviewing your options (and maybe doing one), respond to this chapter's Travel Journal prompt. Your style of expression is again open. Try not to overthink about what exactly you write, draw, or create. This prompt is just to get you started.

Travel Journal

What do I already know about myself, including my personality?

What might be parts of my mind less known even to me?

How can I expand my awareness to these more unconscious aspects of my mind?

JOURNEY REPORT 3.1 Old Wounds, New Healing

My first higher dose mushroom journey (about 4.5 grams) started with a pulse. I'm not sure if it was my heartbeat or some other sensation, but it became so loud it drowned out everything else. I somehow knew then that this was the beginning of a lifechanging experience. Many people I interact with in my daily life, like family and coworkers, came into my inner vision over the course of the journey. I felt each person's energy and explored ways to connect with them so that we could learn from each other. I didn't see their faces clearly, but I knew it was them. Various people appeared at different points. The more central their position, the brighter the light around them. My unconscious surprised me in who I saw. Interestingly, in the months that followed, some of these people actually started to play a bigger role in my life. It was as if my journey foreshadowed this change. In other cases, I was simply reliving the past or indulging wishful thinking. But overall, I felt lovely energy all around me. It was warm, supportive, and without judgment altogether. It just was.

An uncomfortable aspect of my journey involved experiencing heavy weights on different parts of my body. The whole time I was lying comfortably on my back on a soft bed. The heaviness started with my right shoulder and breast and it felt like an elephant was sitting on it. I couldn't shake it and instead just breathed into it actively until it dissolved, which took a while. It was quite painful and stayed with me for what seemed like a long time. I remember thinking, "What if this is a sign that I have breast cancer growing inside me?" I couldn't explain it. Then the pain left my right chest and traveled to my hip. The heavy weight seemed to push me deeper into the bed. I even touched my hip with my hand, but it didn't relieve the pain. Again, I breathed into it for a long time. As with the chest, it remained for a while until it vanished

Report continues on next page

as if it had never been there. I then felt a similar sensation in my hand. Again, I had to actively breath and concentrate on the discomfort until it disappeared so that I could move on with the rest of my journey.

It took me a few days of reflection to realize what the spots symbolized. I had had a motorcycle accident 7 years prior. I broke my right collar bone, fractured a few ribs and my left hand, and had a flesh wound on my hip. I knew I had not completely processed this trauma, but this accident was not even on my mind going into the journey. I was so surprised it became such a major part of my experience. The way it appeared was striking. One part of my body flared up after the other and it forced me to concentrate on each separately, confronting my pain and discomfort, and accepting it by breathing into it. I will never forget what that felt like and thinking about it a year later makes me emotional. Whatever happened in my brain on that day was clearly telling me that I hadn't spent enough time with this traumatic accident even after all these years. In the days after my journey, I felt no discomfort. I went through the same motions in the same positions, but it was as if I was given a break from this psychological and somatic pain. It was truly remarkable. I learned that day to respect the mystery of my unconscious mind and recognize that recovering from old sources of pain takes time and patience. But healing, even if I didn't realize I needed it, is still possible.

—Emilia, Age 29

Note. This account and all others in the book are de-identified and anonymous to protect the confidentiality of the person sharing their story. Minor grammar, spelling, and stylistic changes were made and usually in partnership with the person providing the account.

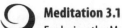

Meditation 3.1
Exploring the Museum of Your Mind (~10 min)

Carefully read this script to get a sense of this meditation. Then, close your eyes and lead yourself through it. Remember it's not about getting it 'right.' As long as you're focused on exploring and observing your own mind to expand your self-awareness, you're doing it just fine. Pace yourself as you need. No meditation is a race to the end.

Find a comfortable, quiet place to relax into your body. Don't worry about where you place your legs, arms, or hands as long as it's comfortable. All things being equal, a symmetrical posture works well. Now, close your eyes and focus on breathing in and breathing out, naturally at your own pace. Ride the waves of your breath until you settle into a relaxing rhythm. In your mind's eye, picture yourself where you are now. Fill this picture with as much detail as comes naturally. What are you wearing? What might you look like now from the outside?

Now, imagine from this outside observing point of view, you're able to peer into your own mind. No longer observing what's on the outside of yourself but what's within….Imagine seeing, if you could, the contents of your own psyche. What do you see?….Are there thoughts?…. Emotions?….Sensations?….How about any images? ….Remind yourself that whatever you see or experience is perfectly okay….The content of your mind that emerges from within can come, and it can go…expand and contract…and all you have to do is observe them as it happens…

Notice too if you feel any judgment about what's coming up….Maybe even judgment about not being able to focus…instead of indulging in self-judgment, just notice the judgment exists. Like any other content that comes to mind, you can observe it without having to change it, fight it, or deny it….If helpful, try saying, "I'm aware a part of my mind is thinking…" and complete the sentence with the contents of the thought. By observing your mind, you're not buying into its contents…or wrestling with them either….

What if you approach every random thought, feeling, memory, or image with curiosity? View each as a single item within the art exhibit of every moment… and understand each moment as existing within the vast museum that is your mind, past, present, and future….What if instead of concentrating on each little piece of artwork, you were to become aware of the 'you' that is the museum itself. You're both the endless array of art inside and the museum that contains everything....What is this perspective like?....Rest here for a moment, simply being the museum as a whole....

From this experience of being the museum in its entirety, begin to shift your attention to your breath...and the experience of breathing in...and breathing out. As you center yourself in your breath, you center yourself in your physical being....Imagine riding the waves of each breath as you've done before.... Being here now, in this body of yours, in this place....Here on Earth....

Still, with your eyes closed, start to imagine the space around you....Fill your imagination with as many details as you can remember....As you reach the limit of your memory, slowly and gently reopen your eyes. Breathe in the air of this present moment, knowing the museum continues to exist.

Experiential Awareness— Four Modes of Experiencing

Drink your tea slowly and reverently, as if it is the axis on which the whole earth revolves—slowly, evenly, without rushing toward the future. Live the actual moment. Only this actual moment is life.

—Thich Nhat Hanh, *The Miracle of Mindfulness*[1]

Journey Waypoint III

While exploring the cosmos and the psyche, we've found a boundless array of mysteries. At the same time, we have more to discover in our quest to expand awareness. In its purest form, awareness is awakening to the present moment and the reverberations of our movement through the eternal now. I hope you forgive such grandiose phrasing. The idea, at the end of the day, is incredibly straightforward. That's what frustrates many writers and thinkers. If I just said, "Be here now," per the title of Ram Dass's well-known book,[2] then I'd be summarizing succinctly a key purpose of this chapter.

A summary, though, won't let us go beyond the basics and unpack the more intriguing nuances. There are many angles from which to experience the present moment. If life is a collection of experiences, then each of us certainly has our own unique mix—a consequence of both our personalities and the distinct situations and life circumstances we encounter. Everyone has habitual patterns in how they experience each moment and by extension their life. These patterns often reflect our personality. It also reflects our ego's efforts to fulfill its 'reducing valve' function by sifting through data and selecting a manageable—or desirable—subset. A thinking-oriented introvert and a feeling-dominant extrovert can experience the same situation quite differently. If they conferred with each other, they might gain a richer perspective that addresses each other's blind spots. Of course, for that to occur, they'd both need to be open-minded—a quality you likely already possess.

In a parallel yet exaggerated fashion, individuals under psychedelic influence can have significantly divergent experiences. Some people see sounds. Some re-examine their fundamental beliefs about existence. Others encounter an emptiness of all thought entirely. Our last chapter opened the door to higher levels of self-awareness. In this one, we'll focus less on the depths of the individual psyche and more on the breadth of every single moment. Although the limits of human perception and ego remain, we'll attempt to locate a realm of awareness less encumbered by overinterpretations and unconscious motivations—at least in theory. It is, after all, yet another Sisyphean task. If we foster greater experiential awareness than previously held, however, we'll uncover sources of not only information but also strength. At minimum, you'll gain a few essential skills for your continuing adventures.

Self-Reflections Check-In

Before getting too far ahead, let's check-in. In the second waypoint along our psychedelic path, we returned to more human concerns. Instead of a resting point after voyaging to the stars, we reflected deeply about the many secrets of the conscious and unconscious mind. Your own consciousness expanded beyond your everyday idea of who you are, and you found questions, if not clear-cut answers, about what may lie beneath. Consider your chosen activities from the list of options. Between that chapter and this one, what did you contemplate, observe, or do? Did you gain a better grasp of your personality and how you compare to others? Did you start uncovering hidden parts of yourself? Perhaps you have more questions to ask now than before. You might find yourself concerned about having fewer answers than desired. That too provides insight. Reflecting on your patterns of emotional reactions will prove invaluable as you continue exploring. These patterns might tell you more about yourself than you realize. Take a few moments to reflect if you want. When ready, you can dive in again.

The Four Modes of Experiencing— A Phenomenological Approach

Few of us sit around and ask questions like, "What *is* experience?" Everyday experiences just *are*. We take them for granted. We move about the world, interact with parts of it, and move on. What if we observed our experiences in a far more complete, systematic way? If we did, we might become amateur philosophers studying phenomenology. Based on its Greek roots, *phenomenology* means studying that which appears. For our current purposes, this approach entails looking directly at 'what appears' in our subjective experience. Of course, we continue to be limited in our starting place, our own point of view—which you now understand is also narrow when we acknowledge the unconscious. Besides, if we overinvest in our own subjective perspective, we may lose sight of the fact that everyone else, outside of us, also has their own. Thus, we should be cautious about unintentionally reinforcing an egotistical mindset. Later in our journey, we'll think more about other people, but to get there, we must focus on expanding our own awareness first.

So, where shall we begin? The lineage of phenomenology is vast, but we can land on a pragmatic model that captures the largest domains. That model I call the four modes of experiencing. It organizes aspects of experience into thoughts, emotions, body, and behavior.[3] These four modes help us describe experiences, including psychedelic ones, without being overly narrow or getting caught up in overinterpretation. Expanding experiential awareness means accessing sources of information our everyday waking consciousness can easily overlook—by habit, by accident, or with some unconscious motivation. Every experience has an array of conscious to unconscious elements. But as

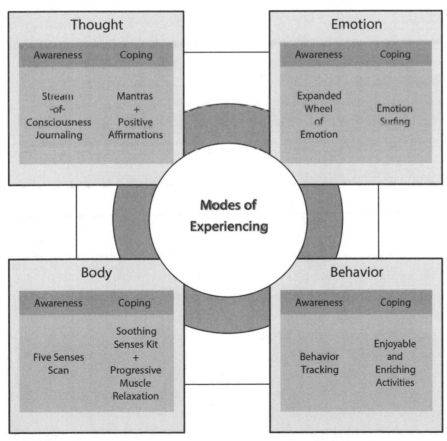

Figure 4.1 Four Modes of Experiencing with Corresponding Awareness & Coping Skills

Jedi Master Qui-Gon Jinn summarized, "Your focus determines your reality."[4] Although the modes are interconnected, I'll introduce each separately and offer skills for expanding awareness *and* coping in times of stress. As previewed in Figure 4.1, these skills are crucial tools for the upcoming trials. And having them will complete our preparations for what lies ahead.

Exploring Thoughts

Overview

Let's start with thoughts. Why? Because they're the easiest to access. In fact, our highly developed brains (in our biased human-centric estimate at least) gifts us with symbolic thought and mental experiences. The thinking mode is not just easily accessible, it also tends to be the dominate mode for how we experience ourselves and the outside world. Entire systems of psychotherapy have arisen either to harness the power of thoughts and transform them (cognitive approaches) or bypass them completely when they act as distractions (behavioral ones). Whether we want them or not, thoughts, language, and other forms of symbolic, mental phenomena are major factors for how we engage with life. The evolution of complex language is likely how our species became so dominant. Language allowed us to communicate with others more directly and efficiently, thus enabling planning and negotiation. It also gave us an internal system of complex self-reflection and understanding. Thoughts transform direct experience into words, which then organize how we understand experiences.

That might seem abstract—one of the benefits and downsides of using language. An example may help. What happens when you hear the word 'apple?' Do you imagine, almost instantly, the taste or smell of an apple? Do you even start to salivate a bit? Most people have some reaction just by hearing the word. If apples don't work, think about something tart like lemons. Or the phrase 'job performance appraisal.' Maybe that jolted you a bit more. These words are symbolic stand-ins for actual objects or experiences. Yet words alone often trigger imaginary and felt reactions by connecting to our memories of past experiences or expectations of possible future ones. These reactions are relevant to psychedelic experiences too. Thinking about the words 'mushrooms' or 'ayahuasca' can evoke elements of prior ceremonies—or even the taste! Words are more powerful than we realize.

How we interpret an experience can also alter the experience itself. Conscious and unconscious patterns of interpretation become habits of mind that often have more to do with our past than our present. Over countless life experiences, we develop an internal system for understanding the outside world, others, and ourselves. Early lessons are usually the strongest and most engrained. They can be updated when we have especially powerful experiences that surprise us and differ from our default interpretations and expectations. This process might explain how psychedelics can lead to enduring changes.

Changing prior beliefs and expectations, however, requires mental energy—not to mention the combination of awareness, motivation, and intention to revise them. Our brains prioritize efficient processing over the more difficult and slow process of contemplation and revision. Words, language, thoughts, and other mental phenomena give symbols to experiences so that we can process them quicker. Our brains look automatically for similarities to what's already been learned. They allow us to think fast and to push farther to more abstract, complex, and theoretical levels than we otherwise could.

This first mode of verbal and symbolic thinking sounds amazing, right? It is! But it has some significant downsides too. That's a point many modern therapeutic approaches make routinely. To the extent that we're 'fused' with our thoughts—that is, believe that we *are* our thoughts and that our thoughts reflect *actual* reality—we're trapped in a narrow (and at least somewhat inaccurate) way of experiencing life.[5]

Have you ever had an extreme or unrealistic thought? Like 'No one cares,' 'Everything's meaningless,' or 'I'll never be happy again.' Of course. We all have. It's part of being human. Sometimes such thinking is easier to dismiss. When it's a swift thought that's clearly overstated, we might catch ourselves before it has too much of an impact. At other times, our automatic thoughts are so strong and dominant that a slower, more deliberate examination of a situation seems impossible. Either way, thoughts and interpretations can directly color our experience and filter what information even enters our minds. If left unchecked, repetition creates belief. Beliefs, in turn, further empower thoughts and transform them into habitual attitudes towards life.

On the other hand, sometimes overthinking becomes the problem. We may overthink a situation to the point that the accuracy of our thoughts no longer matters. We can waste so much energy self-reflecting and thinking that we've totally missed out on hours (or even days and weeks) of living our life. Thoughts are powerful. And they're seductive. They want us to believe they're the only way to experience the world. They want us to ignore the downsides of living life through words, beliefs, and judgments. That's why we're discussing them first and as only one of many ways of experiencing.

Awareness & Coping Skills

In psychedelic or other non-ordinary states, our everyday fusion with thoughts can be seriously challenged. Normal patterns of thinking, including even basic linearity, can break open to reveal chaos—chaos that when harnessed, can create new possibilities. Lucky for us, psychedelics aren't the sole method to alter conscious thoughts, question their dominance, and develop a new relationship with them.

As a skill for building awareness, I highly recommend *Stream-of-Consciousness Journaling*. This approach has been both an optional assignment from the last chapter and a style you may already have used to respond to Travel Journal prompts. Stream-of-consciousness journaling allows us to record our thoughts as they occur. By writing them down, they become external and much easier to examine. Journaling can also disrupt repetitive thoughts that might otherwise bounce endlessly around inside our head. Recording our stream of consciousness can uncover thought patterns that may not surface with more deliberate, focused writing. With either approach, you may notice not only how thoughts can be random or relatively empty in meaning, but also habitual and persuasive, regardless of their usefulness or accuracy.

Given how powerful and even domineering thoughts can be, it'd be a shame to dismiss them outright. Wouldn't it be great if we could harness, at least cautiously, the power of thoughts? Many methods also exist for this purpose. The oldest is probably *Mantra Repetition*, in which sacred sounds, words, or phrases are repeated to induce a meditative state. Examples include the classic Buddhist chant 'Om Mani Padme Hum,' which contains the Buddha's core teachings in a single phrase, and the Roman Catholic prayer Hail Mary, often recited as a practice of meditation, worship, or offering of penance. The meaning of the words contained in a mantra may or may not be as important as the practice of focusing on its intention.

Mantras and prayers have been repackaged for secular purposes as well. In this form, they become encouraging phrases or *Positive Affirmations* to be repeated or written in strategic places as reminders. This approach has become a self-help meme after decades of use. But maybe because it works. For most of my life, I was skeptical of this 'hokey' practice. Then over time, several clients described how their affirmations helped them recover from chronic stress and adopt more positive thinking patterns. I finally broke down my own defenses when a friend and I came across similar practices in a creativity workbook we committed to doing together.[6] Staying true to my 'good student' persona, I acquiesced and created a few personalized 'mantras' to transcribe daily. Lo and behold, they became recurring thoughts that popped up randomly throughout my day. It even made me start believing them. Here I thought my skepticism made me immune. Then again, I'm only human. Even the cynic can learn new tricks.

An interesting yet somewhat unsettling research finding is that optimists tend to have better outcomes even when relatively inaccurate in their positivity.[7] As a science-minded scholar, that boggles my mind. As a clinical psychologist, I totally get it. The power of optimism connects to the now-classic notion of *self-fulfilling prophecies*.[8] Believing good things will come increases the likelihood they do. Be careful. That works for negativity too. There are limits, of course. But the observation that thoughts and beliefs, at various levels of consciousness, affect outcomes is consistent with many psychological theories. Thus, the mode of thinking can both narrow and expand the possibilities of our lives. Thoughts reflect a sliver of our external reality but often a large portion of our conscious experience. The greatest danger is overvaluing our thinking minds and viewing our conscious thoughts as a pure and complete understanding of ourselves and our existence.

Exploring Emotions

Overview

Emotions are critical to how human beings and probably many other animals experience life.[9] They influence our motivations, thoughts, bodily sensations, and behaviors. Numerous theories of emotion exist, but theory firmly lies within the thought mode, which we've already covered. Still, you're reading a book, so we're required to use words to explore experiences going far beyond the boundaries of verbal expression.

In describing the range of emotional experiences, our current scientific understanding outlines three components—valence, intensity, and label. The most purely descriptive elements are valence and intensity.[10] *Valence* refers to the degree to which an emotion is pleasant or unpleasant. For example, feelings of happiness and safety share positive undertones even though they're different emotional experiences. *Intensity* is the subjective force of the emotion. Imagine the times you've experienced happiness. The most powerful memories are usually more intense, even to the point of ecstasy or rapture. You may have other memories of experiences that although less intense, still largely fall along the same dimension of happiness.

How we *label* an emotion is another way to understand and communicate its distinctive qualities. Specific labels can reflect a combination of the emotional valence and intensity, but labels communicate more than a mechanical, two-dimensional description. I could say, "I'm feeling a 10/10 intensity on the highly negative end of the emotional spectrum," and you, stunned by my weird phrasing, still wouldn't know if I was devastated, furious, or terrified. Naming an emotion lets us communicate with others efficiently—and ideally, with greater accuracy. It can also help us make sense of an initially nonverbal experience. In fact, across many different types of therapy, labeling our emotions is one of the first tasks in learning to manage them. These therapies recognize emotions have a purpose, and when we discount them, they don't go away. By ignoring our emotions, we're also ignoring the underlying messages they're trying to tell us about our experience.

Although we have numerous words for describing emotions, several researchers have attempted to distill them into basic, fundamental types. Some approaches look for emotions that are expressed consistently across cultures and/or offer some benefit to survival.[11] Results vary and are constantly being revisited, but they include up to eight core emotions: joy, fear, surprise, sadness, disgust, anger, trust and anticipation. If we created an all-inclusive list of emotion words, though, that list would be absurdly long—even if limited to English. Sometimes words describe a mix of emotions—like contempt being a mix of disgust and anger. Other times they reflect a more specific manifestation of a basic emotion—like worry as a kind of fear. Each of us differ too in how specific and nuanced we are in describing our emotions.[12]

If you're intrigued by the hidden complexity of feelings, you're not alone. Much of our poetry, stories, and artwork expresses the nuances of human emotional experiences. For now, though, we can add just one more layer of complexity—the distinction between primary and secondary emotions.[13] *Primary emotions* come on quickly but fade naturally after the initial trigger ends. Think of feeling surprised upon seeing someone you know unexpectedly while out and about. *Secondary emotions* are slow burns, delayed responses, or transformed reactions to a natural emotional response.

Secondary emotions can also be feelings about other feelings. Guilt that comes after self-reflection is a great example—like feeling guilty after expressing anger towards someone. Note too that although guilt and shame may occur together, they're often confused.[14] Guilt is feeling responsible while being distressed about how our actions have hurt someone else or not met our own standards and values. Shame is feeling bad about our core self and perceived inadequacy, usually paired with a sense of powerlessness to change.

By exploring secondary emotions, we've ventured into how experiential modes are interlinked, in this case, thought and emotion. Arguably, the 'purest' emotions are ones most directly tied to an experience without the need for interpretation. Then again placing such value judgments on emotions can lead us into some tricky conflicts—within ourselves and with others. Emotions we deem as 'not okay' or unacceptable can become parts of our inner exile and/or our projected shadow. On the other hand, emotions we cultivate over time can become our characteristic attitudes toward ourselves, others, and life in general.

Awareness & Coping Skills

Becoming more aware of our emotions is a crucial step in building both experiential and self-awareness. Emotional awareness is, of course, complicated by the hidden layers of the mind. Nevertheless, greater attention to our emotional reactions can expose information that may otherwise reside in the unconscious. My colleagues and I sometimes offer clients a list or visual representation of emotions to get the ball rolling.[15] As seen in Figure 4.2, the *Expanded Wheel of Emotion* organizes emotional labels by their broader domain and intensity. Reviewing such graphics can help pinpoint what's being experienced in the moment or upon reflection. As with thoughts, exploring your feelings over time can reveal patterns. What emotions do you tend to feel the most often? What situations evoke your strongest emotional reactions? Investigating possible patterns can foster significant emotional insight.

Sometimes emotions feel a bit too intense. Emotions are powerful experiences, so we must handle them with care. It's not emotions themselves that are dangerous. It's what they might compel us to do. The danger lies in how emotions can motivate risky or harmful behavior. At the same time, ignoring or exerting tight control over emotions allows them to slip into the unconscious. Even there, emotions can wreak havoc and secretly motivate us. The simplest alternative approach is to slow down and experience the emotion as a wave that peaks and then falls. This image leads directly to *Emotion Surfing*, a coping skill you can practice in these steps:

1. Pause or create space where you can slow down, ideally in private

2. Focus on how the emotion shows up in your current experience. Consider its influence on other experiential modes, such as the emotion

being felt in your body, echoed in your thoughts, or evident in your expressed, desired, or imagined behavior

3. Instead of feeding the emotion (or any other part of the experience), just let it happen. Notice how it slowly changes and fades over time—usually within seconds or minutes

4. Maintain this gentle awareness until the emotion has completed its natural cycle, or you feel more capable of returning to your normal flow of life

This skill's strength is in how it avoids active efforts to control, overinterpret, or judge the emotion itself. In non-emergency situations, emotions naturally come and go when observed without interference. You're not trying to change your feelings. You're merely getting on your surfboard and riding them out. If you're like me, you may fall off the surfboard occasionally. That's alright. There are always more waves to catch.

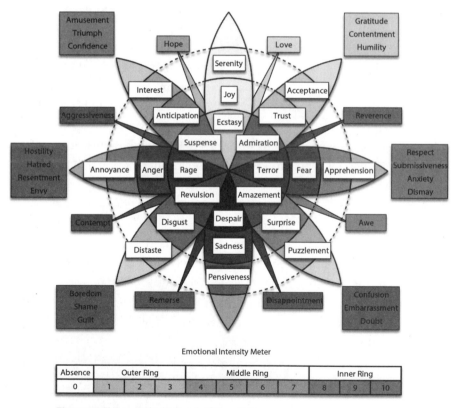

Emotional Intensity Meter

Absence	Outer Ring			Middle Ring				Inner Ring		
0	1	2	3	4	5	6	7	8	9	10

Figure 4.2 Expanded Wheel of Emotion

Thoughts and Emotions—A Curiosity Generator Task

Since we're halfway through the four modes, let's stop to check in. What interests you about thoughts and emotions or how they're connected? Using words like 'interest' and 'curiosity' might make us wonder if they're emotions, attitudes, moods, or something else entirely.[16] Whether or not you suddenly care about these conceptual labels, list at least three questions that do engage your curiosity about these two modes or related skills. Take no more than two minutes now but remember you can add to this list later.

> **As I explore the modes of thoughts and emotions, my biggest questions are:**

Exploring the Body

Overview

And now we find ourselves at the third mode of experiencing—the body. In our mind-dominated modern world, the body can sometimes be left behind. Yet, as far as we can tell, the other modes of experiencing (thought, emotion, and behavior) all require a body—or at minimum, a rudimentary brain. Psychedelics, as well, work through some mind-body connection. Of course, in more intense moments, a journeyer may forget they have a body at all. But psychedelics trigger such experiences first through neurochemical mechanisms.[17] Psychedelics provide but one of many pathways to alter consciousness. Meditation is another route. The nature of the mind-body connection intersects with many profound questions.[18] Can consciousness be reduced to a complex network of neurons firing? Is it an emergent feature of the brain? Or, is the brain merely a gateway to consciousness?

For our current purposes, we need only consider how our bodies provide another method of experiencing life itself. In many ways, the body anchors us to our external world.[19] It's how we interact with other living beings and inanimate objects. It's how we perceive our environment and, at least in part, how we experience our emotions. What, then, do we make of bodily experiences when the mind can dominate much of our everyday life? Many people, in fact, view the mind as superior because it gives us access to reason and rationality—though, to be fair, it's debatable how often we use these abilities. Well over a century ago, Friedrich Nietzsche critiqued the dominance of the mind over the body in the West and attacked its emphasis on "rationality at any cost."[20] He called it a sickness of the post-Enlightenment era to dismiss our 'base' animalistic instincts (the then-dominant perspective in scientific and religious circles alike). Instead, Nietzsche suggested we re-align ourselves with our natural bodily needs and functions.[21] Of course, it's rarely that easy given cultural value judgments on so-called animalistic instincts and desires.[22]

Alas, the debates of mind-vs-body and reason-vs-instinct aren't the only barriers to consider here. Discomfort and disconnection with the body can come from many places. Some of these factors intersect with our upcoming trials. In the meantime, we can understand the body simply as a source of information. Bodily experiences include not only the five senses (sound, sight, smell, taste, touch) but also a range of other sensations. Examples include pressure, temperature, hunger vs. satiation, exhaustion vs. energy, and pain vs. pleasure. We must not forget that the body also plays a role in instinctual 'gut reactions' and intuitions—feelings that evade immediate, conscious correlates in rational thought or discrete emotions. When the mind is dominant, we're left to wonder what information our bodies might also hold. True balance means attending to physical sensations in tandem with mental phenomena. It's not about competition. It's about synergy.

Awareness & Coping Skills

Many modern mental health specialists have worked to re-establish the connection between mind and body—partly for practical purposes. Talk therapy is great, but ignoring the body can limit its effectiveness.[23] Various frameworks seek to remedy this blind spot. The following is but a small sampling:

- **Third-wave Behavioral Therapy**—structured, evidence-based approaches that incorporate the body, such as Dialectical Behavior Therapy,[24] Mindfulness-Based Stress Reduction,[25] and Skills Training in Affective and Interpersonal Regulation (STAIR)[26]
- **Hakomi**[27]—a framework that emphasizes mindfulness, nonviolence, and mind-body-spirit wholeness
- **Holotropic Breathwork**[28]—the practice of rapid, rhythmic breathing (usually with drumming or singing) as a method to induce a non-ordinary state of consciousness

Many approaches to bodily awareness recognize the breath as an anchor to both the body and the present moment. In other words, when in doubt, go with the breath.[29] We've already been using the breath in a basic way in this book's meditations. Holotropic Breathwork is an alternative, noteworthy practice because of its psychedelic roots and connection to Stan Grof, a pioneer of psychedelic psychotherapy. Breathwork can be unexpectedly powerful (while being completely legal). Intense breath work, however, is best left to guided experiences with experts.

For our journey, we're going to stick with some safe and simple yet effective skills using the body. Our awareness skill is the *Five Senses Scan*. Keep in mind the body has more than five senses. Spatial and temporal perceptions are two that conveniently connect to cosmic awareness. Each of us has access to varying levels of each sense, and some we might be unable to experience at all. The five senses included in this skill are places to start. You can adapt these to whatever senses are available, as long as you're working towards increasing awareness.

To practice the standard version, begin by asking yourself, what am I seeing right now? Scan the environment and attend to the visual details, including ones you've ignored. What are you hearing? From quieter to louder sounds; from constant to periodic ones. What about any smells around you? If nothing, then you might bring to your nose something fragrant. Do the same for taste. Taste is intricately connected to smell, so exploring them together with the same object, like a piece of fruit, can be a great option. What are your feelings with your sense of touch? Even without purposely touching anything, we often have internal sensations in our body, like a growling stomach or muscle tension. Similarly, external contact through our skin allows us to notice how the fabric of our clothes feel, for instance. These experiences usually exist far in the background as our minds are distracted by other experiential modes or tasks.

Whatever emerges by scanning the senses, the goal is simply to acknowledge and attend to all sensory experiences occurring in the moment. Since the mind constantly chatters, you'll probably notice judgments, triggered memories, and future-oriented thoughts arising regardless. Sensory awareness, in its purest form, is about observing the present, not evaluations of it as good, bad, or neutral. We can accept distracting thoughts or memories as they come, but instead of following their breadcrumbs or judging ourselves for having them, we can gently redirect our attention to the senses.

This skill is highly portable. Here's another insider secret: if inclined, you can even transform it into a more strategic coping skill. You can do so by creating a *Soothing Senses Kit* that includes your favorite objects to smell, taste, touch, hear, or view. Creating a physical kit allows you to savor these pleasing sensations when helpful or desired. Sensory awareness provides us two skills for the price of one.

Even though senses are great for both awareness and stress management, a real contender for body-based coping skill of the century is the classic *Progressive Muscle Relaxation*.[30] This technique is straightforward as well. Start from your head or your feet and strongly tense any muscles within that area on both sides of your body for 10 seconds, then release for 10 seconds. Move to the next set of muscles and repeat. Once finished, you'll likely notice significant relaxation in your body and probably your mind too. That's because you're both biding your time, similar to emotion surfing, and you're paradoxically tensing muscles in order to relieve tension. The tense-then-relax strategy actively releases stress that is stored within our body. If specific muscles are especially sore or tense, then adding self-massage to this skill afterwards may be a good idea. Another quick tip from psychiatrist and psychedelic expert Julie Holland is left-nostril breathing, which improves relaxation according to several research studies and is part of some types of yoga.[31]

It's all too common to be disconnected with our bodies. As a contribution towards mending this rift, Figure 4.3 offers an extra summary of our three main body-oriented skills.

Five Senses Scan and Soothing Senses Kit

Sound
Scan—What do you hear now?

_____

Kit—What's soothing to listen to?

_____

Sight
Scan—What do you see now?

_____

Kit—What's soothing to look at?

_____

Progressive Muscle Relaxation

Overview
Slowly attend to and tense each muscle group for 10 seconds, then release for 10 seconds. If anything hurts, don't do it!

Scalp

Brow and Eyes

Jaw, Lips, and Tongue

Neck and Shoulders

Smell
Scan—What do you smell now?

_____

Kit—What's soothing to smell?

_____

Taste
Scan—What do you taste now?

_____

Kit—What's soothing to taste?

_____

Touch
Scan—What do you feel now?

_____

Kit—What's soothing to touch?

_____

Mid Back

Biceps / Triceps

Forearm

Hands

Abdomen and Core

Buttocks and Hips

Thighs

Calves

Feet and Toes

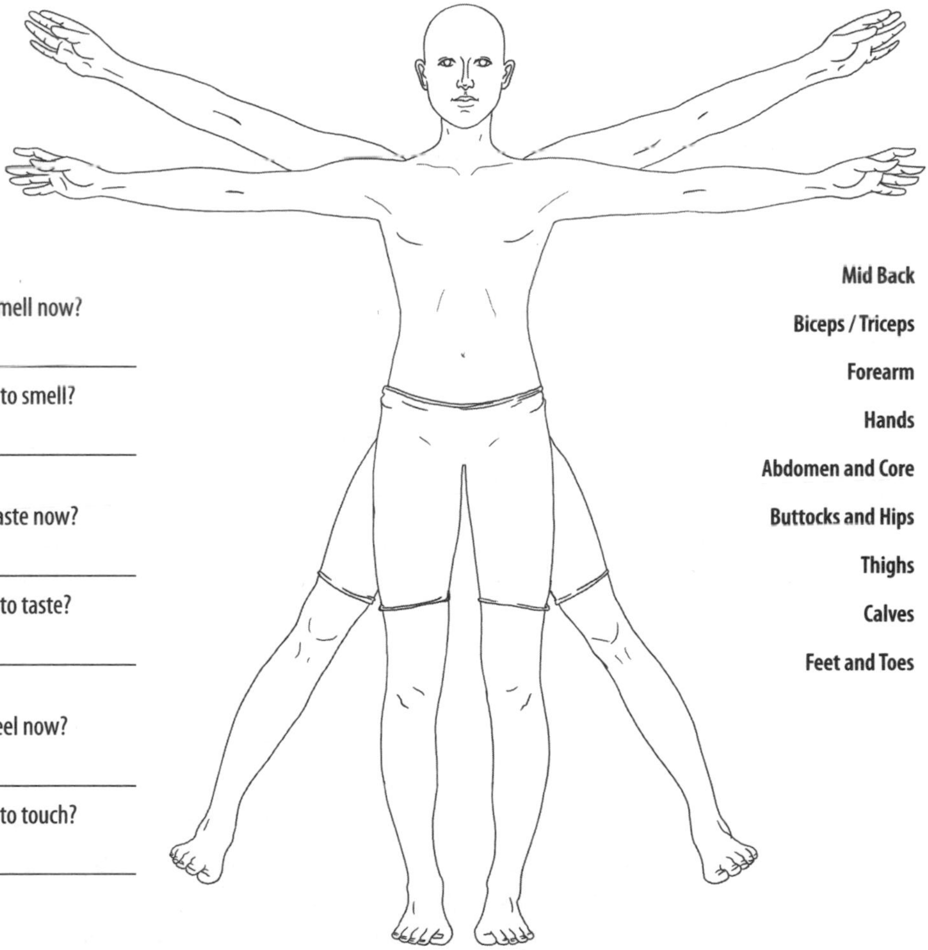

Figure 4.3 The Experiential Body—Awareness and Coping Skills

Exploring Behavior

Overview

Having tackled three significant (and perhaps most apparent) modes of experiencing, we've arrived at the final one—behavior. How is behavior a mode of experiencing? Because how we behave is how we explore and react to the world, and thus access the full range of experiences across the other modes (thoughts, emotions, and bodily sensations). When I say behavior, I mean what we do both consciously and unconsciously, with full intention or by reflex or impulse. Conscious behavior is done by choice with at least some awareness of intent. Unconscious actions, though, might be the most common type of behavior. It's not all about secret motivations—like the person late to the job they dislike after hitting snooze too many times (without realizing it). Much of our everyday behavior is automated. Consider driving to work, scratching your nose when it itches, washing your hair in the shower while singing the latest Tame Impala song—well maybe not that specific, but you get the idea.

Unconscious behavior isn't nefarious—at least the vast majority of the time. It's efficient and adaptive. What if every time you needed to breath, you had to think about it—and if you didn't, you'd suffocate? Breathing is a body-based form of unconscious behavior, but we have many more built-in behavioral reactions that are more situational. Everyone's probably had a doctor give their knee a firm yet painless whack to test their patellar knee-jerk reflex.

More complex examples are behavioral instincts. These behavioral responses are built-in and inherited from our ancestors. Perhaps the most basic is the instinct to escape when threatened. Even imaginary threats can trigger an instinctual response. Think about the last time you were startled while watching a movie. In the tense moment before the eventual jolt, you might remember feeling unease (an emotion), thinking "Why would they even go in there?!" (a quite reasonable thought), and experiencing an increased heart rate (a bodily reaction).

But what did you do? Leading up to the scare, you might've tensed your fingers into a fist or brought your hands to your face. Afterwards, if you recovered quickly, you probably remained seated and reminded yourself it's only a movie. Or, maybe you kept your eyes closed. If the movie felt like too much, you might have even left the theatre. Any response that involved escaping—either literally (leaving the theatre) or figuratively (closing your eyes and thinking happy thoughts)—was in line with our basic escape instinct. This instinct is great for survival in the presence of actual danger. As life diversified, other options arose like fighting off threats. We humans also possess this ingrained fight-or-flight response.[32] The real benefit of more-automated behavioral responses is that they don't require complex thought, careful decision-making, or even awareness. If they did, then when faced with a sudden threat, we'd likely be injured or worse before determining a response—unless that threat came from a movie, of course.

Other less conscious actions come from habits and other learned behaviors. If we were unable to learn from experiences, we'd be unlikely to survive for long. Learning usually occurs by association, consequences (reward-or-punishment), and/or observation.[33] Once we learn a new behavior, by any method, we can start doing them less consciously. That's not necessarily harmful. In fact, most of the time it's healthy. But here, we're tackling behavior as a mode to promote conscious awareness. Automatic, default behaviors and habits can sometimes become less helpful over time. In life, we must balance applying what we've learned from the past (both personal and collective) and responding to new situations with openness to what may be different—or what we could do that's even better.

Sometimes how we behave is misaligned with what we think, say, or feel consciously. In the previous journey waypoint, we learned about defense mechanisms. Defense mechanisms are sneaky. They can transform hidden motivations behind our behaviors into more palatable explanations for our actions. It's, yet again, part of being human. But it's not the only option. As you observe your own behavior, keep this caveat in mind. Note, describe, and attend to your behavior (and that of others), but be cautious in interpreting what a behavior means. Interpretation belongs in the thought mode, for one. More importantly, the more we try to interpret the less we're being aware of behavior in its most unadulterated form. Observing our patterns of behavior is critical to self-awareness, but we should be cautious in overinterpreting patterns and/or simply repeating stories of why we do what we do. With intention and patience, though, fostering genuine insight into our behavior can facilitate our efforts to change patterns that no longer support the life you want to live.

Awareness & Coping Skills

Unconsciously motivated behavior sounds a bit ominous, right? Sometimes it is. But we're cultivating awareness, not judgment or interpretation. Meaning making can come later, after deliberating about what's happened. It also largely involves our thinking mode. Notwithstanding possibly useful insights that come later, having a few behavior-based skills in the moment can improve our ability to make conscious choices in challenging times. From an awareness angle, *Behavior Tracking* provides a great foundation. Because we've now explored all four modes of experiencing, you're ready for this book's comprehensive tracking tool—The Experiential Explorer (Form 4.1). This form modifies traditional versions used by cognitive-behavioral therapists with an important, psychedelic twist: Here, we do not assume a static, causal trajectory among thoughts, emotions, bodily sensations, and behaviors. Traditional behavioral forms trace a linear flow from an antecedent (the situation) to the behavior (one's response) and end with the consequence (or outcome)—the classic A-B-C worksheet.

A-B-C worksheets are convenient for simplifying experience, but when expanding awareness, oversimplifying is a danger we're trying to evade. Streamlined stories of what happened are narratives created *after* we experience or observe a situation. Another distinct quality of our new form is how the four modes aren't presupposed to be in any fixed order. Sometimes we notice a bodily reaction before any thoughts—like when the hair stands up on the back of our necks before knowing why. Other times we react with behaviors before *anything* else enters our conscious mind—like when our hand jumps back from touching a hot surface before feeling the burn or fear of injury. I'm sure you've experienced situations where thoughts or emotions reverberated across the other modes too.

Alright, enough rationale. Here are the steps for completing an entry in The Experiential Explorer:

1. **Jot down notes about a situation that prompted a response.** What was going on around you? Where were you? What started the chain of experiences?

2. **Record what you noticed first about your reaction.** What initially entered your conscious awareness about the situation or your reaction? In the corresponding box, describe your experience. Remember to refrain from explanations or interpretations, as seen in words like 'because.'

3. **Fill in remaining the modes in the order in which you became aware of them.** If you'd like, put a number in each box or draw directional arrows connecting the chain of experiences. If some things occurred simultaneously, place the same number in the corresponding boxes or link them with a double-line (═══) without an arrow. A chain of

experiences may circle back to earlier modes. As relevant, you can record later experiences belonging to the same mode in separate areas of the corresponding box. Or, use a second form for especially complex or lengthy situations.

4. **Note any interpretations, insights, or patterns.** In the final, lowermost section, go beyond 'just the facts.' This is where you explain 'the big picture' by fitting separate pieces into a larger experiential puzzle. You might tell a story about what happened and why. You might also describe any observed patterns about how you experience or react to specific situations or people. Making repeated entries over time will likely reveal personally relevant patterns.

This form can be a powerful tool for your explorations in the upcoming arc. Although our current focus is experiential awareness, this form synergizes with our efforts to increase self-awareness if completed over several days and weeks. All types of awareness are ultimately connected.

As for active coping, the most powerful approach for the behavioral mode is engaging in *Enjoyable and Enriching Activities*. Doing things that are fun, rewarding, and playful is far from unadulterated hedonism and seeking pleasure at all costs. It's about appreciating life. This skill isn't limited to vacations and other big-ticket items. If life were about looking forward to our next escape or 'trip of a lifetime,' we'd be wasting the moments in between—which is most of our lives! That's no way to live.

Instead, consciously engaging with even briefly enjoyable or enriching activities can make your seemingly mundane everyday life much more fulfilling. Certainly, someone under the influence of LSD can spend what feels like an eternity observing the wind blowing through the branches of trees. They can do the same the next day and still appreciate the experience. LSD just opened the door. If tree gazing isn't your thing, then consider what is. Is it more active like going for a hike? Or, is it watching a movie on its opening night? Perhaps being outdoors with your dog? Doing yoga? Whatever it may be, make time for it. That's all this skill requires. It's simple in concept but harder in practice, especially as we get wrapped up in other distractions, ambitions, or responsibilities. Fun, laughter, and joy do not equal hollowness and overindulgence. Trust yourself to know the difference. Armed with this permission, consider brainstorming some fun things to do in the near future. I highly recommend it.

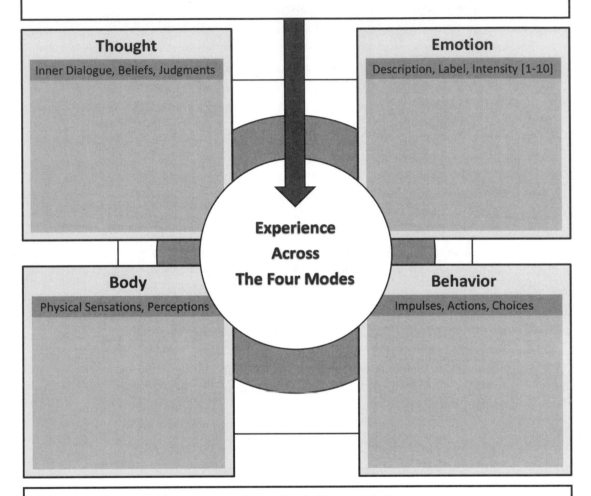

Situation or Trigger

What happened first? What was the situation that prompted your reaction and chain of experiences?

Thought

Inner Dialogue, Beliefs, Judgments

Emotion

Description, Label, Intensity [1-10]

Experience Across The Four Modes

Body

Physical Sensations, Perceptions

Behavior

Impulses, Actions, Choices

Interpretations, Insights, or Patterns

What's your overall story of this experience? Anything to note for further reflection or exploration?

Form 4.1 The Experiential Explorer

Body and Behavior—A Curiosity Generator Task

Now that we're finished with the last two modes, list three or more questions that engage your curiosity to learn more and/or apply related skills to your life. What you come up with can connect to either bodily sensations or behavior, or their relationships with other experiential modes. Use a couple of minutes now, but know you can refine your list later too.

> **As I explore the modes of body and behavior, my biggest questions are:**

A Word of Caution—The Limits of Perception

Alright, we've done it! Now you know everything there is to know about experiencing across the four modes. Well, not quite. But then again, no surprises there. You're used to the limitations of awareness by now. You confronted them with the cosmos and with your own consciousness. In the domain of experiential awareness, we must realize that experiencing isn't the same as understanding. Trying to understand can actually detract from experience. Another dose of humility for us homo sapiens may be in order. Have you ever seen an optical illusion? Maybe a mirage in the dead heat of summer? You don't have to be at Burning Man to realize these waves and ripples in your field of view isn't spacetime bending in front of you. Barring a small wormhole that spontaneously forms on Earth, these mirages occur when light waves bend due to differences in heat. Light plays tricks with our minds, as magicians have always reminded us. Some of our limited awareness lies in built-in human restrictions on perceptions. Our eyes and brains can see only a tiny sliver of the entire spectrum of light—less than 1%. What colors would be possible if we could see it all? Would radio waves look like ever-present static? What about gamma rays? (I mean besides causing instant death)? Certainly, sleeping would be harder. The night sky would be almost as bright as the day. Electromagnetic light is everywhere. All our physiological senses face similar built-in limits.

Beyond our limited senses, we also confront the problem of how our brains automatically process and interpret data. As psychologist Carl Rogers concisely asserted, "We live by a perceptual 'map' which is never reality itself."[34] It's not much of a problem most of the time. In fact, it's a necessary gift. The brain has to make leaps to organize a chaotic world into an abridged version for us to comprehend. Outside of basic science and psychology, various religious and spiritual traditions also emphasize the illusory nature of perception and even consciousness itself. Chief among them is Buddhism. Still, our everyday life is a human one, and we must begin somewhere. Our direct experience of the outside world and ourselves, no matter how limited, gives us a launching pad from which we explore. We just need to realize there's always more than meets the eye, so to speak. Staying humble makes the journey a lot easier.

Fostering Growth through Curiosity about Experiences

Experiential awareness is supported, yet again, by our metaphorical ally for expanding cosmic and self-awareness—the attitude of curiosity. Curiosity might occasionally be accused of killing a feline friend or two, but as long as we pay attention to ethical considerations and the "Do Not Enter!" signs along the way, we can explore a seemingly endless array of experiences. Keeping an eye out for any dangers, like threats to basic safety, is critical. But over-focusing on threats can feed into another major barrier to expanding experiential awareness: *experiential avoidance*.[35] Avoidance shows up in many forms, but it's often triggered by an underlying fear or discomfort, which like other emotions, can be expressed in each mode. The ego minimizes distress it deems overwhelming, so we don't always consciously experience or express our more vulnerable feelings. Defense mechanisms can transform them into something else—even into their opposites. After all, many emotions share several physiological features, such as increased heart rate being part of fear, excitement, and anger.

Curiosity can mitigate the risk of living a life ruled by experiential avoidance. Avoidance can limit not only unpleasant feelings but also enriching experiences and personal insights. What if, instead, we were to approach even unpleasant experiences with curiosity? We might ponder questions like, "What is this experience tied to? Why might I be feeling this way?" We can ask these questions without labeling an experience as bad, wrong, or undesirable. Curiosity motivates us to engage, explore, learn, and grow. It affords us new experiences and possibilities.

As little surprise by now, curiosity has a handy sidekick too—*mindfulness*. Cultivating mindfulness, or present-centered awareness, is the most direct approach to increasing experiential awareness. If you can't yet muster a full attitude of curiosity, simply observe everything you can about the present moment. Do so without fueling judgment—including judging yourself for not doing it right. The word 'mindfulness' itself contains a bit of a paradox. For most of us, being more mindful is really about being more mind-empty— empty of the overpowering dominance of thoughts. Thoughts are seldom about the immediate present. Many thoughts focus on anticipating the future or ruminating on the past—moments near or far from the current one.

A related aspect of mindfulness is how centering on present experience involves *de*centering from our typical perspective, which is entangled with our ego. Experienced meditators describe consciousness as a mirror. When the mind is full of clutter, the mirror is covered in soot. Mindfulness meditation serves to 'polish the mirror.'[36] Emptying the mind, or at least separating it from its surface-level contents, reveals the pure awareness underneath. That clean mirror then provides clarity, allowing a more accurate reflection of 'reality.' By building your mindful awareness, even very slowly, you're strengthening this part of your mind.

With increased mindfulness, we can direct our consciousness by broadening our awareness or focusing our attention. Developmental psychologist Alison Gopnik calls these two approaches lantern and spotlight consciousness.[37] Lantern consciousness lights up our surroundings indiscriminately, allowing us to discover many hidden objects dispersed throughout the environment. *Lantern consciousness* is the default of infants and young children as they learn about the world around them.

Over time, *spotlight consciousness* takes hold and lets us concentrate more discretely, shining a focused beam on the task at hand. Although still capable of both, adults tend to dwell in spotlight consciousness—likely due to pressures of the modern world and a 'Been there, done that' attitude toward our everyday surroundings. That doesn't mean we're particularly good at concentrating our spotlight. Too many shiny distractions exist, like our consistent companion, the smart phone. An antidote is learning to cultivate and recover our 'child's mind,' as meditation experts call it. Using our adult-level skills, we might even be able to combine the lantern and spotlight. Ultimately, if we push this metaphor to its limits, expanding awareness equates to brightening the light of our consciousness so that it can illuminate the entire room with little left in the dark. If even briefly possible, we might see the full experience of each moment as one integrated whole.

Efforts to strengthen this bright light connects us to our *experiential self*.[38] For our current purposes, the experiential self means the part of us that observes the fullness of experience without getting caught up in any one element. It's the part of us that witnesses everything, but is more than our default, conscious personality. That part is busy managing our lives and containing our experience. In other words, that part is our ego. The experiential self, in contrast, integrates all modes as they occur in the present without interference.[39] This perspective observes each mode as interconnected and unified. They're interconnected in how each occurs in parallel with others, even when outside our conscious awareness. Relationships among modes can involve direct and indirect influences, which as discussed, aren't consistently causal in any single direction. Over time, each mode influences the others in all possible directions. They're ultimately unified in how the whole is greater than the sum of each part.[40] No mode exists in isolation, and through their integration, we find so much more. By raising our consciousness of both the parts and the whole, we gain a transcendent perspective that creates space for true freedom—the cornerstone of what awareness can offer us.

Concrete Suggestions & Journey Report

To expand your experiential awareness, Box 4.1 provides some concrete suggestions and examples. For more on how this theme connects to psychedelics, look at this chapter's Journey Report 4.1. Barry had several prior psychedelic experiences in which he attempted to avoid or control his unwanted feelings of shame, guilt, and physical discomfort. Although 5-MeO-DMT is often viewed as a powerful psychedelic, Barry's 'break-through' was more likely due to his newfound willingness to explore his emotional and physical sensations with curiosity, rather than being due to the chemical substance itself. His symbolic experience of death and release in this journey also enabled healing mystical experiences during his later encounters with other psychedelics.

Box 4.1

Expanding Experiential Awareness within Everyday Life

Suggestion	Example
Notice when your autopilot mode of experiencing life kicks in.	You recognize a habit of 'being in your own head.' Your commute to work has become so automatic you're unaware of making each turn. While taking a shower, you rarely attend to how the soap feels on your body or its fragrance. While walking into your apartment building, you're often lost in thought and ignore your neighbors as they pass. You decide, at minimum, to start saying 'hi.' You notice feeling awkward at first but realize that being friendly with them will actually be more pleasant in the long run.
Commit to a regular practice that supports mind-body health and wellbeing. The practice may be as simple as routinely walking or doing other physical exercise.	You've been curious about yoga but uncertain where to begin. You start a trial period at a nearby studio that offers several varieties. After only one class, you rule out Bikram because of its sweltering heat. Vinyasa is better, but other attendees (and the instructor) seem more interested in making it an exercise class. You discover your ideal fit with hatha yoga and its mixture of various poses, breathing exercises, and meditation.
Reflect on how your present experiences or situations are influenced by past ones.	You spend much of your time ruminating about a previous relationship and trying to understand what led to the breakup. Revisiting these memories never seems to lead to helpful conclusions, so you set an intention of moving on. As a replacement for ruminating, you decide to watch *(500) Days of Summer* since your friends keep recommending it to you for some reason.[a]
List five least favorite and five neutral activities in your life. Consider why you feel the way you do about each activity.	Your lists include a dislike of washing the dishes and a neutral feeling about grocery shopping. After reviewing your lists, you become aware the risk of boredom seems to be a common element. You also wonder if these activities aren't nearly as tedious as you judge them to be. You decide to clean the dishes immediately after and forgo watching videos while doing so (your typical approach to escape boredom).
Light a candle and practice a more focused form of experiential awareness.	After finding a candle around the house, you light it and spend 5-10 minutes observing its flickering flame, scent, and warmth. You then focus on the visual experience alone. After a few minutes of intense concentration, you notice a curious shift in the quality and color of the fire and its surroundings.
Connect to the part of yourself that can observe your immediate experience without getting caught up in internal dialogue, past memories, or planning for the future.	You notice how frequently you think about the state of the world. When these thoughts occur, they distract you from what you're doing in the moment. You decide to add "I'm having the thought that..." in front of every thought, assumption, belief, or judgment that passes through your mind—such as, "I'm having the thought that 'the world is going to hell in a hand basket.'" You notice that observing each as a thought and not as 'The Truth' feels different and less all-consuming.

[a] Webb, 2009

Grounding Words—A Brief Summary

In this chapter, you discovered that expanding awareness extends beyond the mysteries of the cosmos and the layers of the unconscious. Becoming more aware is possible every single moment, in the here-and-now of life. As for all of us, your personality and habits of mind often bias your focus and limit your awareness to a fraction of the full range available. As you become more mindful, you observe many aspects of experience previously dismissed or ignored. Conscious life unfolds along the four modes of thoughts, emotions, body, and behavior. By reviewing each mode, you've earned critical tools for enhancing awareness. Moreover, you now have skills to cope with any stressors confronted in our on-going journey and far into the future. Whether by using a systematic approach or by fostering mindful awareness more spontaneously, you know each moment holds so much more than what's typically dominant in your default level of consciousness. You know as well to stay watchful for signs of avoidance, a key barrier to experiential awareness. Your inner curiosity remains an ally in exploring facets of experience that might otherwise hide within your unconscious. All this work you do while realizing that past the reaches of human perception, even more exists—some of which we have discovered and some we have not.

Your Assignment, Your Choice

It's time to choose your assignments for the week. You might notice how the domains of *Reflective-Intellectual* and *Experiential-Emotional* overlap somewhat with two modes of experiencing. That's not entirely an accident, but the choice remains yours. As before, a good approach is doing either the same or a new activity each day before moving to the next waypoint.

Assignments 4.1

Expanding Your Experiential Awareness

Reflective-Intellectual	Experiential-Emotional
☐ Task—Complete entries in **Form 4.1 "Experiential Explorer"**	☐ Task—Review and **practice techniques within the four modes** as showcased in Figures 4.1-4.3
Time—Minimum of 2-3 entries, at least 15 min of reflection	Time—Minimum of one skill practiced per day, 5-10 min each
Aim—To increase awareness of your life experiences, patterns, and any habits or blind spots	Aim—To acquire skills for increased awareness and coping that supplement your existing ones
☐ Task—Read or watch content based on questions emerging from your **Curiosity Generator** responses or about other chapter topics like mindfulness	☐ Task—Practice the meditation in **Meditation 4.1 "Exploring Present Experience"**
Time—No minimum as long as you lose yourself in explorations and learning	Time—Minimum of 2-3x/week, ~10 min each
Aim—To explore topics intersecting with experiential awareness, coping, or healing tailored to your personal interests	Aim—To experience the present moment in its fullness and expand beyond your default conscious awareness

After reviewing options or doing one quick exercise, respond to this chapter's journal prompt. Your style of expression remains open. So, write, draw, or create whatever seems genuine and honest in your version of the here-and-now.

Travel Journal

What aspects of my everyday experience do I often ignore or dismiss?

Why might that be?

How can I be more aware of my thoughts, emotions, body, and behavior?

What could greater mindfulness offer me personally?

Prior to this 5-MeO-DMT journey, I had about a half-dozen psychedelic experiences under my belt (mostly mushrooms and LSD). Each had been fruitful and valuable, but I kept feeling like something was missing. I wasn't encountering any mystical blast-offs or earth-shattering revelations. My experiences were always similar: As the psychedelic would take hold, tightness in the center of my chest would begin. I'd then become anxious and resist the feelings, thinking, "Not again!" The remaining journey would be colored by discomfort. My arms and legs would ache. My jaw would tighten. I often doubled over in a fetal position, clenching my stomach, while experiencing nonstop, recurring themes of shame and guilt. In the worst one, I had the classic reaction of, "Will I be stuck like this forever?" Visually, it was almost never anything but geometric shapes of blacks and greys. Occasional colors offered some brief respite, but not for long. When my journey ended, I kept thinking, "What am I doing wrong? Why are my experiences always so physical and dark?"

Heading into my first 5-MeO-DMT experience armed with this history, my intention was to understand this guilt, shame, and pain that continued to pop up. I was with friends who were experienced travelers. I felt very safe. We took turns sitting for each other as we went under. I don't recall the size of my dose, but it was measured precisely and described as "good for a first timer with a sticky ego." Whatever that meant.

As I exhaled, the room began to blur and outlines of objects became tinged with shades of red, purple, and gold. As my sitter guided my back to the floor, the familiar feeling of anxiety and heavy pressure in my chest surfaced. I remember thinking, "Please, let this time be different!" An unfamiliar feeling then arose—curiosity. What if I followed this tightness, instead of trying to avoid or control it? Where would it go? I started breathing into the sensation in my chest, giving it attention

Exercise continues on next page

instead of wishing it away. The tightness soon transformed into an expanding warmth. It gently spread into my arms and legs, then my neck and mouth, and finally, to the top of my head. My physical body felt like it was being recognized and seen for the first time. The warmth turned into a tingling sensation and began to concentrate in my upper body. As the tingling moved upwards, my body seemed to disappear slowly. What was left began to sink into the floor, as my extremities felt brittle and weak. As the tingling passed into my head, I could feel my lips pull back, and my mouth and teeth became dry. My breathing slowed, and I felt my last breath pass by my tingling tongue as I said, "Just...die." My body disintegrated, and a bright pinpoint of light slowly enlarged until it nearly encompassed my entire view. The edges of my vision, though, began to return to my everyday version of reality. It felt like I had experienced the dying process and how the physical pain of my existence would slowly drift away. It was so peaceful and joyous. I began to sob.

What I realized in that experience is how much my body stored and held onto emotional pain, and how listening to my body and emotions could provide relief. Sure enough, the next time I tried psychedelics, I listened to my body, allowed my shame to come and go, and then experienced the most vivid and mystical journey of my life. Since these experiences, I've become more attuned to my feelings, and how important curiosity is in hearing the insights they have to offer me.

—Barry, Age 33

Note. This account and all others in the book are de-identified and anonymous to protect the confidentiality of the person sharing their story. Minor grammar, spelling, and stylistic changes were made and usually in partnership with the person providing the account.

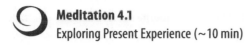

Meditation 4.1
Exploring Present Experience (~10 min)

Read this script to see this meditation's flow. Find a place to sit, stand, or lay down, ideally without major concerns or external distractions. Then, close your eyes and lead yourself through the meditation. If you get distracted, know that's your mind doing what it typically does. It likes to stay dominant and in control. No matter how many times you must return to the present, each return strengthens your muscle of concentration and awareness. Pace yourself as you need.

With your eyes closed, focus on experiencing the natural rhythm of your breath for a few moments to center yourself....With your eyes remaining closed, begin expanding your awareness beyond your breathing....What is the first experience you notice outside of your breath? Attend to whatever emerges in your awareness...Follow it as it changes in form, quality, or strength...

Focus now on what's going on inside your mind. Are there thoughts? ...If so, are they related or unrelated to your meditation? ...Do you follow the thoughts naturally? Or, do you resist them? ...Whatever you do, notice that when you choose to view them as such, your thoughts are simply thoughts. They're not all of who you are and all of what you experience. They flow in and out of your mind but need not dominate your current experience....

Attend now to any emotions you may be feeling. Are any specific emotions present? If so, how are you aware of each emotion? ...How might you describe the emotion? ...Try not to follow the word or label too closely. It might lead you back into the realm of thoughts, bringing you to the past or the future. You can let an emotion word stay, though, if it captures something 'true' about how you feel or lets you experience it more fully....if you're not feeling any noticeable emotions now, just notice what it feels like to be without strong emotions....

Now check in with your body. Are your experiencing any physical sensations? Scan your body for experiences across its core senses. ...what do you feel? ...Perhaps the touch of your clothing or the temperature around you...What do you smell? ...Is there a taste you notice in your mouth? ...What about any sounds? ...Even with your eyes closed, what is it you see? ...Are there colors of any kind? Perhaps you still notice a source of light? ...Or, is there nothing but darkness?

Now observe your behavior. Consider any movement, even if small....Reflect on the choices you made just moments ago that now are part of your current experience. How did your choice to sit, stand, or lay down impact your current experience?...Are you moving now or staying perfectly still?...whatever you're doing or not doing, observe it without judgment....

Expand your awareness, if you can, to include all you've experienced in this meditation and are experiencing now...across all modes, thoughts, emotions, bodily sensations, and behaviors. Rest in this state of broadened awareness, freely observing the present in all its fullness...

From this place of complete presence and awareness, slowly reopen your eyes and reconnect to your surroundings. Know this fullness of the present moment continues onward, moment by moment, even outside of this meditation. —and even when your typical level of conscious awareness, with its limitations, naturally returns.

The Second Arc: Confronting the Existential Trials of Initiation

> It is a bewildering thing in human life that the things that cause the greatest fear is the source of the greatest wisdom.
>
> —Carl Jung[1]

The main phases of the monomyth, as you already know, are Departure, Initiation, and Return. We've completed our departure by heeding the call to adventure and broadening our awareness. These have prepared you well for the next step—the trials of initiation. As we move into the trials, remember the hero's journey, like personal growth, requires facing challenges. In fact, mythology's rampant with stories of heroes who fall at various points on their quest even before taking their first step. You're not one of those would-be heroes. You've prepared for what lies ahead. And, you're not alone. Although indeed challenging, each existential trial contains existential opportunities too—opportunities to flourish by not giving into fears and realizing your underlying strength. Unexpected reactions and temptations present themselves regardless of one's preparation, but that's what makes passing these trials all the more rewarding.

Becoming initiated means entering into a new understanding, community, or realm of existence. Rarely is initiation simply bestowed upon an individual. One way or another, it's earned. Mythic forms of initiation are often intense and a matter of life and death. One of history's most ancient tales is the Sumerian epic of Gilgamesh.[2] Early in its telling, King Gilgamesh achieves victory over his challenger, the 'wild man' Enkidu. Encouraged by this triumph, he befriends and partners with his once-rival to demonstrate their combined strengths to the gods. They succeed. Yet, Enkidu is soon killed. Upon losing his companion, Gilgamesh's confidence erodes and is replaced by overwhelming grief. In experiencing this vulnerability and eventually accepting his own mortality, he ascends to become a king 'surpassing all other kings,' one who appreciates life's fragility. Gilgamesh abandons his former arrogance and chooses to lead not by brute strength, but by genuinely caring for those under his guardianship.

Outside mythic stories, initiation and healing practices often involve tools for accessing alternate forms of consciousness to resolve fears and gain enhanced perspective. Many ancient and indigenous tribes have used psychedelics in initiation rites. In particular, shamans and other spiritual healers may become selected after they face periods of intense psychological or spiritual crisis. Their initiation into shamanic traditions usually involves careful and rigorous training experiences that heal their own wounds while preparing them for their tribal role.[3]

As a parallel in Western science, the MAPS Phase 3 protocol exemplifies a similar approach to healing trauma. During MDMA sessions, the team of therapists provide a safe container and encourage participants to go towards what they fear most, the memory of their trauma. This courageous act supports the process of healing posttraumatic stress. In partnering with the therapists and their own inner healer, these participants can gain new perspectives on the past, connect to personal meaning, and find strength to move forward in the present.[4]

Therefore, as with mythic tales, tribal initiation, and psychedelic healing, we too must pass trials. Three trials stand before us, each focusing on core issues we humans confront in life. They are as follows:

Chapter	Journey Waypoint	Theme / Title
Ch 5	Waypoint IV	Facing Death— Embracing Life and Impermanence
Ch 6	Waypoint V	Knowing Loneliness— Welcoming Solitude and Interconnectedness
Ch 7	Waypoint VI	Encountering Meaninglessness— Discovering the Responsibility of Meaning

Though the material may at times challenge you, you're not in any actual danger. Expanding awareness, alongside your ally of curiosity, has equipped you with all you need. Your efforts have fortified your presence of mind, preparing you for the next step. As we proceed, my hope, and responsibility, is to create space for you to:

- **Access your expanded awareness** to contemplate each trial
- **Recognize any tendency to avoid discomfort**, without judging yourself for this natural response

- **Harness your skills** across the four modes (thought, emotion, body, behavior), as needed, to circumvent unhelpful avoidance and remain steady
- **Consciously explore any underlying reactions or conflicts** related to each theme
- **Begin the process to heal, transform, or resolve problems,** if any manifest
- **Deepen engagement with your life** while accepting the challenges, mysteries, and unknowns inherent to our human journey

These steps are intertwined and before you know it, you'll be doing them with ease. Nevertheless, it's a good time to review your Journey Self-Care Plan (Exercise 1.2). You might make refinements now that you're better acquainted with this book's approach and possess a few more tools.

Why Existential Trials

These trials before us are more than a matter of mythic tales. They're core concerns for humanity that manifest in both archetypal and personal ways. An existential framework is handy here because we're not skipping over hardship as an aspect of the human experience. We must also acknowledge what we don't truly understand. That doesn't mean we can't make 'leaps of faith,' but when we do, we do so knowingly. That is, with awareness—which you've conveniently already been cultivating.

As the saying goes, if you've met one existentialist, you've met *one* existentialist. The individuality and freedom of existential thinking are tantamount to its power. We need not worry about formal definitions. Existentialists didn't invent concerns about death, loneliness, or meaning. They're woven into the tapestry of human life. When we speak of existential trials, we're merely discussing common difficulties of the human experience. You've probably already confronted many of them several times in various forms: from personal losses to hypothetical ones, from conscious fears to ones lurking just underneath the surface, and from intellectual understanding to intimate emotional familiarity. We can revisit each trial throughout our entire life—sometimes because old lessons weren't learned; sometimes because new ones await. What's different here is how you're making a conscious choice to enter into these trials. They're not being forced on you—not by me at least. And what's more, yet again, is you're undergoing these trials armed with greater awareness and clearer intentions. Existential thinkers may not agree on everything, but they do agree that confronting existential concerns can lead to inner strength and a fully engaged life. Discomfort precedes growth. If it helps, remember to use our psychedelic-inspired mantra and go 'in and through.'

Discovering Your New Ally

Before rushing forward, remember your allies. In the first arc, curiosity played an important role, but here we'll have additional support in our new ally— *Acceptance*. This ally, though multifaceted, reflects an attitude of receptiveness or willingness. Upon receiving invitations or offerings, we can accept or decline them. Seeing through fear, delusion, or deception allows us to accept genuine offerings and decline misleading ones, which both in turn lead to passing the test. For mythic quests, the result is receiving a literal or symbolic reward, what Campbell called the "hero's boon."[5] Passing a trial means earning new insights or symbolic powers or gaining liberation from the underlying fear or concern.

Acceptance counters a natural impulse to avoid or deny. Fostering acceptance reveals more possibilities than fear alone suggests. Instead of rolling over in defeat, out of fear or exhaustion, acceptance allows us to stand strong. By using its strength, our curiosity too can return and lead us further down our path. Acceptance is critical to becoming initiated—into a new community, new level of understanding, or both. Starting to connect all the dots? These connections familiarize you with your new ally and the important and occasionally nuanced role it plays. Learning to appreciate acceptance might be tricky because it can, at times, appear less friendly than curiosity. Sometimes it encourages us to be willing to experience or accept things that are more difficult. That's why it's necessary for our second arc.

Do you remember the image or token you evoked for your first ally? I hope that exercise allowed you to contact your own inner curiosity. Keep this ally, along with your image or token, nearby. Appreciate how curiosity helped you make it this far, and realize its role remains significant for this next stage.

To bolster your support, let's imbue your new ally with a similar level of personal relevance. Visualize either a person you know or a fictional character who captures an attitude of acceptance. This attitude may appear as a willingness to experience whatever comes their way, adapt to the changing weather of life, or express genuine equanimity despite facing overwhelming odds or personal hardship. As before, choose someone to accompany you who you'd trust to be present as you face your own trials. Imagine how they appear, even down to the details of their clothing and expressions on their face that communicate their acceptance not only of life, but of you as a fellow conscious being. Recall their image whenever you need.

You can also select another physical token to represent this person or a more general feeling of being fully accepted as you are, including your fears, conflicts, and hidden parts of yourself. This token might be another stone, small figure, piece of jewelry, or anything else that you can mentally associate with acceptance. As you might recall, such tokens are useful in psychedelic journeys because psychedelics too can generate challenging moments. In addition to having a guide, therapist, or shaman, a token can elicit a grounding connection to a journeyer's inner strength and intentions. It follows then that these tokens can act similarly for us, connecting to your own inner resource. They remind you that you can weather fear and pass through gateways to find the insights lying on the other side.

Updating Intentions

Now that you've contacted a personal version of our new ally, we have just one more task before undergoing our first trial. Look at your written intentions for the first arc. How have you done so far? Are these intentions still relevant? Or, could you refine them? Sometimes progress is faster than expected. If that's the case, celebrate any achievements you've already made, even if only with a quick smile of accomplishment. Larger achievements, of course, deserve more than that. We often undervalue progress by moving quickly onto the next goal. As a therapist and as a human being, I know how easy it is to move onto the next thing and forget to acknowledge how far we've already come.

Regardless of your sense of progress, consider too how your initial intentions might relate to these existential trials. If so, or if you want to track them anyways, record them again here. You can add new intentions as well. Whether continuations, updates, revisions, or entirely brand-new ones, write down a renewed set of intentions for this arc. Your intentions will continue to guide you to gifts of insight waiting to be uncovered as you confront and pass each trial. As with psychedelic journeys, though, be prepared for surprises. Intentions help guide us, but hold them lightly. Remaining open to what emerges ensures you can receive what is offered.

In confronting these existential trials, my intentions are to…

Excellent. You've now completed your preparations. It's time for the trials. I'd wish you luck if I thought you needed it. Instead, I'm confident you already have what it takes. Find your footing, if you need, and then charge forward.

CHAPTER 5

Knowing Death—
Embracing Life & Impermanence

Accepting impermanence and our shared mortality requires loosening the story knot: letting go of our concepts, ideas, and expectations...life and death are not separate but intertwined like roots deep in the earth.

—Joan Halifax, *Being with Dying*[1]

Journey Waypoint IV

Here we are. The growing awareness we built in this journey's first arc has led us straight to death. Well, not death itself. But that matters not when considering the reactions the word alone can evoke. Still, it's hard to imagine anything more fundamental to life than death. Confronting death and its eventuality is the first real trial we face in our path. Why start with death? Because it kicks off these trials with arguably the hardest fact of life. Coupled with the broader theme of impermanence, death frames the human journey like no other experience or idea. Birth would be another big one, and obviously a necessary part of the human experience. But how many of us, at this point, are worried about our own birth? Our entrance to this world may be a profound mystery—at least when it comes to the birth of our consciousness. But all of us reading this book (or writing it, for that matter) already passed that first, essential threshold. Shouldn't that be enough?

If only! Appreciation of our birth and the life that follows can play second fiddle to the awareness that it won't last—and that it won't last for any of us, including our loved ones. This reality isn't just about mortality, though. It's connected to a fundamental aspect of nature. Nothing lasts. Everything changes. What we might think are exceptions to this rule are perhaps illusions or fantasies. Some changes that we don't perceive are on timescales outlasting our human one. Here's where I might insert a morbid joke of some kind to lighten the mood. Yet, the best introduction to this chapter may be to sit with these hard facts of life.

Even so, I'll give you a hint. We're going to confront this trial in a way that creates other possibilities beyond denial and dark humor—although the latter is not an entirely bad option. This trial is only the first. At least within the confines of this book, death is the beginning to more adventures, and as such, realize this: As you pass the trial of death, you gain a bit more confidence that the further reaches of your journey are also attainable.

Self-Reflections Check-In

Let's start, as always, with a comforting and familiar check-in. In the last chapter, you worked on building experiential awareness. The four modes gave you a handy framework for exploring your experience either mindfully in the here-and-now or upon reflection. From thoughts and emotions to bodily sensations and behavior, you saw the fullness of each and every moment. What did you do to practice this awareness? Consider the activities you chose from the suggested ones. How did you engage with experiences that were new, interesting, or broader than before? Did you end up experimenting with any specific skills for awareness or coping? How did it go? If you found any skills helpful, keep practicing them. If and when they're needed, you'll have them readily available as we go through these trials. When in doubt, just remember to breathe.

Confronting the First Trial

To start our trials with death might seem a little heavy-handed. Admittedly, it may be. Nevertheless, the shock of starting here (what many people consider the core fear of human existence) heightens our engagement and sincerity with the other trials we must face in this book—and by extension, life. Depending on your point of view, death is an intrinsic mystery or an uncomplicated fact. What assumptions, if any, do you make about death?

Strict materialists may assert the mind (and soul, if they even use that word) belongs exclusively to the neurobiological mechanisms of the brain. After people die, they no longer exist. A religious or spiritual person might declare that the soul exists, and when people die, they go to the great beyond—sometimes heaven or nirvana, other times a dark dimension, or maybe a rinse-and-repeat in the grand karmic wheel of death and rebirth.[2] The pragmatic therapist might throw up their hands and say, "Who knows? Let's focus on improving your life now." It's true, however, that even in the mental health field, we can have a hard time talking about death. We can fall into superstitious thinking and fear that mentioning death or suicide makes it more likely to happen. Spoiler: it doesn't.[3]

All things considered, no one knows what happens after we die. An air of mysteriousness will always exist surrounding death. Despite plenty of subjective reports about near-death experiences, past lives, and reincarnation,[4] nothing definitive can be said from a strict scientific perspective.[5] Any conclusions reached from various lines of inquiry are largely hypothetical. As acknowledged at the beginning of this book, science cares most about 'hard' data and falsifiable ideas. And when possible, scientific communities follow Ockham's razor—the most parsimonious idea (the one requiring the fewest assumptions and least speculation) is most likely to be correct.[6] This perspective may be more about esthetics and simplicity than reality.[7] Interestingly, peer-reviewed scientific publications about the possibility of consciousness existing outside the human brain have increased in recent years.[8] Certainly, it's a common discussion point in many psychedelic communities.[9]

Barring any radical paradigm shifts, it's relatively safe to say we don't know. It's from this place of honest humility that I'll guide our explorations for each of these existential trials. I'll not assert what you should or should not believe about death, for example. Instead, we'll survey the terrain of each trial and explore ways they're intertwined with the very nature of human existence—whether elicited by psychedelics or discovered by simply opening our eyes.

The Human Journey Across Time—
Returning to the 4th Dimension

Before examining your personal relationship with death, it's worth returning to the vast cosmic timescales from our first Journey Waypoint. Since our existential trials are essentially about humans exploring what it means to be human, we can skip the 13.8 billion years prior to our life on this tiny planet. Our species is estimated to be less than a million years old. That's chump change when it comes to cosmic time. The 72-year life expectancy average seems even smaller in comparison,[10] but if we hit that mark, living for seven decades is much longer than previous generations could expect. A commonplace cold, injury, or infection could end everything for a person far younger. Medical advances in the last century have greatly increased our average, but many, many people don't make it that far or even have access to sufficient medical care. Despite some comfort offered by modern medicine, in the grand scheme of the cosmos and our planet, all our lives are short. Our species is new. We all die relatively young.

Yet, in such a short span of time, we have accomplished astonishing things. Today we take for granted the option of traveling across Earth's oceans, getting vaccines to ward off numerous fatal diseases, and accessing unlimited information online. Many astonishing technological advances occurred just in the last century. Even so, as a global community, we've had to face yet again our inherent vulnerabilities. The coronavirus pandemic has reminded us we've not conquered nature with our clever tools. Nature adapts. Yet, as part of nature, we do too. Our technology is infused with our evolution—from the prehistoric ancient past to the all-too-uncertain future. The most luddite among us can appreciate our ability to generate fire, create basic tools, and cultivate crops for sustenance. These advances are groundbreaking and innovative for our species. We're early adopters here. And the consequences of all our technology continue to unfold.

Mortality & Its Consequences

It's time to return to a much smaller scale: the life and death of a human individual—that is, you and me. Us. Our deaths. What are you experiencing now as you contemplate your own death? Check in with each of the four modes. Any thoughts or images come to mind? Emotions? Bodily sensations or reactions? What about feeling compelled to act or do something? Hopefully you're not feeling compelled to stop reading. To be honest, that'd probably be the most common reaction for an average person off the street. I'm not judging them. Death *is* hard. Well, to clarify, as a species, we're pretty fragile, so dying's not *that* hard. What I mean is it's hard to think about death. It's also a mostly human burden. As far as we can tell, we're more acutely aware of our eventual death than other forms of life. A dog is so 'present-centered' that despite funny memes of pets staring off camera looking pensive, they're less burdened by an awareness of their own mortality. Humans don't have that luxury. But we do have a choice. In its broadest form, that choice is between: (1) attempting to avoid our anxiety about mortality or (2) accepting the reality of death with openness and honesty.

The Defense Against Existential Dread—
Loss, Trauma, & Death

Existential dread is the unsettling distress, sorrow, or anxiety we might experience from simply being human. This dread is triggered by problems inherent to "our very nature."[11] When our ego detects a risk for experiencing existential dread, one path available is that of defense. Those defense mechanisms described in our second Journey Waypoint play a big role (see Figure 3.1). No matter what causes distress the approaches for managing it are largely the same. Our minds employ defense mechanisms to protect us from our own death anxiety as well as profound grief after experiencing a significant loss. As Box 5.1 illustrates with only a few examples, defensive reactions can vary considerably.

Box 5.1

Example Defenses Against Death-related Grief & Loss

Selected Defense	Example
Denial	Roberto forgets or ignores that his loved one has died. He talks about plans for when they return home and pretends not to hear when friends and family make remarks about his loss.
Dissociation	When told of her friend's death, Emma stares blankly with no emotion or with emotion that doesn't match the situation. An observer has a distinct impression she isn't really there behind her eyes.
Displacement	Alexis complains about how the dishes haven't been done and the house is a mess. They get so upset they start yelling or crying, but it's clear to their friends that Alexis is really distraught about the loss of their father.
Humor	At his brother's funeral, Noah shares memories of their time growing up together and a few humorous reflections that characterize how his brother was in life. Noah mixes appropriate humor with a genuine expression of loss.

Some losses evoke incredible grief. Triggers might be the death of a parent, partner, close friend, or in especially tragic cases, a child. Each loss can pile on yet another weight—reminders of our own mortality. After losing parents or people around our same age or younger, the pain can extend to knowing we could be next in line. Sure, it's part of the circle of life. But one person's image of a circle is another's downward spiral towards oblivion. As generations above us pass into the unknown, we slowly realize we've unwittingly joined the next vanguard heading in the same direction.

When the young die, we seek further answers. Common questions might be: Did they have 'an underlying health condition?' Were they being 'reckless?' Was it 'their time to go?' Or, did they 'go long before their time?' All such questions and pretty much any response are, at some level, about our desire to confirm an order exists, a rhyme and reason for life and death. Something to hold onto besides uncertainty and fear. If we can't escape death, then at least we can know when it's coming.

These undercurrents lie entirely beneath our conscious mind most of the time. But whether conscious or not, we all have them. In periods of grief, we need additional comfort. Most funeral rituals involve reflections on life and the great beyond, even if the deceased weren't all that religious. The mourning process can extend well into the weeks and months after a funeral. Finding relief may seem impossible. Some of us bury ourselves in work or create distance from others, sometimes to avoid being too attached to people we also risk losing. Although I don't recommend overworking and isolating, I have felt the pangs of grief and certainly understand the impulse.

Confrontations with death and loss aren't confined to funerals. They're also major players in the horrors of trauma and violence. Even when people survive trauma, its effects can reverberate far into the future and across generations. Nowadays, after decades of research in military and veteran populations, posttraumatic reactions are no longer considered signs of personal weakness. But classic PTSD is one of many possible reactions to terrifying experiences in and outside of combat. The great 'secret' is that most people with PTSD aren't combat veterans and most traumas don't come from war. In fact, based on our current definition,[12] around 89.7% of adults in the US have experienced trauma.[13] That's almost everyone. And many people have experienced multiple traumas, the most common being physical or sexual assault (reported by 53.1%). Yet only 8.3% of people meet full criteria for a PTSD diagnosis at any point within their lifetime.[14]

Although war and terrorism aren't the most common causes of death and trauma in the US, they often garner the most attention. The September 11th attacks and subsequent wars ignited a new fervor for understanding posttraumatic reactions beyond classic PTSD. One research-based model led the charge in situating various common reactions underneath one umbrella. Its name, though a bit on-the-nose, helped too—*Terror Management Theory*.[15] As with most existential approaches, Terror Management Theory asserts that acknowledging the eventuality of our death inherently unnerves us. When death does creep into our consciousness, it threatens to push us into chaos. The ego is no fan of chaos. So, in response, it mobilizes efforts to re-establish emotional equilibrium and control. Two related types of motivation shape our defensive strategies: (1) reaffirming culturally sanctioned beliefs and ideas about how to transcend our own death and (2) nurturing our sense of self-esteem, worthiness, and alignment with personal and cultural values.[16]

Various worldviews offer ways to transcend our personal death. Reassurances of the religious and spiritual variety often entail heavenly ascension, reincarnation, or reemergence into some higher plane. For non-believers, comfort can be found by establishing a legacy that will outlive us—either biologically through offspring or socially through students and others we've personally influenced. Perhaps too through symbolic relics of our existence, like creative or scholarly works.[17] Most death-defying strategies are unconscious. In other words, we're largely in the dark about how our behaviors, beliefs, or reactions might ultimately connect to death.

One way or another, our personal and cultural beliefs protect us against the full force of death anxiety. But what if we're wrong? To admit that other people's beliefs might also be valid is to risk diminishing the strength of our own. If and when our beliefs are threatened—even by mere exposure to alternatives—our ego's go-to response is to tighten its grip and reaffirm our existing dominant worldview. Otherwise, the dam could break. Fear can make the ego double-down to protect everything it's built. Its work, after all, lies on a rocky foundation. One truth remains far outside its control. Our ego's story has already been written. And it ends in death.

Our story is the same as the ego's, and if we're not mindful, our response can be just as swift. It's no surprise then that prejudice, in-group versus out-group conflict, and political polarization can be some consequences of death anxiety.[18] That's especially true in the context of war, limited resources, financial inequalities, widespread trauma, and pandemics. Sound familiar? Becoming indignant and blaming others, particularly when they hold different values or opposing viewpoints, are seductive alternatives to sitting with our own anxiety.[19]

The Possibility of Accepting Death

Death anxiety and efforts to contain it can result in reactions ranging from benign to reprehensible, but recognizing that duality is an important step. These defensive approaches are merely default pathways. As ardent explorers who value awareness, we're going in a different direction.[20] Open contemplation of mortality is not only possible but also can promote psychological wellbeing. Benefits can include greater flexibility, gratitude, forgiveness, and inclusivity of one's 'in-group'—extending to all humankind or even all forms of life.[21] These positive effects also align with the phenomenon of posttraumatic growth, which up to 53% of trauma survivors report experiencing.[22]

Does thinking about death just desensitize us to death anxiety? In part, perhaps. When we are intentional, though, something more transformative can occur. As countless contemplators of mortality have concluded, living *is* dying. To be born into existence is to start the march towards our final moments. Can accepting this equivalence reveal possibilities beyond defense and numbness?

It's no coincidence that our modern renaissance of psychedelic therapy has involved targeting existential distress—as seen with cancer and end-of-life anxiety and depression.[23] It also hasn't been the first time Western researchers have recognized the potential of psychedelics in the dying process.[24] Part of what makes psychedelics healing seems to be in how they can facilitate mystical states of consciousness.[25] These states share a combination of the following qualities:[26]

- *Mystical Features (Unity, Noetic Quality, Sacredness)*—intuitive and intellectual insights that feel 'objectively true' and reveal some 'ultimate reality' often with a profound sense of awe and an awareness of the interconnectedness of all things, internal and external
- *Positive Mood*—a deeply felt sense of love, peace, joy, acceptance, etc.
- *Transcendence of Space & Time*—everyday perspective of space and time collapse or are experienced quite differently, including a sense of eternity or timelessness and a felt understanding of the limitlessness of spacetime with nonlocal connections across vast distances
- *Ineffability*—an inability to communicate adequately what was experienced, often associated with an awareness of paradoxical relationships in which opposites are either transcended or coexist and live in harmony

Note that these descriptions are nearly identical with the concept of a Pure Consciousness Event (see Figure 5.1).[27] Mind-expanding mystical or pure consciousness experiences can radically shift attitudes about life and death. According to modern research, self-described atheists become less likely to identify as such after taking a psychedelic.[28] Others maintain their atheism while still expressing benefit from having had a mystical experience. Psychedelics aren't always gateways to spiritual conversion. But conversion isn't the goal. Relief and healing are.

Sometimes psychedelic journeys entail passing through unpleasant or frightening moments. The most well-known involve what's colloquially known as *ego death*. Ego death isn't the actual death of the ego. It's a loss of one's everyday sense of self and identity. An alternative or 'pure' form of awareness often somehow remains after this metaphorical demise. Experiencing a state of consciousness, absent of personal identity, is what may be most transformative about 'ego death'—with or without moments of ecstasy and rapture.

When psychedelics first re-entered modern Western society, the controversial yet remarkable psychologist Timothy Leary partnered with two other impressive scholars, Ralph Metzner and Richard Alpert (later known as Ram Dass) to transform the *Tibetan Book of the Dead* (aka, the *Bardo Thödol*) into a guide map for navigating intense psychedelic journeys.[29] These scholars argued that this ancient, sacred text is as much about the process of living as that of dying—and if one so choses, the experience of rebirth. They described three essential phases, known as bardo states (see Box 5.2).

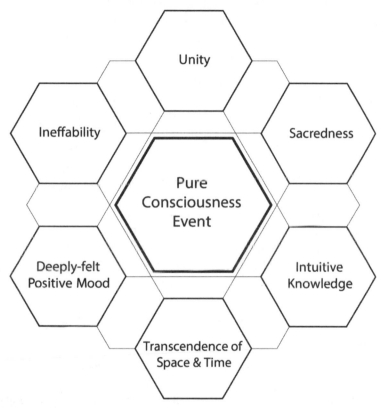

Figure 5.1 Elements of a Pure Consciousness Event

Note. This figure is largely based on Foreman's (1990) description but is also aligned with work by Panhke and Richards (1966) and Richards (2015). To examine the underlying structure of the Mystical Experiences Questionnaire, Maclean et al. (2012) used a statistical technique called factor analysis. This analysis revealed that items underlying Unity, Sacredness, and Intuitive Knowledge (sometimes referred to as Noetic Quality) were highly correlated. When combining these three elements, the authors labeled the resultant broader domain as the 'Mystical' aspects of non-ordinary states of consciousness.

Box 5.2

The Bardo States of Death-Rebirth as Manifested in Psychedelic Journeys

Bardo State	Short Description	Summary	Associated Verse
CHIKHAI	Period of Ego Loss (or Non-Game Ecstasy)	Transcendence of space-time, personal identity, thoughts, external life and work pressures, etc.	Now as the bardo of dying dawns upon me, I will abandon desires and cravings for worldly objects. Entering without distraction into the clarity of the teachings, I will merge my awareness into the space of the Uncreated. The time has come to let go this body of flesh and blood— It is merely a temporary and illusory shell.
CHÖNYID	Period of Hallucinations	Symbolic and visionary experiences, pleasant or unpleasant, that may facilitate insight and/or represent aspects of one's personal life or self	Now as I enter into the bardo of visions, I will abandon all awe and terror that may arise. Recognizing whatever appears as my own thought-forms, As apparitions and visions in this intermediate state. This is a crucial turning point on the path. I will not fear the peaceful and terrifying visions in my mind.
SIDPA	Period of Re-entry	Return to everyday ego self and external world, possibly with insights ready to be integrated	Now, as the bardo of rebirth dawns upon me, I will hold one-pointedly to a single wish— Continuously directing intention with a positive outlook. Delaying the return to Earth-Life as long as possible. I will concentrate on pure energy and love, And cast off jealousy while meditating on the Guru Father-Mother.

Note. This box summarizes the states outlined in Leary, Metzner, and Alpert's (1964/2007) *The Psychedelic Experience*. By 'game,' Leary et al. mean the collection of concerns, drama, and motivations we get caught up in as part of our everyday life and usual waking state of consciousness. In his chapter for *Zig Zag Zen*, Metzner (2015) revisited this work and noted the existence of three other bardo states—waking life, dreams, and meditation. The verses associated with the bardo states come from Metzner (p. 13, 14, 18, respectively).

According to Leary, Metzner, and Alpert, challenges can emerge during any bardo state if the journeyer tries to stay in control and connected to their everyday consciousness. The third state parallels reincarnation, but instead of the soul being reincarnated into another body, the psychedelic journey ends with the opportunity for psychological rebirth and renewal. If successful (including through the integration phase), the result is an expanded sense of self and a more flexible, well-functioning ego. Such a transformation fits with modern research showing lasting personality changes after one undergoes psychedelic therapy.[30]

If you're interested in bardo states—and can handle fictional trauma and violence—I highly recommend watching *Enter the Void*.[31] This brilliant but challenging film does an impressive job of connecting psychedelics (in this case, DMT), trauma, and karmic cycles of birth, death, and rebirth. As such, it's a great introduction to these overlapping, mysterious states outlined here and in Leary, Metzner, and Alpert's classic book.

Death is a trial that we all eventually face—whether it's the complete cessation of consciousness or the beginning of a new adventure. Regardless of what we believe, might we gain something from accepting our death, in advance, while we're still alive? Could it allow greater appreciation for our life and for other living beings? I hope. It remains difficult and slippery, though. When we see ourselves aging in the mirror or when looking at old photos, we're reminded of the passage of time. Of our life inching closer to the end of our journey. What would it mean to accept that (dare I say embrace it) and appreciate our life as we age—even as we become frail, endure pain, and perhaps slowly forget the past? Time will tell.

Death & Loss—A Sentence Completion Task

To help guide your own reflections, I offer a classic exercise from my field: The Sentence Completion Task. This exercise is a new feature for these existential trials. It replaces the Curiosity Generator from our first arc. Although curiosity remains important, the attitudes and feelings that arise during these reflections will likely involve much more. Take a moment, clear your head, and complete the following statements with the first response that comes to mind. You may do this exercise again, after a week or more, to see if your answers differ. No one is going to grade you. This task is only meant to stimulate reflection and personalize your journey.

When I think of death, the first thing that comes to mind is _____

_____.

As a child, I was taught that death _____.

The first person close to me to die was _____. My reaction

   was to _____.

I'm still mourning the loss of _____.

What most scares me about my own death is _____.

Because of my feelings surrounding death, I avoid _____.

To be honest, thinking about death makes me _____.

What I accept most about my own mortality is _____.

If I were to accept death more openly and honestly, I would be able to

_____.

In the end, I would like my gravestone to say _____.

Good job. Some sentences might have been easy, some not so much. Feel free to take a few moments to re-center yourself before continuing onward.

Impermanence—Reducing Suffering by Accepting Change

Death as a topic of conversation isn't very popular, but it does have one close companion: *impermanence*, the inevitability of change. Death and impermanence are natural emanations from the flow of time. Buddhists see impermanence (*anicca*) as a central fact of existence, superseding that of death. Death is just one of many forms impermanence takes.

Impermanence is expressed through changes at the smallest to grandest scales, encompassing all existence. See that flower in your garden? It will wilt. That delicious dessert from last week? Long gone (well, depending on your metabolism). These examples are trivial. What about life itself? Our Earth has had not one, not two, but five mass extinctions—from asteroids and overactive volcanic eruptions to sudden cold snaps. The worst event, nick-named The Great Dying, caused the extinction of up to 96% of marine life and 66% of land vertebrates.[32] That's unfathomable. On much smaller scales, human history contains stories of severe droughts and pandemics far worse than our recent coronavirus. Whatever the cause, the fact they happened is why we as individuals are here today—and why we're even human in the first place. These extinctions and disasters made room for our ancient ancestors to survive and adapt. Thinking beyond life, how about our grand Milky Way Galaxy? Four billion years from now, it'll collide with our closest neighbor the Andromeda Galaxy to form something new.[33] No need to worry. We're unlikely to be around during that gradual but spectacular merger.

Impermanence can easily trigger sadness, but Buddhism goes further. It describes our inability to accept impermanence as the source of *all* human suffering (*dukkha*).[34] In other words, we suffer because we grasp onto sensations, emotions, objects, and relationships that we deem desirable, but even if obtained, they're all doomed to end. They end because all good things end. But let's not be too gloomy. All bad things end too. If we push this train of thought further, then these labels of 'good' and 'bad' are themselves relatively empty—especially when considering the perspective gained from our growing cosmic awareness. Such labels reflect judgments based on how we desire things to be (or not be) and futile attempts to maximize what we evaluate as 'good' and minimize what we deem as 'bad.'

We're not all Buddhists, though, and fortunately, Buddhists aren't offended if we don't convert. I introduce these ideas only because it's hard to think about mortality without thinking about how all things change over time. And, it's hard to contemplate death and change without contemplating loss. Everything is lost over time. We even constantly lose ourselves. In both a microcellular and psychological sense, we aren't exactly as we were just a few days ago, much less after a year or decade. Even with reincarnation, Buddhists emphasize the absence of a permanent ego-self (*anatta*). And yes, Earth shares this same fate. As our sun enlarges and finally bursts, our solar system will transform into a giant, if not also magnificent, graveyard.

For some people, it's hard not to jump to nihilism when facing these facts. A nihilist might argue, "If we all die in the end, and our entire species and home will eventually be obliterated, then everything is meaningless." This conclusion is a leap in logic. Knowing the likely end of our story doesn't mean we should ignore all that came before or dismiss what might occur along the way. Plus, we're not even close to the natural end of our solar system. We're in the middle or even early stages of this story. And you are still alive. If you've been practicing mindful awareness, then you're beginning to appreciate how full each moment truly is—even if ephemeral and fleeting, we're always existing in an 'eternal now.' Everything else is a collection of memories or fantasies of the past or an imagined future. Impermanence isn't some grand esoteric and impenetrable concept. You experience it just by being aware of how each moment shifts into the next.

So, if we're not to become Buddhist monks, then what can reflections on impermanence give us? For one, it can create space for deeper appreciation. Several years ago, I learned of the Japanese sentiment 'mono no aware'—to be deeply moved by the existence of something, even if fleeting.[35] The phrase reflects a poignant awareness of the ephemeral nature of beauty, love, and life. It's resonated with me ever since. Knowing something won't last doesn't need to take away from its underlying meaning or beauty. Acknowledging the fragility that underlies all things can trigger complex reactions. Sadness, anticipatory grief, thoughts of denial, and sometimes, simply a quiet, downward gaze. All these reactions arise from acknowledging the beauty that was, is, and will be no more.

If you've seen *Lost in Translation*,[36] then you've witnessed a modern American film portrayal of 'mono no aware.' This sentiment is interwoven in the deep connection between the lead characters played by Bill Murray and Scarlett Johansson. Knowing they must ultimately part is no spoiler. By realizing this inevitability, both the characters and the audience feel an underlying sweet sadness in the background that culminates in the film's final moments. If we skipped to the end, we might conclude, "Why bother?" Yet the fullness of 'mono no aware' is in experiencing beauty and love *despite* loss. A feeling of deep appreciation intermingles with the mourning of what once was, or could have been, and what we know won't last. Given that all things end, this same sentiment may prove helpful in understanding much of our human journey.

Impermanence—A Sentence Completion Task

With its influence throughout the entire cosmos and within our individual human lives, impermanence deserves its own reflection exercise. These sentences highlight the impact of change or resisting it. Again, take a moment to clear your mind and finish the following statements. Remember there's no right answer, and you can always revisit this task in the future. For now, go with your first response.

I want _____ to last forever and never end.

In remembering what I've lost in the passage of time, I mourn most the

loss of _____.

As a child, one of my favorite places to visit was _____

_____, but now it no longer exists.

If I could make one feeling or sensation last forever, it'd be _____

_____.

If it did last forever, the downside could be _____.

If I could choose never to feel one thing ever again, it'd be _____

_____.

If I got my way, however, the problem would be _____

_____.

The part of myself I'm most attached to is _____.

If I lost this part of myself, I'd _____.

If I could accept that all things change and nothing lasts, I'd be able to ____

_____.

These sentences are only a few examples to stir your mind and heart. You may be inspired to create your own stems. If you do, record them alongside other reflections in your Travel Journal.

Heeding Warnings while Confronting the First Trial

Reading and reflecting about death and impermanence are important, but they're insufficient to pass this first trial on our journey. Completing those sentences, though, is a great start. In my prior work in hospice, I learned an important lesson: People tend to die as they lived. Despite initial hopes, my brief time as a hospice provider showed me not everyone approaches dying with deep contemplation or experiences epiphanies. If a person never valued self-reflection in their days of living, they're unlikely to have a change of heart even while approaching their final goodbye.

When speaking of passing or not passing these trials, I'm using oversimplified language. In all honesty, these trials remain relevant throughout our lives, up to the final moment. Everyone engaging in this journey, though, is already practicing what's required. By continuously expanding your awareness within our first arc, you've set yourself up with the tools needed to confront these trials as they emerge and re-emerge throughout your life.

In this second arc, I'll impart some key considerations (tips, if you will) about how to avoid common 'off-ramps' for our version of the hero's journey. By avoiding these off-ramps (or recovering from them quickly), you increase the likelihood of gaining insights from these trials instead of becoming stuck or relapsing to old habits.

The First Warning—Rigid Defenses (vs. Flexible Coping)

The first warning is relevant for each trial ahead: reverting to rigid or unhelpful defense mechanisms. Earlier in this chapter, we reviewed brief examples of how a person can defend against the significant pain of losing a loved one. The defenses to look out for are ones like denial, displacement, and projection. These approaches transform reality into something at first more manageable, but they lead to additional problems. We shouldn't disparage these defenses, though. They're first learned in infancy and early childhood when they were the most effective, if not the only, options available. Later in life, their downsides become worse than the emotional pain they're intending to avoid. Consider a person who turns to heavy drinking to numb painful emotions after losing a partner. Over time, their living family and friends may slowly turn away because of their behavior while intoxicated. It's heartbreaking to see, much more to experience. Changing such patterns takes patience, awareness, and consistent effort—and ideally, compassion towards the pain hiding underneath the defense.

To stay with the example of mourning, greater healing is possible when we're able to break through denial and feel the loss more fully. Approaching emotional pain is hard. Developing new ways of coping often requires first understanding and having gratitude for the support old defenses offered in the past. What's better than finding new coping skills is realizing we also need to be flexible, moment-to-moment, in how we cope. No one needs to wallow in the depths of pain indefinitely. Flexible coping is nimble and responsive to your needs and the needs of the situation as they change, which they do and will—remember impermanence? Flexibility means being able to move mindfully from using even healthier defenses (like humor and suppression) to expressing more genuinely our vulnerable emotions (like sorrow). Afterwards, we can mix things up and cope in other ways—like seeking the support of a friend.

As a therapist and trauma specialist, I've witnessed people transform their deepest personal pain into renewed energy to create positive change in the world. Sometimes this transformational healing meant studying law and advocating for others who've been victimized. Other times, it meant being fully present as a parent and showing their child the love they seldom received themselves. In other cases, it meant committing to a contemplative practice, which later inspired loved ones to do the same. A single person's healing can spread to an entire community.

In all these cases, these individuals found healing not by getting rid of their 'symptoms', but by working hard in and outside of therapy. They experienced the emotions they kept buried, learned from them, and rediscovered the parts of themselves that knew how to move toward healing and transformation. And most of these people I mention didn't use psychedelics—they found their inner healer in other ways. Many doors can lead to transformation. Finding them and then choosing to walk through them is the tricky part.

The Second Warning—
Staring at the Sun (vs. Respectful Engagement)

Later in his life, the famous existential psychiatrist Irvin Yalom wrote a book on death anxiety with a title as stark as its subject matter: *Staring at the Sun*.[37] Indeed, the embedded metaphor is clear. Being wholly cognizant of one's looming death (and the unconscious, intense anxiety associated with it) can harm the psyche similar to how staring at the sun can damage the retina. Maybe I could have given you stronger warnings before reading this chapter? Still, you've made it this far, so I'm confident your 'eye' (perhaps third eye?) is perfectly alright. What Yalom means is there's a certain foolhardiness in confronting the stark reality of our mortality.

But, you might say, what about psychedelic-triggered 'ego death?' Isn't that a good thing? That's what's so transformative about psychedelics, right? Indeed, a good question—ignoring the obvious caveat that ego death isn't the same as physical death or permanent ego loss. Walter Pahnke, an early psychedelic researcher and psychiatrist, observed that psychedelic-induced mystical states lessened connections to people's individual identities but somehow did so without making them "feel that they have 'lost' anything crucial." Many of them actually felt they had "'come home' and regained proper perspective" about their true nature.[38] Modern psychedelic therapy research studying cancer and end-of-life anxiety has found similar results.

So then what's the risk? The primary one I've witnessed is a kind of compulsive chasing of ego dissolution. Once at a large social gathering, a young man approached me after he heard of my scholarly work in psychedelics. He proceeded to tell me about all the psychedelics he had tried so far—there were a lot—and how he felt as if he hadn't broken through to the 'other side' yet. He wanted my opinion on which drug he should try next. I suggested none. Specifically, to take a break and focus on integrating the experiences he'd already had. That wasn't quite the response he expected.[39] This young man had had ego death experiences, but he had no idea what to make of them.

And he desired more, never being fully satiated or content with his experiences. He was chasing the peak of the psychedelic summit and even though he had arrived (multiple times, in fact) he didn't find it was enough.

When anything, no matter how 'good' it may appear, is lauded as the magic bullet or cure-all for stress, depression, or existential dread, it's sure to disappoint. When that magic bullet is called ego death, then I'm left questioning whether something deeper is going on. Later in his work, Freud spoke of the death drive (*thanatos*), a hidden desire for self-annihilation to return our life to its original inorganic state. The death drive is the less-known counterpart to the famous pleasure drive (*eros*). Freud believed both forces work in tandem but to opposite purposes until finally, in the end, death naturally wins.[40] Taking Yalom's warning to heart as well as Freud's assertion of a death drive within each of us, we must ask: Should we pause to consider whether any hidden motivations are leading us to 'stare at the sun?' I think that's wise, with or without psychedelics.[41]

A cursory understanding of beliefs about reincarnation or an afterlife may suggest the death drive, if it exists, isn't all that irrational. If there's a soul that transcends the body, what is there left to fear? These beliefs are common throughout the world and within psychedelic communities. Mystical experiences often involve contacting a spiritual realm of existence that appears to transcend death. These experiences are very real for the people having them.

What if we found inscrutable scientific proof of reincarnation? The 2017 film *The Discovery* acts as a thought experiment exploring just that.[42] Although reincarnation might sound nice to some Western minds, the film follows a darker (but arguably more realistic) narrative about the impact on society. After the discovery, suicide rates drastically increase. Dissatisfied, unhappy people believe their chances would be better if they 'reset' their current life and begin a new one. If these people first read *The Tibetan Book of the Dead*, they might be better equipped to handle the bardo states between lives—or better yet, the life they were given in this go-around.[43] Whatever we believe about the existence of an afterlife, we should carefully consider our motivations to face death, metaphorically or literally. To evaluate our intentions alongside any potential risks and rewards is to show respect not only for our death but also for our life.

Alongside compulsive death drive motivations, we should also be aware of another sneaky defense mechanism: *counterphobia*. Rather than seeking death per se, counterphobia is about seeking control over anxiety by approaching what we fear with reckless abandon. Now, I admit I learned about counterphobia because I had more of a predilection for it. Being trained in exposure therapy for PTSD and anxiety, I thought facing one's fears was the pinnacle of mental health. As a young male trauma therapist-in-training, I got drawn into the world of motorcycles. Mastering riding was a thrill, but then I started meeting people who barely survived motorcycle crashes and family members of others not so lucky. Ever hear the adage, "A motorcycle helmet only means the difference between an open and closed casket?" Its meaning eventually sunk in. When I examined my motivations, I uncovered desires for excitement, community, mastery, and living up to masculine ideals—all of which contrasted with my graduate program's intense intellectual and emotional demands. Not too bad. But counterphobia was in the mix too. Riding a motorcycle is risky, but the danger is part of the thrill.

It's often true that facing fears is healthy, but we mortals have fear for a reason: self-preservation. When we push through fear, ignore it, or discount it, we may feel tough and strong—especially for us men who are constantly told that's how we should be. Fear, though, has no gender. It's a basic human emotion for a reason. We need some level of fear when facing actual danger so that our fight-or-flight system kicks in to protect us. Skydiving may be safe with highly trained staff and plenty of safety checks, but at the end of the day, it's still jumping out of a plane and trusting all factors line up as planned. The same is true of the emotional risks of powerful experiences like psychedelics. Journeys are best undertaken with the proper preparation and attention to one's mindset and setting going into the experience—and even better in legal contexts with professionally trained support. Taking risks is sometimes necessary and well worth it. We shouldn't live life governed by fear. But deciding whether to take risks is best suited for mindful, balanced decision making, and not defensive impulses.

Passing the First Trial—
Fostering Acceptance of Death & Impermanence

Whether these warnings about rigid defenses and 'staring at the sun' are about hidden motivations or honest explorations, we're left with the question of how to face death and grow from it—instead of being burnt to a crisp. The human trial of death is the most mysterious of all. Why? As far as we know, no one has returned to tell the tale—outside near-death experiences, which appear remarkably similar to some psychedelic journeys.[44]

In passing this trial, my suggestion is to engage with death, in all its forms, with a steady presence of mind, balanced by a great deal of respect and reverence. This attitude means maintaining awareness without giving into either avoidance or counterphobia. This offering then is really an invitation to use our new ally—acceptance. Accepting mortality and impermanence allows us to acknowledge these facts of life. Acceptance doesn't mean we dwell on them, but by not avoiding them, consciously or unconsciously, we can learn to live in harmony with these fundamental truths.

In our everyday waking lives, it is possible to foster greater acceptance of mortality and impermanence. To do so, some Jungian scholars promote active engagement with mythic tales involving cycles of death and rebirth.[45] Examples from ancient myth include that of Osiris, Phoenix, Persephone, and several cosmological creation stories. In the visionary film *The Fountain*, director Darren Aronofsky explores both the mythic and modern struggle with mortality and loss.[46] Through three parallel quests to conquer death, Hugh Jackman's character avoids accepting the terminal illness of his love, Izzi. By focusing on finding a cure, he wastes the precious time he has left with her, who patiently encourages him to be present. In another timeline, a Mayan priest and protector of the mythical Tree of Life exclaims to a different version of Jackman's character that "Death is the road to awe."[47]

Reactions of awe are certainly appropriate when facing the mysteries of life and death. Thus, we might consider keeping respect front and center in these explorations. Respect involves having some healthy amount of fear. But that fear can be balanced with curiosity and reverence. These attitudes support the possibility of mindful and ethical exploration. To pass the trail of death and impermanence in our journey, we must accept their reality. Through acceptance, we may receive our first mythical boon—a more fully engaged life. A life replete with gratitude and relatively free—not from pain or loss, but from the added suffering caused by refuting the unyielding flow of time.

Mystical experiences, with or without ego dissolution, can require passing through trials of distress and fear before one can 'break on through to the other side' (a la The Doors).[48] Life too can work this way. We can ride the waves of fear in life, being honest about its presence yet not turning away. By confronting existential questions and accepting whatever we find, we can discover personal insights through our direct experience. This process is true within psychedelic journeys, but more importantly, it's true in life in general. Facing and accepting our fears about mortality, loss, and impermanence can open new vistas for exploration. This trial may be our first in this book, yet in life, it's the final one for us all.

On the 14th of March 2019, the impressive scholar and co-author of the earlier mentioned book *The Psychedelic Experience*, Ralph Metzner passed away. His friend and fellow psychologist David Presti wrote a touching memorial describing Metzner's dying process. To the end, Metzner practiced what he preached. His approach to dying embraced an attitude of respectful engagement and acceptance:

> In the days immediately prior to his death, Ralph posted small notes near his bed in which he had written: 'intention → attention → awareness'—reminders to remain alert and aware along his dying trajectory—and a testament to the shamanic advice he frequently offered in working with visionary states: stay connected with your intention, your ancestors (those who have gone before, those who have mapped the terrain), your ground, and your light. Good medicine, indeed.[49]

If we remember that living is already dying and the present is all we ever really have, then we too may contemplate death with the same courage that allowed Metzner and our other countless ancestors to face the ultimate journey of consciousness.

This attitude requires a steady presence of mind. One that recognizes any natural anxiety as it arises but is anchored by qualities of stillness and silence. Can we then stare into the void and not get sucked in? Can we avoid the event horizon and its point of no return? The skills you gained in the last chapter can come in handy after all. Whether managing anxiety in a psychedelic journey or as provoked by mortality and impermanence, an attitude of respectful acceptance may guide us 'in and through'—even if our other ally, curiosity, temporarily fails.

Concrete Suggestions & Journey Report

To support your individual work, Box 5.3 offers a few concrete suggestions and examples. Read the list to see if any might be worthwhile in your efforts of passing this first trial. Journey Report 5.1 provides an example of a psychedelic experience involving themes of death and loss. Marianne described her previous conscious belief system as atheism, but this ayahuasca journey, alongside her preceding ceremonies, opened her to other possibilities. She became aware of the spiritual significance of being part of the earth and connected with her loved ones who had passed. Her fears were not erased, but they became less powerful, serving as merely a backdrop to her feeling of gratitude for life.

Box 5.3

Exploring Death & Impermanence in Everyday Life

Suggestion	Example
Meditate on the everchanging present moment, with a physical anchor or object to ground these reflections.	You gather a single ice cube from your refrigerator and sit down and let it gently rest in one hand. You notice the sharp coolness of the cube that crescendos and then slowly fades as your nerves get used to its temperature. You watch the cube slowly but surely melt, absorbing the heat from its surroundings, including from your hand. You continue to observe the cube dissolve, being with it every moment of its passing into liquid form.
Choose a meal of the day to practice mindful eating and acknowledge the once-living components that provide you sustenance.	You prepare your meal, whether a full course of 'meats and potatoes' or a carefully prepared vegan masterpiece. You look at each part of your meal and consider its origins. Was it a plant grown at a farm? An animal you hunted, or that someone else raised? What life was here that's now being used to sustain yours? You eat each portion with this awareness and gratitude for the life that came before.
List five people, places, objects, or experiences from your past that are no longer present in physical form with you now.	You think of your grandmother and the love and support she gave you from a young age, how she encouraged you to follow your dreams no matter where they take you. You remember your favorite restaurant that has since closed. You also reminisce about your favorite toy as a child.
Reflect on any patterns you may have with mourning loss. If helpful, consider stages or aspects of grief, such as denial, anger, bargaining, depression, and acceptance.	You journal about the loss of a family member, a friend, and/or a stranger (such as a public figure). You describe your emotions, from when you first learned of their passing, to the days after, and to the present. You notice similarities and differences in how you mourned (or didn't mourn) each loss. You realize a part of you still fears being overwhelmed by reflecting on the loss of one particular family member.
Connect to the consciousness you had as a child, an adolescent, a young adult, and now.	You scan your memories for standout or representative moments for each stage of your life. As you reflect, you connect with the part of yourself now that feels like the same person, even if as other parts have changed or become less dominant in your current life.

Grounding Words—A Brief Summary

You've done what few of us mere mortals can bring ourselves to do, at least with full awareness. In this chapter, you've confronted some of the most profound and distressing questions of the human experience: What is death? How can we live freely while knowing death comes for us all? You charged forward anyways and learned that beyond the fragility of life itself, all things in the cosmos must bow to the dominance of time. All things fall apart or change, sooner or later. And new things emerge in their place. Yet, here you are at the end of this chapter, perhaps the most challenging of all, and you survived. You gained some wisdom too about the dangers of facing this trial. You know you could just return to ignorance or denial. Or perhaps worse, you could stare at the sun, too recklessly, too directly, or too frequently and lose more than you bargained. But, perhaps also, you're feeling more grounded than before. A part of you may be opening, expanding your awareness to the edges of your deepest fears and the greatest unknowns, and somehow finding ways to manage your reactions with admirable flexibility and care. Having equipped a full set of scuba gear before diving in, you're giving these explorations all the respect they deserve. I'm impressed. And, I know you can go even deeper.

Your Assignment, Your Choice

In this second arc, you might notice some assignments are a bit more challenging to complete. Remember these are your journey's trials. Passing them means you're growing, and growing pains are occasionally to be expected. Fear not, though. I wouldn't suggest anything you couldn't handle after making it this far already. The options will remain divided by their relative emphasis on *Reflective-Intellectual* or *Experiential-Emotional* exploration. The choice, as always, is yours. Try to do at least one activity daily before you turn to the next trial. Because some activities might be challenging in one way or another, you may continue using skills or meditations from the first arc to provide strength. In fact, I encourage it. Nothing's gained by investigating a dark cave without a flashlight or two, right?

Assignments 5.4
Exploring Death & Impermanence

Reflective-Intellectual	Experiential-Emotional
☐ Task—Complete **Exercise 5.1 "Lifeline Reflections"**	☐ Task—**Visit a graveyard** where a loved one is buried. Visit their grave as well as a grave of a stranger.
Time—Minimum of 30 min of reflection	Time—Minimum of 30 min visiting the graveyard
Aim—To reflect on your own life and death and the passing of time	Aim—To notice reactions as you view the final resting place of someone you know and another person you do not
☐ Task—Study the **life of a loved one who passed away.** Note facts about their birth, life, and death. Record any reactions you have to this exercise.	☐ Task—Practice the meditation in **Meditation 5.1 "Being with Impermanence & Mortality"**
Time—Minimum of 45 min to gather information, reflect on exercise, and record reaction	Time—Minimum of 2-3x/week, ~10 min each
Aim—To review the life of someone you've lost and consider the impact of doing so	Aim—To experience the ever-fleeting yet eternal present as it constantly changes

After reviewing options and possibly doing one, respond to the Travel Journal prompt. Write, draw, or create whatever comes to mind related to this first trial of death and impermanence.

Travel Journal

How does contemplating my eventual death change my life?
How might my choices differ if I accepted my mortality and the impermanence
of all things?

JOURNEY REPORT 5.1 The Circle of Life

Before this journey, I received a message that a good friend had died. He had been fighting cancer while maintaining his quality of his life, and when that quality disappeared, he decided to end his suffering in a humane way with palliative care. The year before I lost my mom from a sudden illness, and after that I kept wondering about death and life after death. Being an atheist almost my entire life, I found solace in the idea that there was nothing after life and that the life we lived was the most meaningful part of existence. But experiencing the realms of plant medicine awakened a nascent spirituality within me. I knew my prior mindset was too limited. I was avoiding some feeling inside me.

In one ayahuasca ceremony, I truly surrendered to the experience and asked Grandmother Ayahuasca about death. I thought I might be connected to my friend and my mom, that I would have a conversation with them, as many people have spoken about their conversations with the deceased. Instead, I saw my hands turning black and disintegrating. I got scared. *I wasn't ready to die yet!* I begged her not to take me as I had different things to do. But she was unresponsive. I kept my eyes fixed on my hands hoping it would stop, hoping this would reveal something else. I remembered the shaman telling us to drop resistance and to surrender to the wisdom of the medicine. So I did. Slowly I gave into death and saw my hands being turned into soil, unified with the Earth. At that moment, I understood the circle of life and our interconnectedness. We are all part of the same substance. Being born and dying is reviving from and returning to the Source.

Within the soil, different pathways extended underneath and in front of me. The paths were surrounded by beautiful flowers and plants. Looking at each, I saw that all of them ended in darkness and disintegration. Hovering above was some sort of energy floating. It felt like my friend who just passed away. The energy felt peaceful and calm, resting in the beautiful 'landscape', surrounded by light. As everything faded, I felt my whole body making a deep sigh. Looking to my left I felt a presence, but while opening my eyes I saw only the other people in the circle making the same sigh. Closing my eyes, I looked to my left again. In my 'mind's eye', I saw this big presence surrounded by beautiful small birds and floating bubbles. The presence felt familiar, as I was sure I had seen them before. I felt I was…coming home. They repeated this one phrase that since then has always stayed with me: *We're always here…We're always here…We're always here…* I knew it was true, and I cried silently with tears of joy and gratitude. I felt deeply held, touched by unconditional love and warmth.

Death is inevitable. As part of the human life, it is something we cannot escape and that arouses occasional fear in me. What I learned was that the inevitability of death is intricately connected to birth, nature, and spirituality. That being born is a privilege, and dying is an act of love, giving back to Mother Earth. My biggest fear about death, being alone, is one I can now surrender into more fully. Even though it remains scary, I can hold myself and let it be.

—Marianne, Age 46

Note. This account and all others in the book are de-identified and anonymous to protect the confidentiality of the person sharing their story. Minor grammar, spelling, and stylistic changes were made and usually in partnership with the person providing the account.

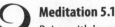

Meditation 5.1
Being with Impermanence & Mortality (10-15 min)

Carefully read this script to understand this meditation's flow. Find a comfortable place to sit, stand, or lay down. Ensure the location is safe and without major distractions. Then, close your eyes and lead yourself through it. Remember, becoming distracted only gives you an opportunity to strengthen your awareness and concentration over time.

Slowly close your eyes, attending to the gradual reduction of your external field of vision….and then shift your attention to what you notice in the present moment… You may find yourself noticing different sensory perceptions, like sounds or scents…or you may notice internal imagery or other sensations your mind generates or perceives with your eyes closed.

Attend to each or any of these, depending on what feels natural in this moment…notice how the sensations change over time…sometimes very subtly…sometimes with clear, decisive movement…settle into the rhythm of the present moment as it continuously evolves…

Now, with a gentle shift, attend to your body…imagine yourself in touch with all the cells of your body, the billions of diverse biological units acting in concert to support your living…some partnering with each other in their tasks…some existing for quite different purposes…what do you notice as you connect with the living organism of your own body?

Now, acknowledge that the biochemical orchestra of your body, of which you are currently aware, is a wholly new one compared to your body of the past. Yet, the *you* here, noticing and appreciating this new orchestra, is somehow the same…Or, perhaps it is not? Stay in this awareness…try not to follow any judgments, interpretations, or questions it evokes…but just be…

Imagine now, if you can, the moment in which your consciousness will dissolve at the time of your eventual death….Try not to get distracted by following fantasies or fears of how you might pass. Just contemplate the exact moment in which occurs the subtle and gentle shift from your life and identity as you know it into whatever the absence of that may be…Rest here in this liminal space…being in the stillness and silence of this moment…

In the span of your next breath, begin to return to the present…return to the eternal now. As you find yourself able, leave behind the moment of your imagined death…and settle back into your body…back to your life…Follow your breath as it anchors you to here and now…and in unison, soak up all the senses, both external and internal, of your current experience…

Still aware of the continuous flow of each moment, anchor your awareness to your body…to your physical location…and slowly reopen your eyes and refocus on your surroundings…knowing that time continues onward and so do you along with it.

Exercise 5.1

Lifeline Reflections

Instructions

1. Enter your date of birth. This date is when you started your current journey in our shared world.

2. Enter your best guess of an estimated or expected age at which your life may end. Consider the lifespan of family members and other people you've known, your current health status, etc.

3. Mark on the line approximately where you think you are in relation to your entire lifespan *Optional Recommendation*—add markers for major life events (like graduation, beginning or ending relationships or jobs, major losses or achievements, etc.). Place these marks relative to other events on your lifeline.

4. Sit quietly considering this image for 5 minutes

5. Afterwards, jot down some reactions in words or images, and across the four modes of emotions, thoughts, body, and behavior, as relevant. If you'd like more structure, complete Form 4.1 "The Experiential Tracker."

Date of Birth: _____   **Estimated Age of Death:** _____

Birth ————————————————————————— **Death**

My Reactions & Reflections:

CHAPTER 6

Knowing Loneliness—
Welcoming Solitude & Interconnectedness

There is a pleasure in the pathless woods,
There is a rapture on the lonely shore,
There is society, where none intrudes,
By the deep sea, and music in its roar:
I love not man the less, but Nature more,
From these our interviews, in which I steal
From all I may be, or have been before,
To mingle with the Universe, and feel
What I can ne'er express, yet cannot all conceal.

—Lord Byron, *Childe Harold's Pilgrimage*[1]

Journey Waypoint V

One down, two to go. You've confronted mortality and impermanence. I hope doing so has imbued you with more life and opened doors that were previously closed. This next trial is a challenge. Not just because it involves another core fear, but because here, we begin to confront paradox far more directly. Perhaps we can take some comfort in knowing that paradox is itself quite psychedelic. Death and impermanence are straightforward—in concept, if not in our acceptance of them. They're facts of life. Yet, this trial contains 'facts' that don't quite add up. The fear of loneliness is intertwined with the fear of deeper connection. They are one and the same.[2]

Few of us, however, consciously feel both sides of this fear. Our personal history, from our first separation at birth to our present life, can be mired by imperfect experiences with other human beings and individual pain often kept private. The pain of feeling misunderstood, unseen, or rejected can be triggered by strangers or our closest loved ones. The need to belong, though, is as fundamental as our need to eat and drink.[3] Although our social needs have ancient evolutionary roots, today we need others perhaps more than ever for our basic survival. Modern life and culture have made most of us dependent on others to have clean water, fresh food, and safe shelter.[4] What happens if these systems stop working? Popular post-apocalyptic shows like *The Walking Dead* are meant to warn us as much as entertain us.[5]

In navigating this next trial, the reflections you've had in confronting mortality will remain very much alive. The boundaries of our existence, birth and death, set the frame—the playground of life, its edges delineated by these truths. But within these boundaries, we face many choices not set in stone. The early lessons we learn upon arriving in this world continue to unfold long after. But the lessons never stop. Old experiences are repeated until we learn to use a different tactic. And the playground continues to change. Countless others join us also trying to find their way, stumbling along or acting with exuberant overconfidence—young and old souls alike, aware of others or too self-involved to notice. And we as journeyers exist between all these possibilities because all are within us—to connect, to distance, to embrace, to isolate, to be alone, to fall into a crowd, to belong, or to be abandoned. Nothing here is quite what it seems.

This trial might involve a few paradoxes, but that's why it's a trial—and a worthy one at that. In transformative psychedelic states (as in mythic quests) a journeyer is never truly alone. At the same time, they must experience separation to find their own path. So it is for us. Others cross our paths, sometimes as fellow travelers, spiritual mentors, loyal allies, or threatening foes. And we can be each of those for other people too. This chapter marks the midpoint of our journey. As you pass the trial, you'll gain insights about relating to both yourself and others. I'll describe the terrain. You'll choose how to explore it.

Self-Reflections Check-In

Before entering our next trial, let's take a deep breath and check-in. How was your experience confronting the first trial? Was it as challenging as you expected? Everyone reacts to reminders of mortality and impermanence in different ways at different times. After completing the chapter, which activities did you choose to do? Contemplating death and impermanence can bring up loss and grief, as seen in many of the last trial's examples. If you're still in a grieving process of any kind, some themes from this chapter may continue to resonate. Contents of one trial can bleed over into the others. Just like the various forms of awareness you cultivated in the first arc, these existential themes are interlocked. Separating each layer of the human journey into conceptual categories helps us examine them, but that separation doesn't reflect the full reality. If you need more time to reflect, give yourself that space. But remember facing each trial allows you to find your own strength. Pace yourself and be kind to the wounded parts of your psyche. That, alongside being brave, is part of the journey too.

Confronting the Second Trial

In this arc's preface, we learned our existential trials are also trials of initiation. To become initiated is to enter a new understanding, community, or plane of existence. Initiation into something new requires leaving behind something old. In many initiation rituals, a temporary withdrawal allows an initiate to be less entangled with outer actions and other people—and thus, better able to engage with solitary, inner explorations. A common theme of mythic initiation is submission.[6] That word alone can be loaded. Our ally for this arc, acceptance, might help untangle its meaning. Acceptance means submitting to what cannot be changed or resisted. Mythic submission corresponds to a genuine attitude of humility and an ability to suspend, at least temporarily, common ego-level concerns and ambitions—including the need to know and understand. In this trial, as in the previous, I won't tell you exactly what to do or believe. As a guide, I'll offer suggestions and simply ask you to reflect on your personal reactions to being alone and with others.

Before we dive into more personal reflections, we should acknowledge the broader problem of loneliness within our modern world. Roughly one out of every five people in the US and UK report frequently feeling lonely, left out, or without adequate companionship.[7] Some feel isolated even when their amount of social contact appears typical. In other words, people don't need to be completely alone to feel like they are. Among people who report loneliness, 60-66% can identify a specific trigger. The most common include the loss of a loved one (13-18%) and the impact of their own health problems (8-12%).[8] Do you see connections to our first trial? If not, then consider that loneliness increases one's risk of death.[9]

The causes of loneliness are numerous and echo across individual and collective factors, including culture. Whether acknowledged or not, we're all individuals *and* we're all embedded within multiple layers of social, regional, and cultural contexts—even when we're seemingly isolated.[10] Many people blame social media and technology, and certainly they do play a role.[11] Reducing our daily social media use to ten minutes per app decreases anxiety and perceptions of missing out.[12] Barring some apocalyptic societal collapse, though, technology is here to stay. And it's developing rapidly. Given how fairly simple inventions have impacted our wellbeing, what could more advanced technology do? In a relatively subtle exploration of this question, the film *Her*, set in the not-so-distant future, explores our increasing loneliness and the temptation to use technology to find connection. Its ending hints that hope for rehabilitating human-to-human connection may still remain, but perhaps not before heartbreak.[13]

Both connection and lack of connection can be frightening. Sometimes it appears we're damned if we connect and damned if we don't. Still, that isn't true. It collapses the dilemma into a one-sided negativity, another nihilistic conclusion that erases possibilities outside the extremes of connecting unreservedly or disconnecting entirely. One side fears loneliness and the dangers of isolation. The other fears social entanglement and the dangers of coercion and loss of self. Your ever-expanding awareness, however, has prepared you to hold multiple perspectives. The trick is finding within each of us both sets of fears. Whether conscious or not, a part of ourselves fears being controlled by others and losing our personal freedom. And another part fears if we don't connect or conform to social expectations and standards, we'll miss out on something vital—and we'd be right. On both accounts.

Other people and groups have the power to influence us in very negative ways, but so can isolation and dogged individualism.[14] If our individual freedom were absolute, we'd be lost without some guidance on how to make the best choices. The best guidance may come from within, particularly when we're listening to our inner healer—a key mechanism of psychedelic healing and transformation.[15] Modern psychedelic research and many ancient and indigenous initiation rites possess a shared tenet: Healing and transformation don't occur in isolation. Occasional periods of solitary reflection are needed, but it's both alone time and time spent with guides or communities that work hand-in-hand with the process of transformation. Even in our modern Western world, individual willpower and perspective are best tempered and refined by wise counsel and learning from the experiences of others.

The Human Journey Across Space— Returning to Cosmic Dimensions

The mysteries, fears, and hopes about isolation and connection we explore as individuals are replicated at several levels, all the way to the cosmic perspective developed in our very first journey waypoint. The core question seems to be, "Are we truly alone?" In our planet's current ecological system, we're one of roughly five million species—of which the vast majority haven't yet been identified.[16] And that's notwithstanding the hundreds of millions of years before we arrived or considering the innumerable lifeforms predating us. But realizing these biological and historical facts appear insufficient to assuage our fears of isolation.

One of the biggest cosmological questions is whether we're ultimately alone in the entire universe— either as complex lifeforms or as self-aware, conscious beings. As far as we can tell, we're the most advanced intelligence in the history of our little planet, so it makes sense to look outwards into the cosmos for answers. One concern this approach raises, though, is the *Fermi-Hart Paradox*.[17] Put simply, if we're not alone, where is everybody? If conscious life is a natural outgrowth of how the universe works, then why haven't we heard from other intelligent life? Beyond science fiction and speculation, this question bridges several areas of study—physics, biology, philosophy, and religion, to name a few. Contemplating this paradox can lead to some fascinating and disturbing possibilities. Although responses are numerous, Box 6.1 offers some plausible or frequently discussed solutions.[18] Scientists continue to investigate such possibilities, but for us, these questions frame our current existential trial far beyond our personal focus here.[19]

At the smallest scales of space—that is, the molecular, atomic, and quantum realms—we face more questions about connection.[21] Some noteworthy implications come from our everyday experience of solid matter being an illusion. Atoms are, after all, mostly empty space. The electromagnetic fields of our atoms and molecules (our constituent parts) repulse or attract each other but never occupy the same location. At the same time, energy and information are exchanged.[20] Barring atomic fusion, which unleashes enormous amounts of power—as seen in fusion-based nuclear reactions in our sun, other stars, and our most dangerous weaponry—fundamental electrophysical boundaries are set between us and everything else. Biologically speaking, though, we can easily share our microbiome with others through casual and intimate contact. Mostly, what we share is benign, but not always. As painfully experienced in the coronavirus pandemic, we're all connected.

The preceding is only from a scientific perspective and not psychedelic conjecture. Of course, it provides the bedrock for many fascinating theories, pseudoscientific speculation, and both catastrophic *and* wish-fulfilling thinking. We needn't dismiss these possibilities, but it's good to admit what we do and do not know. Leaps of faith and intuitive knowledge are necessary and critical in life, but arguments arise when we're overly attached to our version of the cosmic story and cannot communicate with people who think differently— another theme of this trial and a preview of what lies ahead. The fundamental questions remain the same: Are we alone? If not, can we interact with others? If so, how? Regardless of any answers we might eventually discover, we must remember humanity shares a universal context that's *very much* non-human—in terms of our planet's ecological system, the known and unknown aspects of the cosmos, and the fundamental methods and boundaries of interaction.

Box 6.1

Example Solutions to Fermi-Hart Paradox

Possible Solution	Brief Explanation
Limitations of Spacetime	The physical space between Earth and other planets with conscious life is too great to allow communication—either entirely or practically because of time requirements for relaying and receiving messages.
Forerunners Before Expansion	We're one of the earliest forms of conscious life to exist in our cosmic region. Over time, more life will evolve, develop consciousness, and create technology allowing communication.
Missed Opportunity	Conscious life evolved elsewhere before us. They tried to communicate with or visit Earth before we evolved, before our recorded history could document the contact, or before our technology could receive their messages.
Deliberate Silence	Conscious life evolved before us and now possesses advanced technology for interstellar travel or communication, but they're choosing to remain silent. Their silence could suggest disinterest, caution, or competing priorities. Alternatively, they may be waiting until we've demonstrated some prerequisite level of global stabilization, technological advancement, or development of consciousness (broadened awareness, scientific knowledge, and/or ethical understanding).
The Great Filter	Conscious lifeforms have existed in the universe, but they're now all extinct. Extinction occurred due to natural disasters (like comets, lethal gamma-ray bursts), dangerous technological advancements (like nuclear war, scientific experimentation gone wrong, environmental collapse, hostile artificial intelligence), or hostility from other intelligent life (like interstellar invasion or war).
Extraterrestrial Spores	Ancient fungi arrived on earth and seeded life as we know it, including our evolution into conscious intelligence. A mycelial network connects all life and consciousness, and psychedelic fungi and plants facilitate interspecies communication.
A Cosmic Fluke	We are alone. Conscious life is exceedingly rare or random, and it only exists on Earth. There is no actual paradox.

Note. For these and many other proposed solutions, see Ćirković's (2012) and Webb (2015). The extraterrestrial spores idea is a psychedelic 'Easter egg' and comes from the work of people like Terrence McKenna (1992) and self-taught mycologist Paul Stamets (2005).

Attachment & Its Consequences

Shifting from the cosmic to the personal, we may find this human trial no less complex. As individuals, each of us have navigated many unique experiences from our first entry into this world to the present moment. Those experiences have shaped our distinctive personalities, perspectives, and expectations. How we connect to ourselves and other people are intertwined with a system embedded in all our psychology and shared with many other mammals. This system is *attachment*.[22] Attachment is archetypal in that it has many forms and potential manifestations which vary based on experiences. Each person enters their human existence with the ability and motivation to form attachments with others. At its core, attachment arises from how we connected with our early caregivers and what we learned from their responsiveness or lack thereof. The fundamental question is one of basic trust versus mistrust.[23] Attachment is necessary for us humans. Compared to other animals, we require an exceptionally long time to grow up and become self-sufficient. We rely on our caregivers to survive infancy, but early attachment lessons can follow us well into old age.

According to attachment theory, infants inherit an instinct to signal distress when scared or threatened. Such signals typically elicit a response from caregivers. A simple example is crying. Crying notifies a caregiver that the infant needs attention. Over time, infants adapt their strategies based on their caregiver's patterns of response.[24] If the response is consistent, effective, and comforting, then the infant can develop a secure attachment. If the response is inconsistent or consistently intrusive, unhelpful, or relatively non-existent, then the infant can develop various types of insecure attachment. What distinguishes a secure or insecure attachment is how infants respond in the presence and absence of their caregiver. Ideally, caregivers act as a *secure base* from which infants and children can go forth, explore the world, and play. When they become distressed, for whatever reason, these infants and children know they can signal for help or return to their caregiver to receive reliable support in the form of a *safe haven*.

Lessons from our early attachment experiences reverberate throughout our lives.[25] As we grow out of our infancy, attachment moves beyond nonverbal emotional and behavioral reactions and into the realm of core beliefs about connection, our sense of self in relation to others, and expectations of care in relationships. We call this process *internalization*—that is, we internalize lessons we learned from our early interactions with our caregivers.[26] These lessons and associations become further multifaceted over time, but generally their roots lie in these early experiences. Attachment theory may sound like some classic psychoanalytic 'blame the parents' talk, but if anything, we should be grateful that most of us have 'good enough parents.'[27] After all, parents are only human, just like us. The experiences of our caregivers in their own childhood informed their approach to parenting and so on and so on, across all generations proceeding us. Caregivers don't need to be perfect to provide security.

At the same time, unless they're healed, early attachment wounds can continue throughout life. Whereas infant attachment manifests in behavioral and physiological responses to caregivers, adult attachment manifests across all four experiential modes (thought, emotion, body, behavior) and in close relationships of all kinds.[28] In our adult years, attachment intersects with concerns about emotional safety and belonging. Our internalized views and expectations of ourselves and others can turn into self-fulfilling prophecies that influence our selection of partners and personal triggers for insecurity. Attachment is largely stable, but it can change when we have significant experiences, good or bad, that challenge our early conclusions.[29]

To help guide our explorations, Figure 6.1 shows the current understanding of how attachment is expressed in adulthood. As with personality, speaking of types is easier, but the underlying structure of attachment involves dimensions of anxiety and avoidance.[30] *Attachment anxiety* reflects how uneasy and concerned we feel about our close relationships. It corresponds inversely with views of ourselves as worthy and desirable. When attachment anxiety is high, self-esteem is low, unstable, or highly contingent on validation from others. *Attachment avoidance* reflects how emotionally distant we prefer our relationships to be. High avoidance corresponds to views of others as being untrustworthy, inconsistent, demanding, or dangerous. This avoidance can also block access to feeling vulnerable emotions. The combination of these dimensions explains the labels we typically discuss as an easy shorthand. *Secure attachment* involves low anxiety and avoidance and relatively positive (but not unrealistically so) views of oneself and others. High avoidance and anxiety in combination describe *fearful attachment*, which highlights the intense insecurity, distress, and negative views of oneself and others. The other prototypical combinations are *dismissing attachment* (high avoidance, low anxiety) and *preoccupied attachment* (low avoidance, high anxiety).

Intimate relationships offer challenges for everyone. I normalize that for all my clients, because otherwise, we tend to blame ourselves, our partners, our parents, or all the above. But just as the roots of attachment lie within early interactions between our infant selves and our caregivers, attachment remains an interaction between two or more people, each with their own attachment histories. Simultaneously, attachment's impact is present in the absence of others. When secure, we can feel safe and connected even when far

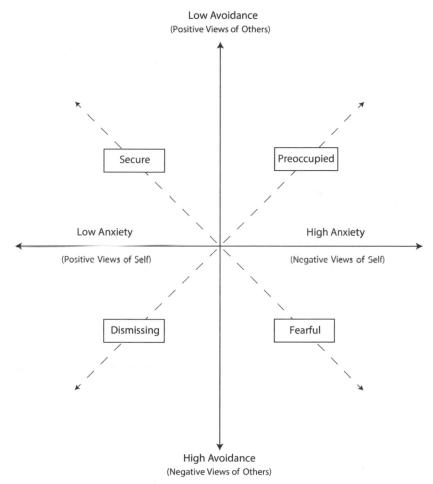

Figure 6.1 Adult attachment dimensions and labels

Note. This figure adapted from Mikulincer and Shaver (2016) and incorporates Griffin and Bartholomew's (1994) formulation of attachment models (labeled here as 'views') of self and others in relationships. A missing component of this figure is disorganized attachment, which reflects an instability or collapse of organized strategies for managing attachment needs and anxieties. As in childhood, disorganized attachment is often connected to severe and unresolved interpersonal trauma (see Main & Solomon, 1986; Liotti, 2004).

apart. When insecure, we can feel anxious and uncertain either alone or in the presence of others. Of course, we might also convince ourselves that we don't need anyone at all and keep others at a comfortable distance. This is how attachment relates to our trial of loneliness. It also highlights how it's a trial about connection as well. In its broadest form, the choice we face is between (1) attempting to avoid our fears of loneliness and our attachment concerns, or (2) accepting our attachment needs and respecting both our individuality and our relationships.

The Defense Against Existential Dread— Avoidance of Isolation & Social Intrusion

Throughout our lives, tensions exist between early lessons and later possibilities. When involving our relationships, a core conflict is between dependence and independence. Our prior experiences and current personalities impact what we consciously desire and fear. Although ultimately connected to fears of mortality and loss, attachment-related existential dread involves fears of either isolation or intrusion by others. Social intrusion comes in many forms, such as trauma, coercion, and limits on personal agency.

As part of the ego, our attachment system uses the same set of defense mechanisms, of which Box 6.2 provides some examples. People with greater attachment security tend to use more complex, flexible, and conscious defenses that can accommodate new information.[31] That is, reality is accepted even if unexpected or unpleasant. In doing so, pathways to connection and repair become possible. Insecure attachment increases the likelihood of forcing new experiences and contradictory information to fit within old patterns and expectations. In other words, reality is distorted or selectively emphasized to support prior conclusions about oneself and others. Even securely attached people, though, have similar options at their disposal depending on their current needs, stress level, and resources available.

Box 6.2

Example Defenses Against Attachment-related Concerns

Selected Defense	Example
Denial	Patrick believes his partner can read his mind. They're like one person. Soul mates who'll never be apart. The two are never physically apart either. Patrick has no idea who he is or where he'd be without his partner.

Box continues on next page

Splitting	Kal believes they can only trust themselves. Everyone else is out for their own interests and in the end will just disappoint or betray. Kal is better off on their own and knows better than to display 'weakness' to anyone.
Rationalization	Maria busies herself with several hobbies, social groups, and volunteer work. She's happy as long as she's not bored or alone. She feels justified in this arrangement because she has important and fun things to do with friends and acquaintances. She often thinks, "You only live once, right?"
Suppression	Ryley is randomly reminded at work about the recent ending of their marriage. They take a breath and compartmentalize, but later that evening, they journal about their feelings and decide to take a relaxing bath to practice some much-needed self-care.

Keep in mind that for most of us, the descriptions I'll present are exaggerated versions of defensive strategies.[32] Attachment, like personality, exists along dimensions. The questions we ask here are not, "What is my attachment style?" but "What am I trying to avoid?" "What am I risking by avoiding this and not that?" "What am I compromising? Is my current approach the best one?"

What's most threatening to each of us depends on what we've learned from past experience. Over time, we internalize implicit and explicit messages about relationships, others, and ourselves. During times of stress, like the infant, we can signal others for support or isolate, turn inwards, and shutdown. Our attachment history gives us internal scripts for how best to cope. Though not entirely conscious, these scripts aren't completely irrational either. They come from our lived experiences in relationships.

If the perceived threat is being isolated or abandoned, we may fight for approval and avoid being alone. The downside is risking conformity over authenticity. In the search for true belonging, the compromise might be to fit in regardless of what's lost. The resulting hollowness of self is like an empty vessel ready to be filled with whatever the outside world wants to store inside. And to be sure, there are predators out there very willing to take charge and give such a person what they think they need. Chief among them are cult-like communities where members subjugate their own will to the will of a 'guru.' Lacking a sense of self makes a person malleable and easy to manipulate. Jung warned, "Resistance to the organized mass can be effected only by the [person] who is as well organized in [their] individuality as the mass itself."[33]

In the other direction, if the perceived threat is being controlled, impinged upon, or losing freedom, we may fight for independence and avoid vulnerability.[34] In distancing oneself from others, the downside is losing true intimacy and avoiding commitment in relationships. Being overly self-focused may ironically prevent deeper connections to our innermost self. People with dismissing or avoidant attachment may appear arrogant or unflappable when it's quite reasonable to feel upset. Asserting our independence can sometimes be guided by unconscious rebellion not only against outside influence but also against vulnerability and social responsibility. Rebellion is a reaction in need of a foe. If rebellion becomes a habitual way of life, then the fight for independence never ends. That's because, in reality, the hidden 'foes' are the rebel's own inner vulnerabilities and inescapable social needs. Unfortunately, dismissing attachment can lead to dismissing the rights and needs of others too, especially when they conflict with the 'right' to do whatever we want.

Dangers may come from outside and within, but our minds learn to perceive threats that fit our prior experiences and expectations. Are we most afraid of losing ourselves and our independence? Are we more afraid of being abandoned by people we love? Do we even care? How willing are we to compromise our autonomy? If we avoid consciously feeling whatever threatens us most, which may be our ego's default, the underlying fears may be expressed or acted out unconsciously. As connected through our fight-or-flight response, fear can quickly turn into anger. Anger feels more empowering than fear. But anger needs a target, whether or not it's the right one.

The Possibility of Accepting Solitude & Connection

Given the problems of isolation and intrusion, it's reassuring that we can become more comfortable with both solitude and genuine connection. Developing this comfort, chiefly by increasing our attachment security, allows greater flexibility in how we manage our fears and mitigate the risks of extreme defensive reactions. If we feel secure in ourselves and with trusted others, we can expand our sense of belonging to include a greater range of other people. We can also manage our existential anxiety in healthier, prosocial ways.[35] Secure attachment isn't naïvely trusting everyone. It's a grounded expectation that with care and communication, we can foster authentic relationships, be comfortable by ourselves, and adapt to life's constantly shifting circumstances, replete with beauty and uncertainty. Secure attachment may appear as an ideal state reserved for people protected from the dark sides of human nature. Yet people gifted secure attachment in childhood still face an eventual fall from innocence—a fact reflected too in almost all myths. Pain is part of life, and to deny that is to escape what we cannot. But the fall from innocence is the beginning of a new journey where life can unfold in all its grandeur and complexity.

If we accept necessary pain, we find greater possibilities. Attachment may start early in our lives, but it's not set in stone. With deep reflection, effort, and healing experiences in later relationships, insecure attachment can be transformed into what's called *earned security*.[36] The past remains important, but when old wounds are healed, our present experience and future outlook become brighter. Development doesn't end in childhood. Throughout life, we continue to learn lessons in relationships—if we're willing. Our brains are capable of learning new things, and we don't need fancy words like neurogenesis to realize that. Like posttraumatic growth, earned security isn't automatic, and it doesn't cover up attachment wounds—that'd be akin to spiritual bypass. Because most severe traumas involve other people (assault, rape, war) and perpetrators are often well-known (family members and intimate partners), positive experiences in relationships can accelerate healing from trauma. These experiences can come from one's community and/or professionals. In fact, the development of a trusting therapist-client relationship is a crucial vehicle for healing attachment wounds in therapy.[37] Wherever they occur, deeper connections can heal and transform.

Attachment security, whether provided early in life or earned later, correlates with the features of a "fully functioning person"—higher openness to experience, engagement in life-long development, dependability, and creativity—all of which resonate with the outcomes of psychedelic therapy.[38] My colleagues and I have also found initial support that attachment influences psychedelic journeys.[39] Higher attachment avoidance can predict more challenging experiences, likely because psychedelics can make people face vulnerable emotions. Higher attachment anxiety, on the other hand, can be associated with more positive mystical experiences, perhaps compensating for distress surrounding their intimate relationships.

Unguided journeys, even when positive, can inadvertently amplify a narrow sense of self-sufficiency at the expense of connection.[40] The ego can experience a type of whiplash moving rapidly from transcendent states and back into the material world. Its response is sometimes to double-down on defense mechanisms to convince us we're in control. Being in a vulnerable altered state of consciousness when surrounded by caring, competent guides can increase emotional and physical safety. Although psychedelics can elicit different experiences when alone and when guided, feeling safe can catapult experiences into new dimensions—so to speak.

However and whenever it's fostered, greater attachment security can lead to exploration and play. When fear is managed, curiosity, compassion, and love can come forward. And being alone transforms into solitude, not loneliness. Alone time allows deeper reflection which in turn promotes integration of insights from various life experiences. A richer inner world promotes a rich outer world. Your work in this book reflects a level of security that you've already gained and are continuing to build upon. By asking questions, you've shown that you want to do more than accept the answers of others without at least first doing your own exploration. You've even been willing to question yourself. Comfort with solitude partnered with mutual respect allows us to learn from one another and become better than we would be in isolation.

Solitude & Connection—A Sentence Completion Task

It's time for some self-reflection and inquiry. These stems are organized into two sections to reflect the two sides of this trial. Pause to clear your head. Then finish the following statements with whatever spontaneously enters your mind.

Solitude

When I'm by myself, I _____

_____.

I feel lonely when _____

_____.

What most scares me about being alone is _____

_____.

Because of this fear, I avoid _____

_____.

I'm content being alone when _____

_____.

What I accept most about solitude is _____

_____.

Connections

As a child, I was taught that other people _____

_____.

When others try to get close to me, I _____

_____ .

I trust people who _____

_____ .

I don't trust people who _____

_____ .

I feel I most belong with people who _____

_____ .

In my close relationships, I avoid _____

_____ .

If I felt more connected and open with other people, I would be able to _____

_____ .

Some important themes may have emerged already from completing these sentences. If so, be sure to explore them further in your Travel Journal.

Connected, For Better or For Worse— Interpersonal Communication & Relationship Patterns

In 1844, upon completing America's first long-distance communication network, Samuel Morse used his name-sake coding system to transmit its first message, "What has God wrought."[41] Although communication technology has made leaps and bounds since this first 'instant message' the embedded question remains relevant. Communication, regardless of distance, is fraught with risks and rewards. A truism in psychotherapy is that relationships are hard. Imperfect people relating to other imperfect people creates imperfect relationships. But, to use a couple more truisms, nobody's perfect and perfection is the enemy of the good. Lucky for us, wisdom can hide in plain sight, even in seemingly empty sayings and clichés. That wisdom is often uncovered within psychedelic journeys, so we do well by not outright dismissing them. We need only disentangle their insincere overuse from their obvious-yet-overlooked meaning.[42]

As we saw with attachment theory, our individual selves first form in interactions with others. Over time, our internalized ideas of who we are (beliefs about ourselves and our identity) and what to expect from others (beliefs about people and relationships) inform our personality. Our default beliefs, most of which remain unspoken or unconscious, form *relationship patterns*, which like self-fulfilling prophecies repeatedly confirm what we 'knew' (meaning learned) from the beginning.[43] After relationship patterns stabilize, it becomes difficult to update them with new information or contradictory feedback. Ego defenses make it especially challenging to acknowledge negative self-fulfilling prophecies. As an example, if we expect others to be unfriendly, our nonverbal expressions (like a look of skepticism) increases the likelihood that we actually receive unfriendly responses—which only reaffirm our pre-existing beliefs. So, to change unhelpful patterns requires conscious, sustained effort to communicate more effectively or find healthier relationships. Uncovering relationship patterns starts with asking questions like: Who am I drawn to, and who do I push away? Who do I attract in my life, and who keeps me at a distance?

A helpful way to understand these communication and relationship patterns is through *The Interpersonal Circumplex*[a] and its dimensions of *Dominance-vs-Submission* and *Warmth-vs-Hostility* (see Figure 6.2).[44] The circumplex was espoused by none other than the controversial if not highly influential psychedelic psychologist-turned-advocate Timothy Leary. As a student, I respected Leary's work well before I realized he was one and the same as the outspoken persona of 1960's counterculture. All controversy and coincidences aside, his model rings true—both intuitively and because of its decades of research support.[45]

Why introduce the circumplex now? The answer lies in how our current trial entails developing both greater self-awareness and awareness of others. As social creatures embedded in a social reality, our personalities and attachment histories are always interacting with those of others—and the situations in which we find ourselves.[46] Every social interaction is a process of sending and receiving signals in a cycle of live, continuous interpersonal feedback, most of which is nonverbal and automatic.

Think about where you feel most comfortable on the circumplex. Consider your typical range of responses when interacting with other people. If you want, draw a shape around the space you feel most comfortable in Figure 6.2. How large is this space? Do you act the same no matter with whom you're interacting? Your responses may illuminate what you bring to the

[a] As Defined by the APA, a circumplex is "a circular depiction of the similarities among multiple variables ... with variables having opposite values or characteristics...displayed at opposite points, whereas variables having highly similar characteristics are displayed adjacent to one another on the circumplex."

table. When you see patterns with specific people, you can learn about what they contribute too—neither your nor their contributions exist in isolation.

Regardless of your everyday personality, think for a moment about times when you've behaved differently. Maybe you were more submissive or passive than normal. Now consider interactions where you've been more assertive. What about moments when you've been uncharacteristically friendly? Or

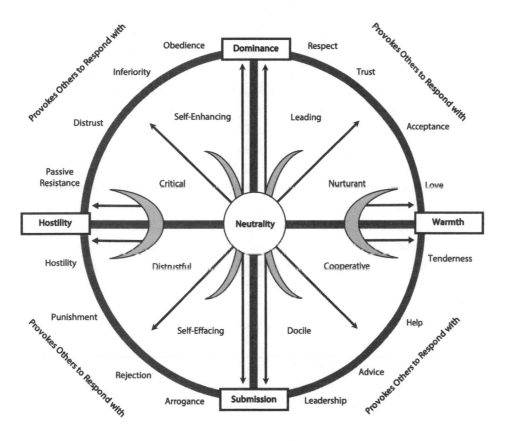

Figure 6.2 The Interpersonal Circumplex—The Non-Psychedelic Legacy of Timothy Leary

Note. In typical interactions, people respond to each other in complementary ways. When one person expresses warmth, the other tends to respond with warmth as well. The same is true of hostility, whether outward or concealed aggressiveness. When one person is dominant, however, the complementary reaction is for the other to be submissive. Although this figure primarily adapts and simplifies Leary's (1957) original circumplex model, I've made two modifications. First, Leary's original label for the horizontal axis Hate-vs-Love have been changed to Hostility-vs-Warmth. Second, although the reactions evoked from others are from Leary's original work, the inner descriptions are adapted from Ghaed and Gallo (2006).

cold? Do you have some relationships or interactions where you've acted less like yourself? Some of these memories may still correspond to your typical personality or relationship patterns. Others may not be so much about how you are generally but how you react to certain people or situations, from one-off interactions with acquaintances to patterns only observable in your most intimate relationships.

In general, psychological health means being able to adapt to the situation at hand. In American culture, our bias is towards seeing warm-dominant personalities as better—with, of course, some exceptions depending on the situation, relationship, and gender. Being willing and able to choose to relent or compromise is important. A neutral, if not overtly hostile, attitude can be necessary too when warding off bullying behavior from people who aren't listening to more subtle messages. Strong personalities are less flexible and almost demand others respond in a certain way.[47] Ideally, though, most social interactions have a natural back-and-forth cadence.

Part of this trial is acknowledging any unintended influences we've had in difficult interactions or relationships. If we ignore 'trolls' who just want to troll, rarely does anyone enter situations with the conscious intent to cause chaos and pain. It happens. But more often, people cause pain because they feel pain. Ignoring pain means it can't be healed. In all relationships, misunderstandings and ruptures occur. Repairing them requires acknowledging the harm done. Although ruptures can trigger guilt, shame, and anger, repair isn't about blame. It's about taking responsibility, which is often shared, while expressing genuine care. If we learn from past mistakes, we can become better at preventing similar ruptures in the future. Every interaction and every relationship is a dance. Missteps happen, but as long as we're willing to keep on dancing, we can find our rhythm again.

Interconnectedness— Interacting Parts of a Greater Whole

The key to navigate tensions between solitude and connection might lie in the concept of *interconnectedness*.[48] Interconnectedness recognizes that every individual exists within much larger complex systems, and every interaction is influenced by exceedingly complex variables. Within such systems, searching for one-to-one, cause-and-effect relationships vastly oversimplifies the reality of multidirectional influence, nonlinearity, probability, and emergent properties. Several fields of science and mathematics have tackled the paradoxical features of complex systems through frameworks like chaos theory.[49] Chaos theory introduced the occasionally embellished but popular notion of the *butterfly effect*. Its name echoes author Ray Bradbury's short story about the unexpected and severe consequences of a time traveler stepping on a butterfly in Earth's ancient past.[50] An everyday example is our difficulty in predicting naturally occurring chaotic systems like weather. That's no fault of meteorologists. At the quantum level too, as we've discussed, probability estimates are, so far, as good as it gets.[51]

As a psychologist and fellow explorer, I can say with a rare level of certainty that human consciousness, neural networks, relationship dynamics, cultures, and history appear no less complex than fundamental aspects of nature.[52] As above, so below. Like hindsight bias, we're much better at creating narratives about causality than predicting outcomes. It's beyond our ego's ability to know and factor in all the relevant details. But it tries, and the results range from creative fiction to conspiracy theories.

From a purely rational scientific lens, none of us are ever separate from the multiple systems connecting our individual psyche to the broader human species and Earth's complex ecosystems, which are influenced by other celestial bodies of our solar system, embedded within our Milky Way Galaxy, and so on and so on. Subjectively, loneliness and isolation are very real, and these feelings affect our perceived connections with others. Given the significant downsides of isolation and the complexities of relationships—from our early attachments to our later interactions—we may sometimes feel out-of-sync and imbalanced as if trapped in a laundry machine where someone else has control of the off-switch. Or worse yet, no one at all. The loss of the individual self in our grand cosmic-to-human, chaotic-but-maybe-orderly universe may appear rational. Even so, within our sphere of influence—our personal encounters, relationships, and community—we certainly have direct impacts. Every individual existence and interaction matters, but how it does varies greatly, maybe beyond our ability to predict even with our best scientific and scholarly minds. Either way, denying our interconnectedness means denying a fundamental aspect of our shared reality.

While facing this manifested chaos and unpredictability, most of us live our lives perceiving some nascent order. Perhaps it's an illusion from our ego's desire for control and predictability. Perhaps it's something else. Regardless, our individual journey is one that's never truly individual. We see this in our mythology and our rituals of initiation. Psychedelics may open the mind to see our profound interconnectedness. That's why we hear heart-felt phrases such as "We're all connected" and "I'm so small but part of something larger."

Indeed. But unless these messages are integrated consciously, we may not realize just how true it is that the development of the individual supports the development of our larger collective. Ultimately, and somewhat paradoxically, periods of solitude promote an awareness of our embeddedness. Each of us, nevertheless, must explore the personal implications of this interconnectedness—if, that is, we're willing.

Relationship Patterns & Interconnectedness— A Sentence Completion Task

With their relevance to all forms of interaction, relationship patterns and interconnectedness demand their own sentence completion activity. As best you can, try not to contemplate theory when responding. Go with your first response. That's usually most accurate to how you feel, not just how you think, which can be tinged with beliefs about what's most desirable—socially or personally. Clear your mind and finish the following statements, going with your gut reaction and realizing you can return later to offer more responses.

Relationship Patterns

Of my current relationships, I feel most free to be myself with _____

_____ because _____.

Healthy relationships require _____.

If I were to guess, my most bothersome relationship patterns revolve around

_____.

On average, other people react to me with _____.

Given the choice between being in charge or following someone else, I prefer

_____ because _____.

Interconnectedness

I feel connected to all humanity when _____.

I experience a deeper connection to the Earth when _____.

I feel most connected to the cosmos when _____.

It's more challenging to accept my connections with _____.

What I appreciate most about my interconnectedness is _____

_____.

If I accepted that we're all connected for better or for worse, I'd _____

_____.

These sentence stems can't do justice to the complexities of relationships and the implications of interconnectedness. If you'd like to continue exploring these concepts, do so in your Travel Journal and through this chapter's activities.

Heeding Warnings while Confronting the Second Trial

As we acknowledge the importance of solitude and connection, we must also heed warnings about unintentionally taking the wrong path. Along our human journey, we have many opportunities to course correct. If you see yourself or past self in any of these warnings, then that's a good sign too. It means you've gained greater self-awareness and applied the insights that resulted. To use the last chapter's metaphor, taking an 'off-ramp' implies there might be an 'on-ramp' further ahead. You just have to know to search for it. Note that these warnings apply to both self-identified introverts and extroverts. Instead of typical personality differences, patterns of over-socializing or isolating may reflect avoidance more than one's deeper nature. Thus, these warnings are relevant to everyone regardless of personality.

The First Warning—
Shallow Connections (vs. Authentic Relationships)

As Albert Camus once stated, "In order to understand the world, one has to turn away from it on occasion."[53] The more intense the need to belong, the more likely a person will avoid alone time and compromise their individuality to fit in. The result is inauthenticity and the absence of true intimacy. Without intimacy, the need to belong remains unfulfilled. Shallow connections can't penetrate the deeper self underneath our outward personas and identity labels.

Authentic relationships are work just like any relationship, but they're simpler in their agenda. Each person is upfront with their reactions and motivations to connect. No games are played. Authenticity requires transparency, and transparency requires vulnerability. In everyday language, authentic people say what they mean and mean what they say. Although authenticity promotes kindness, inauthentic kindness is manipulation. 'Do no harm' is different than 'fake nice.' Besides, most people see through it, and as you now know, hostility whether overt or passive-aggressive pulls for aggression in response.

Everyone, not just rare personality types, can cultivate authenticity. Researcher and author Brené Brown's description resonates with the healing potential of both traditional and psychedelic psychotherapy:

> Authenticity is the daily practice of letting go of who we think we are supposed to be and embracing who we actually are....It's the courage to set boundaries, to be imperfect, and to allow ourselves to be vulnerable— expressing compassion that comes from knowing that we're all made of 'strength and struggle,' and nurturing the connection and sense of belonging that can only happen when we believe we're enough.[54]

Brown's personal authenticity mantra is "Don't shrink. Don't puff up. Stand your sacred ground."[55] In other words, move past defenses and stay strong by recognizing your innate worthiness and owning your experience whatever it may be. The only thing I'd add is that if you're inherently worthy, so are other people. Even when they act in ways unbecoming of their better nature.

Respecting our inherent worthiness requires setting clear yet flexible boundaries that allow us to show up when needed and retreat as necessary to heal and recharge. Saying 'no' or 'not now' is possible without being on the hostile side of the circumplex. But it takes practice. Honing this skill saves us from the built-up resentment that inevitably escapes the shadows of defaulting to 'yes.' As Brown offers, "Choose discomfort over resentment."[56] Of course, the problem may be in the other direction. Well-meaning advice from supportive people can inadvertently encourage one-sided, rigid boundary setting that ignores nuances, spoken or unspoken.[57]

Prior relationship patterns and direct experiences result in stable expectations. Expectations perpetuate dynamics and provide a sense of consistency and order, even when unpleasant. Although working towards healthier patterns is appropriate, changing them within long-term relationships is tough. Experienced psychonauts often jest about first-timers returning home and suddenly ending their romantic relationships and quitting their jobs. Often, these jokes come from personal experiences of doing the same. That is, there's a kernel of truth. Experiencing a profound psychedelic state or insight can cause unrest, especially with people who have little preparation and integration support. As recommended before embarking on this journey, it's almost always beneficial to pause before making major decisions. Even when the end goal or decision remains the same, we need time to clarify underlying problems and weigh options. With on-going effort, we can establish, repair, or recover stronger connections that have gone stale.

People often come into therapy with boundaries tuned either too tight or too loose. The need to belong can lead to boundaries that are too permeable for protection. At the extreme, it can create a loss of self. These feelings of emptiness gain potency when alone. When people avoid solitude, I wonder what exactly is being avoided. Is it feeling lonely? Insecure? Is something lurking below the surface, waiting for a chance to show itself? Whatever it is, it's usually intertwined with what brings someone to therapy in the first place.

For solitude-avoidant people, the key step towards authenticity is to use alone time to build relationships with one's hidden feelings and vulnerable parts. Alone time is different than isolation. Everyone knows the self-help proclamation 'Love yourself.' What does that mean, though? If we replace 'love' with 'accept,' we might be closer to the sentiment I'd like to convey. Self-acceptance can foster greater acceptance of others, and both are necessary for authentic relationships. Practicing self-acceptance isn't complacency or the cessation of growth or change. Impermanence makes sure of that. Instead, self-acceptance promotes courage, and courage promotes authenticity.

The pinnacle achievement of authentic relating is what philosopher Martin Buber called the *I-Thou* relationship, one not obscured by projections, fantasies, judgments, and other defensive distortions.[58] Establishing this type of relationship is inherently healing and transformative. I-Thou experiences can elicit awe where two people can admire and be moved by the totality of the other. It's bowing deeply to the existence of another conscious being. That's quite a high bar to set in our disconnected world, but authentic relationships move us in the direction of I-Thou and away from Me-or-You.[59]

Because they foster mutual respect and dialogue, I-Thou relationships invite disagreement, not conformity or wholesale alignment. As a personal example, I welcome my clients to express any doubts about how to apply abstract or esoteric ideas to our everyday world. It allows us to go deeper in exploring the endless nuances of human experience and the questions we all have. If abstractions have merit, then the work naturally shifts to the next major task—translating, even imperfectly, novel insights into concrete action. It's through authentic relating that we can change for the better. As long as both people are open to 'not knowing,' authenticity flows forth freely even when there's disagreement. That's because each person recognizes the other as a fellow explorer. For my spiritually inclined clients, I talk about *divine disagreements* where each person can welcome not avoid difference and learn from one another. Divine disagreements awaken both people to higher levels of reflection and awareness. After all, to echo Ram Dass, "We're all just walking each other home."[60]

The Second Warning—
Defensive Detachment (vs. Secure Engagement)

On the flip side, detachment might be our go-to defense against vulnerability and connection. Like the dangers of loose boundaries and the risk of losing oneself, aggressively setting 'boundaries' to avoid being influenced by anyone else poses problems. For one, we must acknowledge that we're affected by others because we *are*, even if we try to deny it. Interconnectedness is an observation about reality, both the human and non-human, and the living and non-living parts of the cosmos. When defensive detachment takes the form of reactionary anti-conformity, we should remember that a relationship, even if adversarial, is still a relationship. And it's too easy to project onto other people parts of ourselves we don't want to see. Projection helps us disavow our vulnerable, imperfect, and complicated feelings—all the while protecting or inflating our ego. In an exaggerated but compelling way, Francis Bacon once paraphrased Aristotle as proclaiming, "Whosoever is delighted in solitude is either a wild beast or a god."[61] There might be truth in that notion, but there are certainly warnings too.

That said, functioning in the outside world requires navigating social realities and norms that frequently don't make much sense—or worse yet, harm people who might already feel ostracized. We must strike a balance that facilitates self-protection and autonomy while navigating our complicated, occasionally dangerous world. Defensive detachment forecloses on the possibility of finding authentic relationships in a similar fashion as shallow connections do. For the person who errs on the side of separation, the growth edge is to relax inflexible boundaries and move towards connections while preserving the individual self. Why? Rigid boundaries prevent positive as well as negative influences. As the famously introverted Jung acknowledged, "The meeting of two personalities is like the contact of two chemical substances: if there is any reaction, both are transformed."[62] Our individual selves exist as an ongoing dialogue between our different parts and our interactions with others. Engaging deeply in relationships reveals hidden potential for personal growth that couldn't manifest in isolation.

Discussing the risk of defensive detachment brings to mind a deceptively similar-sounding concept from Buddhism: *non-attachment*. In the previous trial, you learned that a key cause of suffering is grasping for things to remain the same when impermanence rules the cosmos. Non-attachment reduces suffering by loosening our grip on desires, expectations, and surface-level contents of the mind. Mahayana and Tibetan Buddhist traditions, in particular, emphasize how compassion and loving-kindness are natural outgrowths from recognizing suffering and appreciating our interconnectedness. Understanding non-attachment can keep us engaged with others and our everyday life while we accept our inability to control how people respond to our expressions of goodwill. Some Westerners, however, adopt an individualistic flavor of 'enlightenment' that restricts compassion and vulnerability. As a possible example of spiritual bypass, it's worth noting because many of these words—avoidant attachment, detachment, non-attachment— sound similar when in practice they can diverge considerably.

As social creatures, we benefit from having a sense of community, which shared religious belief systems have traditionally offered. Engaging in religious communities may promote mental health—with some caveats for communities that encourage judgment, shame, or self-righteousness.[63] The decline of organized religion and other communities may be a significant player in the modern outbreak of loneliness.[64] Religion of the Ego is a poor substitute for a genuinely connected and caring community, religious in nature or otherwise. Besides being sources of belonging and meaning, part of the healing power of communities is how they offer support in times of need, loss, and transition. Community members can 'show up' for each other in many ways. Sometimes by visiting people in the hospital, bringing food to grieving families, or in happier times, celebrating marriages and births. Whether suffering or rejoicing, community members can feel seen, accepted, and loved. Supportive communities need not be religious in nature, but shared belief systems do provide a powerful glue.

Defensive detachment prevents genuine engagement in communities and often in relationships of any kind. By the end of life, many detached people eventually face their innate vulnerability and need for others. Too often it happens when the only relationships available are professional ones with nurses, doctors, and volunteers in retirement homes or hospice centers. In contrast to defensive detachment, if we foster an attitude of secure non-attachment or simply acknowledge 'mono no aware'—the bittersweet appreciation of impermanence—we can value our connections, even their imperfections, and not take ourselves, our experiences, and our relationships for granted.

For the person choosing detachment over connection, the idea of engaged non-attachment appears paradoxical. Many people who choose detachment learned early that trusting others can be dangerous. Given the reality of cults, coercion, and interpersonal trauma, they're not wrong. Even in safe relationships with attachment security, though, impermanence remains true. Ultimately, engaging in relationships leads to eventual sorrow. Yet, I've never heard someone in the despair of grief express regret for connecting deeply with people they've lost. If anything, it's the contrary. Despite such pain, people value the preciousness of time spent together. By accepting impermanence while still caring about others, we can show up when the bittersweet aspects of the human experience enter our lives. This is true courage. Accepting grief and love, attachment and loss, connection and disconnection, beginnings and endings.

Passing the Second Trial— Fostering Acceptance of Solitude & Interconnectedness

To discover interconnectedness within several domains of our existence provides a resilient sense of belonging. William James, a brilliant psychologist and luminary of exploring consciousness, remarked that it's possible to "experience *something* larger than ourselves, and in that union find our greatest peace."[65] We all enter the world small and powerless, and through our attachment with early caregivers, we confront the necessity of connection. For some, this first human-to-human relationship transforms into a perceived connection with some higher power that transcends our individual lives.[66] This higher power can take various forms—God, the Tao, unitive consciousness, or simply the totality of the mysterious forces that rule the universe.

In a very literal interpretation of interconnectedness, we find all humans are connected biologically, socially, and historically with the grand ecosystems of our planet and with our solar system. Feeling connected to nature is associated with vitality, positive emotions, and overall life satisfaction.[67] And, it's honest. We *are* a part of nature. Even so, nature extends beyond what we can see with our naked eye.[68] No astrology, deep meditation, esoteric philosophy, or New Age spirituality are needed to appreciate interconnectedness. Whether under the influence of psychedelics or simply by stepping outside and looking up at the stars or across a vast impressive landscape, we can find profound connection even when alone and in silence.

Connection is more about heart than about mind. Being vulnerable and accepting imperfection in ourselves and others forms the foundation of secure attachment. Multiple systems are always at play, in every moment, at every level, from cosmic to interpersonal to our inner conscious and unconscious minds, with multiple parts, motivations, and manifestations—all constantly shifting and connecting beyond our awareness. Nothing is ever in isolation—not really. Across time and space, we are all interconnected, yet each also individuals. Accepting both realities is critical to passing this trial. As a tool for contemplation, Figure 6.3 visualizes layers of our interconnectedness beyond what we might typically regard in daily life.[69]

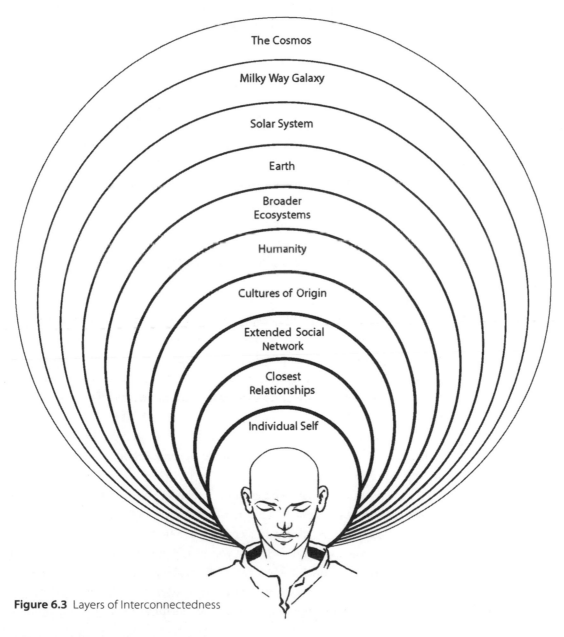

Figure 6.3 Layers of Interconnectedness

Accepting our complexity, warts and all, provides a sense of internal cohesion. Accepting the complexity of others, our relationships, and ultimately, the intricate, mysterious workings of the cosmos, provides a sense of external cohesion. This unity is a key ingredient in psychedelic therapy and ceremonies. Yet it can be found without psychedelics. In passing this trial, the mythic boon is two-fold—fostering greater attachment security and developing profoundly authentic relationships. These manifestations of the mythic boon could also be called love. Yet, this word can be loaded with cultural and personal baggage. Self-love doesn't have to equate to narcissism, and loving others doesn't mean the blurring of boundaries where one party unilaterally subjugates their will.

For now, we need only rely on our ally of acceptance to find deeper connection with ourselves, others, the Earth, and the cosmos. As you know, every mythic journey requires allies, metaphorical and otherwise. Even when alone, relationships exist between parts of ourselves and with the internalized versions of our most significant relationships. Challenges in inner or outer relationships are signals of work to be done. Our families, mentors, teachers, partners, friends and even foils can be explicit or secret allies in our journey. Connections can broaden our awareness and help us reach higher levels of understanding.

Even when people cover up their vulnerability or divert their attention to digital distractions, underneath we're more alike than we know. When acceptance extends to others, a natural result of accepting our interconnectedness, it decreases judgment and increases openness. The human condition, though experienced uniquely for every individual, also binds us. If we hold the tensions of not knowing how our relationships will turn out, not always feeling like we belong, and wanting to attach yet avert the pain of loss or betrayal, we can confront life in its complexity while not falling into fantasy. We can accept and not disavow the seemingly conflicting truths that we're alone, and we're not. We can experience connection alongside conflict. But conflict can be healed. Strength comes from embracing our vulnerability, as experienced in both solitude and relationships.

As you pass this trial and engage more deeply in your life, find other travelers who are doing the same.[70] They're out there waiting to find you too. Jung once echoed an ancient alchemist's encouragement to his pupil, "'No matter how isolated you are and how lonely you feel, if you do your work truly and conscientiously, unknown friends will come and seek you.'"[71] Other travelers can teach us things we may not discover by ourselves. If, however, our relationships reinforce inauthentic, limited, and fearful ways of relating, we risk letting them cloud our minds.[72] As the poet Rilke exclaimed, "I want to know my own will and to move with it. And I want, in the hushed moments when the nameless draws near, to be among the wise ones—or else alone."[73]

Celebrate the genuine connections you've already found in life. Give energy and time to them. Laugh together. And do the same in relating to yourself. Building relationships takes time. Mystical experiences may instill a sense of belonging and hope, feeling connected through sacred love, experiencing universal harmony, transcending everyday limitations of communication, and finding meaning beyond the imperfection of words. But these experiences create change only if brought to life and integrated into your approach to relationships with others and with your deepest self.

Moving towards authenticity takes self-reflection and practice. We can start by asking ourselves questions like, "What impact do I have on my relationships? What might I change so that my impact is the impact I want to have?" If willing, we can break cycles that keep us separate or compromised. The behaviors that lead to positive changes are relatively straightforward. Most often, it's our concrete behaviors that must change before our beliefs and emotions catch up. Expectations can turn into self-fulfilling prophecies through our behavior. We can disrupt harmful cycles by pushing the 'pause button' and allowing silence before response. Over time, fulfilling relationships will emerge that validate our authentic self, instead of some social façade existing merely to perform for others. This authenticity is what can heal loneliness. By fostering intimacy and trust, we can shed light on our hidden parts and welcome them.

As a natural outgrowth, we can also welcome others to express their authentic feelings and vulnerability and show them the same level of acceptance that has healed our own wounds. Some version of the golden rule exists across cultures, but for it to work, the first and most important step is to listen.[74] Be kind and curious. Hear every word. Put aside habits of formulating a response or offering platitudes. Reflect what you've heard and ask questions when unsure. And continue doing the same with yourself. Ask what you need, express what you're grateful for, and wonder what else you have to learn. Let yourself be surprised. Discover new insights and layers of your mind. There's so much within you and within others, whether we realize it or not.

Concrete Suggestions & Journey Report

Box 6.3 offers a few ways to bring this chapter's concepts to life. Some suggestions are about exploring or deepening your relationships while others are

Box 6.3

Exploring Solitude & Interconnectedness in Everyday Life

Suggestion	Example
Establish a routine for quality alone time, free from outside distractions and without your phone or internet.	You protect fifteen minutes each morning for unplugged alone time. During this time, you start with a moment of silence, roughly one minute in length, in which you focus on clearing your head. For the rest of the time, you alternate each day between extending this moment of silence (with an unguided present-centered awareness meditation), doing mindful stretches or yoga, or drawing in your sketchbook.
Watch a series of evocative movies either by yourself or with someone you're close to. If with someone else, discuss the movie afterwards and the moments you found most compelling. Either way, journal about your reactions afterwards.	You and a friend make a commitment to watch four movies together over the course of a month. You choose *Annihilation* and *Arrival,* and your friend chooses *The Tree of Life* and *Mother!* Because your friend doesn't watch many sci-fi films, you're excited to share these two, convinced you can win over your friend. It works. But more surprising is how your friend's selections win you over to symbolic arthouse films. You both find fascinating parallels among the movies related to time, nonlinearity, causality, and relationships.
Interview close friends and family about what they believe is most important in relationships. Show genuine curiosity about their perspective and experiences even if different than yours.	You interview your grandfather, sister, and a long-term friend. To gather their opinions and experiences, you ask questions like, "What makes a relationship last?" "What have you learned about yourself from your relationships?" "What have you learned about other people?" and "After an argument, what's the best way to make amends?" You hear quite different perspectives from your grandfather and friend but areas of overlap with all three. You gain some new perspectives that challenge your own relatively fixed ideas.
Find connection through humor. Humor works as a social glue but also helps us not take ourselves too seriously. It paradoxically allows us to connect more authentically by refueling our reserves to go deep and to return with lightheartedness.	You're a big *Rick and Morty* fan, but the long wait between seasons has become a lesson in patience. A couple friends tell you about a newer series created by one of *Rick and Morty's* writers and producers, *Star Trek: Lower Decks.* The three of you set a date for a marathon. Although not a Star Trek fan beforehand, you get a kick out of the fourth episode's theme of chasing enlightenment while avoiding authenticity. You realize sometimes the way you speak about spirituality sounds a bit like one character's exaggerated spiritual bypass. You laugh about it with your friends and decide to keep an eye on that in the future.
Find albums or create a playlist of songs, with or without lyrics, that capture your feelings about interconnectedness, relationships, and solitude.	You decide to make a Pink Floyd playlist, one of your dad's favorite music artists. Because he passed away a year ago, you figured it'd be a good way to remember him. You hadn't listened to their lyrics closely before, but this time, certain themes and songs hit you pretty hard. You never realized their concept album *The Wall* explored the fallout of the protagonist's loss of his father when he was an infant. Some favorites for your playlist include "Hey You," "Comfortably Numb," "Wish You Were Here," "Breathe (In the Air)," "Time," "Brain Damage," "Eclipse," and "Louder than Words."

about increasing your comfort with solitude. Review these possibilities and do any that seem appealing or helpful in your efforts to pass this second trial. For an example of how psychedelic experiences can elicit themes introduced in this trial, see Journey Report 6.1. Sofía's DMT experience incorporated archetypal religious imagery from her family of origin and universal feelings of interconnectedness and compassion. The thorniest issue, however, proved to be her complicated relationship history with an ex-lover. Unraveling relationship dynamics takes clarity of emotion and intention as well as on-going effort. Whether the two are meant to be 'entangled' or are simply repeating an undesirable pattern is to be seen, but raising the question is an important part of the process.

Grounding Words—A Brief Summary

Following your bravery in facing death and impermanence, you've now confronted the dual fears of isolation and intrusion. Like others, you've inherited the need for belonging but exist in a world facing significant loneliness and disconnection. In facing this trial, you've earned greater attachment security, allowing you to see a path forward where you balance your time and energy in two directions—setting aside space for solitude and self-reflection while investing in authentic relationships. This path has its origins in your past, all the way to infancy, and it leads far into your future. Still, change occurs in the present. You've heeded warnings of how imbalance can occur through either shallow connections or defensive detachment. Neither approach can fulfill the need for belonging or foster acceptance of your most vulnerable parts. By acknowledging these warnings, you've begun to explore authenticity and your interconnectedness with all things, perhaps even the cosmos. You're guided by mindfully engaging with others and welcoming love and friendship while acknowledging human imperfections. True to this trial's theme, you're ready to discover personal insights by exploring these complex issues on your own. Afterward, you'll face your final trial. All that you've learned and explored will soon be brought to bear. And I know you're up for the challenge.

Your Assignment, Your Choice

To guide your efforts in exploring and passing this trial, select your activities from the recommended exercises. Do at least one activity a day before proceeding to the final trial.

Assignments 6.1

Exploring Solitude & Interconnectedness

Reflective-Intellectual	Experiential-Emotional
☐ Task—Complete an **attachment measure,** like the Experiences in Close Relationships Scale[75] offered by OpenPsychometrics.org: https://OpenPsychometrics.org/tests/ECR.php Time—Minimum of one test with time to reflect on the results (1 hr) Why—To explore your attachment style and reflect on its relevance to your relationships	☐ Task—Experience a **sensory deprivation tank** or 'float.' Alternative—If unavailable, go on a **silent, solo hike or visit** to a secluded beach, forest, mountain, cave, or other natural landscape Time—At least 1 hr in either activity Why—To experience solitude without distractions either by immersing yourself in silence or in nature
☐ Task—Review your relationship history with **Exercise 6.1 "Relationship Reflections."** Time—Minimum of 1 hr to complete and reflect on the exercise Why—To reflect on significant relationships and any underlying relationship patterns	☐ Task—Practice **Meditation 6.1 "A Sondering Walk with Interconnectedness"** Time—Minimum of 2-3x/week, 15-30 min each Why—To reflect on the complexity of all human lives and our interconnectedness

After considering your options, respond to this chapter's Travel Journal prompt. Write, draw, or create whatever you feel inspired to while contemplating your personal reactions, strengths, and pitfalls regarding this second trial.

Travel Journal

What might I be avoiding about being alone?

How could I relate to others more authentically?

What are the personal implications of accepting my interconnectedness?

On-going Lessons of Entanglement

My first time doing DMT, I was with my boyfriend: A much more supportive paramour than my previous. I inhaled, holding as long as I could, expecting to need another hit. Eyes closed, I tried to grab the pipe, but I felt odd... like I had no hand...I had no body at all. I was already a million miles away.

I zoomed through dimensions, landing at the feet of a thousand images of the Virgin Mary. It was a homecoming like I'd never experienced before. Every iota of my consciousness relaxed. I felt an acceptance and understanding of every dark part of my—well, and every human's—soul. Then, I attained a vantage point of what I could only describe as heaven, a curious motif since I'm not a traditionally religious person (much to my Mexican father's chagrin). With my DMT consciousness, I was aware that these religious images enabled me to make sense of my experience, but they weren't embedded in any world religion. This experience surpassed all world religions.

From my heavenly vantage point, I became aware that next to me was my ex-boyfriend (not my current boyfriend), also in his spirit form. We watched ourselves on Earth, living this lifetime, making hurtful mistakes as we did in our previous tumultuous relationship. At this elevated soul level, we had endless compassion and understanding for these two misguided incarnations. I said aloud, "Look at them. They're in it," meaning that they were living from their place of limited understanding and learning lessons they needed to.

This deep acceptance and compassion ushered in old memories of past trauma, each memory washing over me, being redressed in this newfound compassion. I awoke from this experience, feeling complete acceptance of everything, and an assurance that everything was exactly as it should be.

Still, I found it odd to be visited by my ex-boyfriend while my current boyfriend was lying right next to me. This experience came at a time when I had blocked my ex-boyfriend out of my life for the umpteenth time, and I was happily moving on. A week later, I was walking near my ex's apartment and decided to walk by, posing a playful test of synchronicity to the universe: I thought, if I walk by his apartment, and if he comes out right when I'm walking by, then I will take it as a sign that I need to stop blocking him, and will be open to whatever role he needs to play in my life. It was a playful gamble, but the closer I walked, the more nervous I got.

Just ahead of me, I saw his door open. My heart stopped. It was him! I couldn't believe it. I felt like the universe was having a big laugh, and I was left to figure out the meaning of it. My whole body was shaking, and in my head, I screamed, "Why, universe, WHY???"

Why was he meant to be in my life? In my Earth-consciousness, I may never know. What I know is that my ex has been in and out of my life since that fateful day, still bringing as much pain and conflict (read: 'opportunities for growth') as ever before. Except this time, when he brings me to my wit's end, I take a deep breath, remember that DMT heavenly vantage point, and say to myself, "I guess we're still in it."

—Sofía, Age 29

Note. This account and all others in the book are de-identified and anonymous to protect the confidentiality of the person sharing their story. Minor grammar, spelling, and stylistic changes were made and usually in partnership with the person providing the account.

Meditation 6.1
A Sondering Walk with Interconnectedness (15-30 min)

Although a recently invented word, 'sonder' describes an important experience connected to this trial's theme. Sonder is a mix of wonder and sorrow upon realizing random and peripheral people in the background of our intricate lives have just as much complexity in their own lives.[76] The sorrow can come from recognizing we'll never know the depths of their emotions, reflections, and relationships. Sometimes it comes after realizing we've unintentionally dismissed the humanity of others because of becoming absorbed in our own complex lives. Your experience, though, will likely involve more wonder than sorrow as you reflect on our innate interconnectedness despite having separate and only occasionally intersecting lives with people around us.

Read this script to understand how this walking meditation works. You can walk in your own neighborhood or in another safe location likely to have people around, even if only inside their own homes. Charting a path that circles back to your starting location may be especially helpful. Keep your eyes open when walking, but if it feels right, you can close your eyes when you're resting in place and wanting time for some internal reflection.

Upon arriving at your chosen location, pause to take a few deep breaths to clear you mind before beginning to walk. If you need additional time to settle into the present moment, take your time. When ready, begin walking at a slower pace than you usually walk in everyday life. Notice the feeling as each foot contacts the ground and rises again to move you forward in space...

Instead of looking down, look at your surroundings at eye level....Scan the environment and observe the mix of living and non-living things that populate your external world...allow your attention to hover without overfocusing on any one aspect of your surroundings....Experience the ways you feel separated from the outside world and ways you feel connected...perhaps you feel connected through your senses, from feeling wind gently or firmly breezing all around you, to smelling a variety of fragrances...

As you look around, notice other people, not by staring at them but by recognizing their presence wherever it may be. You might look up at the window of a home or building, see a light on that hints at the presence of another or see the distant image of another human being going about their day or night. Or if you're walking on a street, you might see people close by...Notice any assumptions you might make automatically about your similarities and differences with these people. Instead of believing them, contemplate how complex their lives must be…their relationships…their jobs…their passions…their fears…their losses…and their inner sources of strength…

Imagine their lives and their consciousness as being just as complex as your own…from the layers of their unconscious minds…to the things they share with others and the things they hold secret…do you see part of yourself in them? …or do you feel completely different, separated by a barrier impossible to overcome? …Take your time to reflect but also stay centered in your present experience, noticing sensations in your body, any emotions that get triggered, you're your decisions to walk in certain directions and not others…

Continue your walk while reflecting on various people, their imagined lives, and the ways your life exists in parallel to theirs. You may also notice other forms of life. Contemplate your sense of connection with these other Earthbound animals, plants, and insects. Do the same with non-living objects you encounter.

When you're ready or have returned to your starting location, pause to take a few deep breaths, closing your eyes if you feel comfortable…As you breathe in, imagine yourself breathing in the world around you. As you breathe out, imagine yourself releasing any tension, uncertainty, or sorrow upon reflecting on being in the world as an individual but being connected to countless others in realized and unknown ways…Slowly open your eyes and refocus on your surroundings. Gently but surely return to your everyday life but try to remember at least occasionally what you experienced on your walk.

Exercise 6.1

Relationship Reflections

Instructions

1. Choose three significant, close relationships to explore from different stages of your life. See the 'Types of Close Relationships' box to the right for ideas.
2. Respond to the reflection questions.
3. Consider whether any relationship patterns exist that cut across these or other relationships. Record any reactions to this exercise in your Travel Journal.

Types of Close Relationships

- Caregivers
- First Significant Childhood Friendship
- Early Romantic Relationships
- Long-term Romantic Relationships
- Important Friendships
- Mentors

Early Life

Relationship: _____   Timespan: _____

What were the strengths of this relationship? _____

What were the challenges? _____

What did I learn? How is this relationship still impacting my life? _____

_____

Does anything need to be healed or repaired for you or the other person? If so, how? _____

_____

Relationship: _____   Timespan: _____

What were the strengths of this relationship? _____

What were the challenges? _____

What did I learn? How is this relationship still impacting my life? _____

_____

Does anything need to be healed or repaired for you or the other person? If so, how? _____

_____

Relationship: _____   Timespan: _____

What were the strengths of this relationship? _____

What were the challenges? _____

What did I learn? How is this relationship still impacting my life? _____

_____

Does anything need to be healed or repaired for you or the other person? If so, how? _____

_____

Recent Life

CHAPTER 7

Encountering Meaninglessness— Discovering the Responsibility of Meaning

And then we were born…And then we discovered reason…And then we realized we were more than what reason and logic dictated…and then we become conscious of our spirit, greeted our spirit and introduced it to the world…and finally, we embarked on our individual quests, searching for meaning in an unexplainable existence, finding our true selves within our purpose through our spiritual essence, and rejoicing when it was all said and done…

—Marie S. Dezelic, *Meaning-Centered Therapy*[1]

Journey Waypoint VI

We've arrived at the final trial of this journey. Everything you've been working towards has led you far down this existential rabbit hole. By accepting death, impermanence, solitude, and interconnectedness, you've been able to explore grand landscapes containing profound sources of fear and hope about our human condition. Now we're left with a deceptively simple question: Why? This question can take many forms. Most, though, are questions of meaning. Why are we here? Why are you here? Why does consciousness exist at all? More than anything else explored in earlier trials, meaning influences everything. It can transform all that came before, all that happens in the present, and everything that's still to come.

Existential philosophers differ in how they discuss meaning, but one way or another, mortality frames their perspective. No fan of euphemistic or poetic questions like Shakespeare's "To be or not to be," Albert Camus bluntly asked what he considered the most important, honest question of human life—that of suicide.[2] Though seemingly about death, his question is really about the dilemma of meaninglessness. If human life has no agreed upon innate meaning, yet we, as conscious beings, nevertheless strive for meaning, then each person must decide how to make life worth living in the face of this inescapable conflict. Like our myth-inspired journey, Camus used mythology to examine our human search for meaning. His work centered on the myth of Sisyphus, a human king who defied the Gods. Sisyphus trapped Thanatos (Death) in his own chains in hopes that humanity could conquer mortality forever. Clearly, Thanatos's imprisonment didn't last. Sisyphus, on the other hand, received an eternal punishment. His sentence? To carry a boulder up a hill only to watch it roll all the way down. Then repeat the meaningless task. Again. And again. And again.

For Camus, we are all Sisyphus. The question of suicide is rhetorical but sincere.[3] People who struggle with suicidal thoughts largely understand it as a last resort. They want to live, but they have suffered from isolation, rejection, trauma, emptiness, or all the above. They see no way out. At first. Going 'in and through' challenging moments alongside learning skills like those introduced in our first arc can help people learn to thrive. Whether Camus's question is taken literally or rhetorically, exploring life's meaning can lead to a temporary crisis of faith. Resolving such a crisis, though, can allow us to re-emerge with a renewed, more resilient way to engage with what life can offer despite uncertainty. Camus himself faced despair during the fall of Paris in World War II, but he rejected suicide, joined the French Resistance, and until his death, encouraged others to engage with life, through pain and all.

As the culmination of this arc, this trial is the greatest challenge you'll face. Remember what you've learned in passing the other trials: you're not alone, even in solitude. You can find strength through authenticity, despite the challenges of communication and relationships. And if living is already dying anyways, what do you have left to fear? By exploring the deepest recesses of this existential rabbit hole, you know too that your return journey will soon be in sight.

Self-Reflections Check-In

In the last chapter, you faced the trial of loneliness and explored solitude, relationship patterns, and interconnectedness. Which fears and concerns resonated with you? After reading and doing your chosen activities, what insights did you gain about being alone or with others? Perhaps you learned more about your relationships and styles of communication. Maybe you gained greater comfort by embracing solitude and finding the gifts of authenticity. Whatever you experienced and discovered will, of course, continue to unfold. The lessons are endless, after all. Some insights from previous trials may resonate here. Think about your intentions for this journey. Let them guide you as you explore your personal sense of meaning. Intellect can only get us so far, so look beyond the words—yours and mine. As in psychedelic journeys, many answers lie between the lines and remain ineffable. But, they're there all the same.

Confronting the Final Trial

Within every community and field of inquiry, disagreements arise about what's right and what's wrong. From contradictory interpretations of scientific data, sacred texts, and modern literature to divergent applications of agreed-upon conclusions, many reasonable disagreements stem from differences in epistemological assumptions. That is, assumptions about how we can gain knowledge and justify what we believe is true. When exploring meaning, we necessarily confront thorny issues about underlying assumptions. Meaning is rarely if ever straightforward, even if appearing so. We need look no further than human language. As a tool for communication, language has allowed us to develop elaborate ideas and stories and share them with others across thousands of years. Yet, look at almost any word in the English dictionary, and you'll find multiple 'official' definitions. Beyond explicit definitions, words hold implicit meanings. Some are shared but many are idiosyncratic and based on our personal associations and experiences. Nonverbal signals aren't safe from ambiguity and misinterpretation either.

Outside language, the best examples of shared and unshared meaning involve rituals. Culturally bound or religious rituals have significant meaning for many people—at least historically. For others, these same rituals are devoid of meaning or have lost it over time. In the vacuum of meaning, we seek replacements, new rituals, ideologies, or other distractions from the sense of loss of what was once important. At the collective level, when the rituals of our cultural origins lose their meaning, we're often tempted to adopt the rituals of other cultures. When done without learning about the culture's history and respectfully engaging with their communities, we end up with cultural appropriation, which not only can harm those communities but also fails to provide adequate meaning to the people searching to fill a void.

In introducing this trial, I can't think of any better exclamation for the innate human need for meaning than that found in Rollo May's title, *The Cry for Myth*.[4] Apropos to the topic of ambiguous meaning, 'cry' means at least two things. When experiencing the deep pain of meaninglessness, we might shed tears of anguish and sorrow before settling into a state of detachment. Alternatively, we can 'cry out' for meaning, searching for it everywhere, because when found, it might help us overcome a loss of purpose or cope with other sources of existential distress. Thus, the need for meaning is perhaps our most essential psychological need. Without it, we're left with a mix of inconsequential pleasure and unavoidable pain.

For the vast majority of human history, various religions and mythologies have formed the bedrock of meaning and provided guidance for meaningful living, but their power has diminished. Self-guided forms of spirituality haven't been able to replace communal needs and the benefits of shared cultural meaning offered by organized religions. As for myth, most people equate the word with outdated fiction and meaningless fairy tales. Though its power has waned, myth is still with us, and if we can reconnect to its underlying messages, hope remains as well.

St. John of the Cross, a 16th century Catholic priest imprisoned for sharing his mystical beliefs, once called periods of psychological or spiritual anguish the "Dark Night of the Soul."[5] By facing the dark, however, we can eventually discover the brighter light of dawn. The loss of meaning, though brutal, can be the beginning of a deeper awakening—if not a spiritual awakening, an existential one. Navigating the loss of meaning requires engaging in a creative process to imbue our lives with purpose more consciously than before, especially if we rebuke surface-level or dogmatic assertions of meaning. This is the key reason our psychedelic and myth-inspired quest needed trials alongside themes of wonder, beauty, and transcendence. Unlike spiritual bypass, which ignores the darker, more complex parts of human life, our journey has taught us that we need only go 'in and through' to come out the other side.

The Human Journey Across Space & Time— The Cosmic Question of Meaning

From the outset of our journey, this trial's theme has been with us. In our first journey waypoint, I described awe as an occasional sidekick or side effect of following curiosity, but awe isn't as simple as our first ally. It disrupts our everyday perspective and can make us feel insignificant. Insignificance is a near-synonym for meaninglessness. Awe-inspiring experiences can lead to questioning our default assumptions, viewpoints, and sources of meaning. That's why we started with the cosmos. What better way to shake up our minds and create room for something greater? Shifting into a cosmic perspective loosens our grip on our everyday mindset of what we understand and what's important or essential.

We crossed that first threshold long ago, but as in our previous trials, the cosmos continues to frame our current explorations. If meaning is a question of 'Why?' then the biggest why of all is yet again a cosmic one—why is there something rather than nothing?[6] Most possibilities evoke a deep sense of mystery, but if we're attached to a specific answer, we risk intense disappointment.

The Fermi-Hart paradox exemplifies this point. If we're not overinvested in any one solution, most possibilities are fascinating. If we're alone in either life or consciousness, that's remarkable given the size of the universe—which we can't even quantify. If life exists elsewhere—even if totally incomprehensible to us humans or devoid of self-awareness—that's amazing too. If we exist for no reason but chance, it's mind-blowing that we exist at all. And more so given that we somehow evolved to become conscious and can ask such questions. We may not always like the answers, but that doesn't make them any less profound.

Beyond the reasons for consciousness and life more generally, the biggest question remains: Why does *anything* exist in the first place? The big bang or any other scientific model about the origin of our universe won't give us that answer. Science asks 'How?' more than 'Why?' and it's conservative (as it should be) by design.[7] Creation stories more often belong to myth, and when taken literally, these stories provide numerous seldomly overlapping answers. Not all creation myths even address fundamental questions about the ultimate purpose or meaning of existence. Nevertheless, opinions aren't in short supply. As you learned at the beginning of our journey, when expanding awareness, we can't disentangle the observer from the observed. In other words, we can't get around the limitations of our place of observation. If we ignore these limitations, we're susceptible to all kinds of illusions. Earth looks like the center of the universe, and our conscious minds treat opinions and perceptions as facts. Absolute objectivity is nearly impossible if not entirely so. All opinions deserve some reasonable amount of scrutiny, but the bigger the question, the bigger the implications. There may be some meaning behind the cosmos, but when we're unable to reach anything near consensus about the meaning of life or consciousness, an exceptionally heavy dose of humility is in order. That humility pairs nicely with skepticism when other people boldly declare their opinions as Truth. We might, nevertheless, be able to face this uncertainty—or in Camus's words, absurdity—and find or create meaning in our individual lives. But we must remember the shaky ground upon which our 'conclusions' stand if we attempt to assert the meaning of the cosmos—or perhaps anything else for that matter.

Meaning & Its Consequences

Ancient myths, religious parables, and perhaps their surprising modern-day counterpart, creative fiction and film, provide us examples of how to find meaning, even as small individuals in a vast cosmos with forces beyond our understanding and control. Without inspirational stories in which we can believe, it's easy to become lost in the material world, which offers little except elusive promises like success and fame. Unless, of course, we value the meaning of our relationships with one another.

But who's to judge? To judge, we must be certain something is right and something else is wrong. Without certainty of meaning, judgment loses its bite—in theory at least. Many of us default to judgment, whether directed inwardly resulting in guilt and shame, or outwardly leading to self-righteousness and rejection of individuals or entire groups of people. It's not always either/or, though. Sometimes judgmental people hold themselves to the same inflexible standards, condemning others to suffer alongside them.

Before going further, let's acknowledge debates about free will and agency.[8] Many existential thinkers conclude something along the lines of *radical freedom*.[9] Choice is inevitable, and within some natural limitations, we make choices every moment. Because of our freedom, we're ultimately responsible for what we do and don't do. In the end, life is a grand cascading series of choices, and one way or another, we're responsible for our actions and non-actions. Whether exploring radical freedom or some milder form, many freedom-versus-determinism discussions get confounded with other debates like nature-versus-nurture. People assume that if environmental factors (mistakenly subsumed under 'nurture') are most important in predicting behavior, it's easier to change such behaviors. In the reverse, if genetic makeup amounts to predetermined destiny, then change is impossible. Logical fallacies abound in most versions of these debates.[10] Numerous genes, environmental factors, and chance all commingle and interact to influence behavior. This example of interconnectedness doesn't mean we're fated to repeat what we've always done or become who we become. For each generation and field of inquiry, the framing of such debates may change, but the battleground is shared with the ancient Greek struggle against the Fates, three goddesses who weave our human adventures into a tapestry of beauty and suffering.

My favorite response to the question of free will comes from the HBO series *Westworld*'s decidedly unenlightened character William, formerly known as The Man in Black. In the third season, William undergoes some nontraditional (and unethical) Internal Family Systems-inspired techno-therapy to heal his broken psyche. When a part of his mind asks whether his decisions were his own or predetermined, he falls into a tortured silence, uncharacteristic of his typical persona. Then, shifting from uncertainty to confidence, he responds matter-of-factly, "If you can't tell, does it matter?"[11]

Without mistaking him as a paragon of philosophical wisdom and ethics, let's go with that sentiment. The pragmatic solution for everyday life is to act *as if* we're free. But freedom comes with consequences and personal responsibility. Lacking confidence in meaning, values, and direction, we stumble into Sartre's conclusion: We're "condemned to be free."[12] If we deny free will, it doesn't save us from responsibility. Choosing not to choose doesn't save us either. Moreover, our unconscious minds are happy to guide our behavior. Worse yet, quite conscious and intentional actors from outside us are also willing to influence our choices through both subliminal and obvious tactics. That's the whole point of marketing and political campaigning.[13] Other people can be co-creators of our lives, but they're not always benevolent or neutral collaborators. And being completely passive or choosing blissful ignorance doesn't let us off the hook.

Consciously exploring our life's meaning, and the responsibility that comes with it, ensures, if nothing else, that we become a key author of our own story. Similar to earlier trials, our options span the gamut between (1) attempting to avoid our concerns about meaning and responsibility and (2) accepting our responsibility to infuse our life with meaning.

The Defense Against Existential Dread— Motivation, Guilt, & Responsibility

As with other sources of existential dread, our ego seeks to protect us. Unfortunately, we confront psychological risks whether life's brimming with meaning or not. Facing uncertainty, complexity, or responsibility can all trigger distress, depending on the circumstances, and regardless of our belief system. Although existential thinking is frequently associated with atheism, Kierkegaard (often called the 'Father of Existentialism'), was a Christian philosopher. Far more important than any philosophy, theory, or theology is the full experience of meaning or lack thereof.

Before diving too deep, let's distinguish the desire for higher purpose and meaning from other motivations.[14] A sense of meaning may motivate us, but motivations aren't always meaningful—not in a deeper existential or spiritual sense. Basic motivations are relatively innate, shared, and driven by physiological needs, so they mostly go without question. Few people argue that satiating hunger, although important, makes life worth living. In the realm of not-so-basic motivations, questions abound. Such motivations may indeed be meaningful, in our current sense, but they can vary depending on culture, personality, and life circumstances.

The most popular model of human motivation has undoubtedly been Maslow's hierarchy of needs.[15] Alderfer organized Maslow's needs into three domains: *Existence*, *Relatedness*, and *Growth*.[16] Alderfer's model makes two important modifications: 1) it removes the assumption that basic needs must be satisfied before 'higher-level' ones become salient, and 2) it describes how the frustration of higher needs can intensify a person's focus on lower ones. Although this trial is ultimately concerned about the human motivation to grow, meaning can be found in several places, some of which connect to previous trials. Whether basic or not-so-basic, motivations exist across levels of consciousness and in various configurations. Each of us, for example, differs in our conscious and unconscious motivations to achieve and gain mastery, to befriend and affiliate with others, and to influence and exert power.[17] Although meaning-related distress can be triggered in several ways, the options for defense remain largely the same (see Box 7.1 for examples).

Box 7.1

Example Defenses Against Meaning-related Distress

Selected Defense	Example
Distortion	Ashley believes everything happens for a reason, and as long as she keeps all negative thoughts out of her mind, her life will be a happy one. She ignores the news and current events, decorates her home with a haphazard collection of religious iconography, and only watches happy-go-lucky TV shows and movies created for younger audiences.
Projection	Avery 'knows' that life's meaningless and nothing matters. He does whatever he wants, seeking all types of pleasure and excitement with little concern about the impact of his choices on others. He laughs at religious people with their 'senseless guilt,' 'fake charity,' and 'judgmental attitudes.' He frequently posts online about how superior atheism is to religion and that religion's only for the weak and self-righteous.
Intellectualization	Dakotah reads self-help book after self-help book, scours religious texts, and searches the research literature on mystical experiences. They can quote several philosophers about the meaning of life and even the fear of meaninglessness, but they rarely feel or express any fear, guilt, or uncertainty about their life direction or apply insights from their studies.
Sublimation	After turning 40, Celia starts questioning her career in finance and realizes her work life isn't aligned with her personal values. That disconnect has become salient after her aunt's recent Alzheimer's diagnosis. Celia doesn't know about any realistic career alternatives, but while she weighs options, she starts volunteering at a local hospice.

In the absence of deeper meaning, we search for alternatives to fill the void. Viktor Frankl described the experience of meaninglessness as an *existential vacuum*.[18] Examples in film might include *Office Space*, in which the main character Peter has a dead-end job filing 'TPS Reports,' which are undoubtedly meaningless. Choosing blissful ignorance or self-righteous pride are seductive alternatives to sitting with meaninglessness and genuine uncertainty. Material success, fame, and various addictive or compulsive patterns (like excessive drinking, gambling, gaming, or social media scrolling) are imperfect but also readily available alternatives to confronting an existential vacuum.

Even though the most frightening existential fear is arguably that of meaninglessness, other forms of distress can arise when meaning is found. Chief among them is the guilt that comes as a consequence of failing to act from our sense of meaning or live up to some preconceived ideal. Guilt is intimately connected with responsibility. Some guilt, like other emotions, is perfectly reasonable and productive. This guilt results from doing something counter to our personal values and ethics. It helps us course correct, make amends, and prevent future misdeeds.

Sometimes we become too attached to an idyllic vision of our potential or other unrealistic standards. The weight of such responsibility is overbearing, and the result can be never-ending guilt. Taking on too much personal responsibility keeps us stuck in repetitive cycles of guilt. These cycles can be used as a defense against feeling empty, scared, powerless, or angry. Defensive guilt is largely unproductive. For one, it can overemphasize our relative influence and control. Secondly, it rarely offers a path towards repairing any damage done (if damage even occurred) or effectively changing our way of life or habits. For guilt to be productive, it must have a practical impact. Unexamined, unyielding beliefs can also conceal underlying uncertainty and doubt about those same beliefs. Rituals can be transformed into compulsive behaviors, empty of their original purpose but functioning to avoid or control hidden anxiety about our own uncertainty. In some cases of posttraumatic stress, especially when involving traumas perpetrated by others, excessive self-blame becomes a safer alternative to feeling powerless or acknowledging the inherent randomness of some tragedies.[19] Guilt can also conceal anger towards perpetrators, which for various reasons may not be 'okay' to feel or express.

According to many existential thinkers, and perhaps common sense, some level of imperfection and guilt is unavoidable merely due to being human in the first place.[20] Box 7.2 describes three 'worlds' of human existence as well as their related triggers of guilt and potential parallels in motivation and the trials we've been exploring in this book. Note that our current trial most closely concerns *Eigenwelt*, but questions of meaning and meaninglessness can impact all domains.

Box 7.2

Parallels among Worlds of Human Existence, Triggers of Guilt, Domains of Motivation, & Our Recent Trials

World of Existence	Triggers of Guilt	Related Motivations	Corresponding Trials
Umwelt—Natural world of physical and biological realities	Being unaware of our physical existence and place in the world; 'separation guilt' caused by disconnection with nature	**Existence** Sustenance, shelter, basic physical and emotional safety, pain avoidance, pleasure seeking	**Death** Nothingness / Non-Existence / Loss / Impermanence
Mitwelt—Social world of relationships and society	Being unable to see things from another's point of view; inadequacy of communication	**Relatedness** Belonging, attachment, power and social influence	**Loneliness** Attachment / Communication / Social Control / Loss / Authenticity / Dominance-Submission / Warmth-Hostility
Eigenwelt—Our own world of self-awareness and purpose	Being unable or unwilling to fulfill our potential; recognizing the impossibility of reaching the ideal version of ourselves	**Growth** Self-actualization, individuation, esteem, mastery, transcendence	**Meaninglessness** Groundlessness / Responsibility / Unrealized Potential

Note. This box summarizes complex concepts described by Rollo May's (1983) *The Discovery of Being* (three modes of the world—or of being—and ontological guilt, which he adapted from Heidegger), Alderfer's (1969) ERG motivation theory (a reformulation of Maslow's hierarchy), and this book's trials of initiation (integrating numerous sources).[21] The hypothesized connections and parallels are based on conceptual similarities and should not be taken as 'fact' or equivalency.

When navigating tensions between uncertain meaning and personal responsibility, we must at some point take *leaps of faith*—a central point made by Kierkegaard.[22] To make these leaps more consciously, we need to clarify our fundamental assumptions about life and its meaning. Sartre believed that attempting to deny our ultimate freedom and responsibility resulted in *bad faith*.[23] Acting in bad faith is being dishonest—in this case, with ourselves. Living in bad faith is the 'sin' of denying or relinquishing our freedom because of externally defined social norms and imprisoning ourselves within the confines of our prior decisions. We stay in an empty marriage because we committed 'til death do us part.' But we avoid engaging in couple's therapy to salvage our relationship. We accept the abuse of our boss because we need the money for our family. But we avoid searching for alternatives. Giving up behaviors derived from bad faith is frightening because it means losing our pre-imposed sense of structure. Deconstructing the 'rules' that have organized our sense of reality and life choices is like dismantling the ground upon which we walk. That's why meaninglessness is also groundlessness.

Yet, nihilism and apathy, seemingly natural reactions to meaninglessness, are themselves defenses to the responsibility of creating one's own life, living by personal values derived more authentically, and discovering meaning in both the obvious and most unlikely places. Facing meaninglessness can lead us down the path of powerlessness. But that too is inaccurate and far from benign. Not only can it lead to depression and helplessness for the individual, but it can also result in the callous treatment of others. If left unhealed, pain begets pain.

Leaps of faith can be scary, but one especially powerful fear related to our current trial is the fear of being unable achieve our full potential. When such growth-oriented fears result in overly constrained ambitions, or self-sabotage, we fall victim to what Maslow called a *Jonah Complex*. This complex involves the "fear of one's own greatness," the "evasion of one's destiny," or in pop psychology terms, the fear of success.[24] What appears at first glance as humility might be a defensive reaction to fears of greater achievement and the responsibility or pressure that comes with it. It might also serve to escape some personal 'Truth' or deeper purpose. A Jonah Complex often contains a hidden arrogance, jealousy, or resentment towards people who strive to do better—or at least try to, even if they're unsuccessful. It's always easier to be a critic. Like nihilism and apathy, a Jonah Complex hurts the individual along with others who become easy targets for projection of their unrealized hopes.

Motivation, Guilt, Responsibility—
A Sentence Completion Task

Before we try to resolve these dilemmas of responsibility and meaninglessness, let's sit with whatever reactions they've elicited. Check-in with yourself—from your emotions and thoughts to anything felt within your body or your impulse to act in some way. Take a few breaths to clear your mind. Then complete the stems below in whatever way makes sense right now.

My strongest motivations involve _____.

I once believed my life's purpose was to _____.

Of guilt, fear, and apathy, I'm most prone to _____ because

_____.

I feel less nihilistic when _____.

In the end, I'm most responsible for _____.

I often believe I have no choice but to _____.

My fundamental assumptions about life's meaning are _____

_____.

It's hard to admit, but my secret ambition is to _____

_____.

If I'm being honest, I might be sabotaging my own potential by _____

_____.

Some responses may point towards authentic personal meaning. If so, these answers will unfold as you confront this trial and continue this book's journey. Be patient with yourself. And be kind.

The Possibility of Accepting Responsibility—
and Engaging with Meaning

If I offered hope at this point, some existentialists (like Camus) would cry foul. When confronting this trial, we might agree there are many ways to remain asleep in the world. But when it comes to waking up, we face numerous opinions about how to do it 'the right way.' Navigating deeper questions of meaning requires a willingness to deconstruct our old approaches to relationships and life. There's no 'one size fits all' here. And when harmed by religious communities, academic institutions, or other foundations of pre-packaged meaning and structure, the temptation is to 'throw the baby out with the bathwater'—a horrible saying but an appropriate sentiment, nonetheless.

To discover resilient sources of meaning while facing absurdity, we must be willing to weather our own "Dark Night of the Soul." During the darkest times, light can shine through to offer us strength in surviving everyday struggles as well as otherwise unimaginable pain. A striking example of this resilience comes from existential psychotherapist and author, Viktor Frankl. In *Man's Search for Meaning*, Frankl described his imprisonment in a Nazi internment camp and how he and others dealt with this horrifying experience.[25] Natural reactions like initial shock and eventual apathy gave way for some to expressions of kindness and hope. According to Frankl, people who found meaning in their suffering were less likely to give up and more likely to survive. Paraphrasing Nietzsche, Frankl asserted that a person "who has a *why* to live for can bear with almost any *how*."[26] A person's attitude was not the primary factor in surviving the Holocaust. Yet, Frankl and others rightly highlight the power of discovering meaning and living with purpose. It can be a matter of survival in times of physical or psychological torment.

Given the challenges life offers everyone, meaning is far more central to our human journey than its use as a last-ditch survival tactic. We can find meaning and resilience in unlikely places. With humor being a sophisticated defense—or perhaps an honest appraisal of absurdity—comedy might be a great place to look. A personal favorite example of how humor supports existential explorations is *I Heart Huckabees*.[27] The film plays with the tensions between American humanism, with its hopefulness and New Age sentiments, and European existentialism, with its emphasis on the muck-and-mire of life, suffering, and meaninglessness. Without giving spoilers, the synthesis by the film's conclusion is beautiful, honest, and definitely absurd. Humor can help us explore issues that otherwise might overwhelm. It empowers us to engage with topics that deserve great reverence through the ironic vehicle of irreverence. When used this way, humor becomes a powerful tool rather than a mere defense mechanism.

Even Disney remakes have hinted at existential questions of meaning and

---

[a] Timon is a meerkat, and Pumbaa is a warthog.

purpose. Touching upon all our trials, Timon and Pumbaa[a] in the 'live' action version of *The Lion King* propose an alternative to the circle of life metaphor. Contemplating such metaphors can transform fears of death, disconnection, and meaninglessness into an empowering vision of our interconnectedness and the responsibility it holds. In one scene, Simba becomes confused after an antelope rebukes his attempts to play. Understanding the would-be prey's natural suspicion, Timon realizes he must dispel the adolescent lion's naivety about how the world works:[28]

> **Timon:** Eh you see, in nature there's a delicate balance.
>
> **Simba:** Oh, yeah. The circle of life. I know that.
>
> **Pumbaa:** No.
>
> **Timon:** No, no, no. I don't know where you're getting 'circle' from.
>
> **Pumbaa:** No, yeah. There's no circle of life.
>
> **Timon:** No, it's no circle.
>
> **Pumbaa:** No, not at all.
>
> **Timon:** In fact, it's the opposite.
>
> **Pumbaa:** Yeah.
>
> **Timon:** It's a line.
>
> **Pumbaa:** Yeah.
>
> **Timon:** It's a meaningless line of indifference.
>
> **Pumbaa:** And we're all just running toward the end of the line. And then one day we'll reach the end, and that'll be it. [**Timon:** That's it] Line over!
>
> **Timon:** Nothing.
>
> **Pumbaa:** Nada. And you can really just kind of do your own thing and fend for yourself, because your line doesn't affect anyone else's lines.
>
> **Timon:** You're alive and then you're not.
>
> **Timon:** Like this guy. [*he proceeds to eat an insect*] Mmm.
>
> **Simba:** You're sure it's not a circle? That we're all connected?
>
> **Pumbaa:** A circle would mean we're all this [*makes circular movement with tusks*] That would mean what I do affects him [**Timon:** Yeah], affects that thing [**Timon:** No], affects that thing [**Timon:** That's not how it goes.] which makes doing whatever we wanted not that cool.
>
> **Timon:** Let me simplify this for you: Life is meaningless.
>
> **Pumbaa:** Yes, that's why you just gotta look out for yourself. That's why you do you, Simba.

Timon and Pumbaa's misinterpretation of 'Hakuna Matata' as nihilistic hedonism doesn't paint an accurate picture of life either. It dismisses Simba's responsibility and ultimate destiny. Moving past his prior innocence does, however, provide him a path to reconnect with his instinctual, animal nature—a point Nietzsche would emphasize for us too. Simba eventually rediscovers his destiny to lead and defend those he loves. To do that, he must also face his guilt about his father's death, his fear of rejection, and his duty to protect the circle of life.

We clearly are not lions, and most of us are not kings. But if we are to find meaning in life, we too must follow a similar path of innocence, struggle, and renewal. What is the meaning of your life? Why are you here? I'm unable to give you *the* answer. Nor can anyone else for that matter. Life offers many possibilities for meaning. If living in bad faith is to be evaded, then each of us must actively explore, discover, and choose the meaning of our life. Because choices continue until the very end, our life's meaning is actually a collection of meanings.

Myths, parables, and other stories provide guidance, if not to follow, to rebel against, rework, and make our own. Our 'inner healer' is present somewhere if we're willing to listen. Powerful dreams, for example, might offer insights about our deeper sources of meaning. They are to our personal unconscious what myth, religion, film, and art are to our collective unconscious. Each of these sources speak in metaphor and symbols, which require interpretation before we can integrate their messages into our lives. The power of dreams is to highlight what we may not be seeing in our everyday waking consciousness. The power of myth is to preview the possibilities of human life, the choices we'll likely face, and the outcomes of taking any number of paths that lie before us.

Countless myths have existed throughout time, across the world's many cultures, and in several forms. So saying that myth is the answer to modern life's groundlessness remains itself a non-directive response to the question of personal meaning. Campbell and other mythologists have suggestions, but they have critics too. Nowadays, little can be said with certainty without someone pouncing on the argument or conclusion. Instead of waiting for outside critics, we could examine our personally held interpretations of meaning, some of which may not hold as much water as we'd like to believe. To reflect in this way isn't the same as being self-critical, insecure, or doubting for the sake of doubting. By excavating the cave of our minds, we can recognize that underneath any dirt we might brush aside, we're likely to unearth treasures too.

Whatever treasures we earn, we must remember to manifest them in our life. Frankl believed meaning can be found or created in three primary ways:[29]

1. Cultivating remarkable or courageous **attitudes** about unavoidable pain or situations beyond our control—what attitudes we adopt toward life

2. Engaging in and appreciating powerful life **experiences**, such as encounters with beauty, truth, and love—what experiences we embrace and receive

3. Exploring and expressing our **creativity** in manifested talents and insights—what creative works we offer to ourselves, others, and the world

Though neither mutually exclusive or exhaustive, each path can impact our lives and the lives of people touched by our genuine expressions of meaning and purpose. Personally, I've found inspiration by witnessing clients confront and heal from traumatic and painful experiences. That alone is an achievement, but many clients then go on to express their healing through artistic projects and foster greater intimacy in their relationships, both of which spread healing and inspiration throughout their community.

The significance of personal growth and effectiveness of meaning-centered psychotherapies have substantial research support.[30] For our current trial, one finding may be especially helpful. Motivations for social influence and power tend to be less fulfilling over time and may represent a compromise after searching for higher meaning to no avail.[31] As a parallel in our mythic journey, the final boon claimed by the hero may indeed be their hidden power, but it's not power for power's sake. It's a power that serves an ultimate purpose, one that transcends ego-driven motivations based on fear, ignorance, or selfish desires.[32]

Responsibility and Engaging with Meaning— A Sentence Completion Task

It's that time again. Take a deep breath. Clear your head of all these concepts and ideas, and as naturally as possible, complete the following sentences.

In the past, my life was ruled by _____.

Now, though, I choose a life guided by _____

_____.

If I have faith in anything, it'd be that _____.

At this point in time, the most personally meaningful aspects of my life involve

_____.

I'm most creative and engaged when _____.

Of all my attitudes and beliefs about life, the most powerful and meaningfully

around _____.

The five most meaningful experiences I've had in life so far include

_____.

Now that you've completed these sentences, you could return to one of your responses within the trial of death and impermanence. The relevant stem is 'In the end, I would like my gravestone to say....' How does your response then relate to any responses you've given here? Has anything changed in this short amount of time?

The Varieties of Meaningful Transcendence— Charting a Path from the Infinite to the Finite

Transcendence, like most words, means different things to different people in different contexts.[33] For our current trial, it may refer to a transcendent source of meaning—like a Platonic ideal or Truth. It may also allude to self-transcendence, going beyond the confines of our ego and personal identity. Or in a more radical form, transcendence might be rising above the question of meaning entirely, being pure consciousness and awareness without interpretation or intention.

To chart a path forward, we must imagine, resolve, or navigate various tensions about our life's meaning—in particular, that between what Kierkegaard called the infinite and the finite.[34] The infinite is the expansive sense of potentialities. The finite is the necessity of choices which inherently collapse such possibilities—what could be versus what is. Its parallel in time is the eternal versus the temporal or every-fleeting present. This tension is one of choice, for sure, but also of meaning. We risk despair if we've overcommitted our life, sense of self, and meaning to be contained within a narrow realm of possibility, a self-imposed prison. This is being lost in the finite. On the other hand, becoming lost in the infinite is falling into an abyss of aimlessness or fantasy by avoiding commitment to any path. In colloquial language, we might get frozen in FOMO (fear of missing out), a fear so pervasive and relatable to many of us today. Experiencing this tension naturally elicits some initial anxiety, just like other conflicts, but anxiety can be managed.

How might we transcend this tension between the infinite and the finite? Is it even possible? This conflict involves an inherent paradox. Transcending paradox is a core feature of psychedelic mystical experiences, but transcending paradox is itself ambiguous in our shared meaning.[35] To transcend the infinite and finite, are we seeking to rise above, combine, or bypass some inner conflict? Even when interpretations are agreed upon, tensions shift to conflicts about application. From a pragmatic standpoint, what are we to do with these intricate issues of meaning, interpretation, and application? Our conscious minds may not choose what intuitively holds meaning. Yet, we certainly can choose to examine our intuitions and upon reflection, make choices based on those that hold up to reasonable scrutiny. By necessity, these choices, no matter how well informed, collapse the infinite into the finite. Each moment, though, gives us another opportunity to try again. Our freedom lies in the present. The past is the finite and the future is the infinite. By existing in the spaces in between, we discover our power.

Although that seems like an answer, it's really the beginning. My answer, if I dare admit to having one, will not be your answer. Your answer is your life. Your choices. Your approach in navigating these tensions. We can learn from each other, though, and let's not forget to learn from our many ancestors as well. That's what myth offers us. Its hidden meanings range from metaphysical to practical, but that's one of its strengths. Myth can speak to all of us. When exploring mythology, we can search for underlying similarities or catalogue conflicting messages. Doing both reveals nuances. Welcoming both our similarities and differences in meaning may offer, in and of itself, a kind of transcendence. Holding such complexity without giving into judgment is a tall order, though. Believing in any transcendent meaning can easily turn into battles of interpretation, which then solidify into narrow ideologies about Truth and Falsehood. Terror Management Theory reminds us that existential distress can make our ego rigidly defend whatever meaning helps us alleviate our fears.

Thoughtful explorations of the meaning can involve metaphysical and secular paths of inquiry. These paths can be at odds with one another, but not all endpoints necessarily diverge. If pulled towards metaphysical interpretations of myth and mystical experiences, we may eventually face exceedingly high standards about how to live our 'normal' lives. Teilhard de Chardin's words might assuage any understandable fears of inadequacy and failure in reaching for what appears unachievable:[36]

> Although only a small fraction of those who try to scale the heights of human achievement arrive anywhere close to the summit, it is imperative that there be a multitude of climbers. Otherwise the summit may not be reached by anybody. The individually lost and forgotten multitudes have not lived in vain, provided they, too, made the efforts to climb.

In seeking spiritual transcendence, we may commit to a specific path or integrate several traditions. We can practice in solitude, with a community, or by balancing both—yet another connection to our previous trial. In the psychedelic world, the prevailing ethos of ayahuasca circles exemplifies a community-focused path embedded within shamanistic, indigenous frameworks—which are much more diverse than often acknowledged by non-indigenous people.[37]

Spiritual transcendence can be sought in less communal ways too. Although not exclusively psychedelic, perennial philosophy has historically and culturally been intertwined with psychedelic-inspired East-meets-West spirituality. Its underlying assumption is that a hidden wisdom tradition is expressed across mystical traditions within major world religions. Perennial thinkers believe an eternal transcendent Truth exists, we can experience it, and doing so bestows enlightenment, equanimity, and liberation from suffering. Although it too has various schools, Aldous Huxley summarized his version as such:[38]

> The divine Ground of all existence is a spiritual Absolute, ineffable in terms of discursive thought, but (in certain circumstances) susceptible of being directly experienced and realized by the human being. This Absolute is the God-without-form....The last end of [humankind], the ultimate reason for human existence, is unitive knowledge of the divine Ground—the knowledge that can come only to those who are prepared to "die to self" and so make room, as it were, for God. Out of any given generation...very few will achieve the final end of human existence; but the opportunity for coming to unitive knowledge will, in one way or another, continually be offered until all sentient beings realize Who in fact they are.

The overlapping rhetoric with psychedelic ego death, Neoplatonic idealism, nondualism, and 'New Age' spirituality is no coincidence. Perennial-esque spirituality can accommodate individual paths towards transcendence, with or without psychedelics. Even still, perennial thinkers often encourage the path of the Bodhisattva—an enlightened one who temporarily forgoes nirvana in order to help others awaken.[39]

Secular worldviews can accommodate transcendence as well. From a non-spiritual or strictly atheistic perspective—if we exclude nihilistic individualism, at least—we might reach a similar conclusion about the value of setting our mark high, even if potentially unachievable. When viewed as a collective effort, the great human experiment is one in which individuals pushing the edges of our potential may benefit us all. Perhaps, though, the reverse is true too. Many paths lie ahead for humanity, and not all are grand and triumphant. Most of our modern challenges aren't exactly new. They're significantly intensified, though. The scales are so much larger than before—in terms of the size of the human population, global economy, cross-cultural communication and exposure, technological advancements, and environmental impact all occurring within an extremely brief historical timescale. The jury's still out about whether our combined biological, sociological, and ethical evolutionary histories have prepared us for what's to come. Transcending our limitations may be a matter of survival.

Perhaps the most meaningful questions for our human collective involve what we still need to learn and how to apply our evolving knowledge to the situations at hand. To do that well, we need not reinvent the wheel. Innovations may be the exciting frontier, but true innovation only exists in relation to convention. Without understanding the wisdom behind conventional solutions to problems faced by humanity, we could get lost in an arbitrary world of 'solution-focused' action, completely disconnected from ancient, time-tested lessons learned the hard way. Progress comes from knowing which traditions to transcend and which to keep.

In our individual search for meaning, whether divine or secular, we're each conducting our own personal experiment. Research might call it a longitudinal, single case study design—a bland description of our most cherished possession: our life. Our interconnectedness, if not treated as a competitive zero-sum game, suggests that with everyone climbing their own mountain, the individuals who can accomplish something profound and unique can help us all ascend. Our sphere of influence may extend farther than we realize, considering the chain of events that unfolds after making even the smallest choice. Akin to a 'social' butterfly effect, we may not be able to predict or know every outcome, but if we can embrace responsibility without being overwhelmed, I'd gamble the net impact would be positive—a hypothesis you might test yourself.

Reflections on Transcendent Meaning—
A Sentence Completion Task

The following sentences may be evocative. Some may seem like I'm guiding you in a specific direction, but remember you're free to respond in whatever way feels authentic.

For me, transcendence means _____.

Although I can't explain it, I deep down believe _____

_____.

My source of spirituality is _____.

The highest achievement of our human potential will be when _____

_____.

Of all the world's religions and metaphysical ideas, the one that most reson-

ates with my personal beliefs is _____.

That's because _____.

If a transcendent reality beyond the material world were somehow proven

to exist, it'd change my life by _____.

_____.

In contrast, it wouldn't change _____.

_____.

If the material world were all there is, I'd change _____

_____.

I wouldn't change, however, _____.

The places where my talents and my passions converge are _____

_____.

The meaning of my life is _____.

The meaning of the cosmos is _____.

Whether any responses surprise you or confirm what you already knew, consider elaborating on your thoughts and intuitions in your Travel Journal.

Heeding Warnings while Confronting the Final Trial

As the culmination of our second arc, the trial of meaning is the most profound. As such, passing this trial can lead to significant changes in your approach to life. But it's prudent to be mindful as you navigate the tensions between possibilities and the necessity of making choices. The following pointers are to help you find your path while avoiding some common pitfalls.

The First Warning—Outcome-Fixated Goal Chasing (vs. Expansive Values-Driven Process)

The desire for meaning and growth can be distorted by the avoidance of meaninglessness and uncertainty. This warning is about one subtle manifestation: chasing after never-ending self-improvement goals or other outcome-oriented expressions of personal meaning. In our modern Western-centric world, we emphasize the active expressions of meaning, like setting and attaining goals. We've even turned enlightenment into a concrete goal. The ego loves goals.

Meaning is not a goal. Unlike needs that can be temporarily satisfied, meaning and growth cannot be checked off a to-do list. In Maslow's hierarchy, our highest growth-oriented motivation, self-actualization, can never be fully realized. Self-actualization's an on-going process of living your values and reaching for ideals, as opposed to achieving a single or even multitude of personal goals. Treating self-actualization as an outcome is doomed to end in frustration. At its core, growth is an expansive process rather than narrowly focused. To allow growth, we must also acknowledge the tension between our highest values and our inherent inability to live them perfectly and consistently. Unreasonable expectations lead us into unproductive guilt or demoralization. Demoralization is not so much about meaninglessness as it is feeling disempowered to create meaningful changes in our lives or the world.

When we start growing and self-actualizing, unintended consequences might occur. Goals, like intentions, should be held lightly. If overly attached to goals and desired outcomes, we might forget the underlying values they're meant to serve, which can be expressed in innumerable ways. Moreover, for every action, there can be an equal and opposite reaction, psychologically speaking. Others may become threatened because of their own competitiveness and insecurity, due perhaps to a Jonah Complex. We might also hesitate as our meaningful actions start to unravel our old, comfortable ways of living. For every light, there's a shadow. For every attachment, there's a loss. If we hold onto ideals too tightly, we can fall into the traps of perfectionism and disillusionment. Alternatively, our ego might convince us that we can attain perfection—or already have. Self-actualization is not self-enhancement or self-aggrandizement. As supported by research, subjective wellbeing is higher when personal sources of meaning transcend self-oriented needs, desires, ambitions, and identity and connect to so-called self-transcendent emotions like awe, love, gratitude, and beauty.[40]

Chasing goal after goal is effective to an extent, but transforming abstract ideals into concrete actions necessarily diminishes them. Denying that can amplify the fear of not reaching our full potential. Here's an insider secret: No one reaches their full potential! Potential lies in the realm of the infinite, not the finite. On the positive side, growth doesn't stop unless we give up or cease to exist. Growth takes courage, but courage is found when we discover meaningful ways to grow and be in the world. The relationship between meaning and courage is reciprocal and expansive. Missteps are miniature trials, which you can continue to pass and learn from. Emotions like guilt, fear, and doubt can come and go without becoming frozen by them. Beneath these emotions may be underlying values you secretly or explicitly hold. Values are guideposts towards a meaningful life. They're flexible in application but can clarify the overall direction of your personal process of living-through-meaning. No matter where you are and where you've been, you can always follow their lead, even if that means turning around.

As a dynamic and fluid process, meaning can be expressed in three ways.[41] Contemplating each can free us from the trappings of rigid and outcome-fixated goal chasing.

> **Being**—a present-centered, radical acceptance of your existence as meaningful, not contingent on specific actions or experiences

> **Doing**—an action-oriented process of living in meaningful ways; may involve goals but emphasizes the process of value-driven living instead of any single outcome

> **Becoming**—a continual growth-oriented process of reaching for a higher or more meaningful understanding of oneself, others, and existence and in doing so, experiencing meaningful transformations, many of which are unexpected but welcomed nonetheless

Self-actualization, growth, or whatever we call the on-going process of discovering and creating meaning is the ultimate journey of life. Like all journeys, though, the destination isn't the point. Is death—the final destination—the meaning of life? Death gives life meaning, as the saying goes, but until that ending, meaning manifests in countless ways. All it takes is realizing what's right in front of us yet fleeting all the same.[42] Contemplating multiple sources of meaning can keep us grounded despite temporary moments of groundlessness and doubt. Shifting our perspective among being, doing, and becoming can help us circumvent any unproductive guilt and regret that locks us into the past and obscures the meaningful actions we can make in the present.

The Second Warning—Unfettered Meaning-Making (vs. Playing with 'Not Knowing')

A breakdown of former meaning is the first sign of a breakthrough. This pattern is yet again why our trials have been necessary. The psychedelic parallel is how ego death and mystical experiences collapse pre-existing mental structures, allowing the mind to open itself to alternatives, and stimulate neuroplasticity.[43] Because these experiences speak through symbols, paradoxes, and riddles, it can be difficult to discern the meaning behind non-waking and non-ordinary consciousness, whether otherworldly dreams or psychedelic journeys. If nihilism represents an excessive response to meaninglessness, then the risk on the other side might be a whole-hearted yet overconfident and arbitrary assignment of meaning.[44]

No stranger to existential questions, author Joseph Conrad once asserted, "One must explore deep and believe the incredible to find the new particles of truth floating in an ocean of insignificance."[45] Learning to swim means more than avoiding drowning in meaninglessness. It means moving towards waters that hold genuine significance. To use another metaphor, it's finding the signal in the noise. In our waking life, certain powerful moments can be as mystical as psychedelic journeys, but their meaning may likewise be unclear. Moments of awe, for example, connect us to something larger than ourselves, but as we know from our first waypoint, a cosmic perspective is readily available. What's different about subjective experiences of awe or meaning?

Whatever causes sudden jolts of meaning, the challenge to ascertain significance in a sea of insignificance is true of many life experiences. Jung spoke of synchronicities, the ambiguous yet personally meaningful co-occurrence of objectively unrelated events.[46] Recently when discussing synchronicity, a friend posed a wise question, "What's the difference between magical thinking and synchronicity?"[47] In Western medicine, magical thinking isn't magic. It's a possible symptom of psychiatric illness.[48] Magical thinking occurs when people significantly alter their behavior based on superstitions or read heavily into arbitrary coincidences and become convinced of hidden messages. It can cause harm when an individual dismisses reasonable alternative interpretations or contradictory evidence and then make important life choices based on their beliefs. In less extreme cases, the line between meaningful synchronicities and magical thinking can be vague.

Then again, meaning itself is often ambiguous. Heeding this warning may require us to reflect on the context as well as the consequences of acting from ascribed meaning. Let's say one person watches an alien invasion movie, reads 'between the lines,' and discovers hidden messages about how to fight a fascist regime from within.[49] After sharing these messages with their therapist and expressing paranoia about current world events, this person gets a tentative diagnosis of delusional disorder. Another person sees the same message, but rather than telling their therapist about it, they write a paper on the subject that gets published in a peer-reviewed journal. What's the difference? The second person is a film professor. This professor also happened to use a one-two punch combo of intellectualization and sublimation to create an effective defense against their triggered anxiety. When under the effects of psychedelics, otherwise strange experiences (like believing oneself to be Jesus or experiencing the world as made of plastic) can be perfectly acceptable and incredibly meaningful. Overly concrete interpretations of these experiences may not only miss the underlying symbolic meaning but also cause significant distress and harm.[50]

Sometimes the difference between magical thinking and genuine meaning is clear-cut, but in our exceedingly complex world, ambiguity appears to be a feature of 'reality.' How can we navigate the ambiguity of meaning? As with any interpretation, it's wise to hold our insights lightly. Attempting to make the ineffable effable is, after all, a Sisyphean task. Holding tightly onto interpretations, no matter how 'good' or popular, is a disservice to what lies beyond words, thoughts, and our culturally sanctioned beliefs about reality—which are based more on consensus than objectivity. Even science, our best tool for finding objectivity, can be treated like a secularized religion. Scientific and pseudoscientific words can become reified as Truth. What's the difference between a ritual and a research protocol? Is describing gravity as magical or the combined laws of physics as the Tao any less true than our scientific-sounding labels? To echo the first line of the Tao Te Ching, "The Tao that can be told is not the eternal Tao; The name that can be named is not the eternal name."[51] If we replace 'Tao' with any other word, does the underlying meaning change?

Beyond issues of semantics or rhetoric, engaging in dialogues about meaning and interpretation can reveal important nuances and layers of possible meaning. Dream interpretation, too often dismissed by modern psychology, is a process that exemplifies a wise if not difficult tolerance of ambiguity in both the dreamer and the therapist.[52] It serves as a great parallel to the interpretation of psychedelic experiences. Different interpretations of dreams, psychedelic journeys, or random life experiences might be understood as complementary layers of meaning, not competing interpretations with only one being true. Holding any single interpretation lightly allows us to accept paradox, a feature of mystical experiences but also of most mysteries lying at the edge of human understanding.

Tolerating ambiguity about meaning-versus-meaninglessness might allow us to rest in a state of 'not knowing,' or what existential Buddhist psychologist John Welwood has called meaning-free-ness.[53] Not knowing requires humility and flexibility, but it's not the same as willful ignorance. We can know things—relatively speaking at least. When paired with the desire to know, allowing 'not knowing' can ease any suffering from the parts of our mind that want to jump to conclusions or understand what we cannot. Another benefit of meaning-free-ness is how it teaches us to surrender an attitude of seriousness which fights to defend our pre-existing 'knowledge.' Although reverence is valuable, seriousness can be a sign of the ego's self-importance. My encounters with Tibetan Buddhist monks, though too infrequent, have struck me in exemplifying a playful yet reverent attitude when approaching profound topics like suffering and transformation. The 14th Dalai Lama models this attitude in how he flows freely between humor and candor. In many of the world's wisest people, regardless of faith, we find a lightness of being, where freedom and ambiguity are not triggers of suffering but sources of liberation from self-seriousness and the necessary tensions of meaning and meaninglessness.[54]

Passing the Final Trial— Fostering Acceptance of the Responsibility to Live through Meaning

The search for answers to what's unknowable is part of the human journey, but when asking questions of meaning, many give up too soon. Some by avoiding the question altogether. Others by prematurely committing to narrowly defined sources of meaning. What then is the alternative? What could it mean to pass this final trial? In attempting to resolve the dilemma of meaning-versus-meaninglessness, we're all in the same boat. If nothing else, that connects us. Spiritually minded people speak of awakening as the attainment of a profound insight about existence and its ultimate meaning. Of course, that meaning may differ for each person and community. These differences might be due to errors of translation, a risk of describing the indescribable. Yet, as individuals, we make interpretations and leaps of faith all the time. Our everyday existence requires it.

Although acceptance has been our loyal ally throughout this arc of trials, it challenges us here like never before. What we must accept is what we've been fated. Nietzsche would tell us to love our fate, that which is necessary regardless of our attitude—our mortality, interconnectedness, and perhaps, absurdity. Our modern-day Fates may not be personified as deities, but the voice of our ally reminds us we must contend with fate, nonetheless. The beginning of our story has been written. We didn't choose our genes, our family of origin, and the world and time in which we were born.[55] Even our past decisions belong to our past self, someone not wholly like who we are now. Despite the necessity of fate, there's room to play within all circumstances, no matter how dire. By accepting that, we find our freedom. By accepting freedom, we must also accept our responsibility. The greatest responsibility is to discover or create meaning and then live from it, but we do this despite inherent uncertainty and the fundamental ineffability of meaning. Living through meaning requires us to transform the infinite realm of possibilities into the finite world of actions and choices. We do so until the day possibilities cease, the day we return to our original home, the state of material non-existence.

It may be necessary to accept these unavoidable tensions, but to pass this trial, acceptance might not be the end goal. Camus would argue we need to embrace these tensions in all their absurdity without hoping to escape them. That's what he meant by suggesting we imagine Sisyphus happy. If we succeed, then we can achieve the status of *Absurd Hero*—a person who recognizes the inherent tension between seeking meaning in a potentially meaningless existence but defiantly chooses life anyways. In choosing life, the Absurd Hero responds to the question of suicide with an emphatic 'No' and gains the power to hold the paradox of meaning, ambiguity, and uncertainty without becoming lost or frozen in indecision or despair.[56]

Sisyphus faced an eternal sentence with no meaning beyond punishment. Our fate, dare I say destiny, involves periods of struggle, but the heroic act of acceptance is not to accept utter defeat.[57] It's to accept responsibility despite not knowing how things will play out. Defeat is accepting temptations to bypass necessary tensions, like buying into rigid black-and-white interpretations of meaning or escapist fantasies. These alternatives serve the ego's efforts to avoid anxiety and uncertainty. The most resilient expressions of meaning are beyond the ego's reign. They're guided by our inner compass, the part of our minds that connects us to transcendent sources of personal meaning but in another paradox, may not belong solely to our personal everyday self.

Acceptance is not a blanket approval of our pre-existing beliefs. We must have the courage to allow doubt while we strive, accept, and live through meaning. Wrestling with occasional doubt can refine our perspective and hone our attempts at putting our meaning into practice. It could also reaffirm what we knew deep down but began to question, either because of an inner critical voice or some outside test of our resolve. It's natural for doubt and guilt to appear as we gather information and experience while needing to make choices along the way. Listening to these emotions instead lets us adapt. In trying to live meaningfully in an ambiguous, fractured world with innumerable distractions and false prophets with pre-packaged meaning, it's prudent to welcome our experience whatever it may be. The voice of doubt or fear may be the voice of wisdom and discernment, but we won't know unless we hear what it has to say and then investigate further. We'd do well to remember that Sisyphus was punished for his hubris. Perhaps there are other ways to be heroic and attain happiness without condemning ourselves to endless cycles of fruitless repetition.

When exploring either personal or transcendent meaning, we can look to ancient wisdom texts, scientific research, or time-tested ideas about ethics and virtues that promote or detract from personal wellbeing, societal stability, or evolutionary adaptiveness. When contemplating meaning leads to an existential crisis, where all hope seems lost, we can remind ourselves that in mythic journeys, the loss of hope often precedes a renewal of faith and determination—often in the face of overwhelming odds.[58]

Although absurdity and uncertainty appear mostly negative and painful, our attitude toward the unknown can be playful. Zen Buddhism demonstrates lighthearted absurdity in the use of nonsensical riddles called koans.[59] Koans, for the most part, have no meaningful solution, but they do have a point to make. They provoke frustration, a natural consequence of fervently searching for an answer to no avail. This meaningless search forces an initiate to confront the limitations of intellect. In realizing the 'real' meaning of koans, a self-deprecating but lighthearted chuckle might be the wisest response.

Laughter helps us approach the 'unapproachable' and move through terror to expand awareness and experience awe. Laughter connects us to fellow travelers who are also learning not to take themselves so seriously and to find joy in absurdity. In describing a healthy alternative to a Jonah Complex, Maslow offered the following: "You must be aware not only of the godlike possibilities within, but also of the existential human limitations. You must be able simultaneously to laugh at yourself and at all human pretensions. If you can be amused by the worm trying to be god, then in fact you may be able to go on trying."[60]

If laughter offers you hope but talk of gods and transcendence turns you off, you might consider a decidedly irreligious example of a strikingly similar attitude. Both the humor and pain of absurdity is found in none other than *Rick & Morty,* a popular animated series that follows the antics of the multiverse's smartest (and most cynical) mad scientist, Rick Sanchez, and his simple-minded grandson, Morty. It pushes the limits of absurdity and dark humor while confronting existential issues connected to each of our trials and beyond. Rarely if ever, however, does it offer good role models or solutions to the absurd—which, now that I think of it, might satisfy Camus. In one psychedelic-inspired scene, Rick, Morty, and a one-off antagonist unexpectedly share a journey full of mythic symbolism, cosmic unity, and infinite mystery that blows their minds. Afterwards, in a line both humorous and insightful, Rick has a warning for Morty that applies to us as well: "Cosmic apotheosis wears off faster than salvia."[61] Apotheosis is the mythic attainment of transcendent knowledge, awareness, and strength, akin to mystical enlightenment. At the peak of the mythic hero's journey, apotheosis is the definitive boon for passing the necessary trials. As we pass our final trial, I can think of no better time to introduce this seemingly irreverent quote—but wise warning—about the importance and challenge of both the integration of psychedelic experiences and applications of any profound source of meaning.

As Frankl suggested, our ultimate freedom lies in the attitudes we have towards unavoidable situations and the consequences of merely being human at this point in history. We can find meaning, ironic though it may be, in our attitude towards the inescapable tensions and paradoxes of absurdity and meaning. Trying to avoid their reality compounds our suffering. We could instead play with absurdity, enjoy it, laugh at it, appreciate it, or fight against it. More realistically, we can do all the above depending on the moment. But to reach our full potential (if such a thing exists) we must dare to find meaning, embrace our responsibility to strive to be better, and remain grounded in both humility and courage. And let's not forget to add a dash of humor and joy.

Concrete Suggestions & Journey Report

Box 7.3 offers a few concrete suggestions for exploring themes related to this final trial. Read the list to see if any seem personally helpful. For an account of a psychedelic experience that highlights this trial's themes, see Journey Report 7.1. This journey exemplifies how transcendent experiences can make a person confront the emptiness of a rigid or ego-centric idea of right-versus-wrong. The ability to laugh at oneself, without undue shame and embarrassment, is a sign of psychological growth and 'lightness of being,' which can help a person foster deeper connections with others and enjoy life—while also expanding one's perspective on their authentic sense of self and their personal values.

Box 7.3
Exploring Meaning and Responsibility in Everyday Life

Suggestion	Example
Outline your basic assumptions about your life's meaning.	You revisit your sentence completion entries and see that your core assumptions are that everyone has a purpose in life, people have free will, and happiness is the reward for living your life's purpose. You reflect on these assumptions and feel largely comfortable with the first two. The third assumption, though, seems too vague because you're not sure what you really mean by 'happiness.' You decide to give this more thought over a few days and then return to either clarify what you mean by happiness or ditch the third assumption for now.
Describe what your superpower might be if you were a superhero. Then imagine a 'real world' version of that power that you can develop, hone, or express in your life.	Your response is immediate—you'd be Rogue from the X-Men comics. Instead of absorbing the mutant powers or memories of others, you absorb people's 'energy' and have been described as 'sensitive' since you were young. However, you found a way to use your sensitivity to good effect. Like Rogue eventually did in the comics, you became a high school teacher. The job is tough sometimes, but you find it very meaningful to have a positive impact on the next generation. You realize too you sometimes get overwhelmed by students who constantly challenge your knowledge. You wonder if there's a way to deflect the negative energy (without dismissing the students) so that you don't absorb it. You decide to speak with your fellow teachers to see how they try to solve this problem.

List 5 things you'd change in life if some eternal divine reality were proven to exist. List 5 things you'd change if no such layer of reality existed. Note especially any overlap.	Your first list includes changing your career, reading more about world religions, not spending as much time complaining, and enjoying more time 'communing' with nature. Your second list includes exercising more, eating better, spending more time outdoors, having kids, and reading poetry. You notice first the obvious overlap with spending more time in nature. Then you realize that the Tao Te Ching is written like poetry and wonder if that might be worth looking into as well. You make plans for an outdoor hike and decide to read one page of the Tao Te Ching each evening before going to bed—with the first week acting as a 'trial period.'
Craft a mission statement based on your top values. The key question to ask is, "What do I want my life to be about?" Write out your statement, or a simplified version, and place it somewhere you'll see regularly.	Your top values are Discovery, Integrity, Perseverance, Autonomy, and Fun. After giving it a lot of thought (and, to be fair, crumbling up some paper with rejected drafts), you come up with the following: "My life is about discovering new possibilities for human consciousness, persevering through difficult and uncertain times, protecting the freedom of everyone to choose their life course (without harming others), and maintaining a sense of integrity— all the while, making sure to have fun along the way!"

Grounding Words—A Brief Summary

You've faced your final trial and have emerged triumphant. Not as an over-confident, rigid adherent to some narrow, pre-determined meaning, nor as a nihilist who dismisses all meaning and chases only pleasure or escapes into oblivion. You realize that although absolute freedom may not exist, you have significant freedom when it comes to meaning and the responsibility you have to live through it. You, like all others, are born into a world with pre-existing and ever-evolving contingencies. Yet to borrow a concept from statistics, you have 'degrees of freedom' that naturally exist, and by accepting your agency, you've seen new possibilities. Armed with awareness and growing insight you can weigh choices, explore, and then commit to action. After action, you know you'll reflect, re-evaluate, and adjust as needed. Then go at it again. Whether fueled by the image of Sisyphus joyfully pushing his boulder, or the idea of an ever-expanding upward spiral of transcendent meaning, reach for your own version of heroic power and choose a path. Many paths lead to meaning, but your path is unique. You approach it now with clear excitement, a dash of trepidation, and an attitude of reverence, hope, and humility.

Your First Required Task—Your Values, Your Choice

As Sisyphus had no choice, neither do we. As a tongue-in-cheek yet suitable twist, this assignment is your journey's first required activity. You have no choice. In all seriousness, though, this task is one I encourage of all my clients, friends, and family to complete. In an example of synchronistic happenstance, I learned only recently that a version of this exercise was part of early psyche-delic studies in the middle of last century. But I first came across it through my non-psychedelic work. Good ideas have a way of coming back around, though, and it's currently being reincorporated in modern psychedelic research.[62] I'm speaking of the Values Card Sort (see Exercise 7.1 on page 225). Values are verbal stand-ins for ineffable sources of meaning or qualities of being. In this activity, you'll review several cards with a word describing a value. Look at each card one at a time. Read the word but avoid being overly concrete about its textbook definition. Look beyond the word to connect to its deeper meaning and the personal associations you have with it. Values are creative, expansive, and complex in application yet simple in abstraction. Although values can be applied in a rigid, legalistic way, a mature application of values isn't moralis-tic.[63] For this exercise, notice but don't give into any guilt that can arise if you compare these ideals with your past or recent behavior. Know you can live these values in infinite ways, and as a gift of the eternal present, your choices now and in the future can be different than those from the past.

There's not a right or wrong in this list. Even if there were, who's to tell you what to believe about your personal values? When exploring personal meaning, what I and others offer should be taken with a grain of salt. Remember to look inside for your own answers. You can't skip to the end, and you can't default to the opinions of others. That'd be denying your freedom and responsibility. Undergoing your own process of values exploration is how you can find the signal in the noise.[64]

Your Assignment, Your Choice

For your final assignments in this arc, embrace your freedom yet again and choose from the options below. The division between Reflective-Intellectual and Experiential-Emotional are relative. Try to do at least one activity daily before you move onto the final arc of your journey. As you've seen before, the themes explored in the activities below will continue to expand in our final arc. As always, you may practice and revisit anything you find helpful or evocative as you continue to move forward.

Assignments 7.1
Exploring Meaning & Absurdity

Reflective-Intellectual	Experiential-Emotional
☐ Task—Use **Form 4.1 "The Experiential Explorer"** to record moments where you've put one or more personal values into practice	☐ Task—Complete **Exercise 7.2 "Oracle Card Reflections—Belief, Doubt, & Application"** to explore ambiguity of meaning and interpretation
Time—Minimum of 2-3 entries, at least 15 min of reflection	Time—At least one card drawn 2-3x/week, 10 min reflection each
Aim—To reflect on your personal values and observe how you express them in intentional and unintentional ways	Aim—To play with ambiguity and the tension between belief and disbelief
☐ Task—Research ideas like absurdity, synchronicity, perennial philosophy, or secular ethics. **Create a 'defensible' list of values** that transcend personal, ego-driven motivations	☐ Task—Practice the meditation in **Meditation 7.1 "Infusing Meaning & Meaninglessness"**
Time—Minimum of 1-2 hrs to gather information, reflect on the exercise, and record response	Time—Minimum of 2-3x/week, 10-15 min each
Aim—To learn about various perspectives on meaning and describe your preliminary synthesis of transcendent meaning and/or socially responsible ethics	Aim—To become aware of and consciously access your ability to imbue random objects with deeper symbolic meaning

After reviewing options, respond to this chapter's Travel Journal prompt and express in verbal or symbolic ways your reflections on this final trial.

Travel Journal

What is meaningful in my life?

What do I fear might be less so?

How can I expand the most meaningful aspects of my life?

Which personal values would I like to translate further into action?

JOURNEY REPORT 7.1 Laughing Out Loud... At Myself

I've used mushrooms several times for healing depression and trauma and developing greater self-compassion and self-acceptance. Many, if not most, of my journeys have been difficult. Although I sometimes experienced glimpses of pure awe, most of my insights until this particular night were dark, scary, and so challenging that I'd ask myself, "Why did I sign up for this?" or "Which part of my brain is going to forget and plan another retreat?" Often at the end of each journey, after experiencing death and rebirth, I'd feel empowered for "surviving" but conclude I'd "never do that again." That conclusion would eventually be forgotten as months later I'd need to "do some more work."

On the night of this ceremony, we gathered in a circle to share our intentions. The setting was perfect. My mindset was "on point" and my intentions clear—including which traumas I'd work on, perhaps why I'm in a job I hate, how I could quit, why I end up in these jobs in the first place, why I always find a boss who's a bully, why I have to fight the system, etc. The journey could address any of these. When others share, there's typically one or two who say something like, "Last time I was soooo high," "I'm looking forward to getting high again," or something similar. I'd always be offended by that language but was too shy to say anything. This time I decided to speak up. When my turn came, I shared I was there for healing, to work on my symptoms, and get to their root cause. And I was NOT there to get high. I also added that using phrases like "getting high" was offensive because we're not getting high, we're trying to heal or grow. So, on that note, I reminded everyone that we should be mindful of our language.

Then, I drank my 'potion' and went in. Only a little while later, my last words kept returning to me. Then, all the sudden, I saw myself as if I were watching a movie, telling people not to use the word "high." I started laughing uncontrollably. I found myself to be ridiculous and absurd, demanding that people not express themselves because I was offended.

Report continues on next page

Seriously?! Who was I to tell people what to say? And to declare that word as off-limits? Since when did I become the authority on language? All these questions made me laugh harder and harder, and while others were crying, I couldn't stop giggling. I laughed for six hours straight, at myself and at the absurdity of my self-righteousness. I had the privilege to see a movie montage of all the times and places when "I knew better" than others or when I was telling people what I thought they should think, or how to be. I couldn't believe I did and said all those things. Each time I remembered sharing another "wisdom," I thought of myself as Big Bang Theory's Sheldon. I was the funniest character in the TV show of my life. I was embarrassed and humbled. The Shaman, who was used to me crying for six hours, came to check on me, asking if I was OK, and I just said, "Oh yes! This medicine is so humbling. I'm not crying. I just can't stop laughing at myself."

Not only was this medicine showing me my own lack of awareness, it also made me realize how privileged I am and how I'm no better than other people. I realized too that no matter what people say, we're all wanting to heal from our pain, fear, or trauma. Some people just aren't as privileged to be doing it in a supervised and safe setting. Others are doing it in dark alleys, without proper support, and nobody to help them integrate. Beforehand, I knew that intellectually, but then I experienced it in the most profound and humbling way. We're all the same. We're all just trying to heal, feel better, and find meaning in our lives. It's that simple. Before this journey, I had an insidious judgmental attitude that existed outside my awareness. Like other kinds of hidden privilege, we often don't realize we have it, but once we do, then the so-called "real work" can truly begin.

—Kat, Age 44

Note. This account and all others in the book are de-identified and anonymous to protect the confidentiality of the person sharing their story. Minor grammar, spelling and stylistic changes were made and usually in partnership with the person providing the account.

Meditation 7.1
Infusing Meaning & Meaninglessness (10-15 min)

Read this script to understand how this meditation works. You can explore your backyard or another safe location, ideally in nature and without the distractions of others. Keep your eyes open for the majority of this meditation, but if it feels right, you can close your eyes when resting in place or if you want additional time for internal reflection.

Start in an upright position. Then, gently close your eyes, and settle into your breath. Ride the waves of each in-breath before it crests and then gently subsides as you breathe out. Continue this focus for a few cycles….Settle into your body. Anchor yourself to your present experience…

Slowly open your eyes. Take in the world around you. Breath in the air, notice any smells. Hear the various sounds. Feel the temperature of the air and the place where your body touches the Earth…

Scan your surroundings for an object that catches your eye. It could be a flower, a stone, a branch, or any other part of nature or your surroundings. If possible, touch the object or pick it up. Experience the object in whatever ways makes sense right now…Focus on this object of your attention, which you've arbitrarily chosen, and imagine it as a symbol of transcendent beauty and perfection. It is exactly as it should be and belongs to the mysterious source of all that was, is, and will be…Imbue it with profound meaning. It has become the most important thing to you in this moment as it represents—or more accurately, as it is your connection to this source of all things…Take several breaths as you fully engage with this experience…

Gently release your gaze on this object of transcendent meaning…Turn in another direction and look for an object as mundane and ordinary as can be found…something that seems as empty as this other object seemed sacred… After you've found this object, whatever it may be, take it into your sensory experience as mindfully as you did the previous object…what do you notice about it? What details emerge as you gaze upon it? What's its texture? Does it have a smell? Imagine this object represents meaninglessness. It is the arbitrary, accidental, or chaotic aspects of existence itself. Imbue this object with your feelings about uncertainty and the difficult realities of life and the world…Look deeply upon this symbol of meaninglessness….

Now pause and realize how you've given it meaning by simply judging it as ordinary or ugly. And then given it further meaning by imagining it as a transcendent symbol of the apparently obscene aspects of our world. What once was meaningless, now is anything but….In understanding this irony, what does this object mean to you now?….What does it symbolize? Or has it returned to its earlier state, empty of all meaning, interpretation, and judgment—that is, as it was before you entered its world?…

If you can observe or touch both objects, do so now. If not, close your eyes and contacting both objects. Imagine each object in its most transcendent meaningful form and experience the totality of both simultaneously….What is this experience like?…

Now imagine each object as simply being an object, without assigning any meaning or value judgment…Observe or experience each as it is in its purest form, not symbolizing or meaning anything at all….What is this experience like?…

Take a few deep breaths now. Imagine that on the in-breath you take in all meaning, symbolic or otherwise, from both objects. On the out-breath you release the meaning each object held and let them exist freely in the world, as they are….Take a few more breaths…and then slowly center yourself in the present…take in all your surroundings…and feel firmly grounded again in the world.

Exercise 7.1

The Values Card Sort

The following exercise is intended to uncover your deepest held personal values. It can be part of the initial method of uncovering or clarifying your values or part of a continual process of revisiting values that guide your life and inform your personal sense of meaning. To prepare the card sort, cut out each card from the printed list of values.

Step 1: With the full deck in hand, go through the deck one card at a time, separating each into one of two piles: **Important to Me** and **Less Important to Me.** Importance is gauged on your personal, intuitive sense. To the extent possible, try not to base your choices on what others think or whether you believe other people should also have these same values.

- Remind yourself that no one is evaluating your choices as 'good' or 'bad.' Placing a card in the *Less Important* pile doesn't mean it's unimportant or that you act opposite of that value. For example, placing the 'Honesty' card in the *Less Important* pile doesn't mean you're dishonest. You're merely seeking to discover values that resonate deeply with you personally.

- Sort the cards relatively quickly on this first pass. Go with your 'first instinct' or 'gut reaction.' You don't want to labor extensively over each choice. If uncertain, you can default to putting the card in the *Important* pile since you'll be reviewing these cards again.

- After finishing this first round, set aside the *Less Important* pile of cards.

Step 2: Take the **Important to Me** group of cards and sort them into three categories: **Incredibly Important, Very Important,** and **Somewhat Important.**

- If you have 5 or more cards in the *Incredibly Important* pile, set aside the other two piles.

- If you have fewer than 5 cards in the *Incredibly Important* pile, add the set of *Very Important* cards and put aside the *Somewhat Important* pile.

Step 3: Repeat this process of making more fine-grained choices until you've narrowed your values to your Top 5. Use **Form 7.1 "My Personal Values"** to record your Top 5.

- Reflect on each value for a moment. You may consider its meaning, associations that come to mind, or example behaviors tied to that value.

- Circle your Top 2 values. Then, if you can, star your top value out of these two.

Step 4: Read and reflect on the following statement.

"If my values get out of balance, I'll likely feel imbalanced too. It's okay to consider if I've left some behind, ignored a few for the sake of trying to feel better, or neglected some while overfocusing on others. No matter my current situation, or the past, I can always realign my life with my deepest values. I can start wherever I'm at and move forward in a way that feels true to me. I know that discovering and living my values is a life-long journey."

Step 5: Continue to reflect on your list of top values and consider using the **Experiential Explorer** (Worksheet 4.1) to record situations where you expressed one or more values or experienced something connected to your values. In time, you may also consider discussing your top values with your significant other, friends, or family, and share this activity for them to complete as well.

Exercise continues on next page

Nurturing	Loyalty
Kindness	Justice
Freedom	Honor
Grace	Fun
Empathy	Discovery
Reliability	Adventure
Courage	Connection
Passion	Surrender
Safety	Growth
Openness	Equanimity

Faith	Dependability
Humor	Understanding
Respect	Knowledge
Vitality	Tradition
Compassion	Service
Trust	Honesty
Learning	Love
Integrity	Support
Gratitude	Truth
Creativity	Patience

Exercise continues on next page

Playfulness	Authenticity
Curiosity	Spirituality
Acceptance	Clarity
Insight	Perceptiveness
Flexibility	Pleasure
Presence	Responsibility
Beauty	Unity
Spontaneity	Benevolence
Uniqueness	Harmony
Complexity	Elegance

Autonomy	Privacy
Awareness	Expansion
Sophistication	Cooperation
Comfort	Reciprocity
Enjoyment	Entertainment
Humility	Wisdom
Hope	Completion
Simplicity	Balance
Discernment	Focus
Perseverance	Ingenuity

Exercise continues on next page

Novelty	Fairness
Leadership	Ease
Forgiveness	Wonder
Mercy	Rationality

Note. This exercise has been adapted from the individual and group psychotherapy versions created by Ortigo & Walser (2012) at the National Center for PTSD. In my current adaptation, value words were derived independently and then supplemented by compiling multiple sources, such as Maslow's (1971) descriptions of metaneeds/metavalues enhanced by peak experiences (p. 102) and Peterson and Seligman's (2004) review of character strengths and virtues.

Form 7.1

My Personal Values—Sources of Meaning & Purpose

Instructions. Write your top five values in any order below. Then describe what each means to you personally, not their dictionary definition. After doing so, check the boxes next to the domains of your life where you feel you're currently expressing each value. The *Relationships* domain refers to all kinds, from romantic partners, family, and friendships to perhaps even strangers. The *Towards Self* domain is how that value is directed inwards. The *Work* domain encapsulates how the value applies to your professional career or work life. And, the *Leisure* domain is the expression of the value in situations involving hobbies, activities, and creative works. It's okay to have some or all boxes left unchecked. That doesn't mean the value is unimportant, just that you have many opportunities to expand your expression of it moving forward.

Top Five Important Values   **Present Domains of Expression**

Value _____

☐ Relationships   ☐ Work
☐ Towards Self   ☐ Leisure

To me, this value represents _____

Value _____

☐ Relationships   ☐ Work
☐ Towards Self   ☐ Leisure

To me, this value represents _____

Value _____

☐ Relationships   ☐ Work
☐ Towards Self   ☐ Leisure

To me, this value represents _____

Value _____

☐ Relationships   ☐ Work
☐ Towards Self   ☐ Leisure

To me, this value represents _____

Value _____

☐ Relationships   ☐ Work
☐ Towards Self   ☐ Leisure

To me, this value represents _____

Exercise 7.2

Oracle Card Reflections—Belief, Doubt, & Application

Instructions

Step 1: Select an Oracle Card Deck.

If you already have access to a deck, there's no need to purchase a new one. Recommended decks, however, include:

The Hero's Journey Dream Oracle by Kelly Sullivan Walden with artwork by Rassouli (2018)

Mystical Shaman Oracle Deck and Guidebook by Alberto Villoldo, Collette Baron-Reid, & Marcela Lobos with illustrations by Jena DellaGrottaglia (2018)

The Spirit Animal Oracle by Colette Baron-Reid with illustrations by Jena DellaGrottaglia (2018)

A Yogic Path Oracle Card Deck and Guidebook by Sahara Rose with artwork by Danielle Noel (2019)

Step 2: Shuffle the deck and draw a card.

You can pick from the top or hover your hands above a spread-out deck and pick based on your intuition.

> **Optional.** Ask a question for the card to 'answer.'

Step 3: View the card and notice any initial reactions.

Before you look up the card's meaning in the guidebook, sit with your own initial reactions and observe them across the four modes as relevant—thought, emotion, body, and behavior.

Step 4: Read the card's meaning from the guidebook.

Find the page in the guidebook corresponding to the card you drew. If the guidebook includes positive and cautionary interpretations, read both.

Step 5: Imagine this card holds a 'real,' meaningful message for you. Reflect on the card's meaning as applied to your life.

Ask yourself the following questions: How does this card apply to my life? What would I do differently if this card were highlighting something genuine and true? What is the value of having drawn this card now?

> **Note.** If the card has multiple interpretations, consider each as applied to your life.

Step 6: Imagine this card has elements that do not apply to your life, either because they're meaningless or could be misinterpreted. Reflect on these aspects of the card.

Ask yourself the following questions: How does this card not apply? If I tried to apply these less meaningful elements to my life as if they were meaningful, what would I do differently? What are the risks of ascribing personal meaning to this card where none exists?

> **Note.** You might interpret the meaningless aspects of the oracle card as being due to the randomness of the card drawing process itself or due to the irrelevant elements of this card's interpretation from the guidebook.

Step 7: Review the parts of the card that might hold meaning and parts that do not. Reflect on the meaning or lack of meaning in this card drawing and interpretation process.

If you believe oracle card readings are random and meaningless, ask yourself: Could the meaning I applied to this card still be valid? Or is it meaningless because I believe the oracle card reading process itself is meaningless?

If you believe oracle card readings are divinations, ask yourself: What risks are there in interpreting oracle cards? What are some dangers in trying to apply their meaning to my life?

The Final Arc: Integrating the Endless Possibilities of the Self & Beyond

> You don't need to be extraordinary. If the world is to be healed through human efforts, I am convinced it will be by ordinary people, people whose love for this life is even greater than their fear. People who can open to the web of life that called us into being, and who can rest in the vitality of that larger body.
>
> —Joanna Macy[1]

You've done it! You faced the trials of initiation and discovered various boons and personal insights as your reward. Although congratulations are in order, we mustn't stop here. The hero's journey doesn't end with passing the trials and gaining new insights and symbolic powers. Initiation into a new existence isn't the real point either. The Return is. Returning to our everyday world gives us an opportunity to share newfound insights and gifts with others. These gifts may come in the form of providing crucial services to the larger community or a subset of it — like the wise village elder who teaches some promising youth the secrets of their craft. A beautiful spiritual example comes from the idea of the Bodhisattva in Buddhism. The Bodhisattva experiences enlightenment and can reach nirvana. But instead of staying in that state, free from suffering, they return to the material world and spread their knowledge so that others may also awaken. If the hero stopped after passing the trials, then the journey would end in failure. Joseph Campbell called this form of the hero's fall as The Refusal of Return. It was one of many ways heroes could fail their quest, and it often led to the ruin not only of their community but also of the heroes themselves.

One version of this failed return is in the 1933 novel *Lost Horizon*. Its protagonist, the British diplomat Conrad, becomes stranded after his hijacked plane takes him to the mystical land of Shangri-La, a heavenly abode nestled in the high mountains of Tibet. By the book's conclusion, after escaping, Conrad second-guesses his decision to leave and then wastes his remaining life in obscurity, obsessed with returning to the sacred land while abandoning his original world. This ending was deemed 'too dark' for the 1937 American film adaptation, which reworked it to see Conrad successfully finding his way back to Shangri-La. Either way, Conrad ultimately failed his hero's journey. He couldn't re-integrate into his own culture and share the wisdom gained from entering this other realm. Like Shangri-La, a psychedelic journey can open vistas of rapture, love, and peace. The point, though, isn't to linger indefinitely in such states or ceaselessly chase the peak of the psychedelic summit. It's to use your newfound knowledge and insights in everyday life—and if you want to become a true hero, to better society as a whole. The hero's ambition is for others, not for their own desires.

Modern film also makes clear this message of responsibility. Think of our friendly neighborhood Spider-Man's mantra: With great power, comes great responsibility. We may not have superpowers, but when we gain insights and heal from personal afflictions and conflicts, we gain a new level of responsibility. This responsibility often lies in using our knowledge and experiences for the greater good. Not with arrogance or for praise, but with authentic humility and compassion. A less pithy version of Spider-Man's famous refrain might better suit us: With greater awareness and insight, comes greater freedom and thus responsibility to make the right choices for ourselves and our fellow beings.

The weight of responsibility can sometimes feel overwhelming. Having increased your awareness and faced your own existential trials, you, like the hero of old, are ready to return and embrace your next tasks. The trials you've now passed will become sources of strength and building blocks for the important work yet to come. The existential themes of impermanence, interconnectedness, and meaning remain relevant. These themes along with your other personal insights will inform your choices moving forward. Meaning must be lived, not espoused. Our journey's final arc is about moving into 'the farther reaches of human nature,' as psychologist Abraham Maslow calls it. In the world of psychedelics, this focus best parallels the continual phase of integration—what happens after a psychedelic, mystical, or other state of expanded consciousness.

Thus, Arc 3 focuses on how to return, re-integrate into the world, and move beyond past limitations while accepting responsibility to both yourself and your broader community. Of course, keep in mind that many of these themes, like before, depend on what world, culture, and community to which you're returning. That's where your personal reflections become even more critical. As in the two prior arcs, we have three themes to explore:

Chapter	Journey Waypoint	Theme / Title
Ch 8	Waypoint VII	Beyond Personal Identity—Towards an Integrated, Flexible Self
Ch 9	Waypoint VIII	Beyond Shadow Projection—Towards the Wisdom of Compassion
Ch 10	Waypoint IX	Beyond the Narrow Life—Towards a Life of Creative Engagement and Renewed Heroism

Like all previous themes, these topics are ambitious, yet I'm more confident than ever that you have all you need to continue your path of growth.

I hear this word of caution, though. Besides the refusal of return, another risk remains—a lack of sustained humility. When some individuals complete an initiation, have a mystical psychedelic experience, or reconnect to significant inner sources of strength and purpose, they can sometimes get ahead of themselves. A sense of grandiosity and overconfidence may be a temporary side effect of especially profound and sudden apotheosis. The humility you've fostered before and throughout the trials stays relevant. As such, when entering this final arc, it's crucial to consider the risk of a *Hero Complex*—overidentifying with the heroic archetype or viewing oneself as *The* Hero, the sole savior of everyone else. Within the psychedelic world, the parallel lies in the person who after their first powerful journey, suddenly proclaims themselves to be a messiah or a 'shaman.' That actually happens. It's a variation of spiritual bypass, a phenomenon in which a person ignores or tries to sidestep the harder aspects of personal growth or the painful parts of human experience.

Offering this caution isn't to diminish any insights or gifts you've discovered. It's simply to remind us all to employ our gifts while staying grounded. Throughout life, we all can continue to grow. There are just too many mysteries and possibilities out there to ever truly master or understand. It's wise to embrace an attitude of 'not knowing' while you continue to search for insights and attempt to apply them. Even as we grow, we remain all too human. Therefore, the two cautions are: 1) refusing the return by failing to integrate insights or accept greater responsibility, and 2) becoming overconfident and proselytizing as a 'Hero' above all others.

Invoking Your Next Ally

Remember, we're not alone in this journey. Others join us as allies, companions, and teachers, and our final arc is no different. We're now ready to meet our third and final ally. When considering potential allies, curiosity and acceptance were natural, intuitive choices for our first two arcs. For this final one, though, so many qualities and attitudes could aid us. Humility, flexibility, compassion, and responsibility were all contenders, and certainly these themes are critical. But despite each being important, they don't quite capture the overarching theme. Our ally here needs to be even more multifaceted than acceptance and more profound than curiosity.

While contemplating these qualities, an epiphany struck. I realized each one is a facet belonging to our greatest ally—*Wisdom*. Wisdom, after all, involves not only knowledge and insights, but also the ability to use them in myriad ways. Not just learning from past experiences, but also discerning how best to approach the present so that we can create a worthwhile future. Of course, true wisdom requires humility to acknowledge our limits in the face of baffling mysteries and forces out of our control. And yet within our sphere of influence, wisdom means embracing our personal agency and power. In these moments, true wisdom comes from accepting responsibility and offering to ourselves and others what we have to give.

Before I too fall victim to proselytizing, though, let's pause and let your own unfolding experience speak for itself. Like our previous allies, we benefit from having a personal image or token to represent the abstract quality of wisdom. Keep your allies of curiosity and acceptance, along with their images and any other symbols. We're adding to these resources, not replacing them. Each still has a role to play. To imbue your new ally with even greater personal relevance, take a moment to select and visualize yet another person in your life or fictional character who signifies wisdom. A wise person garners trust. They share their council for any who are willing to take it to heart. Imagine what this person looks like for you and fill their image with as much detail as you can muster. Create a complete version of this character and imbue them with life. Recall their image as you learn to embrace your own wisdom.

Bring with you, too, another physical token connected either to your personified ally or as a reminder to contact the resource of wisdom. Your token can take many shapes and forms. They might be like your others for curiosity and acceptance. Or, they could be completely different but complementary—stones, figures, jewelry, fabric, candles, and so on. The options are infinite, like the ways cultivating wisdom can serve us throughout our lives. Your external token for this ally and personified image of the same can trigger your own internal resources allowing you to find your path within the dense jungles of life in all its limitless complexity.

Reaffirming Your Intentions

As we've done at the outset of each prior arc, it's time to revisit your intentions, update them, and consider any others that apply to our journey's final leg. You likely have a good handle on your progress so far. For intentions you've already satisfied, consider whether facets remain yet to be explored. In our last arc's investigation into the existential underworld, you might have discovered things you hadn't considered before. New or reimagined intentions are always welcome too.

As I begin integrating my insights and putting them into practice, my intentions are to...

CHAPTER 8

Beyond Personal Identity—
Towards an Integrated, Flexible Self

"We forget all too soon the things we thought we could never forget. We forget the loves and the betrayals alike, forget what we whispered and what we screamed, forget who we were. I have already lost touch with a couple of people I used to be…"

—Joan Didion, *Slouching Towards Bethlehem*[1]

Journey Waypoint VII

By landing here, you can rest assured you've succeeded in perhaps the toughest part of your journey. You've weathered the trials and explored some fundamental mysteries about the human experience. The insights you've gained may still be evolving, but your journey continues. Just as with psychedelics, the work doesn't end after the 'medicine' wears off. In fact, many dedicated psychonauts believe the next phase is where it's all at. How do we make sense of the strange, beautiful, or transcendent experiences we've had? How do we return home and make dinner, do the dishes, and brush our teeth after staring into the depths of the cosmos, ourselves, and our fellow living beings? The previous chapters undoubtedly felt like deep work, and to be sure, they were. But here we push further, seeking to bring burgeoning insights into a new world and a new you. In the words of the *Tibetan Book of the Dead*, you're entering the final bardo state of re-emergence. The critical task is choosing the 'new' life you want to live, one governed by your personal values, not your previously existing habits of mind and behavior that do not serve your greater sense of purpose.

As it is for anyone who has had a profound experience, the question for us is one of integration. What do we want to bring back with us? And how do we integrate these experiences into our everyday life? To start answering these questions, we'll revisit some themes from earlier waypoints that offer clues about integration. In our first arc, as you prepared for the trials, you became more aware of your existing personality and characteristic defense mechanisms. Now, we're looking beyond that status quo. Instead of describing what has existed before, we're moving to a more complex, sophisticated understanding of who you are and who you can become. These newer reflections can help you not only integrate the insights you've gained along the way, but also set you up for more adventures to come.

Rest assured, as Campbell described, the attainment of the ultimate boon or insight "is always scaled to [the hero's] stature and to the nature of [their] dominant desire: the boon is simply a symbol of life energy stepped down to the requirements of a certain specific case."[2] In other words, you've received only as much as you need and are capable of putting into practice at this time.

Self-Reflections Check-In

Before we dive into our journey's final arc, let's reflect and check-in. The last chapter completed the existential trials by exploring the search for meaning in a complex, incomprehensible universe. You used all your growing awareness and insight to discover your deeply held personal values and create meaning through your attitudes, experiences, and actions. You balanced the humility of not knowing what is meaningful at the largest cosmic scale with the centeredness of having intuitively derived sources of personal meaning—meaning that despite it all, meaning still somehow exists. What did you choose to do after the last chapter? What elements of personal meaning did you reassert? Which did you newly discover? Keep these values in mind as the remaining journey will weave them into the fabric of your life and the world around you.

Our Friend, the Ego—
The Necessity of Defense Mechanisms & Identity

Moving beyond our typical ego strategies and personal identity may be this chapter's theme, but before we can do that, we should stop to appreciate what they give us in our lives. Integrating a new understanding of ourselves still involves our ego. For all the talk psychedelic 'ego death' gets, it may seem the ego is the enemy. Tyrannical egos exist, for sure, but in general, our egos are doing the best they can with the knowledge and resources they have available. Its toolbox of learned defense mechanisms assists us in coping with a challenging outer world and complex inner one. Alongside these handy defense mechanisms, the other important function of the ego is the creation and maintenance of a personal identity. An identity helps us understand who we are as individuals, what our roles are in society, and how we compare to others. It's prudent, then, for us to go forward, as always, with mindful awareness, respect, and clear intentions. Before deconstructing our ego and personal identity, let's consider their benefits. Doing so will help us discover what to keep as we move beyond their limitations.

Navigating Multiple Realities

Despite what we've heard from some intrepid psychonauts, the ego is generally a close ally. As you learned in the trial of death and impermanence, chasing 'ego death' can backfire by becoming either a compulsive distraction or a dangerous counterphobic defense against existential dread. An ego is necessary to function within our shared physical and social realities. One of its most critical tasks is to balance our conscious and unconscious motivations with our external, consensus reality.[3] 'Reality' may be a misnomer, though. The world is infinitely complex and can be quite confusing to our limited human minds and personal perspectives. Not everyone agrees on even seemingly mundane aspects of reality—from the number of spatial dimensions to the proper method of mounting toilet paper.[4] Reality, no matter how we understand it, can be overwhelming. It's hard to be aware of the utterly unfathomable expansiveness of the 'known' universe and its mysteries while also trying to deal with modern-day minutia.

As a result, to reuse Aldous Huxley's turn of phrase, our ego's "reducing valve" helps us manage a complex reality.[5] Restricting our awareness to a manageable slice of reality is equally as important as keeping unsavory feelings, thoughts, and motivations outside our conscious awareness. By focusing on the most relevant information in each moment, the ego helps us survive. For our ancient ancestors, that's quite literally what it needed to do on a regular basis. 'Reality' in the ancient past was made especially simple. Notice threats, avoid them, or deal with them if forced to do so. Living in a tribe helped with noticing and dealing with physical threats. It also added new layers of complexity. Our egos had to factor in threats to social belonging and status. If they didn't, they'd risk exclusion, which for our not-so-distant predecessors was also a question of survival.

Our modern world, though, makes biological and social realities much less straightforward. It's not about the tiger nearby ready to pounce—not usually at least—or about our small, tight-knit tribe judging whether we're an asset or liability. In facing 'reality,' our egos must factor in what countless others do, too. These beliefs are largely bound by culture. In our multicultural world, linked through technology and globalization, our egos must cope with multiple 'realities' that appear to exist simultaneously. That's a lot for any ego to manage. Of course, it can take the much easier approach and outright reject many, if not all, competing 'realities.'[6]

To navigate these complex realities, we must understand both ourselves as individuals and our larger social context. This understanding largely involves our personal identity. Identity encompasses our outwardly portrayed persona, but it's much broader. It's who we think we *are*, not just the masks we wear for others. A personal identity provides consistency. It forms a narrative around how we've remained the same even as things change over time. Our adolescent years anchor our identity with stronger roots, but we're free to revisit earlier conclusions at any point in life. Significant loss, social rejection, growing doubt, or difficult life transitions can all trigger an existential crisis of identity. Crises aren't the only way to grow beyond outdated identities. Throughout this journey, you've been intentionally asking questions about yourself. That's not to say you've never dealt with any losses, doubts, or changes. These experiences are part of the normal human life course. That's why we faced them in the trials of initiation. That act of courage equipped you with a greater capacity for the next step, expanding your identity and sense of self.

Although personal identity is largely about our individuality, our social context plays a critical role throughout life. As you know from our second trial, we're all interconnected and possess the human need for attachment and belonging. From the first moments of forming an identity, we compare ourselves and make conclusions based on similarities and differences with others. Are we more outgoing? More adventurous or more cautious? Friendlier or argumentative? Receiving direct feedback can be especially potent. Earlier in life, we're more open to incorporating feedback from influential people like our parents or friends. We receive feedback, though, throughout life. It's given at the workplace, within intimate relationships, and in therapy. Over time, we gain numerous labels for ourselves and others. These labels can have a life of their own and can convert into self-fulfilling prophecies.

These social influences are embedded within our larger culture and society. Our broader community shapes both what's most salient about ourselves and what's most valued. People in relatively homogenous communities may ignore what they share—like language, broader racial identity, ethnicity, and/or religion—and highlight differences in interests, occupation, personality, or political ideology. Of course, rapid globalization has changed things here too. We're no longer ignorant of how people from other cultures differ from us, even in our basic understanding of 'reality.' Our interconnected, multicultural planet has forced everyone to confront these differences, with both inspirational and sometimes far-reaching consequences.

A Brief Summary

The ego protects us from biological, social, and psychological dangers it perceives in our external reality. The characteristic ways it learns to do so shape our personality. Over time, we learn to understand ourselves by developing an identity. This identity itself is embedded within a larger social context. The reality is that personality, identity, and social surroundings all continuously interact and affect our patterns of relating to ourselves and others. Our ego defenses and identities partner in managing the complexity of these interacting factors. They make meaning out of our experiences and create narratives to help us understand them. These narratives are never completely accurate. They're limited by our ego's 'reducing valve' and by complex social influences. Nevertheless, they create order out of apparent chaos. Our sense of self must respond to pressures from social comparison, interpersonal feedback, and cultural expectations. All imbue our individual identities with greater relevance and richer descriptions. At its best, a personal identity gifts us a stable, continuous feeling of individuality and social belonging. Achieving a more complex understanding of ourselves may help us, in turn, navigate the complexities of the world.

The Trappings of the Ego & Constraints of Identity— Rigid Control vs. Psychological Flexibility

Many aspects of our everyday ego and identity can be deconstructed, deemphasized, or transcended within powerful psychedelic states of consciousness—predominantly through so-called 'ego death' experiences. Given the advantages the ego bestows, why would anyone benefit from its temporary metaphorical demise? What happens during psychedelic-induced ego death is, in part, a downregulation of our brain's *default mode network*. This complex network of brain regions is active when we're at rest, daydreaming, self-reflecting, remembering the past, or thinking about the future. To call the default mode network the neurological analogue of the ego is a bit simplistic, but certainly some of its key features are present here—including our typical sense of personal identity.

Although having a sufficiently strong ego and a solid identity are markers of psychological health, too much of a good thing has its costs. If an ego's too rigid and narrow, it cannot adapt easily to the complexities of a diverse world constantly in flux—a la our trial themes of impermanence, interconnectedness, and ambiguity of meaning. Less mature defense mechanisms like denial and projection can cause problems, for sure, but so can more sophisticated ones if we have only a limited range in our toolbox. Even a good sense of humor has its limits if not paired with other possibilities. Even with a variety of tools available, it's a problem to try relentlessly to control what we're really feeling or thinking.[8] Throwing everything we can at some psychological pain is a natural impulse if we fear becoming overwhelmed. In the lingo of internal family systems therapy, this is the key strategy of our inner firefighter—the part that comes out to help us escape immediate pain no matter the long-term consequences. The mindful awareness tools across the four modes are antidotes to this kind of experiential avoidance. Pure mindfulness is being present to what's occurring naturally, without impulsive reactivity or intervention.

Pragmatically speaking, the problem of psychological control is twofold. First, it's not always, and possibly never ultimately, effective at reducing our suffering. Whatever's suppressed eventually finds new opportunities to surface. Painful emotions often tell us something important about our current situation, life circumstances, or some loss we're ignoring to the detriment of ourselves and possibly others. Second, it distracts us from living our life, acting in the outside world, and expressing our core values.

In these ways, an ego that tries to control too much actually can create more suffering. Some therapists use the metaphor of a Chinese finger trap puzzle.[9] The more we try to forcefully pull our fingers out of the trap, the harder it is to set ourselves free. Instead, we must relax and push our fingers together, towards the trap's center, to release ourselves slowly. To alleviate psychological pain, sometimes we need to stop resisting and go into it. In other words, per our psychedelic mantra, go 'in and through.'

What about our personal identity? It too, if held tightly, can unnecessarily restrict our options for interacting with the world around us and adapting to change. Even expected life transitions can highlight the problems of a narrow identity, such as: The overzealous person who dedicated their life to work and then must retire; the committed parent who battles 'empty nest syndrome' after their last teenager leaves home; the professional athlete who's injured and can no longer play; the soldier who finds themselves lost after returning to a community unaware of the true horrors of war. Indeed, these transitions can be hard. But they don't need to be devastating. If we foster intimate relationships, maintain hobbies outside of work or school, and access numerous sources of purpose and belonging, we can face transitions with relative ease and possibly excitement.

A rigid identity or outward persona can cause problems for people of all ages. What is it like for the fledgling social media star who skyrockets to millions of viewers on their YouTube channel at the tender age of 19? Their whole life could easily become swept up in this unexpected role of being an 'influencer.' They might become overidentified with their public persona and lose touch with their deeper authentic self. If so, as they get older, they begin suspecting they've missed an opportunity to become a concert pianist—an early childhood dream. Instead of pursuing this dream, they ignore it and recommit to filming uninspired content. Only years later after declining viewership do they experience the powerful regret evoked from recognizing their unfulfilled potential. Their 'YouTube star' identity, despite initial success, prevented them from becoming something else. This example might appear dramatic, but even in small ways, tightly held identities limit our options for dealing with the present and the future. As our digitized egos and personas become larger and more curated, they become further removed from our authentic selves.

A balance must exist in accessing the benefits of a solid identity and ego while mitigating the downsides of overly constrictive ones. This balance is largely about *psychological flexibility*.[10] In fact, increases in psychological flexibility might explain how psychedelic experiences lead to decreases in depression and anxiety.[11] Flexibility means adapting to changing circumstances, needs, and information. It requires embracing our agency and freedom—radical freedom even—to make choices more aligned with our authentic needs and values, undeterred by false constraints. Every choice has consequences, to be certain. Some are predictable, some not. But, when we artificially shackle ourselves to our self-imposed identities and habitual strategies, we may sever our access to better alternatives.

As you've come to know, impermanence is an apparent feature of the universe. Everything changes, including how we define ourselves over time. Consider the roles that were once so important to you, and perhaps the prior foundations of your personal meaning. Changing circumstances can reveal our old identities no longer fit reality. We then have a choice: update our sense of self or try to change reality. The latter is impossible for things outside our control. If we hold too tightly to an identity or let our egos reign too supreme in facing changes, we might shortchange our ability to adapt more honestly and effectively. The healthiest coping strategies adapt our approach to fit the complexity of the 'real world' and offer practical coping strategies. We can adapt by revising aspects of our identity that no longer serve us. To prepare for these revisions, we need not wait. We can start now. By adopting multi-faceted, sophisticated identities, we can become flexible enough to handle the disruptions that impermanence and an increasingly complex reality would otherwise produce.

That's why we've saved this leg of the journey until now. We had to face the reality of death and impermanence, the interconnectedness of all things, and the crucial yet fraught search for meaning before we could fully embrace the next task—integrating a broader and more flexible sense of self. This task is where the rubber meets the road, where you nurture the nascent insights you've already learned while nimbly adapting to new realities as they unfold.

Identity—A Focused Brainstorming Exercise

To support self-reflections for this final arc, we'll be doing another classic psychological exercise: *focused brainstorming*. Unlike the previous arc's sentence completion task, focused brainstorming involves creating exhaustive lists of possible responses. To do this activity, jot down whatever comes to mind, making sure you have at least a few responses to each prompt. Take a moment to clear your head. Then write words or brief sentences, draw pictures or symbols, or do whatever else seems natural in response. The purpose of this first set is to explore your existing identity. We're only looking at what's most salient and important for you now. Take no more than 2-3 minutes to respond to each prompt.

I am...

I am not...

Great! You may also consider how your responses here overlap with your responses to sentence stems from our first trail in Chapter 5. The two most relevant are "The part of myself I'm most attached to is…" and "If I lost this part of myself, I'd…." Has anything changed from your responses then to your answers above? Either way, consider adding your reflections about these activities to your Travel Journal. Later, if inspired, you can expand upon these reflections and others in this chapter's optional assignments, especially Exercises 8.1 and 8.2.

Rediscovering the Self through Individuation

If a core psychological problem is rigidity and the solution is flexibility, how can we keep our ego in check while receiving its benefits? If we're too loose, we risk becoming too permeable and unanchored. Our mind may lose its individual purpose, contact with reality, and understanding of its place on Earth and in the cosmos. By now, you know I wouldn't lead us to this conundrum without a workable (if tentative) path to consider. In fact, when considering expanding self-awareness, seeds were planted long ago that we've been nurturing ever since. And they're now ready to bear fruit. As poet W. H. Auden exclaimed, "The center that I cannot find is known to my unconscious mind."[12]

This center isn't ego or identity but a much more inclusive organizing principle of all consciousness—what Jung called the archetypal *Self*. The Self represents the whole of our personality, incorporating our conscious and unconscious minds. It's the sum of all our parts and more—the center that harmonizes the complex dynamics of our psyche. When we experience the Self and its perspective of transcendent inner unity, we often notice it has a distinctively divine quality. The Self is the source of our inner healer, the cornerstone of psychedelic therapy.[13] In internal family systems therapy, the Self serves a similar function as the inner healer by demonstrating the Eight Cs—Calmness, Clarity, Curiosity, Compassion, Confidence, Courage, Creativity, and Connectedness.[14]

How does the Self differ from and address the problems of a rigid ego and narrow identity? First, the ego seeks to control and manage while the Self seeks to develop and integrate. Our first arc's focus on expanding awareness coincides with this central goal of the Self. Second, the ego has conscious and unconscious components whereas the Self contains *all* conscious and unconscious material, personal and collective. Thus, the Self includes and supersedes the ego. It's the psyche's center and its totality. As such, it's the wellspring of endless flexibility and possibility.

Back in our first chapter, when you made the choice to go on this journey, I shared the iceberg metaphor of the psyche. That model's psychedelic extension was a playful preview of the mysterious layers of the deepest Self—and a suggestion that more might exist than even the personal or collective unconscious. If the individual ego is an iceberg, then the Self would be the entire ocean with indeterminable depths remaining unexplored. Figure 8.1 updates the more technical image seen from Chapter 3. This version includes the Self and its relative position to the ego.

Whichever images or words we prefer, psychedelics, by manifesting the mind, can give people a taste of these profound inner mysteries. Yet without conscious efforts to integrate such fleeting experiences, they remain ephemeral—or worse. If not prepared for and respected, a quick taste of the boundless mysteries can be like drinking from a firehose. One can become overwhelmed by the sheer force of the unconscious. The greatest risks then are either disintegration or despair. Alternatively, even a full-blown mystical experience, with its swift dive into profundity and rapture, can lead to overconfidence in one's sudden 'enlightenment.' An overgrown ego is what we're trying to avoid. By now, it should be clear that humility is more than some moralistic dictum. It's being honest. There's so little we truly understand, as a species, much less as individuals. At the same time, according to Jung, the Self is often experienced as an inner God-like voice that demands to be heard, and the ego (meaning our everyday self) has no option but to obey.[15]

Despite these risks, Jung believed all humans over their lifespan move naturally towards the Self and greater psychological wholeness. We do so through the process of *individuation*.[16] Individuation advances our own distinctiveness, but it isn't the same as being individualistic, rebellious, or 'unique' for the sake of being unique. By its very nature, individuation creates challenges. As Maslow described as well, "We fear our highest possibilities (as well as our lowest ones). We are generally afraid to become that which we can glimpse in our most perfect moments, under the most perfect conditions, under conditions of greatest courage. We enjoy and even thrill to godlike possibilities we see in ourselves in such peak moments. And yet we simultaneously shiver with weakness, awe, and fear before these very same possibilities."[17]

Armed with deeper respect, and perhaps aided by curiosity and acceptance, you're ready for this journey's ultimate purpose: contact with the Self and its offerings of unending complexity, greater flexibility, and an infinitely expanding awareness. You've trained for this step all along, and now you can grapple with individuation in all its glory—at least intellectually. It's a

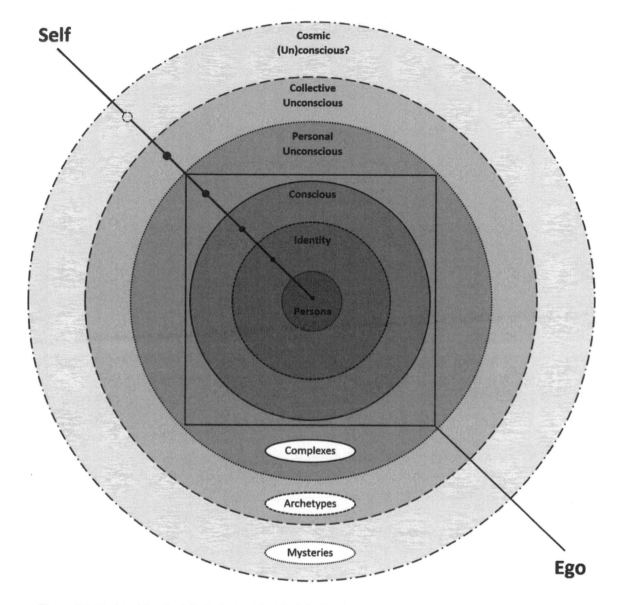

Figure 8.1 Updated Psychedelic-Inclusive Model of the Psyche

Note. The Self extends further into our unconscious than the personal ego. As a possible example of synchronicity, long after I created this figure, I learned of Jungian analyst Edward Edinger's (1960) formulation of the ego-Self axis. The axis is a metaphor for how the ego and Self require on-going communication and partnership. Edinger believed repairing any break in this axis was a central goal of Jungian analysis.

lifelong process after all. Psychedelics provide just one type of catalyst that can kindle individuation. Confronting existential trials is another. Both can connect us to the Self, but it's real work to continue that process. It requires dying to our old self—our former ego and identity—and being reborn anew. Again, and again. Being a Christian minister's son, Jung sometimes pointed to Jesus as one of many symbols for how the limited ego must perish for the Self to experience renewal.[18] You may recognize similar motifs from Gandalf in *The Lord of the Rings* and Neo in *The Matrix*.[19] Within Hinduism, the Self might correspond to the atman, essentially the enduring soul.[20]

Individuation requires two complementary approaches—the first towards separation and the second towards synthesis.[21] *Separation* is about dividing our consciousness and inner parts into pieces, analyzing them, seeing which ones are dominant and which ones less so. We engage this process when we first separate physically and psychologically from our caregivers. Separation further intensifies when we form our personal identity, usually around adolescence.

In contrast, *synthesis* is about creating an increasingly complex yet steady balance, one that surpasses the narrower personality and identity of the old self. In its later, more sophisticated forms, synthesis also entails recognizing our interconnectedness at all levels of consciousness and with the outside world. Awareness of a more complex, interconnected Self also shifts the emphasis away from our personality as static and towards understanding ourselves as a system of continuously unfolding features.[22] As Carl Rogers asserted, "A person is a fluid process, not a fixed and static entity; a flowing river of change, not a block of solid material; a continually changing constellation of potentialities, not a fixed quantity of traits."[23]

By vigilantly exploring this book and its activities, you've naturally been working through both movements of individuation. Now in this final arc, we'll concentrate on integrating your insights by:

- addressing limited aspects of your personal identity and personality
- encountering your personal shadow as well as our collective one

Both require moving beyond ego-driven constraints. This chapter emphasizes the first, but your efforts here will prepare you for the shadow work to come.

How Individuation Expands Personality

When expanding self-awareness, we focused on the Big Five personality traits. Individuation within that particular model may mean avoiding extremes on either end of a trait, or creating new adaptations to our environment.[24]

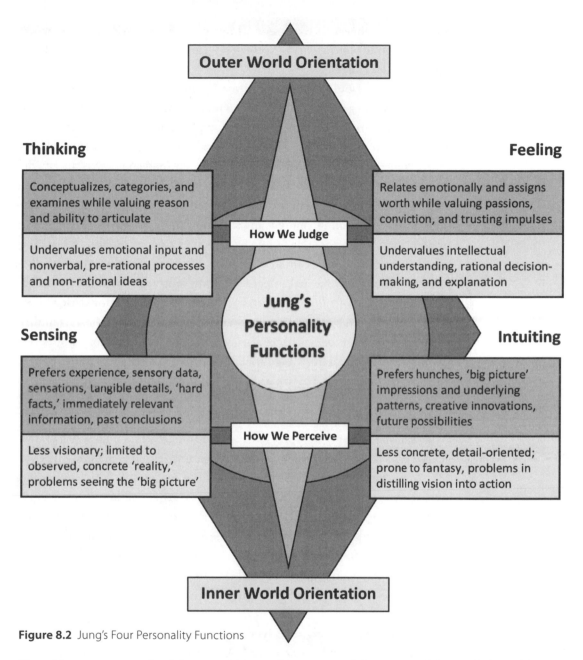

Figure 8.2 Jung's Four Personality Functions

Note. The top segment of each box provides a positive-to-neutral description of the psychological function whereas the bottom segment lists potential downsides or blindspots of each function Jung's concepts of Extroversion and Introversion are similar but distinct from the Big Five's trait domain of Extraversion. In this figure, I've focused on the psychological functions and note Extroversion-vs-Introversion as one's preferred orientation and application of these function towards the external shared world or one's inner one. See Wilmer, 2015, pp. 155-168 for a succinct overview of Jung's original personality concepts.

Increasing Openness to Experience, however, is in line with our larger aim and corresponds to the effect psychedelics can have on personality and psychological flexibility.[25]

Previously, I only briefly mentioned Jung's personality concepts and types.[26] To avoid getting bogged down with details, consider reviewing Figure 8.2's summary of Jung's major concepts, which come in oppositional pairs. The first major distinction is between a preferred orientation towards our shared 'outer world' or our own inner one—what Jung considered the key difference between Extroversion and Introversion. We'll focus instead on the four psychological functions, which can be directed outwardly or inwardly—Sensing, Intuiting, Thinking, and Feeling.[27] Out of these four, we develop habits of mind and preferences due to our basic temperaments, talents, upbringing, life circumstances, social environment, and culture. Thinking-vs-Feeling is primarily about how we make decisions, judgments, or evaluations. Sensing-vs-Intuiting is about how we perceive different types of information. Both sides of each pair have their place, but we all have strengths and biases in their use or neglect. Everyone has access to what's otherwise overlooked or undervalued—but it takes effort. Like other aspects of identity, if we overidentify with our personality 'type,' we limit the full potential of our Self.

Transcending a Limited Personality

By synthesizing opposing forces, individuation creates a balance that transcends what came before.[28] Put simply, we must explore outside our comfort zones and habits to see the value of the 'other side.' No longer can we use the excuse of identifying as an 'extroverted thinker,' for example, to avoid being alone and acknowledging the power of our own emotions. Such excuses restrict our options for adapting to changing circumstances. Addressing limitations of our personality requires the same flexibility discussed earlier. It also requires embracing paradox and dialectal opposites to form an evolving synthesis.[29] We must discover the 'both/and' to transcend the 'either/or.'

Thinking-and-Feeling. The synthesis between thinking and feeling might be what's been called the *wise mind*.[30] A wise mind state of consciousness and decision making incorporates information from both our emotional reactions and our verbal and systematic thinking processes. A wise mind doesn't overreact emotionally, nor does it ignore emotion. It doesn't overthink, nor does it shut off reason. It values insights gained through both and is therefore better equipped to make mindful, informed decisions that address various parts of ourselves, our experiences, and our values-driven intentions. The Thinking and Feeling functions overlap with two modes of experiencing. By increasing experiential awareness, you've already been implicitly assimilating these functions, and thus, accessing your wise mind.

Sensing-and-Intuiting. It may also be possible to combine the detail-minded conscious-oriented sensing function with the implicit 'big picture' mindset of intuition. This combo could look like an enhanced capacity towards *absorption*. As a trait, absorption is the degree to which a person easily gets 'caught up' in an experience, either engaging in inward imagination or outward sensory stimulation.[31] States of absorption can become all-engrossing and even transcendent, whether prompted by sudden flights of fancy or admiration of visionary art or natural beauty. Curiosity plays a role—yet another reason it's been a key ally throughout our journey. We all differ in our proclivity towards and specific triggers for becoming absorbed.

To illustrate this idea, it's helpful to consider a caricature of an absorption-prone person: an artist with an intense sense of creative appreciation. This person might, for example, become struck by the composition of a fellow painter's artwork at a gallery, staring for several minutes longer than other onlookers. They then would be able to articulate their impressions with heightened sensibility and clarity. Whereas an 'art snob' may curate a similar persona, someone who is authentically absorbed *experiences* the art with keen awareness and appreciation verging on awe. These experiences aren't exclusive to quirky personalities. They can be cultivated with practice.

Transcending through Flow

We've gathered, at this point, some clues about surpassing otherwise opposing psychological functions. Now, we're ready to explore the transcendent state of *flow*. Flow occurs when we become "so involved in an activity that nothing else seems to matter."[32] As an "experiential state," leading flow expert Mihaly Csikszentmihalyi has described flow as:[33]

> The holistic sensation present when we act with total involvement....It is the state in which action follows upon action according to an internal logic which seems to need no conscious intervention on our part. We experience it as a unified flowing from one moment to the next, in which we feel in control of our actions, and in which there is little distinction between self and environment; between stimulus and response; or between past, present, and future.

Figure 8.3 displays the typical necessary conditions of flow alongside common features of the subjective experience. The most profound varieties of flow combine elements of wise mind and absorption. We planted the seeds of flow early in our journey. Flow, by definition, encompasses all experiential modes of emotion, thought, body, and behavior. It balances a mindful, present-centered focus with an implicit awareness of relevant insights from the past and a vision for the immediate future, often guided by our underlying values and innate curiosity. Despite typically involving an eventual goal, a person experiencing flow loses themselves to the tasks at hand while simultaneously feeling calm and alert.

These states are usually enjoyable, but the situation that provokes flow may itself be tense. As a modern film example, consider the scene in *Star Wars: The Rise of Skywalker* in which Rey, on foot, prepares to confront Kylo Ren as he speeds towards her in his TIE-fighter on Kijimi.[34] In the film *Hidden Figures*, NASA scientist Katherine Johnson enters an intense flow state when needing to confirm complex mathematical calculations to ensure astronaut John Glenn's safety during America's first orbital spaceflight.[35]

How about a real-world example too? Athletes may enter flow states when they feel 'on fire.' After months of training, a runner experiences flow when finding their groove on the day of their race, noticing how their heartrate matches the beats of their footsteps, enjoying the beautiful scenery along their path, and keeping a steady pace until crossing the finish line.

The role of thoughts, emotions, body, and behavior are probably obvious in this example. Another, more hidden factor here might be intuition. Intuition comes into flow states because of the need to respond quickly—almost automatically—to changing variables, often through creative problem-solving. It requires attunement to unseen patterns below the surface of sensory inputs, conscious emotions, and explicit thinking strategies. This attunement and creative problem-solving allow increasingly complex layers of strategy and interconnection. The marathon runner knows the race will inevitably involve unforeseen challenges. Instead of ignoring this possibility, they train in diverse terrain and weather conditions, which prepares them to adapt on the day of the race. They learn about possible injuries and strategies to address them without giving up. In the middle of the marathon, they know their sudden left knee pain isn't just a nuisance to ignore; it's a signal to fix their stride and shift their weight. Adaptation entails both past preparation and present attunement, including awareness of sensory inputs as they change moment-to-moment.

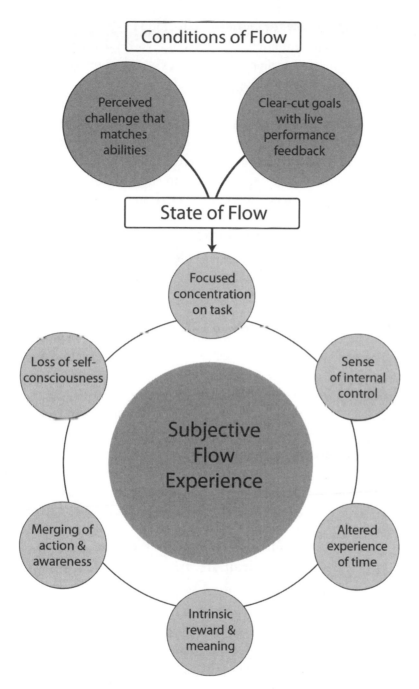

Figure 8.3 Conditions and Qualities of Flow States

Note. Content of this figure is based on Nakamura & Csikszentmihalyi (2011), p. 195-196.

For these reasons, flow requires an adaptive form of absorption that brings together sensation and intuition. Moreover, it involves the same wise mind balance of thinking and feeling. Simultaneous access to internally derived emotions and thoughts aid the engagement of an externally directed creative process. Thus, the true potential of flow lies in the synthesis of sensing, intuiting, thinking, and feeling and its flexibility in navigating inner and outer worlds. When it happens, it's quite powerful. No one, however, can be 'in the flow' all the time. Even so, exploring neglected fragments of our personality and experience arms us with more options to engage in our life. Realizing more options allows us to attain greater freedom and flexibility.

Concluding with a Word of Caution

Given the above, the ideal personality might be summarized as follows: A flexible, open-minded person who uses their wise mind and enters absorbed, flow states of consciousness with ease. Yes, that sounds pretty great. Even having that ideal, though, can cause problems. It can become just another identity, and an unrealistic one at that—one that doesn't allow other normal or less idealized human experiences.[36] We all become imbalanced occasionally, and during times of stress, maybe frequently. That's just being human. Idealizing some 'optimized' personality and chasing flow states gives us something to judge ourselves (and others) against. Becoming either too self-conscious or too self-centered are, in fact, big barriers to entering flow; an overconcern with oneself redirects energy away from present experiences and tasks.[37] Becoming judgmental or self-critical are bigger topics for the next chapter. For now, just try to be mindful, flexible, and in touch with your deepest values. And, recognize when judgments about falling short of an ideal take hold.

Wise Mind, Absorption, Flow— A Focused Brainstorming Exercise

Let's do some more personal reflections. Perhaps you've already had experiences of connecting to your own wise mind that synthesized your emotional and intellectual reasoning. Or, you've become fully absorbed in something that commanded your attention and supreme interest. Take a couple minutes to jot down ideas to each prompt.

I'm in touch with my wise mind when…

I become totally absorbed when…

I enter a flow state when…

Integrating Insights from the Undiscovered Country— From Ego Death to the Birth of the Self

Jolande Jacobi, a colleague of Jung, once remarked that "Every transformation demands as its precondition 'the ending of a world'—the collapse of an old philosophy of life."[38] In confronting the existential trials, you too have examined your 'old philosophy of life.' If you took them to heart, the trials might have helped set you free from some of your prior assumptions and approaches to life. This shedding of the old ways can involve a loss of known order, one restricted by the past. Some previous life lessons may not apply as readily to the present—or the future you want to create. By doing this challenging work, you've communicated to the unconscious that you're ready to hear what it has to say. And, the unconscious is ready to speak.

Beginning in this chapter, you'll gain new perspectives about your broader Self and its many aspects. The overarching goal is to bring these parts into accordance with one another.[39] Moving past old, restricted, or false expressions of yourself requires asking deeper questions—something you've already mastered. In exploring the Self, we can occasionally get into some fairly esoteric ideas—not that we haven't already.

Contacting your deepest Self means shifting away from the part of you that's overinvested in your conscious mind. A now-classic metaphor involves imagining a game of chess.[40] Your thoughts, emotions, and sensations are all pieces on the chessboard. Our default is to make judgments about our mental content and activity. Some are 'bad,' others are 'good.' Think about the contents of your mind that you deem negative or unwanted as being on one side of the chessboard—perhaps the white pieces.[41] The desirable ones belong to the other team. These teams are in constant conflict, each strategizing to win the game. Sometimes one side does win. But rather than ending the conflict, the game just resets. And new pieces are brought to the board.

Who are the players in the game? Sometimes it's different parts of your conscious mind. Your protective parts versus your vulnerable parts. Sometimes your ego on one side and your unconscious on the other. We all start the game identifying with one team—usually our everyday consciousness, our ideal self or our ego and its judgments on what's 'good' and 'bad.' You now understand that. Yet understanding alone may just add more pieces to the board or tweak your strategy in fighting your opponent. No matter how many times you update your strategy, though, your opponent eventually adapts. What worked in the past doesn't work anymore. Or to 'win,' you must sacrifice too many pieces, only for a temporary moment of satisfaction.

Where then is the Self? Perhaps it's the chessboard, the ground upon which the eternal game is played. It provides the context for every game, yet it remains neutral and intact regardless of who wins. Perhaps it's more than the board. It could be the surrounding environment encompassing everything— the board, the pieces, and the ever-changing strategists who ceaselessly continue to play. It's the collector of all experiences. The container of all parts, competing motivations, conscious, unconscious, positive, and negative. This Self remains steady regardless of what happens. It observes. It witnesses. It is strong and formidable.

This is the power of the Self. A temporary death or 'downregulation' of the ego permits this new form of consciousness to emerge. The Self is the context of all mental phenomena.[42] One of its emanations is the experiential self that observes all modes of experiencing as they occur. Living in the realm of the indomitable spirit, the Self is pure awareness. From ancient religions to hidden mystical traditions present today throughout Earth's many cultures, there's a convergence. Another convergence lies where ancient knowledge meets modern psychological approaches to healing—not only through Jung and psychedelics but in evidence-based therapies too.[43] Psychedelic science is providing just one bridge amongst these esoteric but compelling landscapes. Whether or not the chessboard metaphor resonates, we can discover the Self by approaching it from a few additional angles.

The Self is Beyond Assumed Identity. Yes, you already know this quality of the Self. I also know we can push further now and be more radical than before. How? By deconstructing one of the most fundamental aspects of identity across Earth's many cultures: that of gender. From our very first moments of entering this world, either weeks before or at the moment of birth, gender is the first identity assigned to us. It's embedded in our name, the primary way the outside world refers to our individual existence. For most of us, it goes unquestioned. In my clinical work, though, I've learned much from my clients who explicitly explore their sense of gender. Some transition to a gender different than assigned at birth. Some choose to break down the shackles of gender-based expectations of who they can or cannot be and how they can and cannot act. Deconstructing the 'givens' of gender can lead to sincere questions about many other parts of ourselves. It's intensely existential work. My clients have taught me that examining gender is valuable for all of us. Jung, in fact, pointed to encountering the Anima/Animus as another core task of individuation. The Anima/Animus represents gender expressions counter to but complementary with our conscious identity. It's most often inclined towards 'desirable' qualities. Projecting them can play a crucial role in romantic love, especially during early infatuation when information's scarce and intimacy's underdeveloped—the perfect recipe for projections of all kinds.[44]

Culture defines many gender expectations and thus also informs the contents of our personal Anima/Animus. What did you learn about how a man or woman should behave? What's okay and not okay to feel or do based on your gender? You don't need to go full 'Gender Studies' to see the restrictions these expectations place. Like the persona, gender can be more of a performance than an expression of deeply held personal qualities.[45] That's why we distinguish gender identity (how one feels inside) from gender expression (how one performs for others). Conforming to gender expectations can constrain authentic self-expression. By exploring these unexpressed parts, we may uncover buried facets of our Self, freeing us from unnecessary constraints but without demanding we change our core sense of gender.

The Self is Beyond Conscious Memory. Memories are funny things. We all have them, yet they're often distorted or missing significant details. Core memories influence our autobiography, our narrative of who we are and where we came from.[46] It's also why dementia is so frightening to many of us. What do we become when our memories fade or disappear entirely? Memories encode our past experiences, which then help us adapt to future challenges. Yet memories fade for us all. And many things aren't consciously remembered at all. Not everything's meant to be remembered. But think of those precious memories that you hold dearly and that are central to your personal identity and history. Perhaps your first kiss, your childhood best friend, the day of your graduation or wedding, a moment of overcoming significant hardship, the birth of a child, or the death of a parent. What would you be now if all those memories disappeared? Would something remain that at its core is still you? Or, would you be an entirely new person, a new conscious entity with no prior history? A blank slate free to develop into whatever this new you desires—or is destined to become? These are indeed profound questions, even for those of us with memories mostly 'intact.'

The Self is Beyond Explicit Understanding. The intellectual understanding emphasized by academics and the like can be seen as woefully incomplete and occasionally a barrier to the emotional insight emphasized by psychotherapists and artists alike. Intellectualization, after all, is a defense mechanism, and not as sophisticated as it sounds. The risk of intellectualization is relevant to this book. We're talking a lot about concepts, theories, frameworks, etc., all while using a lot of big words. I try to toe the line, but I'm only human. The activities I've included are to combat this risk. Still, emotional understanding has its limits too. The growing complexity you've developed throughout this journey has hopefully affected you both intellectually *and* emotionally. To accommodate such complexity requires ever-increasing levels of differentiation and integration, both of which parallel the movements of individuation.[47]

Even the smartest, most insightful person might overlook the truly mystifying layers of Self beyond language, concrete facts, and contents of the mind. These qualities of the Self may ring familiar. They overlap with common features of mystical consciousness, which as discussed previously in this book, include: An experience of the overarching unity of all things, to the point of paradox; a feeling of transcendence; the download of intuitive insights; and the quality of its ultimate ineffability, where words fail. These features point to the limits of our everyday understanding. Words, theories, concepts can only feebly express a fraction of one's genuine experience. Remember too, "The name that can be named is not the eternal name."[48] So too it is for the Self. That's quite a dilemma for us thinking-oriented minds. But metaphors, poetry, and images assist in painting this larger landscape. By systematically exploring your internal and external worlds, you will continue to form a scaffolding for the larger project at hand: Not to understand the Self per se, but to develop a productive relationship with it.[49]

An Evolving Sense of Self—
A Focused Brainstorming Exercise

As we discuss so many esoteric ideas, we risk abstracting ourselves out of existence. So, let's pause again and do another brainstorm. You know what to do by now. Look at the prompts and take a couple of minutes to respond with words, images, or both.

What was that like for you? Some of these brainstorming exercises might have been easier than others. Some more provocative. Whatever emerged, consider revisiting these prompts in the future. It'd be interesting to see how your responses continue to evolve.

I was once...

I am now...

I could become...

Fostering Wisdom by
Embracing Flexibility & Self Complexity

Throughout this journey you've been growing in various ways. Each step has built upon the ones that came before, allowing you to rise to higher levels of complexity. Complexity means little, though, without wisdom. Long before coming to this book, you passed through the necessary stages of forming an ego and a personal identity. These prior achievements remain critical to the success of your current journey to move beyond unnecessary constraints. Deconstruction doesn't mean, however, complete and permanent disintegration. It simply allows a greater synthesis to form as you undergo the process of individuation. A parallel exists for psychedelics. A mystical experience, with or without 'ego death,' is not the end. These experiences beg for deeper integration long afterwards. Otherwise, it's a mere novelty, containing little significance to oneself or the world.

If we want the insights we've earned to be relevant, then how do we apply such profound experiences and abstract ideas to our everyday lives? We still live in this world and have various responsibilities that demand attention. We must do laundry and pay the bills. Many roles we play are important to ourselves and the people we care about—including, for example, being supportive parents who love their children, the next generation of seekers, or doing work that relieves the suffering of others. It'd be irresponsible and harmful to abandon all of our responsibilities. Giving up empty distractions or meaningless duties might make sense, but usually only after we pause to reflect and plan for any consequences.

With its gifts for planning and weighing pros-and-cons, the ego for sure stays relevant. It maintains equilibrium and keeps us safe, at least as best as it can.[50] Yet through individuation, its functions begin to serve the underlying motivation of the Self: psychological integration and wholeness. Instead of being weakened by this process, our ego and self-worth can become more resilient. This resilience lies in being less attached to our social roles or specific parts of our identity. We can feel whole and intact, even as the particulars of our psychological reality shift, the circumstances of our life change, and the abilities of both our mind and body fade. We can and should mourn losses and difficult transitions, but armed with a sense of fundamental wholeness, we have less need to resign ourselves to more inadequate forms of coping.

Unyielding self-doubt and shame, as well as their apparent opposites— conceit and self-centeredness—are all signs of more work to be done. No one's immune to them, as we'll revisit in the next chapter. But they aren't the end goal either. And they tend to be less effective attitudes in the long run compared to honest humility. Self-worth grounded in humility is resilient. When facing life's toughest challenges, each of us can practice healthy, flexible approaches to coping without grasping onto false attachments, dipping into self-centeredness, or becoming needlessly rigid.

Wisdom comes from understanding who we are while recognizing there's more that lies underneath the surface. Humility is wise because we're still human after all. Our psyche's darker sides can continue to surface. Knowing our personal triggers helps. But when challenges pile up too quickly, our internal resources can be drained.[51] Growth continues here too, but it often means knowing when and how to take time to heal and adapt. An image to aid us during difficult times is one of bamboo. By cultivating wisdom and its facets of humility and flexibility, we become stronger—able to bend when needed instead of breaking under pressure.

Concrete Suggestions & Journey Report

Per usual, Box 8.1 provides some suggestions for applying this chapter's themes in your daily life. Review the list and consider doing a couple. You can choose activities that help you gain new insights or integrate already-existing ones by putting them into practice. Journey Report 8.1 offers a ketamine experience that exemplifies how psychedelics can thwart the ego's efforts to maintain control and re-assure itself. Julia's experience was frustrating. She had trouble letting go of a specific interpersonal disagreement, partly because it challenged her identity as a 'good mother.' After feeling threatened by unwanted feedback, she became attached to proving herself 'right.' This desire was encoded in her intention for the ketamine session. Although she talks about the ego, she hadn't connected the dots between her intellectual and emotional understanding. The interpersonal entanglement complicated her perspective, as it can for all of us. Despite the session's irritating aspects, the next day she felt energized and settled. She had moved on. She reaffirmed her identity as a mother alongside the personal meaning it carried. Instead of needing to prove herself 'right,' she let go, refocused on the present, engaged with her family, and embraced her continuing life.

Box 8.1

Integrating an Expanded Self in Everyday Life

Suggestion	Example
Find your earliest memory, then follow a trail of other significant memories leading to today. Consider how you'd be different if you lost all these memories. Then consider how you might remain the same.	You recall the day of your sibling's birth. Then, your first field trip, your extra fun 7th birthday party, your first sleepover, the time you felt alone at a family reunion, your teenage angst about being 'cool' enough, then your excitement after finding friends also passionate about anime. You reminisce about graduation and your first years as an 'adult.' Your first serious job, relationship, etc. until arriving at more recent memories. With closed eyes, you imagine each memory disappears. You first feel grief. Then realize you'd have no reason to be sad, if you completely forgot they happened at all. You wonder who'd you be, how you'd feel, and what you'd do without these pieces of your original story.
Set aside a few days to make choices 'opposite' of ones you'd normally make. While ensuring your choices are harmless, adventure outside of your comfort zone and typical personality.	Your weekends are always packed with going out with friends or organizing upcoming events, all the while you're constantly on your phone. You decide to try a different approach this weekend and go on your first solo hike. You're afraid you'd get bored. And, you are at first. Then, you get distracted by scurrying geckos, a screeching hawk above, and some unusual foliage along your path. You reflect on how your ancestors must have lived. You lose track of time but are never lost. After coming home, you realize you haven't checked email all day. You smile.
Reflect on former parts of your identity, either no longer accurate, relevant, or salient in your current life.	You journal about a period of your life that was quite different than where you are now. Your job, your romantic relationship, your friendships, and even how you expressed your personality all changed since that time in your life. You describe these old parts of yourself and consider whether to let them go completely or bring some back into your life.
Create several index cards that each describe different parts of yourself, such as your identity, personality, roles, interests, etc. Shuffle them, then randomly remove 5. Imagine you must choose between keeping either these 5 or the remaining deck.	After making about twenty different cards, you realize you've captured the most important descriptions of who you are, including how you think other people probably see you. After shuffling the deck, you spread them out and hover your hand over them as if you were selecting an oracle card. You choose your cards but wait to view them until you've selected all five. Your cards are 'Brother,' 'Engineer,' 'Gamer,' 'Filipino American,' and 'Agnostic.' You're surprised how hard this decision would be in real life. After several minutes comparing your two sets of cards, you wonder if reshuffling and selecting different cards would make your choice easier.

Grounding Words—A Brief Summary

You've embarked on the last stage of your journey, ready for the challenges ahead. The goal now is to integrate all you've been exploring, especially any insights gained from confronting the previous trials. Instead of reemerging from those depths with overconfidence and jumping back into your prior self, you've started to move beyond rigid attachments and narrowly defined aspects of your previously held identity and personality habits. You're realizing the options are much greater. And the depths much deeper. You know your sense of self can evolve to meet the challenges ahead. There's still much to explore and experience. Thus, armed with twin virtues of humility and flexibility, facets of your growing wisdom, you can adapt to an ever-changing reality—the old purview of the ego—and embrace higher levels of complexity and wholeness—the realm of the Self. Beyond identity, memories, and words, the Self is the wellspring of insight and possibilities. The ego's efforts to control inevitably breakdown when facing unavoidable changes and overwhelming pressures in the outside world. The Self, by allowing a larger range of movement, remains intact and strong. So too are you at your core. Now go and contact that center of your deepest Self. It was here all along.

Your Assignment, Your Choice

In this third arc, you might notice your ally curiosity returning and encouraging you to choose different types of assignments. If you've gravitated towards *Reflective-Intellectual* activities, you might consider choosing *Experiential-Emotional* ones. Alternatively, you could try a mix-and-match strategy, certainly fitting for this chapter's theme of extending beyond your everyday proclivities. Try letting your Self guide you, whatever that may mean to you. Do at least one activity daily before moving to the next chapter. As we continue the theme of integration, you may want to revisit previous assignments, worksheets, or journal entries. Doing so could help you reflect on your journey as a whole, but be careful not to become too distracted as forward momentum is important too.

Assignments 8.1
Moving Beyond Identity

Reflective-Intellectual	Experiential-Emotional
☐ Task—Complete **Exercise 8.1 "Layers of Personal Identity"**	☐ Task—Complete **Exercise 8.2 "Creating a Self Box"**—a physical or virtual collection of images, memories, songs, movies, etc. that capture your multilayered self
Time—At least 1 hr for completing and reflecting on the exercise	Time—At least 1 hr where you get lost in the flow of creating this collection
Aim—To reflect on your conscious identity and parts more or less salient or significant, while attempting to peel back these layers	Aim—To contemplate your multifaceted nature, including your conscious identity and core interests as well as less routinely emphasized ones
☐ Task—Read or watch content about the **process of individuation,** self-actualization, or similar psychospiritual framework	☐ Task—Practice the meditation in **Meditation 8.1 "Chipping Away Identity"**
Time—Minimum of 1 hr to gather information, reflect on knowledge gained, and record your reactions	Time—Minimum of 2-3x/week, ~15 min each
Aim—To learn about various models of growth that go further than simply describing personality	Aim—To access a state of consciousness larger than your everyday ego identity and contents of your mind

You know the drill. Review your options and select a couple activities for your continued exploration. Now or after doing one, respond to this chapter's journal prompt by writing, drawing, or creating whatever comes to mind and in whatever way rings true.

Travel Journal

What parts of my identity and personality might I hold onto too tightly?

What are the pros and cons of doing so?

What might be possible if I loosened my grip and fostered greater flexibility around my personal identity?

JOURNEY REPORT 8.1 Frustrating the Ego's Intentions

Do you know the feeling of being really invested in proving you're right? For me, it's like my ego digging in its teeth like a bulldog with its favorite rope toy. No matter how hard someone else pulls on the other side, I'm not letting go. Only one viewpoint makes any logical sense—and of course, it's mine! The other point of view, in fact, seems so unequivocally wrong, it's infuriating.

A situation like this brought me to my first ketamine journey. I was in the midst of some stressful exchanges with my daughter's daycare worker. After learning that I'd brought her and her friends to a local event, this daycare worker suggested I was "trying too hard to be a fun parent." Suffice it to say, I strongly disagreed. How dare she imply that something was wrong about my approach to parenting? I'm a proud mother, and I'd never do anything to hurt my daughter.

Around the same time, my friends started sharing their intriguing experiences with ketamine-assisted therapy. I jumped through the hoops and got a legal prescription from a nurse practitioner who'd also act as my 'sitter.' I was ready and prepared to win my internal tug-of-war, me on one side, hints of self-doubt on the other. To help, I made sure to equip my mantra: 'I'm right!' I guess it also served as my 'intention' for the journey. After the two 100-mg lozenges dissolved in my mouth, I swished them around for about 15 minutes, as instructed. When I put on my eyeshades, I descended into the weird world of ketamine. As I listened to the swirling music, I became disoriented in a way that only a truly novel experience can provoke.

My mantra didn't help me navigate this world as I had hoped. Instead of a straightforward tug-of-war, I faced something more like whack-a-mole. Every time I thought I was about to get a solid hit by bringing down my metaphorical mallet, the 'mole' would disappear. My ego was not winning this game with ketamine. As I tried to think about the day-care worker's words, I'd see in the distance what looked like an insight, knowledge, or proof of being right. As I got closer, ready to smack it and win my prize, it'd disappear! I kept chasing that thing, knowing it contained my 'Ah-ha!' moment, proof of my righteous perspective. I almost had it. Several times. But it always escaped, and I was left tripping from the force of my almost-successful whack.

Out of frustration, I told the nurse, "I don't know how to navigate this ketamine." In hindsight, my ego was trying to maintain a calm façade. Her reply was something along the lines of, "This is your first time trying. Stay with it." So I did. Not that I had much choice. I did my best to go along with the experience rather than trying to fight and force it to fit my expectations. "Wait," I thought for a brief moment, "Was I doing that with my mantra? Forcing it?" My tightness and confusion continued, despite ditching my now-former mantra. I remember thinking, "This medicine's so weird." My mind kept slipping back into the whack-a-mole game. When the journey was over, I felt disoriented as if my typical points of reference had shifted. West was east and north was south.

The next morning, I woke up feeling strangely energized and happy. When I reflected on the situation with the daycare worker, it didn't seem to matter like before. It happened and was unpleasant, but my ego no longer had its teeth in it. Its emotional weight had seemingly vanished, just like the mole. What previously seemed so personal now felt like it had very little to do with me. So I let it go. Perhaps the frustration my ego faced in the ketamine journey helped me move on. I realized that morning all I really cared about was my family and being a loving mom. Of course, that's what mattered most all along.

—Julia, Age 42

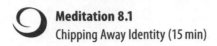

Meditation 8.1
Chipping Away Identity (15 min)

Read this script to preview this meditation's flow. Find a comfortable, safe place to sit, stand, or lay down without major distractions. Then, close your eyes and lead yourself through it. Remember, becoming distracted offers you more opportunity to practice strengthening your concentration. This meditation is longer than previous ones. To help you recall the main themes, consider reading the script multiple times before practicing the exercise.

Begin by closing your eyes and enter into a state of being grounded in the present moment....if focusing on your breath helps, then do so...

Once centered, bring your attention to your current sense of self....Imagine describing yourself to a stranger...what would you say? ...notice what comes to mind first...then next...and after that....Are these things the most important to who you are? Or are they only the most salient at this time? ...Take a few more moments to flesh out these parts of your personal identity...from your personality...your hobbies and interests...to the roles you occupy, either through your work...your family...or your community...even the things so obvious you sometimes forget them...maybe your gender, age, ethnicity, and cultural heritage, if not already acknowledged. Even your identity of being a human, living on this Earth...

Now imagine each of these parts, your personality, interests, profession, family roles, gender, culture and so on, are all represented by different wooden blocks. These blocks are meticulously stacked inside a large container...blocks that are more surface-level qualities or roles are on top...and the ones most important and central to how you see yourself form the bottom layer...You are all these things. Rest here for a moment with this image...

Shifting from this awareness of the totality of these parts, neatly organized in this container, gently begin to remove the blocks near the top, one at a time. For each block you remove, pause to give honor to this part of your identity and the role it plays in your life. Then imagine that as it's removed from the box, it disappears along with that part of you...Take your time...

Notice which blocks are easier to remove...and which are harder to let go... think of letting each block go as a gentle exercise, not motivated by fear or anger but by your willingness to release these parts of yourself...

You now move onto the deeper layers of blocks, parts of your identity that you hold closely...maybe the roles most important to you...ones that shape how you understand yourself...how you even access personal meaning...these too you gently pick up, one at a time, and let disappear...Allow yourself as much time as you need. After all, these fragments form the essence of your personal identity and core sense of self...

Once you've finished removing each block, pause to take a deep cleansing breath...look into the emptiness of this container which once held all the pieces of you that you just let vanish...what's this emptiness like? What thoughts or emotions, if any, come to mind? Notice them. Then let them go too...

Now, from this place of emptiness, imagine becoming one with this empty container...you are remaining somehow present and aware but without the precious identities and mental content that once filled the spaces in between... as these aspects of yourself re-emerge, acknowledge them as ephemeral signs of the mind's habit of filling the space of this container and let them fade away...Simply allow yourself to be...as pure consciousness and awareness...

Still in contact with this broader Self, begin to imagine the blocks reappearing one-by-one with the most important returning first...your pure consciousness remains and takes each block and places them in its respective stack, in its relative order of importance to your everyday self...The order may be the same. It may be different. Their size also may have changed, if upon reflection, some parts of your identity have shifted in importance....Slowly, each part returns to the container. Thoughts, emotions, physical sensations also return, as we welcome them to fill any remaining crevasses...

Now being full again with the contents of your mind and your personal identity, sit with a feeling of being all these things, including the container, in its totality....

Consider whether more blocks can fit inside...or perhaps there's not enough space...either way, expand your awareness outside of the container, to the imagined space you—as the container and its contents—are in...See all possibilities that surround you, either formed as blocks, or simply ideas and unconsidered options... reaching infinitely into the surrounding space...

As you become aware of this infinite space, you realize even the container, whether full or empty, encompasses only a fraction of possibilities....through this expanded awareness, you shift to being more than the container itself. You become the space all around...this breadth of awareness may feel as infinite as the cosmos...Or perhaps not. Regardless, you see that it's larger than what you had before...and yet is somehow still connected to you...

From this place of expanded consciousness, take a few deep breaths...intentionally taking everything in...being all these things and more...

Take a couple more breaths while in this expanded state....Feel cleansed and renewed by this fresh perspective and clean air...Then, gradually center yourself back into your body, your physical container in our shared material world...and with breath, inch closer to re-entering this present moment but keep your eyes closed...

Take your time and allow yourself to make a gentle return. There's no rush... become centered and aware of both yourself and your surroundings...When you're ready, slowly reopen your eyes and reconnect to your location and surroundings in this small yet important corner of time and space.

Exercise 8.1

Layers of Personal Identity

Step 1—Use the top box to brainstorm about different parts of yourself. These can range from your personal and professional roles to your interests and hobbies and even your deepest held values, political beliefs, and religious or spiritual convictions.

Step 2—Once you've created a thorough list, place each one in the concentric circles below, with the innermost circle reserved for the parts of yourself that are most central to who you are and your identity.

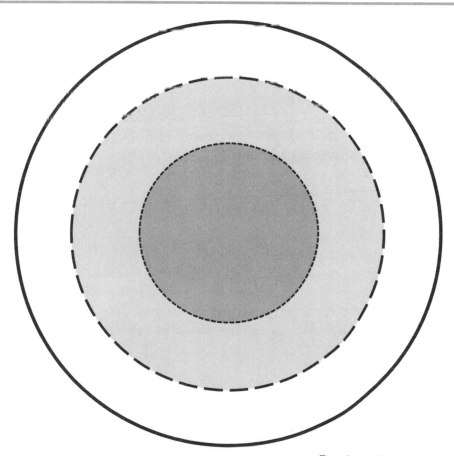

Exercise continues on next page

Step 3—Looking at the layers of your identity, imagine each one as a mask. Look at the outermost layer for a few moments, then close your eyes and imagine taking off each of these masks. How does that feel? What if anything has changed?

Do the same for the second layer of your identity. Note how removing this layer felt. What has changed?

Finally, imagine removing the innermost layer of your identity, what you consider core to who you are. How do you feel now? What is left?

Step 4—As best as you can, keep these masks off and go for a walk outside. Try not to speak with anyone and just be present-centered and walk in the world without giving into the dominance of your everyday identity and sense of self. What is this experience like?

Step 5—Throughout the next few days, notice any moments where you experience different layers or parts of yourself—or even the 'empty' self from Step 4. Record your experiences in your Travel Journal and/ or use Form 4.1 "The Experiential Tracker" to make more systematic notes about these experiences

Exercise 8.2

Creating a Self Box

Purpose. To express and document the many parts of yourself, your identity, and beyond. This collection can be a virtual or physical one but will include a range of items. Below is a list of suggested categories that can stir your imagination and get you started. It's not exhaustive, though, so feel free to add your own personal spin to the task. The empty space allows you to jot down initial ideas while you brainstorm possible content. The final collection, however, should include much more than words alone.

Types of Content	Personal Brainstorming Notes
Memories Earliest and/or most significant	
Images Photographs, paintings, visual metaphors, and/or other graphics	
Songs, Lyrics Favorite or particularly meaningful music, audio recordings, and/or lyrics	
Movies, TV Series, Videos Favorites or especially meaningful movies, series, or episodes	
Poems, Stories, Books Fiction and/or nonfiction, authored by yourself or others	

Exercise continues on next page

Quotes
Inspirational, funny,
or otherwise

Material Objects, Items –
Tokens, souvenirs, memorabilia

Symbols of the Sacred –
Archetypal, mythic, or religious
images or figures that represent
the divine, mysteries, or your
highest Self

Miscellaneous –
Any other content not captured
by the above. Be creative!

CHAPTER 9

Beyond Shadow Projection—
Towards the Wisdom of Compassion

The shadow is a moral problem that challenges the whole ego-personality, for no one can become conscious of the shadow without considerable moral effort. To become conscious of it involves recognizing the dark aspects of the personality as present and real. This act is the essential condition for any kind of self-knowledge, and it therefore, as a rule, meets with considerable resistance....[and] frequently requires much painstaking work extending over a long period.

—Carl Jung, *Aion: Researches into the Phenomenology of the Self*[1]

Journey Waypoint VIII

Although we're far into our mythic journey, perhaps no other waypoint has been as critical as this one. Our path hasn't been easy by any measure, but lurking just outside our awareness, in the things said but not heard, and in many things not said at all, the shadow has been with us all along. Do not worry. Where there is light, there is shadow, and where shadow, light. As the natural counterpart to our conscious ego, the shadow is unavoidable. But the all-too-human default strategy is to attempt to avoid it anyways.

Like many of life's challenges, though, avoidance can pose bigger problems than it solves. Psychological and spiritual growth requires shadow work, and as per the theme of this final arc, the major task is one of integration. If we do not explore the shadow, it doesn't disappear. It becomes stronger and eventually can destroy us from within.[2]

If we use all our allies and all our insights in this ultimate challenge, we might approach the seemingly impossible and see the dark and light as intertwined in obvious and mysterious ways. In this chapter, we make the shadow manifest and acknowledge its existence throughout this book's journey. By doing so, we find wisdom not in conquering, denigrating, or projecting the shadow onto others—our ego's default strategies—but by continuing to accept our innate challenges while fostering greater compassion. In the end, we'll sketch out a path for how to hear what the shadow has been trying to tell us all along.

Self-Reflections Check-In

In the last chapter, you wrestled with some larger perspectives about your sense of self that expand beyond your ego, personal identity, social roles, and the surface-level contents of your mind. What most resonated with you from the first waypoint of our final arc? What didn't? The parts you could relate to and the parts you couldn't are all informative and welcome. What activities did you choose to explore or practice? Did they provide you intellectual or emotional insights about your Self versus your everyday identity? Remember the individuation process is lifelong, so pace yourself as much as you need, just as I hope you've been doing throughout this journey. If helpful, take a few deep breathes to ready yourself for this next chapter. Then proceed.

What Once was Lost, Now is Found—
Seeing the Shadow in Human History & This Book's Journey

As an archetype, the shadow has numerous possible expressions. In its simplest form, the shadow is that which is unseen or unconscious. That definition is largely true but not particularly illuminating. Let's look to one of Jung's later works, *Aion*, for some especially shrewd words on the matter:[3]

> [Characteristics of the shadow] have an *emotional* nature....Affects [emotions] occur usually where adaptation is weakest, and at the same time they reveal the reason for its weakness....Although, with insight and good will, the shadow can to some extent be assimilated into the conscious personality, experience shows that there are certain features which offer the most obstinate resistance to moral control and prove almost impossible to influence. These resistances are usually bound up with *projections*, which are not recognized as such, and their recognition is a moral achievement beyond the ordinary....[S]ome traits peculiar to the shadow can be recognized without too much difficulty as one's own personal qualities... [When projecting the shadow, however], the cause of the emotion appears to lie, beyond all possibility of doubt, in the *other person*. No matter how obvious it may be to the neutral observer that it is a matter of projections, there is little hope that the subject will perceive this himself. He must be convinced that he throws a very long shadow before he is willing to withdraw his emotionally-toned projections from their object.

As we know, it is not the conscious subject but the unconscious which does the projecting. Hence, one meets with projections, one does not make them. The effect of projection is to isolate the subject from their environment, since instead of a real relation to it there is now only an illusory one. Projections change the world into the replica of one's own unknown face.

In this excerpt, Jung has summarized the most relevant aspects of the shadow for our current purposes. As individuals, it is unseen by our conscious minds but can be hinted at when we have intense emotional reactions. The shadow is by default projected onto others, not seen as part of ourselves. So as an example, if we're unconsciously afraid of being incompetent, we're likely to see incompetence in others and judge it harshly well before we acknowledge our own areas of incompetence.

In internal family systems therapy, the shadow is most directly correlated with the exile parts of ourselves. This Shadow-as-Exile is denied by our ego (the manager and firefighter parts) because it feels overwhelming. It exposes deep pain and/or shame. When the exile emerges into our conscious awareness, it can be healed, but this healing takes effort and care—and the forging of new alliances with different parts of ourselves. This is why the Self is such an important concept in our final arc. The Self helps mediate relationships between our ego and our shadow. Defenses like projection and denial only perpetuate the polarization of our inner and outer worlds.

Forgotten Histories

Much of this book has dealt, one way or another, with the shadow—multiple shadows, in fact. In this book's prologue, I quoted *The Lord of the Rings* while introducing the notion that myth comes in many forms and not all are from the distant past. Galadriel's words spoke of a growing shadow, one felt but not seen, and the fear that the knowledge needed to weather the coming storm had been lost to history and disbelief. Everyone's heard the saying that if we don't know our history, we're doomed to repeat it. Hearing about history is quite different than putting ourselves in the shoes of our various ancestors. If we were to do that, we'd better understand the depths of our historical and collective shadows—war, slavery, infinite intergenerational trauma, starvation, greed, tremendous loss, and promising innovations with unforeseen consequences. Not every aspect of the shadow is conventionally evil or horrific, even at the collective level. The shadow is anything which we don't know or prefer not to see, think about, acknowledge, or dwell on—and sometimes that which has been lost to time, including personal stories of bravery, love, and resilience. But if we cherry-pick our history, we miss perhaps the most important lessons and warnings. At the same time, we must acknowledge that the vast majority of human history was never recorded. Our written records only date back roughly to the last 5000 years.[4] That's out of the 305,000 years of our species' existence. And what has been recorded is unquestionably incomplete and biased.

At a more personal level, what do you know about your own family history? How far back do the stories go? Even when narrowly defining 'family' as our direct genetic ancestors, we confront quick escalations in scale. Two parents become four grandparents, become eight great grandparents, become sixteen great great grandparents, et cetera. Five generations back may get us only to 100-150 years ago. In America, many of us can trace our ancestors to multiple continents and cultures. Genetic test kits are also revealing occasional, if not frequent, surprises. Either way, what are the personal implications of your ancestral heritage? What various religious, ethnic, and racial histories are relevant to your lineage? Where might there be gaps?

When we think about history, personal or cultural, sometimes we focus on the stories of beauty and resilience and the courageous acts of previous generations. These stories are inspiring and important. In the last decade, I worked with several veterans to support their healing from various posttraumatic reactions, whether due to combat, sexual assault, or childhood abuse. My knowledge of trauma and world history had to become much more than 'just the facts.' With most veterans I had the honor to work with, I witnessed over time the posttraumatic growth mentioned in our first existential trial. As part of my American culture, I appreciate tales of courage and resilience.

But stories of heroism, survival, and recovery don't undo the horrors that humanity has experienced and inflicted as well. Hearing positive stories of the past can be like reminiscing about the good old days—but that's not quite right. Most of us never lived in those 'good old days.' Yet somehow, thinking about the historical past, the parts we like at least, can feel like reminiscing. When we slow down and consider the atrocities that actually happened in the past, even outside of war—and those that continue to happen—it can feel soul-crushing.

Even so, thinking about the horrors committed by others is far preferable than thinking about the ways we've fallen short (or our own ancestors did). And as we've explored, discovering personal values, a critical boon of our final trial, can lead us directly into the shadow too—guilt, shame, perfectionism, hypocrisy, and fears about not living up to some unobtainable ideal. Let's not forget, though, that myth is full of tales of redemption and reconciliation. Those stories are only possible when misdeeds are acknowledged and present actions align with one's expressed desire to repair previous mistakes.

The Shadows of Our Journey

The shadow has played a role throughout this book. To help manifest possible shadows, Box 9.1 summarizes a few major themes as oppositional or complementary pairs, some of which were explicitly incorporated in this book's content. Others were left to endnotes, explored in activities, or existed only 'in between the lines.' You might turn this box into another activity in which you reflect on other missing pieces of this book's approach. Notice that what appears to be shadow very much depends on one's perspective. Our trials, in particular, demonstrated that bringing the shadow into focus can reveal hopes and strengths hidden underneath fear, which may be more conscious. As an author, however, my shadow work has come in accepting that no amount of writing, reflecting, researching, citing, and editing can bring to light all the shadows that play a role and need to be seen and heard. That's where you and others come in.

Since our journey broadly follows the hero's myth, we might reflect on the shadow of the hero as well. Broadly speaking, the hero of this book is anyone exploring and partaking in its journey. But not all heroes are alike. The popular understanding of Joseph Campbell and his work can admittedly be too simplistic and narrow, but like all of us, Campbell was a person of his times and had blind spots despite his brilliance.[5] Ideally, valid criticisms lead to refinement, not abandonment. Identifying common structures and elements to myth across the world's cultures and time necessarily brings to the shadow mythic stories that appear to break the mold. Campbell was a European American, Irish Catholic-raised man in the 20th century. He survived two world wars, the Great Depression, and several other tragic historical events. How would the monomyth be different if it were described by a woman from another culture, of another ethnicity, and during a different time period? I've continuously asked the same of this book while writing it. Try as I have to educate myself, though, I cannot speak of what I do not know. Besides doing copious amounts of independent research and reading, I've tried to do my due diligence and address personal gaps of knowledge and perspective as much as possible. I've required my own allies in that task—friends, family, and colleagues who come from many walks of life, cultural backgrounds, and political beliefs to offer their perspectives. This book's acknowledgments name them specifically. If there's ever to be a second edition of this book, I'm sure I'll have many refinements based on my on-going explorations and conversations. Growth is a lifelong process.

Box 9.1

The Light and Shadow Elements of this Book—
Example Tensions, Paradoxes, and Double-edged Swords

Instructions. What is shadow and what is light depends on your perspective, situation, personality, lived experience, culture, etc. The columns could be labeled and ordered in various ways, even by myself. My ordering or pairing should not be taken as exhaustive or as a value judgment about what should be considered light or shadow. The key questions are ones of possible synthesis and dialogue. The 'light' side of each pair may correspond to what's more emphasized in a chapter or what's culturally or personally valued, desired, or believed to be beneficial. The 'dark' side may be the reverse or what's undervalued, feared, or believed to be harmful, either personally or by one's culture or society at large.

Book Section	Spoken and Unspoken Tensions, Themes, Paradoxes, and Double-edged Swords		Your Reflections, Synthesis, Notes, or Additional Entries
Prologue / Entire Book	Western Perspectives	Indigenous Traditions	
	Myth / Religion	Science	
	Everyday Life	Transcendent Experiences	
	Subjective Reality	Shared Reality	
	Intentions	Expectations	
	Non-Legal Psychedelic Use	Legal Psychedelic Use	
Introduction to Choice	Freedom of Choice	Responsibility	
	'Yes' to the Journey	Reluctance / Refusal of the Call	
	Previewed	Unforeseen	

Arc 1–Preparation		
Major Theme	Awareness	Obliviousness
	Expansion	Restriction
	Knowable	Unknowable
Ally	Curiosity	Apathy
Cosmic Awareness	Humancentric Perspective	Non-Human Reality
	Order	Chaos
	Creation	Destruction
	Awe	Sublime
Self-Awareness	Conscious	Unconscious
	Self as Observer	Self as Observed
	Personal	Collective
	Protector Parts	Exile Parts
	Expressed Personality	Suppressed Personality
	Openness to Experience	Closedmindedness
Experiential Awareness	Outer Experience	Inner Experience
	Perception	Illusion
	Broadened Awareness	Concentrated Focus

Box continues on next page

Arc 2—Initiation		
Major Themes	Deeper Engagement	Escape into Fantasy / Nihilism
	Approach	Avoidance
	Heeding Warnings	Ignoring Warnings
	Passing a Trial	Abandoning a Trial
Ally	Acceptance	Denial
Death-Impermanence	Death	Life
	Grief	Love
	The Temporal	The Eternal
Loneliness-Interconnectedness	Solitude	Isolation
	Interconnectedness	Separateness
	Social Belonging	Social Conformity
	Attachment Security	Attachment Insecurity
	Dominance	Submission
	Harmony	Hostility
	Vulnerability	Defensiveness
	Authenticity	Deception
Meaninglessness-Meaning	Freedom	Responsibility
	Free Will	Fate
	Motivation to Grow	Fear of Failure / Demoralization
	Humility	Arrogance
	The Infinite / Possibility	The Finite / Choice
	Shared Meaning	Personal Meaning

	Clarity	Ambiguity
	Faith	Doubt
	Harmonized Values	Conflicting Values
Arc 3–Return		
Major Theme	Integration	Disintegration
	Lived Insights	Forgotten Insights
Ally	Wisdom	Foolishness
Beyond Ego Identity	Self	Persona / Identity / Ego
	Complexity	Simplicity
	Wise Mind	Biased / Imbalanced Mind
	Absorption	Boredom
	Experiencing Flow	Becoming Stuck
	Flexibility	Rigidity
Beyond Shadow	Ego	Shadow
	Hero	Villain / Dark Hero
	Shadow Seen by Self	Shadow Seen by Others
	Unconditional Love	Fear / Hatred
	Compassion	Indifference / Cruelty
Beyond the Narrow Life	Symbolic	Literal
	Appreciation	Criticism
	Creativity	Conventionality
	Future	Past
Epilogue	Continual Unfolding	Ending / Saying Goodbye

My Enemy, My Shadow— A Focused Brainstorming Exercise

Every hero has a shadow, and most stories have a villain. In reflecting throughout your own journey, where have you found evidence of your shadow? If you're the protagonist for this mythic quest, you likely have one or more antagonists out there in the 'real world.' Have you been aware of one all this time? Maybe someone in your life who's taking up more mental space than you'd like. Maybe someone in your professional world full of criticisms and too little praise or acknowledgment. Has your relationship with this person changed at all as you've been working through this book? The prompts below refer to your 'enemy,' but 'enemy' is a stand-in for any competitor, challenger, critic, or person who has gotten under your skin or represents everything you fight against or hope you are not. These antagonists within your journey may be specific individuals, 'types' of people, qualities, or attitudes. After each prompt, respond with words, names, pictures, or symbols. Take no more than 2-5 minutes to respond to each. How was this activity for you? What was it like thinking of your 'enemies?'

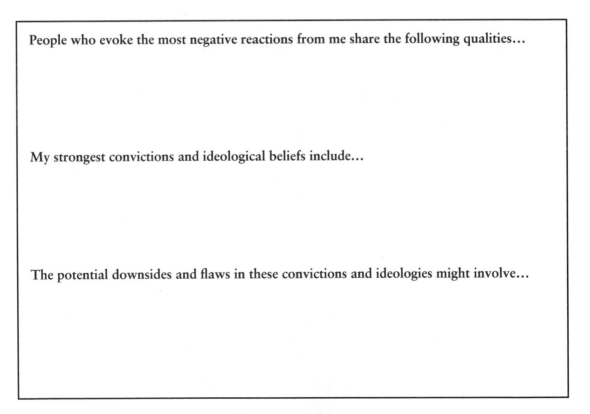

People who evoke the most negative reactions from me share the following qualities...

My strongest convictions and ideological beliefs include...

The potential downsides and flaws in these convictions and ideologies might involve...

For some people, that word alone is difficult to use. For others, it's perfectly acceptable. Your level of discomfort or ease might suggest something about the contents of your personal shadow on top of what you entered as your responses.

How Individuation Involves Encountering the Shadow

Until we can see the light and shadow as part of a transcendent whole— emanations of reality or consciousness, personal or collective—individuation, wholeness, and integration are but pipe dreams, so to speak. Shadow work is a harm reduction approach because it reduces the damage the shadow can do if unacknowledged. It also allows us to access the hidden gifts and strengths it might offer.[6] In the previous chapter, we discussed some benefits of shadow integration without using the language of the shadow. Balancing personality through the individuation process means incorporating the natural human functions that our default personality doesn't express openly. If these unexpressed qualities are viewed in a positive light, they might be incorporated into our personal Anima/Animus. For example, we might seek a partner, consciously or unconsciously, who's more emotionally open. When finding that desired partner, after the initial infatuation wears off, we might become upset with their emotional expressiveness. But ideally, over time we increase our own emotional awareness.[7]

Our deepest shadow isn't usually manifested outwardly in our typical behavior, except perhaps in our 'worst moments' or in our most secret thoughts. Polishing the mirror of consciousness is recognizing our distorted views of others as reflections of our own consciousness. We need a mirror to see our shadow because it's always behind us or out of sight, especially if we're only facing the light. Dreams, mythic stories, fantasies, and psychedelics can illuminate the shadow, but it takes effort to reveal and apply their symbolic messages.

As Maslow stated, "Seeing is better than being blind, even when seeing hurts," but we must have strength in facing the shadow.[8] Recognizing our hidden parts may at times lead to momentary despair, shame, and guilt.[9] No wonder we avoid the shadow. These experiences sound awful. Awe-full? Yes, hiding right before our eyes, awe has a shadow too—what has been called the sublime.[10] The shadow in its most sublime form might be a cosmic Black Sun, an alchemical symbol of dark light so intense that it extinguishes any timid light unprepared or unable to withstand its power.[11] Sounds like a black hole, doesn't it? The analogy fits. Unlike pure fear, the sublime beckons us to approach rather than avoid its source.

Its cosmic and collective parallels aside, the personal shadow is inside us. Denying it breaks it off from our consciousness. The more a shadow is splintered from the ego, the stronger and more autonomous it becomes over time—meaning it becomes more dangerous to our conscious, idealized view of ourselves. The shadow rejects the ego because the ego rejects the shadow. Both are unaware of the higher perspective of the Self, which encompasses ego and shadow. In healing this split, the Self can help mediate these natural tensions, but as Jung explained, "One does not become enlightened by imagining figures of light, but by making the darkness conscious."[12]

In reducing the harm of our shadow, though, the most important process is removing the especially harmful effects of shadow projection. When the shadow's projected onto an entire group or member representing that group, we commit the grave error of *othering*. Instead of seeing real human beings, we see distorted images formed through the filter of an egocentric perspective (promoting personal shadow projections) or from an ethnocentric perspective (promoting cultural shadow projections). Like all forms of awareness in our first arc, we're biased by our starting place and have built-in limits to our perceptions regarding the shadow. The trials of initiation, however, helped us confront basic human fears that often influence the shadow's potency. Although the shadow takes many forms, we'll focus now on a few particularly relevant angles left unexplored in previous chapters.

Shadows of Personality—The Dark Triad

Personality comes in many shapes and sizes, but not all are considered 'healthy' or desirable. As introduced in our second trial, the interpersonal circumplex hides some especially harmful manifestations of the shadow in its hostile-dominant quadrant—the *Dark Triad* of Narcissism, Psychopathy, and Machiavellianism.[13] Like most personality characteristics, the Dark Triad describes dimensional traits, not distinct types of people (except in extreme cases). Though highly related to each other, each trait has some fairly distinct qualities. People high in narcissism value leadership and making positive first impressions (which tend not to last). People high in psychopathy are more impulsive and motivated by revenge. People high in Machiavellianism use strategic networking to ascend social ladders and obtain greater power. The Dark Triad is most consistently connected to lower Agreeableness from the Big Five, with a dash of higher Extraversion and/or lower Conscientiousness depending on the study. And, sorry guys, we tend to be higher on these traits than women.[14]

Recently, Dark Triad researchers have described another triad to counter-balance these shadowy traits. Of course, one person's shadow is another person's light, so take these labels with a grain of salt. The *Light Triad* consists of Humanism, Faith in Humanity, and Kantianism, all of which positively correlate with one another and Agreeableness.[15] Figure 9.1 combines both triads into an hourglass image with brief descriptions of their defining features. These light-dark labels suggest they're in opposition, but we each have varying levels of both dark and light traits. It may be relieving to know that people tend to be higher on light (relative to dark) traits and that extreme scores on the Dark Triad are less common—at least when describing ourselves.

Since our shadow depends on our expressed personality, personal values, and cultures, shadow work involving these traits can come in many forms. For most of us on the 'light' side, recognizing the darker parts of ourselves and others may have some tangible advantages. First, we might reap the benefits of increased confidence and comfort with appropriate assertiveness while striving for positive changes. Second, being too trusting of others, especially strangers, can open ourselves to exploitation and manipulation—the core expressions of the Dark Triad's motivations for power.[16] On the flip side, for those higher on the Dark Triad (particularly Narcissism), taking cues from the light side may make sense. Working towards higher agreeableness, honesty, and humility while managing more destructive tendencies (like callousness, antagonism, grandiosity, impulsivity, and manipulativeness) can increase personal wellbeing and success. In other words, a win-win might be more possible than people might think. Even if so, we might heed cautions of researchers that "the absence of darkness does not necessarily indicate the presence of light."[17] Shadow work must come hand-in-hand with the cultivation of authentic virtues.

From another angle, we might consider the shadow elements of traits viewed as ideal in American society—Extraversion, Conscientiousness, Agreeableness, Openness, and low Neuroticism. Outliers (extreme scores) in these traits can have significant downsides. As a thought experiment, we could brainstorm what these downsides might be. For high Extraversion, weaknesses might include the inability to be alone, remain silent, or practice introspection. For high Conscientiousness, the struggle may lie in being too rigid, perfectionistic, or rulebound. High Agreeableness may result in conflict avoidance and an inauthentic, overly pleasing persona. A person unusually high on Openness might become too ungrounded, lack clarity on 'right' and 'wrong,' or be unwilling to commit to a specialized career or

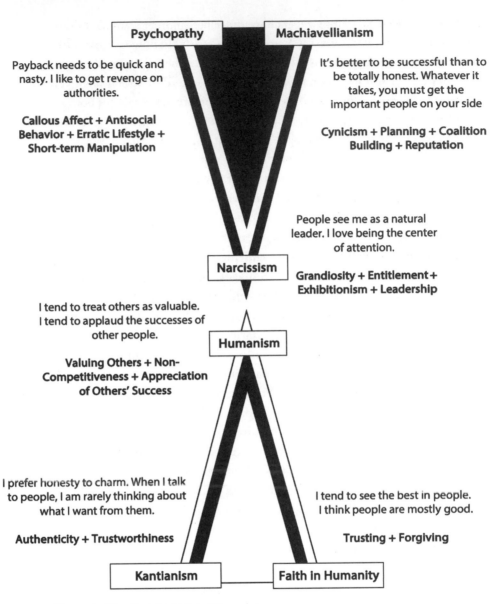

Psychopathy

Payback needs to be quick and nasty. I like to get revenge on authorities.

Callous Affect + Antisocial Behavior + Erratic Lifestyle + Short-term Manipulation

Machiavellianism

It's better to be successful than to be totally honest. Whatever it takes, you must get the important people on your side

Cynicism + Planning + Coalition Building + Reputation

Narcissism

People see me as a natural leader. I love being the center of attention.

Grandiosity + Entitlement + Exhibitionism + Leadership

Humanism

I tend to treat others as valuable. I tend to applaud the successes of other people.

Valuing Others + Non-Competitiveness + Appreciation of Others' Success

I prefer honesty to charm. When I talk to people, I am rarely thinking about what I want from them.

Authenticity + Trustworthiness

I tend to see the best in people. I think people are mostly good.

Trusting + Forgiving

Kantianism   **Faith in Humanity**

Figure 9.1 The Dark-Light Triad Hourglass

Note. Bolded words are summary descriptions of the relevant trait whereas the non-bolded statements come from self-report measures of the Light and Dark Triads. The first Machiavellianism and second Narcissism descriptions were originally reversed. To avoid confusion, I transformed all statements into their descriptive form. The original reverse-scored items were, "It's better to be totally honest than to be successful," and "I hate being the center of attention." See Jones & Paulhus, 2014; Kaufman et al., 2019.

spiritual practice requiring steady devotion. Even high emotional stability (low Neuroticism) may hide opportunities to feel and express vulnerability, which in trusting relationships, increases intimacy—and when alone, allows us to face deeper fears and uncertainty, all of which promote growth. These examples are merely possibilities. One way or another, however, the shadow side of our expressed personality is always with us.

Shadows of Emotion—Paths to the Dark Side

Emotions guide us in ways reason cannot, and even when our preferred mode of experiencing life and making decisions is thinking, emotions continue to influence us. Clues about our personal and collective shadows are found when intense emotions rise to the surface. Jung believed disproportionally intense emotions were indicators of weaker defenses and personal complexes. Remember the ego is largely our friend, and though imperfect, having more complex and flexible defenses helps us adapt to most situations.

Some situations that trigger the strongest emotions involve perceived danger and thus activate the energy-mobilizing fight-or-flight response of our sympathetic nervous system. Except when overridden by a protect-and-connect response (the parasympathetic alternative), fear and its transformation into anger are our biological defaults.[18] Anger is seductive because it feels far more empowering. Once it finds a target, anger if indulged and left unchecked can turn into hate. Although emotions aren't inherently destructive, acting impulsively or turning an emotion into an attitude can be. Yoda's warning, though a bit simplistic, got it right: "Fear is the path to the dark side…fear leads to anger…anger leads to hate…hate leads to suffering."[19] This suffering can spread from the individual to the collective.

With access to the worst news all around the globe, in an admittedly dangerous world where mortality is lying in the background of our minds, it's easy to trigger fear and its consequences. Emotions are helpful and important, but we should be cautious about cultivating them as attitudes or habitual reactions. When directed inwards over time, short-term fear might transform into chronic anxiety, shame, guilt, or a self-hating attitude. When directed outwards, it can become a self-protective or hateful stance towards others. Hate is a powerful indicator of shadow projection. As author Herman Hesse noted, "If you hate a person, you hate something in [them] that is part of yourself. What isn't part of ourselves doesn't disturb us."[20] Us-versus-Them dynamics are hard to dissolve once they form. Our target may be another person or entire group or demographic. Regardless of the target, it can feel like a fight for survival as if we're actually physically fighting for our lives. Sometimes it is, but more often it's not.[a]

Relationships and groups amplify our emotions which can lead to actions that heal or harm.[21] Groups can encourage us to push our boundaries and behavior past our typical individual limits. We might find ourselves asking, "Everybody else is doing it, so why can't we?"[22] Diffusion of responsibility is powerful—if others are doing risky or harmful things, we find it much easier to do the same. The expectations of others can affect our own behavior and performance, for better or for worse. Nowadays, we can find groups of all kinds, online and in person, that can offer a sense of belonging, even if only with virtual counterculture or fringe groups.

A more frantic search for belonging may be borne out of actual or feared rejection. But emotional pain can transform that vulnerability into the empowerment of hate and blame. What happens when more and more people become afraid, desperate, and already feel rejected by 'mainstream' society? Increased suicide rates, mass shootings, radicalization, and rampant social upheaval.[23] Echoes of Yoda's warning ring true yet again. But remember Yoda didn't invent that wisdom. Our wisest ancestors did.

Whatever its roots, fear, anger, and alienation, if left unhealed, can motivate one to find a sense of safety and belonging, somehow, somewhere— whatever it takes. Giving up freedom and truth isn't reserved for isolated or radicalized people. We do it all the time in the name of security and protection. If we explore these tensions and problems consciously and not hold out for fantasized 'perfect' all-or-none solutions, we might move from personal and collective shadow projection to psychological and societal renewal, even if more incremental than ideal.[24] Another tall order, I know. It takes on-going commitment and effort. But the difficulty of shadow work is why self-reflection, psychotherapy, and deeper psychedelic integration are so valuable, arguably necessary, given the complexities of our present world and the strengths and weaknesses of our human minds.

Reflections of My Shadow—
A Focused Brainstorming Exercise

Shadow work is and should be challenging. It requires a degree of raw honesty and openness uncharacteristic of most people. Before or after responding

---

[a] Of course, the truth of this statement depends greatly on one's life circumstances, demographics, location, and the specific situation.

to these next prompts, you might consider reviewing your responses to the previous chapter's brainstorm, "I am…" and "I am not." Responses to the latter may contain hints about your shadow.

If you're ready for a more intense challenge, it might be good to ask permission from your ego first. These reflection questions may be provocative, but answering them doesn't mean you're in any actual danger. When ready, close your eyes and envision someone you dislike immensely, or at times even hate—or would hate if you met them. If you're having trouble imagining this person, go into the treacherous realms of political and religious ideologies for some inspiration. Imagine yourself at your most stressed out or judgmental state. Flesh out this real or imagined person in terms of their personality, values (or vices), assumptions, and behaviors. Imagine telling them exactly 'how you feel,' no holds barred.

That could have been exceedingly easy or difficult. Either way, now try to imagine this person saying the exact same thing to you, with perhaps a few tweaked words to account for their different perspective. Now, take a few deep calming breaths. Then ask yourself this most vulnerable question: In what ways might they be right? Jot down some notes or reactions to this exercise of imagination in your Travel Journal. Afterwards, respond to the following prompts.

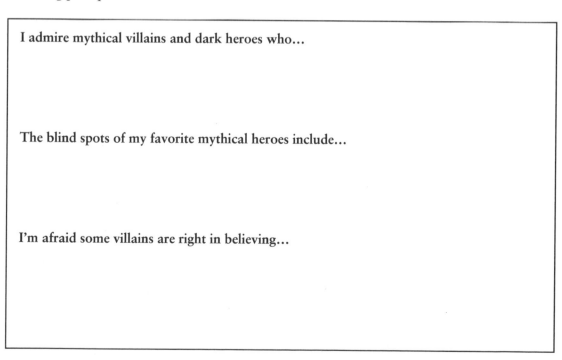

I admire mythical villains and dark heroes who…

The blind spots of my favorite mythical heroes include…

I'm afraid some villains are right in believing…

The Mythic Shadow—The Dark Hero as a Messenger

In mythic tales and their contemporary counterparts like film, the shadow is most often portrayed as the ultimate enemy or evil. Many of us have been seduced by superhero mythologies for decades now. These stories are just plain fun. Besides ego-satisfying identifications with the superhero, we also appreciate the fantasy of it all. One dangerous fantasy, though, is relying on some symbolic savior to protect us from ourselves and the effects of unchecked greed and an insurmountable history of skirting responsibility. Superman, or some political equivalent, will fly in to save the day…eventually. Or, 'scientists' will invite new technology to protect us from the harm we continue to do to the planet—well before it gets too bad, right?

The chosen form of our superhero represents the 'light' side of our personality, culture, or hopes for the future. Yet the downtrodden, wounded shadows of our mainstream or empowered segments of society also have their own saviors. In other words, for every Batman, there's a Joker. Despite a half-century plus of Batman-vs-Joker media, the Joker, like all shadows, continues to be reinvented. In *The Dark Knight*, Heath Ledger's performance marked the peak of the character's portrayal as the Shadow-as-Chaos, an enemy to order, reason, and meaning.[25] This Joker embraced absurdity to the max, convincingly offering contradictory origin story after origin story to explain his madness.

The Dark Knight's other antagonist, Two Face, represented the Shadow-as-Fallen-Hero motif. Harvey Dent, the righteous politician advocating for societal improvement and justice, poignantly warned, "You either die a hero, or you live long enough to see yourself become the villain."[26] Dent was unwittingly previewing his own fall. After losing his fiancée and undergoing a drastic medical intervention to save his own life, Dent's fate revealed a darker possibility than death. The righteous politician was transformed into the deadly rogue, Two Face.

In an even more unexpected twist, the overplayed Joker character was able to escape from his heroic vigilante counterpart's shadow to star in his own film, unceremoniously titled *Joker*.[27] Joaquin Phoenix's portrayal of the relatively benign social pariah allowed the audience to empathize with the marginalized, disempowered outcast of an uncaring Gotham City. Unlike the chaotic villain without a 'true' origin, this Shadow-as-Dark-Hero showed us the Joker's 'origin story' not as a single event but as a series of slights and disadvantages that left him without a bottom to hit and anything else to lose. His violent response in the end wasn't intended to spark a revolution or increase his social or political power. But it did act as a call to arms, not unlike our call to adventure, for the disillusioned and alienated—a collective powder keg ready to explode. In this story, who is the true villain?

Joker's message isn't that we need to create stronger heroes to fight against powerful evils. It's that we must listen to existing shadows and decode their messages if we're to prevent increasing unrest. Their sources of suffering are likely concealed by anger or behaviors we misinterpret or discount as irrational. But those same qualities are within us, whoever we are. The shadows portrayed by our superhero mythologies need to have a voice, or our 'real world' ones will intensify in power. No hero, villain, or ordinary person is perfect. But the imperfections of others, whoever they may be, are easier for us to see than our own. After all, we have fewer reasons to explain them away. What would be possible if we each took more time to understand the 'origins' of people we'd otherwise easily reject?

The Mythic Shadow—A Focused Brainstorming Exercise

In whatever form your favorite mythologies take, whether ancient or modern, create a list of answers or possibilities in response to the following prompts.

I have an easier time feeling self-compassion when...

It's hardest for me to feel compassionate towards...

Atonement is possible when...

Practicing discernment requires I...

Shadows of Psychedelics

Stan Grof famously described psychedelics as "nonspecific catalysts and amplifiers of the psyche."[28] As such, psychedelics can be gateways to shadow material, which is part of their transformational potential. If treated without respect and care, psychedelics might do psychological harm.[29] Although Jung confessed to knowing "far too little" about psychedelics (and denied ever taking any), he offered several warnings about their use. His most frank and colorful explanation was in a 1954 letter to his friend and English Dominican priest, Father Victor White:[30]

[T]here is no point in wishing to *know* more of the collective unconscious than one gets through dreams and intuition....The more you know of it, the greater and heavier becomes your moral burden, because the unconscious contents transform themselves into your individual tasks and duties as soon as they begin to become conscious. Do you want to increase loneliness and misunderstanding? Do you want to find more and more complications and increasing responsibilities? ....I should hate the thought that I had touched on the sphere where the paint is made that colours the world, where the light is created that makes shine the splendour of the dawn, the lines and shapes of all form, the sound that fills the orbit, the thought that illuminates the darkness of the void....I am profoundly mistrustful of the "pure gifts of the Gods." You pay very dearly for them...

This is not the point at all—to know of or about the unconscious—nor does the story end here; on the contrary it is how and where you begin the real quest. If you are too unconscious it is a great relief to know a bit of the collective unconscious. But it soon becomes dangerous to know more, because one does not learn at the same time how to balance it through a conscious equivalent. That is the mistake Aldous Huxley [*Doors of Perception*] makes: he does not know that he is in the role of [the magician's apprentice] who learned from his master how to call the ghosts but did not know how to get rid of them again...

It is really the mistake of our age. We think it is enough to discover new things, but we don't realize that knowing more demands a corresponding development of morality.

Psychedelics are undoubtedly powerful. Anything powerful demands respect and thoughtful consideration. To explore this point when speaking about psychedelics, I've used the admittedly dramatic analogy of nuclear power. Nuclear reactors have the potential for supplying a cleaner energy source than fossil fuels. Yet the first thing we did with nuclear technology was build a bomb. Similarly, psychedelics have a profound potential for facilitating growth and healing. Yet in the 1950's, the CIA's MK-ULTRA program attempted to use LSD and brainwashing techniques to manipulate people.[31]

In light of promising modern research, Jung's warning isn't so much about psychedelics per se. It's about the care we should take in their use and the immense importance of ethics and the responsibility of integration.[32] As religious scholar Houston Smith also highlighted, integration is the decision point between a spiritual *experience* and a spiritual *life*.[33] Integration takes practice, effort, and awareness of the pitfalls to which none of us are immune.

Timothy Leary and the Historical Shadow of American Psychedelia

In hindsight, the psychedelic '60s appears now either like an era of wonderful yet naïve hopefulness (a 'light' interpretation) or a period of wonton hedonism and irresponsibility (an alternative 'shadow' one). Like most things, the truth requires understanding multiples perspectives. Since Timothy Leary casted the largest shadow as a representative of that age, it's apropos to return to him yet again. Upon accepting his identity as a counterculture hero, Leary took to heart media theorist Marshall McLuhan's advice to express unwavering confidence and always be smiling—a perfect recipe for an alarmingly large shadow.

Later, Leary put aside his public persona when he described his first LSD journey and its aftereffects. It was terrifying. He experienced himself as a witless character in a plastic world acting out a comedy routine (or tragedy from his perspective) orchestrated by an unseen cosmic puppeteer. The most troubling part was his account of lifelong, paranoia-inducing 'flashbacks' of this journey. These 'flashbacks' occurred frequently in random moments where he'd suddenly recall his Shadow-as-Puppet role: "I'm the pathetic clown, the shallow, corny, twentieth-century American, the classic buffoon completely caught in a world of his own making, and not realizing that the goals and ambitions he strives for, the serious games he struggles with, are simply the comic relief, a brief clown act."[34] For many people during the 60's and in today's hindsight judgment, Leary's antics and their consequences indeed represent that shadow of a 'fool' caught up in his own desires and ambitions for societal transformation.

As for all of us, Leary and his actions were not all good nor all bad. It's easy to criticize others, especially when reflecting on the failures of the 1960's counterculture.[35] Leary contributed a great deal while knowingly and unknowingly putting his shadow on full display for the unforgiving eyes of the public and our abridged historical summaries.'[b] Instead of judging Leary and others in overly simplistic ways, though, we might learn from their successes, failures, and biases while advocating for a more mindful path forward. Reflecting on his own psychedelic experiences and later observations, Houston Smith again gave sage advice for the new generation of psychedelic explorers, "Be cautious, go slow, but do not give up the quest."[36]

Psychedelic Guides, Sitters, Therapists, or Shamans?

Since Jung and Leary's time when psychedelics re-entered Western cultures, scholars have clarified the significance of dose, mindset, and setting in reducing the likelihood of harmful experiences. Typically, the setting includes the presence of an experienced 'sitter,' spiritual healer, or professional therapists(s), which can greatly reduce risks. Decriminalizing and rescheduling psychedelics for psychotherapeutic and spiritual use have a benefit of allowing more people to be systematically trained and, if needed, held accountable.[37] Adhering to ethical standards is critical to psychotherapy of any kind as well as the care provided by spiritual leaders. Unfortunately, ethical violations still occur—including sexual violations. The world of psychedelics isn't immune to these transgressions, and a growing contingent of psychedelic communities is calling for more transparent and public denouncements of 'known' predators.

While psychedelics remain criminalized in many Western countries, psychedelic tourism has become a workaround for people with the financial means. It's ripe with shadow elements, and the burden is unsurprisingly weighted towards indigenous communities. The influx of money and attention, so valued in Western societies, can have negative consequences all around. Untrained 'shamans' can advertise their services to unsuspecting, naïve tourists with ease. Respectful cultural exchange is possible, but it's too seldomly modeled.[38] In the West, 'pop-up shamans' are becoming increasingly common—people who after a few journeys feel ready to sell their services as healers without undergoing the intense training experiences offered by either indigenous or Western traditions.

---

[b] Leary indeed harmed some people—for example, by advocating for LSD as a conversion therapy. Conversion therapy is an ineffective and unethical practice of trying to change someone's sexual orientation and gender identity to be heterosexual and cisgender. See Alexander Belser's (October 17, 2019) Chacruna article for more information on heteronormative practices in psychedelic science and communities of practice. See also the joint statement by Herzberg et al. (December 18, 2019) about increasing equity and inclusion more broadly.

Upon returning home, most Westerners also aren't prepared for the importance and challenges of integration. We live in communities quite different than indigenous ones and without a shared cultural understanding of what psychedelic experiences actually mean. A cone of silence can descend upon people who return to a society where psychedelics are illegal and/or stigmatized.

Until very recently, the West's closest non-religious parallel to spiritual healers like shamans has been psychotherapists. Training as a psychotherapist is often intense—as it should be, given the ethical responsibilities—but the requirement of extensive personal therapy for therapists-in-training has long been out of vogue. For psychedelic therapy specialization, above ground training programs cannot encourage or connect trainees to sources of illicit substances outside authorized research, religious, or other exempt settings.[39] Some limitations are temporary if governing bodies decide to reschedule, decriminalize, or sanction certain uses of psychedelics. But the responsibility held by the role of a psychedelic guide or therapist cannot be taken lightly. When challenging parts of journeys emerge, skilled therapists know how to guide journeyers through difficult experiences without rescuing them or allowing them to harm themselves or anyone else.

During a group retreat in Amsterdam, for which I was a guest co-facilitator, an older gentleman well into his journey called me over, asked a personal question (which my intuition told me to answer honestly), and then proceeded to describe me as remarkably kind and wise for my age. My ego was perfectly happy to receive the compliment. But because of my professional training, I knew better. I was on the receiving end of a positive transference.[40] I suggested he might be seeing a part of himself in me. At first, this surprised him. Then he began appreciating his own kindness and the lessons he learned in his early life.

This type of transference is fairly benign, but if such compliments are uncritically accepted, then it wouldn't take long to develop an overinflated ego. Worse yet, accepting them would be a missed opportunity for journeyers to reflect on their own positive qualities or potential. In this instance, the journeyer, as an older straight man, might not have expressed as freely his own kindness in his youth. He also may have been projecting his own wisdom that can only be gained through age and experience. Other psychedelic-inspired transferences can be far more intense such as experiencing another person as a deity or devil figure. Regardless of what occurs in any given journey, the power contained in the psychedelic therapist role is one to recognize as a source of responsibility and temptation for the unprepared or insufficiently vigilant. In other words, we need to be acutely aware of our own shadows as well as journeyers'.

Unrealistic Expectations vs. Lightly Held Intentions

Another psychedelic shadow deserves special mention: unfulfilled expectations. Western models emphasize intention setting as a critical part of psychedelic preparation—a key reason why it's incorporated into this book. Unfortunately, intentions can be misunderstood as expectations. The downside is three-fold. First, unmet expectations can lead to disappointment. This is especially relevant when people expect psychedelics to be the 'magic bullet' that will solve all personal and societal problems. There is no magic bullet. Second, being overly focused on one's pre-established intentions can sometimes close off a journeyer to other meaningful themes and surprises that emerge during a journey. Third, we might remember the astute adage, 'Be careful what you wish for.' While discussing his use of sacred mushrooms, R. Gordon Wasson said it well, "In common parlance, among the many who have not experienced ecstasy [or ecstatic mystical states], ecstasy is fun…But ecstasy is not fun. Your very soul is seized and shaken until it tingles."[41] These potential downsides can be minimized by having clear yet flexible intentions and an open mind to whatever occurs. Common guidance is to have 'intention without expectation.'[42]

Threshold Guardians— Dangerous Entities, Illusions, or Surprising Allies?

In many psychedelic communities and professional circles, people espouse the 'No-Such-Thing-as-a-Bad-Trip' idea. That's largely the case in settings with mindful and generous amounts of time devoted to screening, preparation, and integration as well as careful consideration of appropriate dosage and support. Research settings have several checks-and-balances for assuring ethical protocols, well-trained personnel, and adequate contingency plans. Religious and indigenous communities have different but parallel mechanisms for outlying appropriate ceremonial rituals and standards for facilitators.

At the same time, scary moments can and do occur during some journeys. One type of shadow figure can emerge during the onset or midpoint of a journey, often taking the form of a leviathan, serpent, dragon, or demonic-looking monster.[43] The general guidance is to acknowledge the figure, remain steady with courage, and ask, "What do you have to teach or show me?" The idea is that scary figures and images are actually guardians of a threshold that can grant access to a more transformative phase of a journey. This perspective corresponds to how shadow work is a necessary part of individuation. It's also a parallel to the demonic-looking figures adorning some Buddhist temples, which ward off the unprepared.[44] Informed visitors understand these figures as guardian deities or materialized illusions serving as a test of courage necessary to pass prior to entering a temple. In mythic stories too, shadow figures can transform into allies and protectors that defend a journeyer from inherent dangers of the underworld. These variations of the shadow figure provide special knowledge and courage, which may reflect elements of the timid journeyer's unrealized strengths.

Nevertheless, some indigenous and Western journeyers understand certain entities as genuinely dangerous if not approached with caution. Are these figures threshold guardians, as we've discussed, projections of our own mind, or something else? Psychedelic retreat facilitator and Buddhist interfaith chaplain Daan Keiman originally advocated for the above approach in addressing such scary figures.[45] After gaining experience with journeyers from different religions and cultural perspectives, he speaks now in broader terms and offers alternative approaches based on one's personal intentions and cultural background. Keiman describes this shift as a way to respect the "spiritual integrity" and autonomy of journeyers coming from diverse worldviews. Cultural respect and humility, however, is valuable for all of us. There's no one-size-fits-all approach, and no matter our experience—personal or professional—having a 'beginner's mind' helps us respect not only psychedelics but also each other.

Heroic vs. Microdosing—
Or, High-Intensity and Low-Intensity Ego Training?

When journeys are wholly or largely positive, a different and thornier shadow can arise, mostly due to uneven or incomplete integration work. Spiritual bypass has already been alluded to throughout this book, and many of the warnings touched upon in our existential trials addressed common traps of spiritual bypass. Ego inflation is one pernicious example that can impede personal growth. Having a few journeys with escalating 'heroic' doses can correspond to a 'high-intensity ego training plan' where intense experiences become a badge of courage (resulting in bragging rights), not catalysts for psychospiritual transformation. Repeated ego dissolution followed by a rapid return to 'normal' may also illicit 'ego whiplash.' In response to this whiplash, our everyday egos can reassert control without integrating any new insights.

Or, we may choose to focus on the easier lessons offered by psychedelics while ignoring the harder ones that require larger shifts in our behavior, mindset, or lifestyle.

At the other end of the dosing spectrum is 'low-intensity ego training.' The key examples are microdosing and non-psychoactive alternatives that remove the 'side effect' of mystical and non-ordinary consciousness. These alternatives are appealing to many people and businesses because they fit nicely within already accepted methods of psychopharmacology, prevailing financial interests, and existing social frameworks that'd rather avoid all the 'weird' psychedelic effects.[46] On-going research will explore the relative effectiveness of these alternatives, but the advantages they offer in their ease of fit within dominant, traditional approaches to psychopharmacology and societal institutions are also clues to their limited transformational potential.

Beyond the Confusion of Grey—Compassion as a Mediator with the Shadow

In facing numerous personal and collective shadows, we might become confused by seeing only the grey, an amorphous blending of shadow-and-light, good-and-evil, a disorienting menagerie. Or we could adopt an overarching cynicism that discounts all 'light' or 'good' in the world. But that's not the point either. It simply switches shadows. Instead of confusion, cynicism, or returning to our prior naivety, we might envision the possibility of wholeness instead of fracture. A well-known symbol for this wholeness is Taoism's Yin-Yang, which represents how two 'opposing' forces are brought into a steady, complementary balance. The greater synthesis is not erasure of difference but respectful collaboration and open dialogue.

While finding our own version of this synthesis, we benefit from keeping the lines of communication open, even when we're unclear of the way forward. Communication between shadow and ego supports integration through an on-going process of negotiation and collaboration, whenever possible. Like individuation more broadly, psychedelic and shadow integration both require, as Jungian analyst Scott Hill suggests, "bringing released unconscious material into a constructive relationship with consciousness."[47] So what might be constructive? That's the big question for each individual, and perhaps for humanity as a whole.

Based on my personal and professional experiences, I've come to regard one attitude and practice as especially vital in shadow work—*compassion*. Compassion, far more than intellectual knowledge alone, recognizes the complexity of human beings and the world. In its highest form, it's an innate quality of the Self. Compassion, like the shadow, however, can be misunderstood. Sometimes it's equated with empathy, other times with love. Although empathy is connected to compassion, feeling the emotional suffering of others can lead to becoming overwhelmed, burned out, or numb. There's just too much to feel, and that's based solely on what we can access through daily mainstream news. We can't process all that emotional experience and intellectual knowledge, much less in a sustainable way.

Love might be a close relative of compassion, but it carries its own baggage. For good reason too. Love comes in several quite divergent forms.[48] Romantic love alone possesses three features—passion, intimacy, and commitment—each of which vary across time, person-to-person, and relationship-to-relationship.[49] In contrast, non-romantic forms of love like agape or loving-kindness are most relevant here.[50] They're natural outgrowths of recognizing universal suffering alongside our interconnectedness.

As with most multifaceted ideas, a strict definition of compassion can be hard to nail down.[51] Nevertheless, our now-familiar model of the four modes can help us explore its facets (see Figure 9.2). In its highest form (or most basic, depending on your perspective,) compassion involves an experience and/or attitude that naturally arises from fully recognizing the suffering of oneself or others. A compassionate attitude is difficult to master in our action-oriented (and judgmental) world. At the level of emotion, body, and behavior, what appears to be compassion may actually be the result of avoidance or unattuned perspective taking. Examples can include feeling anger in response to another person's suffering (to avoid feeling empathic pain), crossing one's arms in a defensive posture (to avoid vulnerable, physical expressions of openness), or jumping to save, give advice, or problem-solve without the other person's permission (to avoid sitting with discomfort by acting out of impatience or inadvertently underestimating the sufferer's own coping abilities).

Even with compassion serving as a mediator, it's wise to maintain respect for the power of the shadow, in all its forms, before jumping to conclusions about how to respond to its messages and impulses. If the shadow is partly a moral problem, as Jung suggested, then compassion might be one moral force capable of transcending that problem.[52] The shadow, by definition, has been rejected, sidelined, and/or projected onto others. That's got to sting. The shadow is familiar with non-compassionate responses like indifference, denial, or outright malevolence. Schadenfreude, relishing or laughing at the suffering of others, is one all-too-common example of anti-compassion.

Keep in mind that even as we cultivate compassion, the shadow doesn't magically disappear. As an inevitable aspect of the human psyche, the shadow is not so easily dealt with—yet another reason to start with compassion as an attitude or inner experience, not a behavior. When we jump to action, we may do more harm than good. If we grow our compassion as an attitude first, we do not diminish its potential as a harm reduction strategy. At the personal level, cultivating self-compassion can reduce the damage of overactive self-criticism. At the social and collective levels, cultivating greater compassion

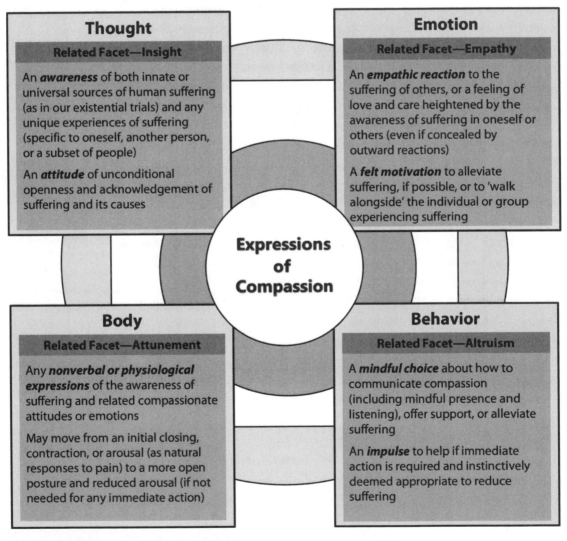

Figure 9.2 Expressions of Compassion Across the Four Modes

towards others (from loved ones to strangers to outright adversaries) can reduce the societal harm of shadow projection and the splitting of others into good-vs-evil categories.

Integrating Insights from Unseen Realms— Compassion as a Gateway to Atonement & Discernment

In general, we're more successful when moving towards something meaningful or positive versus only trying to move away from old or harmful habits. This general principle is helpful as you continue the lifelong process of shadow work. Maintaining awareness of the shadow requires we acknowledge and observe pain, suffering, and darker emotions like shame and hate in ourselves and others. To balance this awareness, we can access our compassion and dare to hope, not in some fantasized outcome, but in the possibility of healing connections and experiencing personal and collective transformation. The following explores some especially tricky but important nuances of expanding compassion. A common theme is allowing an awareness of complexity to coexist with an acceptance of responsibility.

Compassion Moves Beyond Shame. For people prone to feeling excessive guilt or shame, self-compassion may appear to be, at minimum, self-indulgence. Fostering self-compassion, however, can help us tolerate and learn from especially vulnerable emotions. Having personal values can sometimes be intimidating. Some values can be treated like impossibly high standards against which to judge ourselves and our behavior. Values are ideals, directions to move towards, not attainable destinations. If we don't take that to heart, it's easy to fall prey to perfectionism and excessive guilt, if not outright shame. Shame is particularly powerful. It's up there with sheer terror, probably because our ancestral instincts equate social rejection with death. Even when experienced in solitude, shame comes with the impulse to hide or disappear. Being publicly shamed then must feel exponentially more intense—and in the era of online data and smart phone video uploads, there's no place to hide. The panopticon—the equivalent of Sauron's all-seeing eye—is pretty much realized, and that's downright terrifying.[53]

In this context, how do we feel safe enough to lower our guard and be authentic? We need not ignore harmful behavior, but practicing self-compassion bolsters our sense of fundamental worthiness. When we feel worthy at our core, it's easier to dismantle unhelpful social programming about meeting other people's standards. Instead, we can focus on living our own genuine values and enjoying life while we do so.[54]

Sometimes people really do mess up, including ourselves. We can have a bad day, say something we later regret, or betray our own values in a moment of weakness. Then again, we sometimes take more than our fair share of the responsibility for negative outcomes or painful experiences. Self-compassion lets us accept our complexity and imperfections, not as a blanket approval of all our behavior, but as a source of renewal and positive energy as we strive to do better. By being comfortable with solitude and accepting our interconnectedness, we can take time for self-reflection and give space to others who we might have hurt. Then, if needed, we can council with our most trusted friends and allies about our actions and ways to move forward. If we did mess up, then we can work towards *atonement*—the process of seeking forgiveness and making amends for our mistakes. Atonement is, in fact, a core theme of mythic journeys.[55] It's also a theme shared in many therapeutic approaches to posttraumatic healing and addiction recovery.[56] If we strive only for perfection and forget our human foibles, we're only setting a trap for our eventual fall.

The ins-and-outs of atonement, of course, differ by situation and depend on the parties involved, but believing in the possibility of atonement—itself perhaps a choice or a leap of faith—opens a doorway to a brighter, more hopeful future for us as individuals and for our relationships. Shame and guilt can weigh us down without leading to tangible improvements in our personal behavior or social environment.[57] On the other hand, emotional avoidance can lead to skirting responsibilities and projecting fault onto others. A productive yet counterintuitive alternative is to go into the experience of shame or guilt, letting it rise and fall like emotions do naturally, and then reflect on what happened before deciding what if any action is needed to make amends. Compassion is the salve for any temporary pain that may result. It supports us in living our values, despite our imperfections due to being human and having, by necessity, a shadow.

Compassion Moves Beyond Retaliation. It feels empowering to hold others accountable for harmful behavior. After all, accountability is an essential ingredient of justice. But the shadow of justice isn't as simple as injustice. It includes the myriad ways calls for justice can transform into witch hunts (scapegoating), mob 'justice' (groupthink and diffusion of responsibility), and other uneven, disproportionate, or impulsive reactions.

As shadow work reminds us, no one is immune to the temptations of retaliation, self-righteousness, and misuses of power. That doesn't mean we give into these impulses. Justice is complex. Intuitively, most of us have a sense of what justice entails, but when we drill down to details, it's no wonder most justice systems, formal and informal, are so convoluted.[58] Besides, wielding judgment as a sword ensures it cuts both ways. If we're convinced we've mastered our virtues, then we've absolved ourselves of all guilt, shame, and wrongdoing—past, present, and future, right? Of course not. Those disavowed feelings and motivations simply slip into the shadow instead, where they arguably can do greater damage. The shadow denied becomes the shadow projected. Calls for swift and harsh judgment can serve as smokescreens for retaliation or powerplays.

As a response to the ethical problems posed by the shadow, compassion does *not* equate to abandoning justice as a personal and societal value. If compassion offers any alternative to the double-edged sword of harsh retribution and judgment, then it might come in the form of a shield and staff paired with a honed power of discernment. A shield defends the vulnerable—the vulnerable parts of ourselves, others, and society at large. The staff channels our energy into healing and advocating with compassion. But only a wise mind, with its access to both emotional and intellectual insights, can discern how best to defend the vulnerable and strive for justice, all the while keeping an eye open to all the shadows at play. *Discernment* is the ability to perceive what may be obscured (the various shadows of ourselves and others) in order to choose a wise course of action without giving into judgment.

Compassion sometimes inspires us to offer constructive feedback. Giving time for self-reflection can safeguard the risk of communicating from a place of self-importance or inadequate information. Compassionate communication unlocks but doesn't guarantee the possibility of repair. Compassion helps us look past our fear and righteous indignation and see into the tender hearts underneath the masks of others (their personas) and the diverse weaponry of frightened egos and vengeful shadows.[59] But make no mistake, those weapons are real. As rules of thumb, the best predictor of future behavior is past behavior, and if words are misaligned with deeds, then actions do speak louder than words. Yet, the shadow reminds us that in the right circumstances, we too could fall prey to the same temptations of power, greed, fear, and vengeance. Harshly judging others is easy, but on average, we're quite willing to make excuses for our own problematic behavior.[60]

Perhaps the most crucial connection between shadow and compassion involves our last waypoint's theme: identity—the problem of in-group versus out-group. This problem centers all the prejudices that endanger efforts to broaden our circles of compassion and sense of shared humanity. Our in-group is informed by our personality, values, beliefs, culture, demographics, and the people we believe share them. The parts of our identity most connected to our social relationships and places of belonging coalesce to form our social identity.

When ethics and justice are applied only to our in-group, whatever that may be, then the shadow is projected onto an out-group because it's a far safer target. If the enemy is out there, then we can band together, strengthening our bonds and determination without any risk to our sense of belonging. If instead we understand the shadow within and expand our compassion in turn, then we're committing a bold act in the face of larger-than-life cultural shadows—classism, racism, sexism, homophobia, biphobia, and transphobia, to name a few.[61] Holding tightly onto our social identities and ideologies can be risky for our personal wellbeing and for society at large if it breaks down communication and collaborative problem-solving.[62] Putting it mildly, Jack Kornfield summarized, "People with opinions just go around bothering one another."[63] If unabated, 'bothering' each other turns into blaming each other, which eventually devolves into an almost inseparable divide. Appeals to our shared humanity work best when we don't try to erase our differences but instead respect them alongside our similarities.

Fear strengthens the path of blame and shadow projection. The 'other' becomes a heathen, infidel, deplorable, racist, criminal, or any other label that separates our shadow from our idealized sense of self or own community. Worse yet, it can demote others to the status of non-human. Dehumanizing the 'other' is a classic strategy of political propaganda, not an honest or mature application of ethics or morality. The most dangerous 'other' is often in us as much, if not more, than in 'them.'

As mere mortals, trying to comprehend complex ethical and social issues can lead to giving up.[64] Justice and ethics, like politics and religion, belong to a critical but immense can of worms. As you work through various challenges offered by the shadow, consider how your personal values might work as broader ethical principles. Then explore how they wouldn't work. Playing devil's advocate to your own ideas is a great way to challenge your strongest opinions and give your shadow a voice without letting it loose.

As Jung warned, "The more a [person]'s life is shaped by the collective norm, the greater is [their] individual immorality."[65] Besides conformity to mainstream norms and political ideologies, the risk also includes becoming a victim of dangerous cults. I'm referring specifically to insular groups that assert control over their members and may also pose a risk to non-members.

Compassion for self and others both come into play when trying to discern whether one has encountered a genuine cult. Personal humility is best tempered by healthy amounts of hesitation and mindful observation of others—but not to the point of hypervigilance. Powerful substances and experiences like those offered by psychedelics attract wolves in sheep's clothing, and as any promise of collective light increases, so might the collective shadow.

An Evolving Circle of Compassion— A Focused Brainstorming Exercise

As before, take a few minutes to respond to the prompts below about your experiences with compassion, atonement, and discernment. Come up with at least three responses to each.

I have an easier time feeling self-compassion when...

It's hardest for me to feel compassionate towards...

Atonement is possible when...

Practicing discernment requires I...

Fostering Wisdom by
Meeting Shadow with Compassion

To embrace shadow work, we must bring all our allies to the table. First, we must accept the shadow will always exist, regardless of our desire, insight, or progress—psychological, spiritual, cultural, or otherwise. Second, we must be curious about what the shadow has to say so that we can listen to it. Finally, in an on-going process and in especially difficult times, we must rely on our inner wisdom to help discern how to integrate messages from our shadow while reducing the harm it may pose if projected or let loose upon the world.

Using myth as a guide for this seemingly impossible task, we might reflect on how various archetypal heroes and mythic figures resisted the temptation of their own shadow selves. Since I used the words of Galadriel at the outset of this journey and echoed them again in this chapter, I find myself returning to that character now and her embodiment of wisdom and compassion. She too had to face her shadow. And the brighter one's light, the darker one's shadow. Representing Galadriel's ultimate trial of temptation, Frodo offered her the ring of power. Her response initially took a dark path:[66]

> I do not deny that my heart has greatly desired this. [*Her eyes widen, the background darkens, and her voice and countenance become imbued with ethereal power*] In place of a Dark Lord, you would have a Queen, not dark but beautiful and terrible as the morn, treacherous as the sea, stronger than the foundations of the Earth! All shall love me and despair! [*Waking from the temporary possession by her Shadow's thirst for power, she returns to her normal form, momentarily stunned*]...I pass the test. I will diminish, and go into the West, and remain Galadriel.

Galadriel didn't turn away from her shadow and deny its presence. She allowed it to speak openly, but in the end, she resisted the temptation of absolute power. She understood it would end in destruction, regardless of her conscious intention.

As a remarkable yet fallible human, Jung also recognized the importance of staying grounded while confronting the unconscious in all its wonder, power, and terror. In his memoir, he offered the following reflection, "It was most essential for me to have a normal life in the real world as a counterpoise to that strange inner world. My family and my profession remained a base to which I could always return, assuring me that I was an actually existing, ordinary person."[67] If Jung was an "ordinary person," then it shouldn't be that hard for the rest of us to practice humility—if, that is, we value honesty.

Humility paired with compassion helps us avoid shaming ourselves or other people into submission. When cautiously exploring the shadow, we find wisdom in realizing that not all that is unlit is evil. It's unconscious, disavowed, or assumed to be outside ourselves. Power, like responsibility, can be scary and thus be hidden in the shadow, but the destructive side of power can be tempered by regular, mindful reflection—the opposite of unconscious impulse and defense. Unconscious power can be projected onto political leaders, gurus, or therapists—all of whom can be idealized while undermining one's own abilities and agency. Poet Nayyirah Waheed said it nicely, "Knowing your power is what creates humility. Not knowing your power is what creates insecurity."[68]

Given the complexity of our shared reality, anything approaching genuine transcendence requires some integration of *all* phenomena, irrespective of our labels of 'good' and 'bad,' 'self' and 'other.' In other words, we must confront sincere problems, not just skirt over or bypass them spiritually, psychologically, or culturally. We must ask our shadows, "What are you trying to tell me? Or us?" If we keep all our eyes open, asking these questions doesn't mean becoming consumed with darkness or frozen in doubt. And, like before, remembering to laugh while acknowledging our imperfections can go a long way in healing pain and realizing hidden potential.

To close this chapter, let's revisit the metaphor of bamboo that ended our last waypoint. When considering the wisdom gained by respecting the shadow and cultivating compassion, a Chinese proverb offers guidance: "Be like bamboo. The higher you grow the deeper you bow."[69] Remember, though, that other people have their shadows too. But they may not understand what they project onto you is likely part of themselves. Self-compassion ensures we're willing to protect ourselves if needed. To borrow a lesson from martial arts, when you bow, keep your eyes open and remain ready.[70]

Concrete Suggestions & Journey Report

Suggestions for applying insights from this chapter can be found in Box 9.2. After reviewing the list, consider doing any that seem interesting or relevant to your life. For an example of how shadow and compassion can emerge in psychedelic experiences, see Journey Report 9.1. This intense journey acts as a caution for issues of preparation, dose, setting, and continual respect for the power of psychedelics. Calvin was able to navigate this journey only because of his substantial prior experience and integration practices, which included compassion meditations. That said, even he agreed it was an experience he'd rather not repeat.

Box 9.2
Integrating Shadow and Compassion in Everyday Life

Suggestion	Example
Interview a friend, relative, or acquaintance who has a very different political, spiritual or ideological perspective. Be inquisitive, practice active listening, and avoid debates, hostile questioning, or imagining rebuttals. Reflect on places of overlapping values or perspective.	You call your aunt, which whom you have differing political views, and invite her to share more about her perspective for the purpose of dialogue, not debate. From a place of genuine curiosity, you ask the following questions: • "What do you believe is going well in today's world?" • "What's not going so well?" • "What concerns you about the future?" • "If you were in charge, what changes would you make to create a better future?" You find some agreement in values, if not all the policies she'd advocate putting into place.
List your top five favorite love-to-hate fictional villains in movies, novels, or comic books and describe what you like and dislike about each. Determine whether any of their qualities might teach you something about your approach to life.	Your list includes Magneto, Emperor Palpatine, and the Alien Queen. Two are devoted to their cause like Magneto protecting his community's rights at all costs and the Alien Queen's strategic but ruthless protection of her progeny. You hate Emperor Palpatine's thirst for absolute power, but you admire his cunning and ability to operate patiently in the shadows. When considering what you can learn from these characters, you wonder if having greater patience in playing the 'long game' might be an effective approach to living your values and serving your broader community. You still reject, however, an 'ends justifies the means' mindset.
Revisit your top personal values selected from the values card sort. Describe what might be the shadow of each value if lived too rigidly or only selectively.	Upon reflection, your top values of growth and kindness appear to have some potential downsides. In valuing growth, you realize you've felt a perpetual dissatisfaction with life as it is. You push yourself constantly and feel guilt when resting or not making as quick progress as you'd like. As you reflect on kindness, you see that you've been kind to others to a fault by sacrificing your own needs. You have an 'a ha!' moment and understand that personal growth now may mean practicing greater kindness to yourself.
Establish 'compassion triggers' that remind you to practice compassion for yourself and others. Consider a combination of regular 'triggers' and sporadic, even random ones.	You put a sticky note with your favorite inspirational quote about compassion or kindness on your bathroom mirror. Your daily practice is to read it aloud before taking your morning shower. As for your 'random' triggers, you decide to set two different prompts. You turn impatience when waiting at stoplights into a reminder to feel self-compassion, and every time your phone receives an incoming call that goes to voicemail, you imagine sending a brief message of compassion throughout the world.

Grounding Words—A Brief Summary

Nearing the end of your quest, you've now looked into the eyes of the shadow and caught a glimpse of your own mind. Undeterred by fear or shame and unwilling to give into outrage, you remained steady and saw the enemy within. But instead of an enemy, you found a wounded part of yourself that needed to be heard. Although not all it had to say could be taken at face value, you learned the wisdom of questioning your assumptions about other people, especially people who represent disavowed aspects of yourself. This challenge has not been easy, but you've realized the shadow has been with you and your journey all along. You've gained strength by exploring your deeper fears and the complexity of human consciousness and life. With this strength and your evolving insights, you've found a greater capacity for compassion than previously realized. Meeting your shadow with compassion has provided you with the key for unlocking more of your hidden potential while living your values. No longer a source of shame or self-righteousness, your values now can take their place as guideposts for a meaningful life. Compassion for self and others has gifted you the wisdom of allowing forgiveness and atonement while practicing mindful discernment. You've now passed the final test.

Your Assignment, Your Choice

Before proceeding to our final chapter, review and select activities from your recommended assignments, ideally cutting across the two broad domains of *Reflective-Intellectual* and *Experiential-Emotional*. Engage in at least one activity daily before moving onto the next waypoint. As you see fit, also consider revisiting any previous activities or worksheets from throughout your journey, as long as they connect to your overarching intentions and the themes of shadow and compassion.

Assignments 9.1
Moving Beyond Shadow Projections

Reflective-Intellectual	Experiential-Emotional
☐ Task—Complete Form 4.1 **"The Experiential Explorer"** to reflect on situations that trigger shame, righteous indignation, and/or compassion	☐ Task—Create **Shadow Masks**—a physical or virtual collection of cartoon-style faces that represent your less understood or accepted parts of self. See Exercise 9.1 for instructions.
Time—At least 2-3 entries, up to 30 min each, with a minimum of one shadow-related and one compassion-related entry	Time—At least 1 hr where you get lost in the flow of creating these masks and reflecting on the activity
Aim—To gain insight about personal triggers that activate either your shadow or your natural reactions of compassion	Aim—To visualize parts of your shadow that can be seen most easily in others and not as part of your everyday sense of self
☐ Task—Explore mythic and cultural **representations of the Shadow archetype** with at least one from your culture(s) of origin and one from another culture	☐ Task—Practice the meditation in **Meditation 9.1 "Expanding Compassion and Kindness"**
Time—Minimum of 1 hr for research with additional time to reflect and journal about your reactions	Time—Minimum of 2-3x/week, ~15 min
Aim—To understand shared and distinct qualities of the shadow within and across cultures	Aim—To cultivate greater compassion for yourself and others including those who represent your shadow

After reviewing your options, assign yourself a few tasks to complete or practice before going into our final journey waypoint. Then respond to this chapter's journal prompt however you see fit.

Travel Journal

How might cultivating compassion help me better express my values?

How might self-compassion help me better engage with life and live my personal values?

JOURNEY REPORT 9.1 An Ocean of Lost Souls

Two years ago, I had the not-so-bright idea of doing a high-dose journey (about 7 grams of mushrooms) for my first outdoor experience. The location was breathtaking—a secluded beach with an eroding but vertical rocky cliff separating me from the rest of society. It was a stunning location, but I planned to journey inwards, per my usual protocol, by lying down with headphones and eyeshades. I had a friend with me to make sure I was safe, but he was inexperienced with psychedelics so not the best choice for support, especially with such a high dose. I was resolute, though, to make it happen, and I trusted myself and the mushrooms since I had several journeys before in that approximate dose range, including by myself.

Once I had eaten the mushrooms, the experience intensified faster than usual. The music seemed louder too, but I remained calm. I focused on breathing and kept my eyes closed despite the intensity. The visuals were at first very minimal, if not completely absent. Instead of 'ego death' or anything like that, I felt a hollowness, like being empty of human emotions, no joy, no fear, nothing. It might sound disturbing now, but it wasn't at the time. Probably because I was empty of all such feelings. The visual experience eventually kicked in, though I can't say when since time was completely altered. It started with me imagining (or seeing?) an interwoven fabric of space and time, at the subatomic level it seemed, with pulsating orbs connected by strings of energy. It was beautiful and awe-inspiring, but I didn't *feel* awe per se since I remained relatively empty of human emotions.

Then, a bit of fear, or at least concern, started to creep into my experience. For good reason too. I began to hear the screams of dead souls crying in pain. They appeared envious of my lifeforce. I saw a legion of them clawing at me, trying to enter my body and mind, to possess me. I breathed deeper but steadied my heart and mind, partly by keeping my rate of breath slow. Instead of becoming frightened and shattered, I trusted in the invisible shield that kept my soul protected. I didn't consciously imagine or create this shield but because these dead souls hadn't already taken over, I knew it was there regardless. Something must have been protecting me, right?

I witnessed these souls from my relatively safe point of view and saw they were suffering greatly, some with intense fear, others with ravenous hunger and envy, and others with outrage. Because I could see their suffering, I felt profound compassion, but without being overwhelmed by the sheer magnitude of their suffering. I used each out breathe to offer some kindness and wish that their suffering would cease. Eventually, I took off my headphones and opened my eyes. I saw the ocean and cliffs around me with intricate patterns of swirling circles, as if parts of the world were dying and being reborn, again and again. I was in awe and smiled with appreciation, still feeling the universal compassion in the face of so much fear and pain. I can't say I'd ask for this experience again. I gained a deeper respect for the power of psychedelics to say the least—and the power of compassion to navigate these scary moments within journeys and in life in general.

—Calvin, Age 35

Note. This account and all others in the book are de-identified and anonymous to protect the confidentiality of the person sharing their story. Minor grammar, spelling, and stylistic changes were made and usually in partnership with the person providing the account.

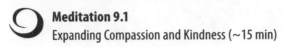

Meditation 9.1
Expanding Compassion and Kindness (~15 min)

After reading this meditation script to preview its flow, find a comfortable, safe place to sit, stand, or lay down where you'll be free from any major distractions. If you do become distracted by other thoughts or outside interruptions, remember you can gently refocus without getting lost in distractions or judging yourself for losing concentration. Note that authentic compassion and kindness can take practice over time when directed at especially challenging people or explored as universal non-conditional expressions of care. Like any skill or attitude, practice eventually will pay off, so try to be patient with yourself if parts of this meditation are difficult at this stage.

Close your eyes and begin centering yourself in the present moment....if thoughts distract you, use your breath to ground yourself...

Picture yourself in your most tranquil and caring state of mind...perhaps in a specific place where you feel most connected to nature and can easily recognize the interconnectedness of all things...In this expanded state, take a few deep breaths...

Now, take a moment to imagine your personal shadow as taking the form of a small child. This inner child may be scared...angry...hurt...or simply unaware of its place in society, the world, or the cosmos...What does this child look like? What emotional expressions are they making?...See this child as separate yet connected to you. As such, it's connected as well to your higher Self with its greater perspective, wisdom, and experience...

Remaining in a state of meditation, open your arms to this inner child in an expression of acceptance and care...allow the child to respond however it might...perhaps with reluctance, doubt, fear, or anger but know that you both remain safe...Once your childlike shadow softens and becomes still, repeat the following:

> May I recognize you in all your forms and accept my imperfections with grace
>
> May I listen to the sources of suffering that you try to communicate with me
>
> May I reduce the harm I might do when denying or ignoring you
>
> May I express compassion and kindness to all parts of myself in all my complexity

Imagine this inner child now feeling calm, safe, and cared for...they then come towards you with arms open ready to embrace...hold this childlike part of yourself as the child hugs you too...

Now shift your imagination to see a loved one. This person may or may not be present in your current life or alive today. Either way, lock eyes with them and smile...see them with all their strengths and challenges...and all their sources of pain and joy...Open your arms to them and repeat the following:

> May I accept your imperfections with grace as I hope you accept mine
>
> May I understand your sources of suffering
>
> May I atone for any harm I've inadvertently done by ignoring or dismissing your pain
>
> May I show you compassion and kindness in all your complexity

Imagine embracing each other with a smile. Feel each other's warmth and your deeper connection...

Shift your attention now to a person, real or imagined, who represents your personal or cultural shadow in whatever form that may take currently... Perhaps a person with a different life philosophy or political ideology...Or a person who has harmed you directly or hurt someone you care about...Know that imagining this person may be especially hard but give yourself time to adjust and reaffirm a feeling of safety, openness, and compassion...

Look into each other's eyes and see their challenges as well as their strengths... Where might they be suffering?...Where do they experience pain, either because of the carelessness of others or because of their own doing?...

Imagine for a moment, you both are willing and able to be vulnerable with each other and give up any pretense or defensiveness....When you're ready, open your arms to them and repeat the following:

> May I recognize the shadow in all its forms, including what we project onto each other
>
> May I accept your imperfections with grace
>
> May I understand our sources of suffering
>
> May I discern how best to reduce the harm we can do to each other
>
> May I feel compassion and express kindness in recognizing you in all your complexity

Imagine, if you can, smiling, shaking hands, or even embracing each other and feeling a sense of deeper connection than either of you might have expected otherwise. If you cannot muster these imaginary expressions, simply expand your compassion as an attitude and a nod of respect...

When ready, re-center yourself in your expanded state of compassion towards your personal sources of suffering and shadow as well as those of others... take a few deep breaths, imagining on the in-breath that you're taking in the suffering of all sentient beings, not feeling it but recognizing it. And on the out-breath, provide newly cleansed energy free of suffering and full of kindness...And repeat the following:

> May all beings be freed from their sources of suffering
>
> May all beings feel safe, accepted, worthy, and loved
>
> May all aspects of light, shadow, and everything in between be brought into greater balance

From this place of universal compassion and kindness, take several deep breaths...allow everything to be as it is while sending out your well wishes for the world...

Then, as you feel ready, gradually begin to bring yourself back into your body and your current coordinates of space and time...Allow yourself a gentle return...And slowly reopen your eyes to end this meditation.

Exercise 9.1

Creating Shadow Masks

Purpose. To express and visual parts of your personal or collective shadow as faces or masks so that they may be more easily recognized when activated.

Note. Be sure to practice self-care and active coping upon completing this exercise, if needed. The compassion meditation from this waypoint may be especially helpful and relevant. Shadow work is emotionally evocative so should be done with care.

Step 1—Review the types of shadows and jot down ideas for your version of each. Note that the examples are not comprehensive and universal, so take them with a grain of salt.

Step 2—Draw or create your own version of each mask in two- or three-dimensional form.

> *Alternative*—Find images that capture the essence of each shadow. For your final collection, it's best to avoid images of real people since that may reaffirm the default understanding of the shadow as outside and not within.

Step 3—Imagine putting on each mask one at a time (or do so if you created physical masks). Look through each mask's eyes and experience its perspective for a few moments. If using your imagination to wear each mask, close your eyes to engage with the experience more deeply.

Step 4—After imagining the perspective of each shadow, take a few moments to recenter your everyday sense of self. You can do so by taking a few deep cleansing breaths or by practicing any skill or meditation from this book that has personally resonated with you.

Step 5—Record your reactions to this activity in your Travel Journal. Note what it was like creating each mask, viewing each from the outside, and putting them on to embody temporarily what they represent. Did you have any surprising or especially powerful reactions at any point in this exercise? Were there any messages from these symbolic shadows that might be important to continue reflecting on?

Exercise continues on next page

Types of Shadow	Examples	Personal Notes
Fear-inducing— Evokes anxiety, distress, or terror	A person with an angry scowl A ravenous predatory animal thirsty for blood	
Anger-inducing— Evokes irritation, hostility, outrage, or hate	Someone with a passive-aggressive attitude A corrupt leader secretly abusing their power	
Shame-inducing— Evokes intense guilt, self-blame, or humiliation	Someone hypercritical and blaming An overzealous critic publicly chastising you and expressing contempt	
Mythic— Evokes experience of sublime, bafflement, or insignificance	A powerful force of destruction An inhuman figure with great power but indifference to human concerns	
Inspirational— Evokes admiration of strength, courage, and/or our unexpressed talents	An admired artist who expresses confidence while working at the cutting edge of their artform A deity of cosmic mystery beyond human understanding	

CHAPTER 10

Beyond the Narrow Life—
Towards a Life of Creative Engagement
& Symbolic Renewal

Wakanda will no longer watch from the shadows. We cannot. We must
not. We will work to be an example of how we, as brothers and sisters
on this earth, should treat each other. Now, more than ever, the illusions
of division threaten our very existence. We all know the truth: More
connects us than separates us. But in times of crisis the wise build bridges,
while the foolish build barriers. We must find a way to look after one
another, as if we were one single tribe.

—King T'challa, *Black Panther*[1]

Journey Waypoint IX

Having faced the fears of human existence and confronted the inescapable
shadow, we arrive at the final destination of our journey. Although endings
can be bittersweet, this one is where you transition to the open road. All training wheels are off. It is your task now to transform the infinite possibilities of
your life into a series of courageous acts of creativity, problem solving, and
authentic meaning.

If that feels both exciting and daunting, then you're tuned into the right
frequency. Of course, if you're feeling calm, cool, and collected, you probably
are too. Occasional encounters with mystics and humanists alike have convinced me of the usefulness, if not necessity, of having hope. Some understand
our current polarization and intense reactions to entrenched social problems
as the temporary death throes of collective trauma being worked out. Eventually these cries of pain will give way to the reprieve of silence. A pause before
a rebirth in which we'll reflect and envision a new way forward.

If we remain optimistic while avoiding nihilism and complacency, we just
might turn that hopeful vision into a new reality. It doesn't need to be perfect.
But it will take effort and time. Lucky for us, we're not alone. And the resilience of human consciousness lies in our individual and collective creativity.
All hands on deck. It's about to get interesting.

Self-Reflections Check-In

The last chapter's themes of shadow and compassion were likely challenging for you in one way or another. Did your reactions to the material change after doing any of your selected activities? What about experiencing moments of compassion? Compassion seems like it'd be an easier topic than the shadow, but I've learned from my clients and my own experience that what sounds easy usually isn't when trying to put it into practice—that is, integrate it into daily life. On the other hand, every step in that direction starts to loosen our grasp on unhelpful judgments and attitudes. You've made it this far, and that's a significant feat. For whatever challenges you still face, pause and take a moment to feel a sense of compassion and gratitude towards yourself. As we explored with the shadow, overcoming challenges is often about working with them, not getting rid of them. When ready, press onward. One more time.

Beyond the Narrow Life—
The Possible Meanings of a More than Ordinary Existence

Going beyond the narrow life is like going beyond identity, ego, and shadow. In going beyond, we aren't escaping the inescapable. To live in the world, we need our egos, and whether we like it or not, we need our shadows too. But what is a narrow life? At first glance, 'narrow' in this context means "limited in extent, amount, or scope" or "restricted."[2] By the very nature of being human individuals who're making choices and searching for transcendence, we indeed face limits. Yet some limits are self-imposed. A narrow life may come from a restricted and rigid perspective, a narrow-minded understanding of our potential and the broader possibilities of deeper meaning. The opposite would be an open mindset that allows the continual attainment of greater insights and fosters the flexibility necessary to engage with life's complexity. If psychedelics can open one's mind, then integration can open one's life.

In an ironic twist, though, living *beyond* a narrow life may be akin to choosing a path that's inherently narrow. That is, narrow in the sense of being a focused path that although available to many, is taken only by a few adventurous souls—or even a single traveler. Despite the similarities of many core human concerns, each person must walk their own path and come to their own conclusions. Engaging deeply in that personal journey is embracing a more than ordinary life. Profound expanded states of consciousness may become more widely available over time if psychedelics enter mainstream culture. Even so, a profoundly engaged life entails courage and commitment. It requires, in other words, an ever-unfolding task of integration.

Because religion can be understood as an especially powerful expression of mythology, we might consider two classic voices representing the Self according to Jung—Jesus and the Buddha.[3] As a Western symbol, Jesus explained the difficulty of taking the narrow path in his Sermon on the Mount: "Because strait is the gate, and narrow is the way, which leadeth unto life, and few there be that find it."[4] This passage may not be the most optimistic line of his sermon, but it highlights life's challenges—even when a roadmap like organized religion exists. We also might contend with the risk of falling off the edges. It's wise to heed the warnings of others—either people who've successfully traveled farther down the road or those who've become cautionary tales after having fallen. As Campbell echoed as well, "a narrow path is a very dangerous path—the razor's edge."[5]

The Buddha, an Eastern symbol of the Self, advocated for the Middle Way, a path that avoids the excesses of self-denial and self indulgence. Lama Surya Das reminded us, though, "[T]he Middle Way is not like a narrow yellow line down the center of the road. It has plenty of lanes on either side for us to enjoy at our different speeds and in our different ways."[6] In the end, what divides a 'narrow' from a 'not-narrow' life may be perplexing—paradoxical even. In other words, we're right at home in the world of psychedelic experiences.

How Individuation Involves Exploring Symbols & Creativity

Undertaking the lifelong challenges of integration and authentic living is where individuation really kicks into gear. It also requires charting your own course. Maps that can approximate the terrain exist, for sure, but maps can be incomplete and tell only one part of the story. That's true of myths as well. Mythic stories have a *symbolic* core—their figurative expression of some transcendent, non-literal meaning. If signs point the way, symbols *are* the way. Symbols have multiple layers of meaning that speak to us in different ways. If taken too literally, we're left with overly complicated interpretations and contradictory sets of dogma and rules. Attachment to tradition or rationality can quickly overshadow the spirit and emotional subtext behind even the most powerful myths. To remain meaningful, myth must stay alive. Living forms of mythology require updates and refinements—a natural consequence of the passage of time (impermanence) and the evolving needs of a culture or community.

In a person's (ideally) more innocent years of childhood, myths take the form of fantastical stories which reaffirm the magic of life as lived through a child's eyes.[7] They impart a few life lessons in the process. As we age, innocence is no longer an option. Escaping into fantasy to avoid pain might be possible but only temporarily. Choosing rebellion is tempting, but it too eventually faces roadblocks. From adolescence to young adulthood, rebellion against authority and the status quo may be an important stage. But it can also mask another kind of escapist fantasy—belief in a romantic, idealized future. As both innocence and rebellion prove ineffective, everyday demands of modern adult life can drain the magic out of our early mythologies and fantasies. After a period of disillusionment, many of us abandon our childhood mythologies—including religions. In the Netflix series *Messiah*, the mysterious Savior-like figure al-Masih echoes a real-life commencement speech by David Foster Wallace, "Everybody worships. The only choice is what we worship. Some people kneel to money. Some to power, [others] to intellect."[8] Opting for an ordinary life means taking a packaged deal. That may be necessary for a time, but some paths lead deeper than others. Some may shortchange or ignore the symbolic meanings underneath the surface.

Individuation itself is a myth. It's another symbolic expression—one for personal growth and development that goes beyond the ordinary. We could outline concrete steps to individuation, but that betrays its complexity, non-linearity, and individuality. At the same time, we need translations of symbols into digestible stand-ins or starting places. For example, the symbolic mono-myth becomes Campbell's hero's journey which then becomes *Star Wars*. Or in reverse, *Star Wars* becomes a gateway to the hero's journey which hides another doorway to the larger symbolic monomyth. Applying the same logic, we can understand a symbolic growth process involving a soul as being translated into Jung's individuation process involving the Self—which then inspires this book's approach. No translation of symbols is 100% accurate or comprehensive. That's why 'training wheels' (any pre-packaged framework) need to come off eventually. As Bill Richards concluded in *Sacred Knowledge*, "What is *is*—stretching beyond our most favorite words and concepts."[9] Still, our journey isn't done yet, so I'll attempt to impart a few more thoughts or images, partial as they may be.

Creative Symbols—Integration & Individuation

Regardless of our explicit artistic talents, each of us can access creative symbols to help integrate our various life experiences. As a personal example, one powerful image emerged while writing this book: channeling chaotic oceanic waters (ideas, feelings, paradoxes, nonlinearity) into a steady, more manageable and concentrated stream for you, the reader. While discussing her book *Consciousness Medicine*, Françoise Bourzat has used tapestry metaphors like weaving to visualize both the process of writing and editing as well as psychedelic integration.[10] In his work on individuation, Jung spoke frequently of the *mandala*, the Sanskrit word for 'disk' or 'circle,' as a critical symbol of personal transformation. The mandala represents wholeness and the integration of conscious and unconscious parts. Nowadays, mandala drawing has become a tradition of holotropic breathwork. After breathwork ceremonies, journeyers create mandalas as a method for jumpstarting their integration process.

Creating mandala-like images symbolizes individuation by imposing a boundary around the totality of the Self. Having this boundary focuses our attention on what's contained inside (our consciousness), but its circular structure encourages us to find the most efficient use of space, which usually involves balanced and symmetrical relationships. In these ways, mandalas encourage finding harmony over chaos and serve as helpful tools for working with paradox and conflict. The Taoist Yin-Yang image symbolizes this balance of opposing forces as complementary, not conflictual. In various other Eastern religions, the mandala is a tool for contemplation, particularly on impermanence and the illusory nature of everyday reality. As a striking example, Tibetan Buddhist monks spend weeks to create highly intricate mandalas out of colored sand. When finished, the monks engage in the ceremonial destruction of the sand mandala as a practice of letting go. The collected sand is later released into a river or stream to spread blessings for the cessation of suffering.

Psychologically speaking, the creation and destruction of mandalas is analogous to the creation of our increasingly complex individual self and the eventual necessity of its deconstruction—ultimately meaning death.[11] Jungian analyst Marie-Louise von Franz suggested the image of an "ascending spiral" to describe the path of individuation.[12] The spiral develops as a balance is formed between two forces—the expansive creative force of the unconscious, which pulls outward like a centrifugal force, and the conservative force of consciousness, which pulls inward towards its center like a centripetal force. The optimism of an upward spiral is appealing, but our perceptions of what may be the center (or even up) are not necessarily accurate or enduring.

Highlighting this theme of change is both Yeats's poem "The Second Coming," and Achebe's echoing of this stanza in the title and opening pages of his novel *Things Fall Apart*:[13]

Turning and turning in the widening gyre
The falcon cannot hear the falconer;
Things fall apart; the center cannot hold;
Mere anarchy is loosed upon the world.

For us as individuals and our respective societies, reflecting on cycles of life-death-rebirth may loosen our grip on our more naïve or overconfident world-views as well as our more apocalyptic doomsday prophecies. Reflecting on the cosmos, the focus of our first waypoint, reminds us our point of view is always limited, and time changes everything. Depending on where we are in such cycles, that may be humbling, comforting, or both.

Creative Engagement—Symbolic Amplification & Appreciation

To engage deeply with symbols, we can practice the art of *amplification*. Amplification involves connecting our personal concerns, passions, and experiences with exaggerated or more powerful symbolic expressions in their collective form. Amplification uses analogy and metaphor to intensify our understanding and relationship with partially or inadequately expressed unconscious content. In using the myth of Sisyphus, Camus, as an example, amplified his reactions to meaninglessness in a way that let him wrestle with and understand them better as well as express his conclusions with others. Like Camus, each of us has several ways to amplify the meaning of symbols most relevant to our lives.

Film and Art. As stated, myths have always needed to be retold. Religious scholars can speak best to the mythic undertones of world religions, but appreciating symbolic meaning within mythology can exist independent of religious beliefs. As referenced throughout this book, the largest modern vehicle for mythic storytelling is film and television—particularly imaginative fiction.[14] It also has the benefit of cutting across ideological and political aisles.

From a mythic perspective, the continuing proliferation of sequels and remakes isn't merely a money-making scheme. We've always retold stories—from ancient oral traditions to more recent written works. Stories are revisited, reworked, and reimagined. That's how they stay alive. Cynics remind us there's no such thing as a new idea. But when viewed as symbols, repeated ideas often speak to something that transcends any single manifestation.[15] Different elements of stories need to be emphasized at different times and for different people. Each telling has its own shadows, blind spots of various kinds.

As children or adults, we might overidentify with certain archetypal characters, including the hero. In doing so, we can adopt the hero's blind spots too. Original *Star Wars* fans (including myself) needed to see how Luke Skywalker could fail even after he triumphed over Emperor Palpatine in the original trilogy. New fans (younger generations especially) needed to see other types of heroes arise—especially those with no special background beyond their intuition or innate talents, and those with ancestral lineage of the most treacherous kind.[16] If a movie doesn't speak to you, then it may not be *for* you. Or, if you really hate a film, it may have messages about your shadow you're unwilling or not ready to hear. Of course, sometimes it's just a bad movie.

As creators of myth, artists can transform the world. Becoming more sensitive to art deepens our appreciation of its symbolic meaning. Art that resonates personally as well as art that feels dissonant can teach us more about ourselves, our culture, or humanity as a whole. Even if we possess no artistic ability, the fact that we all have an unconscious means we already have something inside us that's endlessly creative—and at times bizarre! Trying to force creativity, however, misses the point of its spontaneity and ephemeral nature. It's like trying to remain in flow states. Adding too much pressure backfires. All artists and creative people have occasional blocks, but everyone regardless of their creative talents can feel inspired by the creativity of others. Allowing ourselves to be inspired connects us again to our

Box 10.1

Artistic Appreciation of Images and Stories

Why does this image or story speak to me?

How does it make me feel? Describe emotions and bodily reactions.

What are my favorite parts or scenes? Why?

What about my least favorite? Why? How would I change these aspects or scenes if I were the creator?

What are the messages embedded within this story or image that speak to me personally?

If I were to apply these messages to my life, what might happen?

What messages might there be for society at large? Or for certain people or groups?

Are there warnings embedded within this story or image? If so, what are they?

own imagination. Besides, artistic appreciation is rewarding in and of itself. If you'd like to hone this deeper level of engagement, Box 10.1's example questions can guide your reflections about any powerful images or stories that you encounter.

Dreams and Active Imagination. Besides the ready-made collective expressions of symbols, personal symbols can be accessed via two central gateways: dreams and active imagination. As far as dreams go, thoughtful interpretation of their symbols can communicate areas of unfinished business or messages our conscious minds have minimized or ignored.[17] It's crucial, however, to realize not all dreams are particularly meaningful or enlightening. Showing up naked for class, at least in a dream, may simply suggest anxiety about overlooking something important or being unprepared.

More meaningful dreams come in two forms: 1) reoccurring dreams (suggesting its message hasn't been fully heard), and 2) unusual dreams that evoke a strong emotional response. When dreams involve feelings of awe, mystery, or sublime disorientation, we might unpack several layers of meaning.[18] To explore possible interpretations, ask yourself what comes to mind when you reflect on each part, figure, or symbol in the dream. Brainstorm several possible responses, including other images or ideas that are harder to articulate. Follow the emotions first. Ideas and theory can come later, if they're helpful at all. If you don't remember your dreams (a common problem in adulthood), don't give up. The best starting place is to set the intention to remember your dreams. Then capture fragments of dreams by saying them aloud or writing them down as soon as you wake up. That will usually lead to recalling details more fully and frequently over time. This journaling approach works with psychedelic integration too.

Jung and Jungian analysts have also emphasized another gateway to personal symbols and creativity—*active imagination*.[19] Active imagination is simply allowing images and stories to unfold like daydreams but without predetermining the twists and turns and eventual ending. Generally, active imagination is best saved for working with professionals. In therapy, people can start with an image from a dream, a piece of art, or something more spontaneous. Then, they close their eyes and act as if they're watching a film. Active imagination is undertaking a semi-conscious choose-your-own-adventure story. It can be hard to do on your own—the ego is after all quite comfortable with controlling a story. Through active imagination, our ego can dialogue with our unconscious to amplify its messages while maintaining its balance. Just be cautious about getting too lost in imagination and fantasy.

The everyday world still needs your presence and attention too.

Creative Problem-Solving—
Where Ingenuity and Talents Meet Need

Like art, creativity comes in many forms. Research and public interests have been mounting about how psychedelics might augment psychological growth and creativity, especially in terms of technological and applied innovations.[20] Keep in mind, however, that growth at the personal or collective level can involve growing pains. Being at the cutting edge of progress is exciting. But the cutting edge has risks, and as our collective power to push past these edges intensifies, so does our collective responsibility to wrestle with tough ethical questions—before our capabilities catch up to our ambitions. Sometimes progress occurs by slowing down, not by speeding up. As Frankl stated, "Since Auschwitz we know what man is capable of. And since Hiroshima we know what is at stake."[21] We *have* the ability to anticipate risks and problems, not all of them but certainly many big ones. We also have the ability to prevent or reduce the harm they pose.

Directly and indirectly, film and television communicate messages of hope and caution, but like dreams, we have to listen to these messages and take them seriously without becoming overly concrete or demoralized. Most messages aren't hard to decode, but the problems they outline are complex. When facing complex problems, the Yerkes-Dodson curve applies: We perform best at moderate levels of arousal, not when under aroused (being overconfident or relaxed) or overstimulated (being overwhelmed or feeling hopeless).[22] This arousal-performance pattern applies to worry as well. When we worry about a complex situation at a moderate level but can remain focused on a specific challenge, worry motivates us to problem-solve.[23]

When looking to our current mythology, we see this balance of hope and caution. For every *Close Encounters of the Third Kind* and *Contact*, there's an *Independence Day* and *Alien*.[24] Although apocalyptic and dystopian sci-fi stories can be real bummers, they're necessary. There's not much we can do about aliens—besides achieving world peace and stability. But we don't need aliens to realize that. We do, however, need to consider how developing newer technologies might easily get ahead of us, due to our willful ignorance, impatience, or unchecked ambitions. Simply put, we need shows like *Black Mirror*. Granted, I work in Silicon Valley, and like many of my peers, friends, and clients, I've developed apps and web programs as well as dabbled in newer technologies.[25] It's fun, creative, and meaningful when they have the intended positive impact on people's lives. But the benefits and promises that come from old and new technologies alike also have their shadow counterpart in significant downsides.[26]

Ancient myths give us plenty to work with for most challenges of human living. Some newer myths, though, are confronting relatively newer problems, and many are needing to do so at a breakneck speed—specifically when involving the *technological singularity*.[27] 'Singularity' is another word for a black hole, and as with a literal black hole, looking past the event horizon to see what's on the other side (or inside) isn't possible. So, following the metaphor, the technological singularity is a point in the future where we cannot anticipate with any accuracy or confidence the real long-term impact of future 'disruptive' technologies. Here are some example dangers explored in film:[28]

- **Nuclear weaponry?** Check—See *Godzilla* and countless international spy movies

- **Big data, surveillance, and privacy?** Yep—Consider *The Circle*, *A Scanner Darkly*, *Inception*

- **Artificial intelligence?** Nothing new—*2001: A Space Odyssey*, *The Matrix* trilogy, *Ex Machina*

- **Ecological collapse and forces of nature?** Of course—*Interstellar*, *Contagion*, *2012*

To address possible future challenges, we need to find a sweet spot between ignorance and awareness, or naïve optimism and panic. Awareness of perceived threats can quickly lead to what Alvin Toffler called *future shock*—an individual or collective disorientation in the face of rapid changes.[29] Some people are all too familiar with bigger problems and might understandably feel overwhelmed. To dampen unhelpful negativity, I'd 'prescribe' a dose of utopian, visionary film with plausible messages of hope. *Star Trek* might work.[30] Others, however, may too readily dismiss 'negative thinking' and believe the future is infinitely bright and all life's problems will soon be solved. How about a *Terminator* marathon?[31]

The good news is twofold: 1) We're not alone, and 2) We haven't yet arrived at a fully dystopian future—not to dismiss our existing problems. If enough people engage thoughtfully with thorny issues, we can do something about many problems before they happen or get worse. Let's add to our repertoire of higher-level coping skills by considering *anticipation*—the ability to foresee potential problems and brace for any expected pain or when possible, work towards prevention. At the collective level, most complex challenges require several workgroups to address each issue from different angles, ideally with interdisciplinary teams that balance specialty areas with at least a few generalists—including ethicists.

Regardless of the focus and scope, the most effective problem-solving strategies involve applied creativity, focused brainstorming, and critical thinking. Applications of each start earlier than finding a solution. We must define, as best as possible, the underlying problem and contributing factors. The general steps of creative problem-solving work for smaller, present-centered personal issues and larger, future-oriented collective ones. Figure 10.1 outlines a synthesized approach to problem-solving across these applications. You can adjust and elaborate these steps to fit your needs. Without reflection, we can forget too that sometimes the best action is non-action. If all we have is a hammer—or programming skills, meditation expertise, sheer force of will, or whatever else our favorite tool is—then everything becomes a nail.[32] If you feel overwhelmed or powerless, then go smaller in scale. Whatever your focus, remember to consider your sphere of influence and to trust your ability to create positive changes while working through complex issues.

Figure 10.1
Creative Problem-Solving

This figure was inspired by steps taught by Future Problem Solving Program International and supplemented with the concept of SMART goals. Because SMART goals can be hard to formulate, here are a few examples:

- "For the next month, I will limit my intake of candy bars to one per week so that I can reduce my reliance on sugar as a mood lifter."
- "I will start every day for the next two weeks reciting three positive statements about myself and others to increase my sense of hope and connectedness."
- "To help stretch beyond my social comfort zone, I will attend one community event each week by myself and strike up a conversation with at least one friendly looking stranger also in attendance."

To measure the outcome of these goals, you can record the number of times you were successful in your practice, journal about your reactions and sense of progress, and/or complete measures specific to your goal (such as a mood inventory or an objective measurement).

Figure continues on next page

1.	**Select a Higher-Level Area of Focus**	
Anticipate future challenges and threatening scenarios within your speciality area and sphere of influence		Reflect on important domains of life, personal values, and concerns of interest

2.	**Brainstorm Problems and Identify a High-Impact, Workable One**
List all possible problems within your domain and choose one critical problem likely to have a solution. To clarify an issue or its causes, ask 'Why is this a problem?' and 'What has led or will lead to it being one?'	

3.	**Brainstorm Solutions for Chosen Problem**
List all possible solutions by asking, 'What if...?' Hold off on evaluating solutions as better or worse. Premature evaluation of ideas shuts down creative brainstorming.	

4.	**Rank Solutions on Anticipated Impact, Consequences, and Alignment with Values**
Ask questions like, 'Will this solution prevent the problem or only mitigate harm?' 'Will it create more problems?' 'How might this go wrong?' 'Which values align or conflict with this plan?' 'Which solutions instill the most hope?'	

5.	**Clarify SMART Goals for Highest-Ranked Solution**
Form SMART Goals = Specific, Measurable, Achievable, Relevant, Time-bound. More complex solutions will require separation into smaller specific goals.	

6.	**Create Step-by-Step Action Plan for Each SMART Goal**	
Decide who will do what based on expertise and skills and what resources will be needed.		Outline what you'll need to do first, whether you'll need help, and how you'll stay focused *and* practice self-care.

7.	**Execute the Plan while Observing Impact**
Address both anticipated and unanticipated issues as they occur. Celebrate mini-successes to maintain morale. Be willing to abort the plan if significant problems arise.	

8.	**Review Impact and Lessons Learned. If Needed, Revise Action Plan**		
What went well? What worked as planned?	What, if anything, went wrong? In hindsight, what could be done differently?		What could be even better next time?

Note. When a step has separate elaborations, the left side with darker shading corresponds to its application to a future-oriented collective problem, and the right side with lighter shading corresponds to a more present-centered personal one. When choosing an area of focus, evaluating potential solutions and clarifying your goals, consider reviewing your top values from Exercise 7.1.

---

[a] See FPSPI.org. For an overview of SMART goals, see, for example, Bovend'Eerdt et al., 2009.

Engaging Creativity—
A Focused Brainstorming Exercise

It's time for more personal reflections on symbolism and creativity. Respond to each prompt below with a list personalized to your particular experiences, tastes, passions, values, and talents. Brainstorm a minimum of 3-5 responses to each prompt.

When reflecting on my journey of personal growth, images that come to mind are...

Creative works that most resonate with me personally are...

My most meaningful or strange dreams include...

With the tools of creative problem-solving, I feel empowered to...

Manifesting a New Hero—
A Symbolic Vision for New Generations

When understood as symbolic, the monomyth, our hero's journey, cannot be mapped out in concrete ways with straightforward answers that apply to all people at all points in history. Realizing the incompleteness of such monolithic ideas, however, is the *starting* point for revising our old maps and incomplete mythologies. If Campbell's monomythic hero is too traditional and outmoded for some, then Camus's absurd hero is too idiosyncratic and impractical. By this point in our journey, we've explored both types of heroes. But now, we're ready for a new vision.

When considering the shortcomings of our outdated myths, we should remember that it's far easier to see the shadow of others and criticize their efforts. But to embrace our creative potential, we must dare to add to our collective lore and actually create, or co-create, something. In *The Courage to Create*, Rollo May argued, "[W]e must be fully committed, but we must also be aware at the same time that we might possibly be wrong."[33] That's yet another tall order. But I'm sure you're used to that by now. To support our efforts in manifesting a new hero, let's formulate the existing core problem and play with a possible solution.

The Overarching Problem—
Fractured Realities, Shared Challenges

Academic and non-academic social commentators alike have criticized naïve, inadequate, and harmful aspects of institutionalized religions, philosophies, and ideologies and their tendencies to overgeneralize and ignore many of their own shadows. Although much of this criticism has been warranted, we've deconstructed the ground on which many modern societies and cultures were built. 'Truth' has been replaced with radical skepticism and aggressive irony. The enemies have become traditional wisdom and grand overarching narratives like cross-cultural mythologies.[34] Nothing has been sacred and above reproach. It was inevitable that a collective groundlessness and demoralization would take hold in many of us.

Professing that Truth is an illusion, however, doesn't make it—or the desire for it—go away. Like the risk of 'ego whiplash' for the individual, another kind of whiplash seems to have occurred. More than ever, we seem quite confident about our opinions. No group or individual is immune. Research on the relationship between confidence and competence has exposed the Dunning-Kruger effect: We don't know what we don't know, meaning we're overconfident about topics we know only a little about.[35] There's so much to learn, relearn, and explore that everyone is guilty of this problem to varying degrees.

Without any shared understanding or belief in a knowable 'Truth,' we've returned to a tribalized Us-vs-Them mentality where competing mini-truths (narrow ideologies and identity-exclusive mini-myths) can be worn like uniforms and badges of honor. We've transformed our faith in the Divine into faith in narrowly defined scientific understanding, inscrutable skepticism of 'The Mainstream,' or any other ideological camp that promises order in chaos and a right-and-wrong simplicity of understanding. When contemplating global issues, we confront innumerable, often conflicting records of our concurrent, parallel modern histories, spanning the globe of billions of humans with their unique collection of experiences. We've been divided into regional tribes, each with our own versions of past, present, and future realities. All our histories are being recorded live but without the perspective offered by hindsight or foresight. In the cacophony of these conflicting voices, it's no wonder we confront personal and collective confusion.

To put it simply, we face a *global crisis of meaning* while confronting complex issues that require a *commitment to collaborate to find workable solutions*. Are 'transcendent' values and concrete actions possible in a world where we can't agree on much of anything? How can we give adequate voice to alternatives while having a shared vision for the future?

A Proposed Solution—New Renaissance, New Heroes

To turn the awareness of these global problems and our limited knowledge into inspiration to grow and take effective action is *the* turn of a new hero. In most our lives, despite modern challenges, we still find beauty, even if imperfect and occurring alongside pain. Recognizing the complexity of our world is a critical step to make, but how might we move forward? We can't and shouldn't return to naïve, constricted worldviews. Instead, we're in need of a countermove to deconstruction—that of synthesis. From a broader perspective, the strengths of traditional ideas are clarity and confidence while the strengths of critical frameworks are complexity, diversity, and caution. Each sees the other's shadow—naivety and oppression versus impracticality and problematizing-without-fixing. In the absence of respectful dialogue and repair, the seductiveness of shadow projection has overpowered the need for newer and more flexible and candid mythologies.[36]

As an archetypal symbol of renewal, the Cosmic Tree or Tree of Life is one cross-cultural mythic metaphor for the multifaceted aspects of life and the multilayered nature of reality. As explorers of Truth, our tools for investigating this Tree are diverse. Science, humanities, religion, philosophy, and their competing branches of thought may all be studying parts of this same Tree. But the point isn't competition or that they're all wrong. It's that they have different perspectives and areas of knowledge. They know their part of the Tree very well. Moreover, in each field, some of us err on the side of skepticism, criticism, and 'disruption' of conventional wisdom and practices. Others err on the side of overconfidence and trust in traditional frameworks.

Science, for example, is one of our most powerful tools. It has many strengths, but scientific knowledge accumulates slowly. To grapple with complexity, science and other scholarly fields have required increasingly disjointed subspecialties. In this fragmentation, we've lost track of the big picture—the Tree with its innumerable branches, leaves, fruit, and unseen roots. But solely looking at the largest scale can keep us stuck too. Specialists can lose the forest for the trees while generalists can ignore the astoundingly nuanced details and diverse foliage.

To reach our potential, we need to keep ourselves and others honest, but that means remaining humble in our limitations yet hopeful in our possibilities—as individuals and as parts of our communities, cultures, species, and our little planet. All the while we remember that we exist within an infinitesimal sliver in space and time—with many elements of our past lost and our future unknown. We need everyone included in this new renaissance, and we especially need kindhearted people who value and understand the necessity of balancing clarity with complexity. In other words, we need a new generation of heroes who act as stewards for a better future.

A Creative Elaboration—The Meta Hero

Taking inspiration from myth, film, and psychedelics, let's create a new paradigm to support this ever-unfolding journey of integration in our complex world—what we can call the *Meta Hero*.[37] 'Meta' is a delightful word because of its multiple layers of meaning, from its ancient Greek roots meaning "beyond" or "after" to its pop culture uses indicating something that's "self-referential" and aware—or in gaming parlance, the "most effective."[38] This heroic archetype seeks to transcend the one-sidedness of both traditional and post-Truth thinking while bridging the divide between past and future. Instead of a fragmented pastiche, a patchwork Frankenstein's monster abandoned by its creator, we can envision a hybrid figure who has experienced love and transcended fear and hate. A hybrid integrates opposites—that is, the shadow and the light.[39] Such notions are figurative, but they give us something to play with, and being willing to play is fundamental to both creativity and wellbeing.

Our new hero must be psychologically flexible enough to understand complexity without drowning in it. Unlike protagonists of classic myths, meta heroes exist throughout the world's many cultures, and they don't require stories to be told of them. Their motivation comes from within, and their heroic acts come as a natural consequence of their everyday life.

Psychologists, among others, love creating absurd if not occasionally helpful acronyms and mnemonics. So, however tongue-in-cheek it may be, I'll do the same to describe some core features, attitudes, and values of this new meta hero. My chosen acronym is *AGILITY*. 'Agility' refers to the ability to move quickly and effortlessly while adapting to the situation at hand. As an acronym, it encapsulates several qualities: Authenticity, Gratitude, Inspiration, Love, Insight, Transformation, and Youthfulness. Figure 10.2 elaborates on each quality and provides example mantras to match.

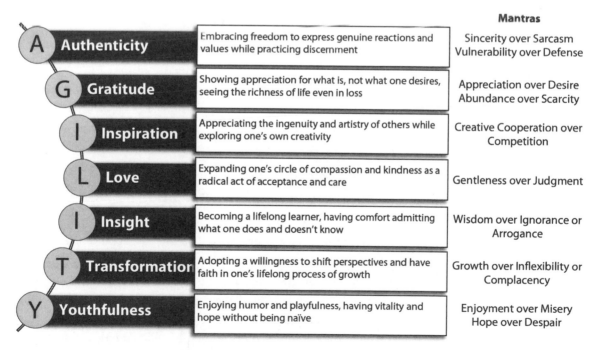

Mantras

A Authenticity	Embracing freedom to express genuine reactions and values while practicing discernment	Sincerity over Sarcasm / Vulnerability over Defense
G Gratitude	Showing appreciation for what is, not what one desires, seeing the richness of life even in loss	Appreciation over Desire / Abundance over Scarcity
I Inspiration	Appreciating the ingenuity and artistry of others while exploring one's own creativity	Creative Cooperation over Competition
L Love	Expanding one's circle of compassion and kindness as a radical act of acceptance and care	Gentleness over Judgment
I Insight	Becoming a lifelong learner, having comfort admitting what one does and doesn't know	Wisdom over Ignorance or Arrogance
T Transformation	Adopting a willingness to shift perspectives and have faith in one's lifelong process of growth	Growth over Inflexibility or Complacency
Y Youthfulness	Enjoying humor and playfulness, having vitality and hope without being naïve	Enjoyment over Misery / Hope over Despair

Figure 10.2 The Meta Heroic Qualities of AGILITY

Manifesting New Heroes—
A Focused Brainstorming Exercise

What's your reaction to the idea of this new hero? Do any of the qualities of AGILITY surprise you? Would you add others? Remember these ideas act as a starting place, not the final word, so respond to the following prompts in the spirit of creativity.

When I reflect on the qualities within AGILITY, my strengths lie in...

At the same time, my growth edges may be...

If I created a new myth to inspire myself and younger generations, it'd be about...

Developing New Alliances—
The Gifted Child, The Playful Trickster, and The Wise Elder

Too often mythic and real-world heroes are understood in isolation. As in many myths, we've had allies in our journey—curiosity, acceptance, and wisdom. Although this book's journey has been a personal one, many other people, unknown to you or me, have also been on their own adventures. There's never been only *one* hero. Countless people throughout human history have worked together and in parallel to make us who we are today. And, of course, sometimes in opposition to one another. Mythic and absurd heroes alike have often leaned towards a serious tone, which makes sense given the demands of their role as community protector or their simultaneous rebellion against meaninglessness and any temptation to escape it. Being overly serious or weighed down by responsibility, however, can block access to creativity and reinforce suffering.

As opposed to the stereotype of a tortured artist, creative works require playfulness and fantasy. As Jung stated:

> Not the artist alone, but every creative individual whatsoever owes all that is greatest in his life to fantasy. The dynamic principle of fantasy is play, a characteristic also of the child, and as such it appears inconsistent with the principle of serious work. But without this playing with fantasy no creative work has ever yet come to birth.[40]

In his writing, Jung tended to be serious, but that's true of many academics and writers in especially serious-minded times, including today. But whether creativity is applied to solving problems, creating art, or just playing around, we benefit from being spontaneous and enjoying the moment. Play is critical to life satisfaction. Various Hindu sects speak of *lila*, divine play, which is not only the source of human creativity but is also the underlying creative principle of the universe.[41] To be creative is to be connected to the cosmos.

Evolving Allies

Three allies support the creative potential of the new hero and the qualities of AGILITY—the Gifted Child, the Playful Trickster, and the Wise Elder. Each ally serves as a parallel to our metaphorical allies throughout this journey, and together they can continue to help us on our evolving adventures. At times we find representations of these allies in others. At other times, we find them within. Although described as human symbols, they could easily be expressed as elements, animals, or other symbolic forms, if you're so inclined.

The Gifted Child. In our first arc, curiosity led our way to expand awareness. Curiosity is a quality of childhood too often abandoned in our adult years, if not sooner. The child is constantly expanding their awareness and confronting the limitations of their pre-existing knowledge. At the same time, children can occasionally see to 'the heart of a matter' because they're less encumbered by preconceived notions and frameworks. Us adults can get stuck in a rut and through hardship, boredom, or obliviousness, life can lose its enchantment and mystery.

Reawakening a child-like wonder can break through the world of ideas and a narrowed thinking mode of experience to reveal a playground right before our eyes. A common instruction for mindfulness is to see through the eyes of a child. An especially gifted child can perceive things us adults have forgotten or dismissed. Their gifts, however, come in several forms—intuitive insight, unprompted compassion, radical optimism, and appreciative joyfulness.[42] To engage fully with life, we can rediscover our inner child by witnessing the surprising wisdom of children as they follow their curiosity and lead by example.

The Playful Trickster. In our second arc, acceptance helped us face fears our inner child could not and in doing so, become initiated into adulthood and join a broader community of explorers. At one level, we had to accept the unavoidable consequences of being human such as mortality, loss, and uncertainty of meaning. An overly serious adult mind, however, could interpret acceptance as defeat or take our initiation into a new community as permission to abandon all others. The playful trickster counters this risk by infusing humor into our lives and reminding us that not all is as it seems. It plays with ambiguity and questions our assumptions about shadow and light.[43] That's because the trickster is a figure of the shadow, either our personal or collective one. Like the mythic hero, the trickster lives in between the divine and the mundane. Unlike the traditional hero, the trickster possesses an enormous range of perspectives and doesn't shy away from irreverence. They understand the depths of their beast-like animal instincts and the heights of divinity.

When we respect the trickster, they can help us examine and connect with these depths and heights of our nature and potential—and hopefully discover some workable middle path. When we become overconfident, the trickster's tricks can snap us out of arrogance so that we can continue to grow. When we become overburdened, their tricks remind us to be lighthearted.

The trickster can encourage us to face the practical and ethical implications of our favorite theories, ideologies, and habits including looking at their actual (not fantasized) impact personally or in recorded history. Not all tricksters are insightful, well-meaning, or effective allies. Some are trolls or fools. Yet even these forms of the trickster can teach us things. The more benevolent and playful trickster has a different perspective than we do, but its trolling-like behavior isn't malicious or meant to be an unwitting tool for destructive ideologies. We don't always know when a trickster figure is a playful ally or a disguised adherent of the Dark Triad. Of course, that keeps us on our toes too. As an ally, though, the playful trickster reminds us to see things from the other side and avoid getting too set in our ways. Ensuring we avoid black-and-white thinking and the trap of shadow projection, the trickster keeps us humble. They also bring messages from other communities and remind us unexpected allies come from every walk of life.[44]

Understanding your own inner trickster and the well-meaning versions of others helps us understand the world as it is, not as idealized. Admittedly, my trickster side might be present in how I've used the hero's journey as a bit of a Trojan horse, a way to appeal to our desires to be like the courageous, classic Hero of Old, or like our fictional heroes of the not-so-distant past; to be Luke Skywalker—from the original trilogy, at least. But like us, heroes can fall (and hopefully be redeemed). And many other stories need to be told so that we all can aspire to be better.

Playing with irony, a quality of the trickster, is fun, but getting seduced by this type of play—trolling because it's entertaining not because it offers insight—turns satire into an enactment of an uncaring, willful ignorance. If the troll cannot troll themselves, then they're not playing the role of a wise or well-meaning trickster but that of an immature jester. When forging an alliance with either our own inner trickster or someone else's, we can remember that the goal should never be to harm another person, including ourselves. It's to keep us lighthearted, joyful, alert, and always willing to learn so that in the end, more of us discover how to play.[45]

The Wise Elder. As we've worked towards integration, wisdom has become our strongest ally. If curiosity speaks to our inner child and acceptance supports our maturing adult self, then wisdom moves us to attain, over time, the broader perspective of an elder. The wisdom of our elders comes from their diverse personal and collective experiences, which form a treasure-trove of lessons learned. The lessons never end, though, and as we age, each of us can add to our collective insights and lore. Our ancestors have lived through amazing and horrific experiences. Some wounds have been self-inflicted, and too many have been inflicted on others. If the wheel of time is to be one that moves towards progress and not entropy, then it requires us to take these lessons to heart. Looking to the past, we might ask ourselves: How have previous mighty civilizations fallen? Whose stories have already been told? And whose have been forgotten?

If you're reading this book now, you have greater access to information than any previous generation. Not all that information is trustworthy, reliable, or practical to apply. But wisdom doesn't require knowing everything or being the smartest person alive. If it did, then we'd be all out of luck! Wisdom certainly doesn't end with knowledge and data. It weaves emotional insights and intuition into its tapestry. We each have threads to weave into the larger project, and by doing our own work to integrate personal and collective lessons, we can get closer and closer to our potential. We can't skip to the end. Impatience can get us into deeper trouble.

At the same time, if the train has already left the building, can we course-correct? The qualities of AGILITY are about being nimble and acting with foresight. Small changes in the individual can trigger bigger changes in our collective. Remember, it's about the long game. Taoism uses the metaphor of water and erosion to illustrate that, given time, gentleness can overpower raw strength—and also like water, kindness can simultaneously nourish all life.[46]

The way forward isn't found by fantasizing about an ancient or future utopia. It's also not found by envisioning dystopian realities and possibilities. It's found by seeing all these desirable and not-so-desirable realities before attempting to discern a course of action. Of course, the winds of destiny are beyond our control and will have the final say, whatever that is. But if we account for their trajectory, we might shoot our arrows in an arc and get closer to our target than we ever believed was possible.

Within our modern superhero mythology, one especially powerful scene highlights the unyielding nature of time and how if we accept our responsibility, we'll be ready when we're needed most. It comes, appropriately so, from the most psychedelic and mystical of all Marvel films, *Doctor Strange*.[47] Before fate forces our protagonist to confront a multidimensional cosmic evil, Dr. Strange's mentor and soon-to-be-predecessor, The Ancient One, imparts a final lesson:

The Ancient One:	Arrogance and fear still keep you from learning the simplest and most significant lesson of all.
Dr. Strange:	Which is?
The Ancient One:	It's not about *you*.

It's not about you, and it's certainly not about me. It's about all of us and our unfolding story. Before undergoing his journey, Dr. Strange had plenty of brash overconfidence, but when his wounds opened his mind to higher paths, he got more than bargained for. Respecting the wisdom of our elders isn't blind hero worship, but we all have many things to learn. If we do our part, then when our time comes, we'll be ready. And because time slows down for no one (infinity stones aside), we eventually must become the wise elders ourselves— elders who can pass the torch and impart our wisdom to the next generation.

Diverse Alliances & Collaborations

Do you know what's better than a gifted child, playful trickster, or wise elder? A whole council of them. Many heroes are out there, and most aren't in the spotlight. In his charismatic appeal for change, Timothy Leary offered a mantra to the 1960's psychedelic youth: "Find the others." More recently in *Star Wars: The Rise of Skywalker*, Trickster-turned-Heroic-Elder Lando Calrissian shared a message better fitting our times, even when the odds appear overwhelming, remember "There are more of us."[48] You're not the only 'hero.' Together change is possible. It may occur slowly with occasional leaps and false starts, but our impact isn't always immediately obvious. If we want change to be a net positive, then we should continue to learn from our shadows and the shadows of others. There may be more of us, but many of us are hidden. Sometimes to find the others, we must let ourselves be found. That can happen more naturally by being kind and respectful towards others, especially when interacting with people who think differently than we do. We're unable to see our various shadows if we remain in echo chambers. Temporary retreats to solitude or our 'inner circle,' however, recharge our energy for the more challenging parts of personal and collective transformation.

Teamwork starts with establishing some ground rules. Yes, rules are made to be broken, and being creative requires a willingness to bend the rules. But, like myth, such rules are living documents, which can be challenged and revised. Box 10.2 offers a few takeaways from this book's journey that you might consider adopting—but only after wrestling with them first!

Box 10.2

Suggested Meta Rules and Guidelines for Engagement

In paradox is Truth, but we might never fully understand it.

Fight for what's right but be willing to consider you might be wrong.

Play your role but be mindful of the masks you wear. Meet others who're also aware of their masks with a nod and a wink.

Always be willing to play but realize when someone gets hurt—including yourself.

Discover the divine in the mundane parts of everyday life. Or, if you can't see the mandala in the toilet bowl, you're not looking close enough.

The most effective path is not always a straight line. Know your terrain.

Perspective is everything. A line may belong to a much larger circle. And that circle may actually be a sphere.

You may not be alone, but sometimes you've got to go it alone. Just don't forget anyone you left behind.

Because absolute power corrupts absolutely, remember to share power and rotate leadership.

If you think something could be done better, ask yourself how. Then do it—or partner with others and do it together.

Forging Alliances—A Focused Brainstorming Exercise

The brainstorming prompts below may elicit responses involving real world people in your life now, from the past, or who you'd like to ally with in the future. You can also respond by describing parts of yourself you'd like to integrate further. For example, your inner child may represent your childlike curiosity, compassion, and/or parts of yourself you haven't expressed as much in your adult life. More than likely, your responses to each prompt will contain a mix of inner and outer allies. Come up with at least three responses to each and see where you're creative brainstorming takes you.

My ally, the gifted child, can be found by…

Allying with the playful trickster requires I…

My wisest elders speak to me through…

If I were to create a team of heroes (mythic, fictional, and/or real world), it'd consist of…

Integrating Insights with Creativity—
In Search of Your Elixir

Turning straightforward intellectual insights into behavior is hard enough. Turning creative inspiration into something we can share with others is a whole other story. In some myths, the hero or an ally must discover or create an *elixir of life* to awaken their abilities or transform their community.[49] Thus, either directly or indirectly, the elixir serves the needs of the larger whole. The question is, then, what might be your elixir? It's not as easy as copying someone else's recipe, but that's where creativity comes into play.

Creativity Exists Beyond Innate Talent. Some people have innate talents that surpass all reasonable expectations. They're outliers. But even the most gifted people have weaknesses and eventually will face challenges that cannot be surpassed without practice, trial-and-error, and commitment. If innate talent was all that mattered, then we'd all be in trouble.[50] Like other gifts, creativity comes in many forms. If painting doesn't come naturally to you, then sure, you could improve your painting skills with practice, but you might be better off developing other more natural talents.[51] What are your natural talents? What have other people told you they appreciate about your abilities, attitudes, or perspective? We can take our personal strengths for granted by thinking they're no big deal, focusing on the talents we don't have, or comparing ourselves unfairly to genius-level outliers. Campbell famously encouraged people to "Follow your bliss."[52] What he meant is to follow our inner inspiration, not chase states of rapture or seek pleasure alone. If we realize there's enough 'bliss' to be had by all, then we'll be able to let go of competition and comparison and focus instead on honing our craft and creating our own unique elixir, whatever it may be.

Creativity Looks Beyond Reification. Reification is what happens when we believe an abstract idea, theory, or model is 'real,' tangible, and factual. To use an example from this book, the four modes of experiencing model has acted as a figurative tool, a symbol, for understanding various aspects of experience. It's imperfect like all models, but with any luck, it's served a practical purpose. The risk of reification intensifies when such tools are especially good in their practical applications, popular with experts within a field or the current zeitgeist, or easy to understand and remember. Having survived the test of time, conventional wisdom and traditional thinking are helpful—until they're not. On the other hand, thinking outside the box (what's sometimes called divergent thinking) can be ineffective and inefficient, or cause more problems than it solves.

We often equate thinking outside the box with creativity. But if everyone is trying to be innovative, then who's advocating for what's already working? We each have strengths in thinking in or outside the various 'boxes' of the world, but as we've explored with the shadow, it's a matter of perspective. The mandala metaphor works here too. Individuation brings more of what's perceived as outside ourselves or separate into the boundaries of our 'circle' (our consciousness). Now and then we reach the limits of the circle and must choose whether to abandon our old ways, rearrange them so they fit with the new, or transcend those boundaries by making the circle larger than before. But remember, the box, the circle, and even the words we use are symbols and metaphors, *not* reality.

Creating Elixirs—A Focused Brainstorming Exercise

It's time for this arc's final brainstorming exercise. As you consider your responses, be open, creative, and willing to follow your inspiration wherever it takes you.

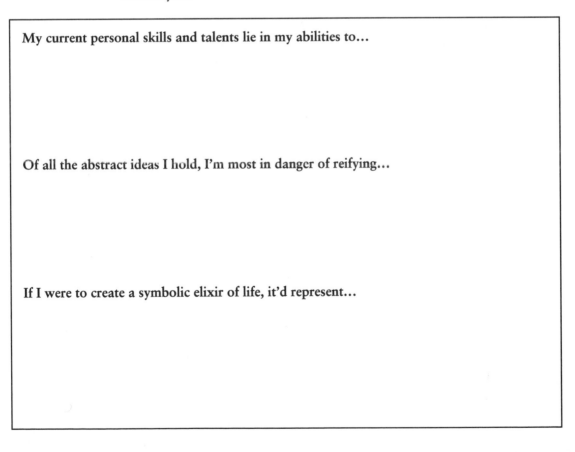

My current personal skills and talents lie in my abilities to…

Of all the abstract ideas I hold, I'm most in danger of reifying…

If I were to create a symbolic elixir of life, it'd represent…

Fostering Wisdom by Engaging with Our Evolving Mythology

As we integrate insights from personal experiences, dreams, or psychedelic journeys, the metaphor I use with clients is to think of integration (and individuation) as building a cathedral, not a house of cards. Genuine integration requires thoughtfulness, patience, and openness to refinement. As our journey comes to a close, ponder the revised image in Figure 10.3 as yet another symbol for what living beyond the narrow life entails. How much more aware have you

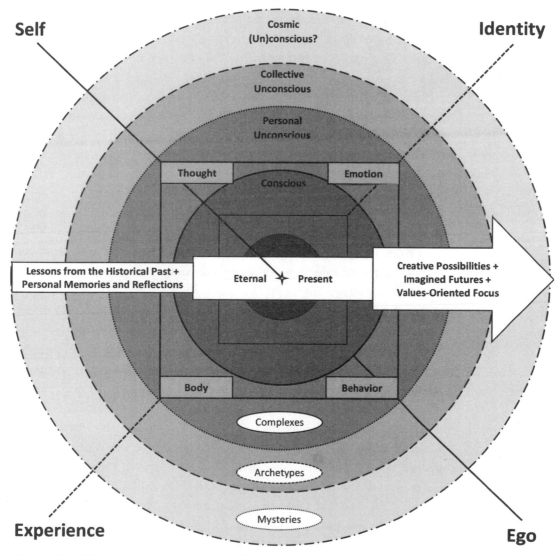

Figure 10.3 A Symbol for Living the Narrow Life

become during this journey? What parts of this symbolic roadmap deserve more of your attention as you move forward? Based on your personal experiences, values, and culture, what additional pieces would you add to this map?

In the end, *your* life is the real symbol you're responsible for creating. Like an archetype, it can take many fascinating forms. In uncertain or difficult times, we might rely on the optimism Bill Richards has offered, "When we trust and act in the world, a meaningful process unfolds within us. Each of us is still being created and crafted as a work of art."[53]

As a symbolic expression of our modern mythology, film reminds us too that behind the roles are actors and behind the scenes are numerous players outside the spotlight.[54] As in a movie, we have select roles to play, parts to embody. Our part is important for the other actors, and each one is essential for the grander scheme—the Great Play, whether it's a tragic drama, an inspiring adventure, a joyful comedy, or all the above. If we were to abandon our role, how would the story unfold? On the flipside, if we become overidentified with our role, do we risk losing our higher Self? That may not be bad for Method actors, who give it their all. But when our part is over and we're done with our role, we must surrender it. If we hold on too tightly, we risk forgetting who we really are. Letting go lets us re-emerge from the depths of the performance and rest in an expanded state of awareness and possibility. We may rest there temporarily—in that space in between—before taking on other roles. Ultimately, though, we must relinquish all roles and allow ourselves to retire—or enter that Great Beyond. And yet, long after we are gone, the grand mythology continues.

To take part in this symbolic story, you don't need to become a monk, shaman, or hermit or disengage completely from this world. But you also don't need to be front and center. The everyday heroes are not politicians, entrepreneurs, or influencers. They live amongst us. As we play our roles, whatever they may be, take time to reflect and remember that each of us is more than any one part we play. You and only you are performing your role in a greater narrative bigger than any of us. But you're not *only* that part. You're much more. So too are others, whether they know it or not. When others drop out, either by choice, illness, or death, you can choose to step up and take on a new role, letting old ones fall to the side if no longer needed. Or, letting them go to the next generation, perhaps offering to help them learn the ropes. And so forth and so forth. As the great story unfolds, each must play their part. Because the play must go on.

The idea of a grand production, for me, illustrates both the deepest esoteric mystery and the most pragmatic side of individuation. It's a perspective that transcends the paradox of ego versus shadow, and perhaps that of Self versus Other—in both their individual and collective aspects. When performing our roles, balancing flexibility and humility with courage and sincerity promotes an ever-increasing awareness. These attitudes cultivate wisdom by embracing the endless layers of complexity of all things. Wisdom is both the fuel that sustains and the byproduct that results from the lifelong process of individuation. When we become stuck, overwhelmed, or overconfident, we can look up at the stars, as our ancestors have always done, and allow ourselves to wonder. Afterwards, we can return and choose to move forward, uncertain of what lies ahead, but ready to discover more with each step. This practice of renewal will undoubtedly need to be repeated, but each moment, the heroic response is to say 'yes' to life.

To close the final chapter of this arc and our journey, let's return to the metaphor of bamboo one last time. Bamboo is narrow and hollow, but these qualities allow songs to be played as if it were a flute. In life, learn to play your music but also rest in silence so that you can listen to the music offered by others and the many sounds of the wind. Not all people are like bamboo, nor need they be. A forest is filled with many kinds of trees, plants, animals, and other forms of life, non-life—and let's not forget, the countless secrets and unknown parts hidden within. It's never been about you or me. It's about us, our evolving story, and the mysterious music of all that was, is, and will be in time.

Concrete Suggestions & Journey Report

In Box 10.3, you'll find a few suggestions to continue your journey. Some are ongoing practices while others are activities you can do once and revisit later as you feel inspired. Journey Report 10.1 tells of Sarah's remarkable ayahuasca experience in which she had to navigate fear before and during a journey of symbolic death and rebirth. The communal aspects of the ayahuasca experience, as well as the support offered by the pajé (medicine man), were essential to her healing. The meaning behind acknowledging herself and others as 'beings of light' is open to interpretation, but regardless of how these symbolic experiences and words are understood, this journey captures many themes explored throughout this book.

Box 10.3

Integrating Creativity in Everyday Life

Suggestion	Example
Commit to keeping a dream journal to record and reflect on messages from the unconscious.	You can't remember the last time you recalled a dream, but you start a dream journal anyways and keep it by your bed. Instead of grabbing your phone first thing in the morning, you grab your journal. You jot down fragments of dreams at first, but over time, you begin to remember more. You observe a recurring theme about becoming lost and being alone. While the circumstances are different each time, the emotions of confusion and anxiety are prominent. After reflecting on situations in your waking life that evoke the same reactions, you realize your conscious frustration with unresponsive friends hides these same emotions, which imply feelings of vulnerability. You decide to talk with two close friends about your reactions.
Draw three overlapping circles. List your values in one, talents in another, and needs of your community in the third. Focus, in particular, on where these three circles overlap.	You find the most overlap with your value of discovery, your talent of perspective taking, and the societal need of having productive dialogues among people with opposing ideological viewpoints. You start by gathering data and information about how to have effective discourse about polarizing topics. You discover the central role of emotional reasoning and the importance of avoiding 'trigger words' that shut down conversations and evoke people's defenses. You outline basic guidelines for having tough conversations and try them out with trusted friends and family members who have opposing opinions. You revise your guidelines and write a blog post to share them with a broader audience. Then you update them again based on additional feedback.
Reconnect to your child-like creativity and inspiration by listing five play activities or hobbies from your pre-adult life. Reincorporate at least one into your current life.	As a child, you spent far more time outside playing by yourself and looking at interesting plants and insects. You also made models of sports cars (but never painted them). As a teenager, you played the trumpet and was part of your school's volleyball team. You also wrote poetry and published a few under a pseudonym in your school newspaper. After graduating college, though, you stopped writing poetry. You decide to give your inner poet another shot and set a goal to write one poem per week for the next couple of months to see what happens. You assure yourself no one else will read these poems—unless, that is, you decide otherwise.
Apply the creative problem-solving process in Figure 10.1 to a challenging but important area of your life. If helpful, invite others to join your efforts.	You work on a software development team at a large tech company, but you realize your team and likely many others focus solely on fixing bugs and optimizing user experience. You rarely discuss how things can go wrong socially or psychologically for your users. You follow the steps of creative problem-solving and set a higher-level goal of increasing awareness and discussion. After brainstorming solutions and strategies, you decide to take an indirect approach. You start an extracurricular sci-fi interest group where people discuss both dystopian and utopian fiction. You have a hunch that conversations within this group might facilitate a greater sense of responsibility to foresee and prevent problems introduced by innovative technologies under development. By pulling from employees throughout the company, this interest group 'seeds' a growing collective responsibility across several teams and divisions, spreading its impact beyond your local team.

Grounding Words—A Brief Summary

Although you've reached the final moments of this book's journey, you realize the adventure continues. Perhaps still uncertain of what living beyond the narrow life truly means, you have a few clues about what could lie ahead. You know to look beyond the surface of everyday life by finding inspiration in art, myth, film, dreams, and imagination. Symbols like mandalas and circles hold promise as you explore and integrate, but other metaphors may light the way too. You appreciate the back-and-forth nature of interpreting and creating symbols as well as the practicality of creative problem-solving. The problems you choose to address will depend on your circle of influence, values, talents, and chosen life direction. Some will intersect with your overarching life's purpose. But you remain willing to change focus and adapt strategies when situations evolve, as impermanence ensures they do. As our shared mythologies respond to our changing needs, new heroes are entering the scene to usher in brighter futures. They come with different skills, perspectives, and concentrations, but they know how to work together—and when needed, in parallel. Your allies evolve just as you do. The Gifted Child, Playful Trickster, and Wise Elder exist 'out there' in the world, within others, and inside your own mind. The roles you'll play will vary, but you find comfort in knowing you're much more than any one part. Now you begin to smile as you imagine all there is left to explore, discover, and create.

Your Final Assignment, Your Continuing Choice

Although you've completed this book, the journey continues. To mark the occasion, review and select activities from the recommended assignments below. I've removed the labels of *Reflective-Intellectual* and *Experiential-Emotional* since each activity is about creating a greater synthesis across these imperfect and narrowly defined divisions.

Assignments 10.1

Moving Beyond the Narrow Life

☐ Task—Create a **Journey Altar** to revisit when you need a reminder of the insights gained in your journey. See Handout 10.1 for instructions.

Time—Approximately 1-2 hrs including brainstorming its contents, collecting material, and creating the altar

Aim—To have a touchstone to remind yourself of the insights gained in your journey and stay connected to your sources of wisdom and inspiration

☐ Task—Create a **Mandala** representing your Self in all your complexity, including any paradoxes. See Handout 10.1 for instructions & Handout 10.2 for a full-size image of the circular outline.

Time—At least 1 hr in which you create your mandala and then reflect on your creation

Aim—To symbolize your process of individuation including unconscious elements that have become more integrated within your consciousness (forming a greater balance or synthesis)

☐ Task—Draw an **Upward Spiral** symbolizing stages of your life and related challenges, joys, and ways you've grown. See Handout 10.1 for instructions.

Time—At least 1 hr to create and complete the various elements of the spiral and then reflect on the activity as a whole

Aim—To reflect on meaningful life experiences and significant markers of personal growth

☐ Task—Practice the meditation in **Meditation 10.1 "Visualizing a World Network"**

Time—Minimum of 2-3x/week, ~10 min each

Aim—To imagine how you and others are working towards positive changes and are connected despite being spread around the world

After you've reviewed your options, make a plan for completing your selected activities and perhaps do a short one before responding to this chapter's journal prompt. To mark the end of your guided journey, review and reflect on your previous experiences, insights, and entries in your Travel Journal. Before or after doing so, respond to your final formal prompt.

Travel Journal

What does living beyond the narrow life mean to me?

How can creative appreciation and expression play a role moving forward?

What qualities of the so-called 'Meta Hero' would I like to develop further?

How might I forge alliances with other such heroes and potential allies during my ongoing adventures?

JOURNEY REPORT 10.1 From Being Ego to Being Light

Earlier this year I went to the Ashaninka people, an indigenous community situated in the Amazonian state of Acre, Brazil. After a few days living with the community and experiencing Ayahuasca, 'the vine of the spirits,' almost every night, I became somewhat anxious about the next night's journey. Visions had been overwhelming, and upon waking every morning I'd feel somewhat confused and tired with a dizzy mind. But these feelings were also accompanied with a sense of deep gratitude.

The fourth morning I awoke knowing we were going to drink in the woods, under the open sky, calling in the spirits of the forest. I felt something was going to be different, and I was afraid of what was coming. We entered the forest after drinking our first cup, fully experiencing the nature and appreciating the fertile grounds upon which we walked. While everybody was gathered around in a circle, sitting on banana leaves, singing beautiful songs that called in the spirits, I got spooked. I felt my anxiety rising and I saw small animals of the forest walking all over me. I panicked and wanted to go home, to be away from all the fear and feel safe again. A medicine man (a pajé) came and began blowing sacred pipe tobacco on me to clear negative energy. I felt the darkness washing away and a clear sky appeared. I could feel my back straighten and I sighed deeply. While tears fell down my face, I felt astonished.

Sitting down for a little while longer, appreciating the magical powers of the forest and their guardians, I found the courage to drink a second cup. Sitting down again I recognized the fear returning. This time I was able to welcome it. While the creatures of the forest were crawling up my legs and my body tightened, I rested my back against the tree and closed my eyes. A deep, warm womb appeared in my mind, encompassing me, asking me to let go and to surrender. I realized I was holding onto some observing and analytical part of myself, trying to figure out what all this meant. In the process of letting go and sur-rendering more, the womb pulled me inside and I became nothing. There was no *me* left, no thoughts or feelings, nothing but that endless all-encompassing womb. From that place deep down I heard a call to sit up, coming from a voice full of compassion. The voice said that it was ok to lean against the medicine man and lay down in his lap. It was my boyfriend's voice, and I was so deeply grateful he was still there, as I had to let him go deep down in that womb too.

Lying in the medicine man's lap, I looked up (but with my eyes remaining closed) and saw him smile at me while bathed in the most beautiful shining bright light. He placed his hand on my head, and I felt deeply cared for and safe. As I lay there, I realized too that everybody was gathered around me, supporting me. Thoughts appeared randomly, reflecting my confusion about what was going on, questioning what was happening to me. I wondered what I did to deserve that attention, or what I did wrong. Confused, looking up again at the medicine man and his light, I realized that there was only one question to ask that was most important to me. A question that was rationally not worth asking, but I knew I had to because I understood that on a deeper emotional level, I really didn't know the answer.

Looking at the medicine man's bright eyes and beautiful smile, I asked the question, "Why do *I* deserve help?" My shiver of fear was immediately washed away with an even brighter light, filled with warmth and love and the answer, "Because you are a light being." *I* am a light being? I *am* a light being. *I am a light being.* Next to him my mom appeared, who had passed away a year before. She smiled at me too with a profound, unconditional love. And I got it. *We all are beautiful beings of light.*

—Sarah, age 47

Note. This account and all others in the book are de-identified and anonymous to protect the confidentiality of the person sharing their story. Minor grammar, spelling, and stylistic changes were made and usually in partnership with the person providing the account.

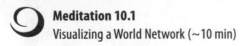

Meditation 10.1
Visualizing a World Network (~10 min)

After reading this meditation script, find a comfortable and safe place where you'll be as free from distractions as possible. If you become distracted by unrelated thoughts or interruptions, remember you can return to the meditation with ease.

Close your eyes and begin by taking three deep breaths to center yourself in the present moment. If you need to take a few more deep breaths, feel free to do so now...

With eyes remaining closed, see yourself as you are now, being in the same position and in a relaxed meditative state...Visualize your consciousness as extending beyond your body...As it does, imagine you become one with the winds of the Earth flowing in complex, beautiful patterns all around the globe...then you become one with the waves rising and falling in the middle of the oceans with no one around to witness their splendor....see your consciousness extend to the underground terrain curving and weaving to fill unseen caverns...encounter too underground hot springs heated by the Earth's mantle...

Now see all the living parts of our planet, the plants, animals, microbes, fungi, the mycelial network, and all forms of life...including us...our intricate cities and small villages...the indigenous communities still thriving...and the ancient ruins of civilizations long past...

Imagine in each of these locations around the world there are known and unknown allies, other heroes...some are only children...some are near you in age and experience...some are teachers, others inventors...some scientists, others artists...

Maintaining this awareness, center your mind in your current location... and envision a signal, a column of light radiating from where your body is in contact with the Earth, traveling through your entire body and beaming upward into the sky...this signal has a sound, a steady hum at a frequency uniquely tuned to your consciousness...

Your signal is noticed by the others...It grabs their attention and inspires them to channel their own light and tone...the light from all around the world pools above the Earth and fills the sky...the tones harmonize and create an ethereal music, a hymn...you hear this music and are reminded you are not alone. You knew this in your heart...and now you see and hear just how many others are out there...They were here all along...Take a few deep breaths, breathing in this collective energy and breathing out your own to share with the others...take in all you need and give all you can...

Now the music slowly softens and the song gradually reaches its natural conclusion...The light too begins to recede, not because its energy has faded but because its being channeled into your body and mind...Feeling energized yet calm, rest in this moment of silence and allow yourself simply to exist...With your eyes still closed, begin to reconnect with your surroundings. Gently let yourself return...and in case it hasn't happened yet, let yourself smile.

Handout 10.1

Instructions for Creating a Journey Altar, Mandala, or Upward Spiral

Journey Altar

1. Choose a space to form an altar. Consider whether you want to place it in your regular site of vision (like in your bedroom or living room) or in a separate area less frequently visited.

2. Select items that symbolize important values, qualities, insights, metaphorical allies (like curiosity, acceptance, and wisdom), and/or people involved in this book's journey (or others like it). You can diversify your items by including various sensory experiences (like touch, smell, or sound) and symbolic verbal and nonverbal elements.

3. Arrange your items in a symmetrical or near symmetrical manner. You may have a centerpiece that highlights especially meaningful symbols of your journey.

4. If you have a mantra or quote that inspires you, consider saying it aloud whenever you engage with your altar. Taking a moment of silence to reflect, even if only briefly, is another option.

Example Mandala with four quadrants

Mandala

1. Create or draw a circle on a piece of paper or canvas. If by hand, use a round object of appropriate size to trace the circumference.

   Optional—Jungian mandalas usually have four quadrants of equal size, but it's up to you what form yours will take.

2. Draw or write within the mandala whatever you'd like to express about your Self in all your complexity, including any paradoxes or light-shadow combinations. You may also create this mandala without preconceived notions of its meaning or content.

3. Consider journaling about the mandala's meaning and any symbols contained within it.

Upward Spiral

1. Draw a spiral that ascends and expands upward, with each turn representing an important stage or chapter of your life. Mark the start of the spiral as your birth and its top level as your current life.

2. For each level of the spiral, designate one side as representing challenging experiences and the other as experiences that inspired you or evoked joy.

3. For each ascending turn leading to a higher level, mark the ways you made this transition, such as learning a lesson, achieving something significant, or healing prior wounds—including what they were.

4. Near the top of the ascending spiral, where a turn has started but not yet completed, consider writing what you believe might help you reach the next level or chapter in your life.

The Ever-Unfolding Journey

Traditionally, an epilogue serves as a story's conclusion, a coda, an ending. But as is the nature of many psychedelic journeys, our story was never truly a linear one. Our journey comes in the form of a circle—another expression of the mandala symbol. The beginning is the end is the beginning. This epilogue acts only as a final transition to your ongoing adventures. The personal takeaways of the journey you've just completed are yours alone. What did you experience, discover, or reaffirm by accepting your call to adventure and continuing your quest to its completion? Perhaps certain passages in this guide spoke to you in a deeper way. Or maybe it was the experiences you had outside of your reading, either through the activities or life itself, that facilitated your growth. Regardless of their source, the insights you earned are ones I encourage you to continue nurturing throughout your life's many adventures. In this epilogue, I'll speak more generally and share a few parting thoughts. To connect our work yet again to myth, I'll situate these musings within the final two stages of the hero's journey—the *Master of Two Worlds* and the *Freedom to Live*.

Master of Two (or More) Worlds

For Campbell, the mythic hero's ultimate transformation entailed becoming a Master of Two Worlds—these worlds being the transcendent or spiritual and the manifest or everyday material reality.[1] Psychologically speaking, we could also understand these realms as our subjective experiences and our shared social realities, or the conscious and unconscious parts of our mind. A so-called master can move freely back and forth between these realms without getting lost or confused. Becoming a fully-fledged 'master' isn't the goal for most of us, nor need it be. Neither do we all need to agree on how many 'worlds' there are or what they're fundamental nature is. We can simply understand this language as a metaphor for various layers of reality and experience (psychological, social, physical, spiritual, or otherwise).

Whatever we understand these 'worlds' to be, human life remains complex—but as basic physics continues to remind us in a more fundamental way, complexity isn't a quality exclusive to life. Still, many of us have somehow lost a sense of enchantment and awe as we've gone about our lives. This disenchantment, though understandable at times, is more a matter of perspective than reality itself. Against all odds, we *exist*. And not only that, we exist as *conscious* beings who can observe and explore our inner and outer worlds. Are these worlds sacred or mundane? Ordinary-and-uninteresting or endlessly fascinating? From Campbell's perspective, the two (or more) are one. The transcendent can be found in the ordinary.

Taking cues from these ideas, we can return to our first journey way-point—cosmic awareness. In only contemplating what we do and do not know about the cosmos, we may understand that true 'masters' are people who realize how little they truly comprehend.[2] But in that humility, they find wisdom and a perspective on life, as mysterious and minuscule as it is in the grandest scales of time and space. This perspective, whether encountered through science, spiritual practices, or within a psychedelic journey, is one at first unstable. How do we reconcile our very human egocentric concerns with the greater reality as we understand it?

Throughout human history, perspectives on whether our everyday world and the cosmos as a whole are inherently meaningful and sacred or empty and mundane has vacillated. These interpretations in their extreme form are like two opposing positions on a swinging pendulum. Today, as in times past, this pendulum continues to swing. Maybe it always will. But as it swings, we might remember that a pendulum's center of gravity lies in the middle and not in extremes. With any luck, as our societies and cultures evolve, our descendants might see a net benefit emerge over the course of our history. That benefit, in part at least, is to be good stewards of the earth and its complex ecosystems, of which we are a part. We are, if I were to guess, still early in our story of humanity and consciousness. Progress isn't as simple as a straight line rapidly driving upwards. Our faith may best be placed in the long game. But while contemplating the future, we can remember that what's immanent in our everyday world now also deserves our attention and respect.

We are, though, at a crossroads it seems. And with a perspective that can be sorely lacking and shortsighted. But we are not powerless, even as individuals. The psychological and societal transformations that may come will likely begin small, as they nearly always do, with fits and false starts, but given enough time, a single spark can light a fire which ignites into a blaze. This blaze is not about destruction but renewal. One mythic symbol that may help us in such times of transition is that of the phoenix. The fiery phoenix is an eternal celestial force, but its immortality comes through its voluntary cycles of death and rebirth, destruction and restoration. Each time this firebird combusts it soon is reborn, and the cycle begins anew.

If we reflect on how the phoenix manifests in our personal lives, how we have been transformed through various life experiences, we may also realize that what has affected us as individuals often reverberates throughout our larger networks. Is this how our cultures evolve too? Each of us is never isolated from our larger social context. We humans naturally move towards a sense of community and often a deeper connection to something beyond ourselves or some higher power. Through these connections, however we understand them, a kind of self-transcendence is fostered. These connections were intertwined with how we evolved because they spoke to what we *knew* in a fundamental way. Most essentially, our ancestors experienced our interconnectedness with and dependence on nature in their daily life. We've merely forgotten our deeper connection with one another and nature itself. We *are* nature. A part of ourselves has always known this because in our origins we were so intimately connected to the earth, knowing so little about our place on the planet but knowing we were one small part of a much bigger mystery. Maybe that part of ourselves, passed on through our genes, our ancient cultures, and our living sources of indigenous wisdom, can re-emerge to create a new balance—one not idealizing the past but learning from it, all of it, shadow and light, to bring us forward to a new stage.

The exaltation of the humancentric perspective and our own cleverness has left much to be desired, but it was never the big picture to begin with. Basic science and cosmology may teach us this, but so do many ancient, modern, indigenous, esoteric, and even mainstream contemporary wisdom traditions.

A distinctly modern challenge, however, is that now we must reconnect to this higher perspective while integrating and holding space for a greater awareness of diverse experiences, complexity, and ambiguity. We live in a multicultural world, most of us not belonging to a single 'tribe,' and this world contains many distinct belief systems and meaningful mythologies. Remember, though, that any single myth is not to be believed in a concrete, reified manner but to be *lived*. And to be lived alongside other myths that speak to us, as part of a greater network of meaning and mystery. By applying their symbolic lessons in our everyday shared reality, they by necessity must themselves evolve and adapt to our expanding insights and needs—both at the personal and collective level. Critical blind spots can and will be addressed. And different stories need to be heard at different times. The hero's journey is one of many patterns of human storytelling. It alongside others may allow us to reconnect to our inner wisdom and perhaps reconstruct some core elements of lost traditions as we move forward in time.

In a letter written less than a year before his death, Jung shared this same perspective about essential knowledge re-emerging when it's needed most:[3]

> It seems to me that nothing essential has ever been lost, because the matrix is ever-present within us and from this it can and will be reproduced if needed. But only those can recover it who have learned the art of averting their eyes from the blinding light of current opinions, and close their ears to the noise of ephemeral slogans.

Platitudes, uninformed assumptions, and propaganda do not point the way. The path to deeper work and transformation may seem at times lonely for people who ask profound questions, but by being comfortable in your solitude, always willing to learn, and authentic in your expressions of Self, you will, I believe, discover that you were never actually alone. In the same letter, Jung echoed a similar sentiment, and it continues to ring true to me in doing this work and writing this book:[4]

> Thus an old alchemist gave the following consolation to one of his disciples: "No matter how isolated you are and how lonely you feel, if you do your work truly and conscientiously, unknown friends will come and seek you."

How? We first must be willing to tell our stories. To share what we've learned with people who have open ears and minds while we remain humble and curious. Perhaps more importantly, through this openness, we can encounter and listen to others who also speak authentically about their perception of Truth, especially when they're speaking to the edges of our own understanding and growth. Truth is bigger than any one of us. And far grander than our little human species alone. For this reason, I believe Truth is and will always be one and the same with Mystery. For explorers of consciousness and life, whether we become 'heroes,' 'masters,' or everyday people working toward a brighter future, that awareness of Mystery can re-enchant the world as it *is* and break through the illusion of boredom, banality, and hopelessness. Sometimes all it takes is stepping outside and looking up at the sky.

Freedom to Live—Savoring, Loving Awareness, & Embracing the Eternal Moment

In the 'final' stage of the hero's journey, the hero transcends any remaining ego-level concerns and by doing so, they learn to live without fear.[5] That mythic attainment is likely too high of a mark for us to strive for. Fear is embedded in our psychology and our bodies, but so are love and joy. A major theme of our journey, especially the trials, has been that with awareness comes freedom. By becoming conscious of when and how fear and its consequences can take hold, we become more liberated from its destructive influences. As we work towards mastery in navigating our multiple 'worlds' and solving problems as they emerge, the ultimate outcome may be right in front of us—engaging more fully and freely with our lives.

A part of this engagement is the capability and practice of savoring our life experiences. Savoring is an act of appreciation and joy for life, which can enhance our sense of vitality. What should be savored? Of course, that's up to you. It's your life, after all. Your freedom of choice continues. At any moment, though, even the most difficult, remembering the miracle of our very existence, especially as conscious beings, can rejuvenate and heal. Ram Dass used a simple phrase to capture this sentiment, "I am loving awareness."[6] This deceptively straightforward mantra has layers of meaning, which in different moments may speak to us in different ways.

If we are loving awareness, then we are free to explore this awareness in a myriad of ways. We humans tend to be explorers. So, by all means, we should continue to explore, discover, and have that sense of wonder as we experience this life we've been given. What do you want to continue exploring? This is where Campbell's suggestion of following your bliss comes into play. 'Bliss' here is suggesting a path of intrinsic joy and meaning, which is individualized to your nature and values, not what others tell you you should do. We each must walk our own path. As you engage with life, follow the paths that ring true, even if you can't fully explain why. But as countless explorers have learned, do so with a measure of caution and reverence. Even when you're on the 'right' path, know you too will experience occasional setbacks, but these are only new trials which you can pass, just like the ones you did in our journey. Each experience is a teacher that can help you grow, refine your insights, and see where your next frontier may lie.

In the end, that's all that any of us can do. And it's enough. Part of loving awareness is a profound acceptance of what that awareness is showing us.

When the weight of the world appears to be on our shoulders, we can take time to just breath and remember that sometimes progress happens by just allowing what *is* to be. This is resting in our awareness and grounding ourselves in the profound mystery of the cosmos. The result is a cultivation of equanimity. It is a challenge and a counter measure to the productive yet limited action-oriented, problem solving hero archetype. Our notion of the new meta hero and their strengths is one attempt to navigate these multiple worlds, full of ambiguity, while staying engaged in active creative problem-solving. But implicit in these ideas is the option to allow greater space for non-action, a central tenet of Taoism that's especially hard for us Westerners. Recently, the 29th stanza of the *Tao Te Ching* has resonated with me in this regard:[7]

> Do you think you can take over the universe and improve it?
> I do not believe it can be done.
>
> The universe is sacred.
> You cannot improve it.
> If you try to change it, you will ruin it.
> If you try to hold it, you will lose it.
>
> So sometimes thing are ahead and sometimes they are behind;
> Sometimes breathing is hard, sometimes it comes easily;
> Sometimes there is strength and sometimes weakness;
> Sometimes one is up and sometimes down.
>
> Therefore the sage avoids extremes, excesses, and complacency.

Another way to think of non-action is to revisit the three expressions of meaning discussed in our final trial—being, doing, and becoming. Non-action is resting in *being* and focusing less on intentional goal-oriented doing or becoming. The latter can and will unfold naturally from whatever is.

In cultivating the freedom to live, the concept of being can act as a touchstone in even the most difficult moments where we're uncertain of what to do next. In truth, being in the present moment is all we ever really have and are guaranteed. In a 1932 seminar, Jung spoke eloquently of the *eternal moment* in a similar fashion as Campbell did when discussing the freedom to live:[8]

> [T]his [now] is the eternal moment, and if you do not realize it, you will
> have missed the best part of life. You will have missed the realization that
> you are the carrier of a life contained between the poles of an unimag-
> inable future and an unimaginably remote past. Millions of years and

untold millions of ancestors have worked up to this moment....One should take each moment...as if nothing were ever going to change, not anticipating a faraway future. For the future always grows out of that which *is*...You must live life in such a spirit that you make in every moment the best of the possibilities.

This attitude of appreciation and present-centered engagement is one way we can cultivate equanimity and both savor life's beautiful moments and endure its more difficult ones.

A Journey to Be Continued

Throughout this book, a hallmark of each chapter has been a brief summary. For this epilogue, if I were to summarize some key elements of our journey together, it'd be something like the following:

When our curiosity is first sparked and our vision expands, we may revel in the mysteries we discover. But in time, we also must confront the challenging aspects of our human existence. Curiosity leads us to awareness, and awareness leads us to the necessity of acceptance—acceptance in experiencing both the joys and sorrows of our world and the profound impact of our impermanence, interconnectedness, and search for deeper meaning. After we accept this greater whole, we can develop wisdom through awareness of the light and the shadow while choosing compassion and love over fear and hate. This growing wisdom also helps us discern what's best for ourselves and within our circle of influence, recognizing again we're all interconnected, belonging to the earth and the cosmos itself. The mysteries of intuition and wisdom need not be explained away for us to continue to explore, expand, and engage deeply along our individual path, gaining comfort in both our solitude and our authentic and intimate connections with our fellow travelers. Like our ancestors and allies before us, we can play an important role in our shared mythic story, even if many roles remain private and unseen. Interspersed throughout our lives will be moments where we can rest and be at peace, knowing too that in the end this peace will be our ultimate destination.

If you were to summarize your personal journey, what would you say? What moments have stood out? How were your intentions addressed over time? Even a far-reaching journey like ours, however, leaves some territory left to be discovered. If you were to add another chapter to this journey, what would it cover and what activities would you include? Or, if you're especially ambitious, what would your 'sequel' to this journey be about? If you're a writer, I encourage you to write about it. An artist? Create art as your contribution to our on-going adventures.

For the rest of us, we may simply deepen our engagement with our lives and our continual process of growth. When in doubt, consider listening to the myth makers, our modern-day artists, filmmakers, and writers who are actively exploring and expressing the stories that help point the way and chart our possible futures. The messages that you personally need to hear will resonate as long as you're paying attention.

You too may contribute to our living myth. How can you keep the story alive? This question is not only for the young or young at heart. In our old age, we can contribute through our willingness to share our hard-earned wisdom and pass on meaningful roles to the next generation. Unlike most movies, the story doesn't end after the credits roll. Each of us is living our own multi-part, unfolding journey that goes beyond linear narratives. Life marches forth in a continuous flow, moving towards an unknown future with many possibilities. What do you want your life to be about? Where do you go from here? There's no need to have everything figured out ahead of time—which isn't even possible to begin with. Trust that if something is truly important, you'll hear a new call to adventure and can choose to embark on yet another journey of growth.

For all humankind, as we continue to confront challenges and possible futures, we might also ask ourselves, "Will we be a warning for future generations or a source of inspiration? Will we reach our own potential in time? Or will we be the fallen ancient civilization (or species) that serves as a cautionary tale for future conscious life?" In the grand scheme, all possibilities may be ultimately meaningful, but as a human, I choose to work towards our survival and development alongside that of the planet and its diverse and beautiful ecosystems. If it's a Sisyphean task or not, it doesn't matter. If our ancestors didn't display courage and try, against all odds, to survive and adapt, we wouldn't be here today.

For now, we can work for what's possible in the present and near future while having a vision for the long game. A great story, as ours continues to be, requires people who are willing to work towards that brighter future. Such 'heroes' are manifestations of every generations' evolving consciousness. They're stewards of the future and the unfolding development of all life. Whether through science, mysticism, or art, 'follow your bliss' to the path that beckons you and plays to your strengths—while respecting others who choose a different path in good faith. We can all welcome the attitude of being a lifelong learner and realize there's more than one meaningful path laid out for us.

I'll end this book by sharing that once in my life, my greatest fear about my adult years was that I'd inevitably become bored. Now I've learned again and again that boredom is merely a sign that my eyes have yet to open further. I offer this journey with a deep bow of respect to you and all your unique and shared experiences, whatever they may be. As best you can, as your adventures continue, connect more fully with yourself. And with each other. And the world we share. Stay humble. Stay grounded. And don't forget to have fun.

Travel Journal

Who am I?

Who are we?

What might be my way of contributing to the world and our on-going adventures?

ACKNOWLEDGMENTS

Writing a book as ambitious as this one requires undergoing a journey, a journey replete with both joyous and sorrowful moments as well as unexpected encounters and opportunities of personal transformation. And that's overlooking the fact that although I first outlined this book in early 2019 and drafted the initial chapters that same year, the majority of work really occurred in the unforgettable 2020. Who knew that exploring mortality, loss, interconnectedness, and existential issues would be brought to life in such a way in 2020 that my inner and outer worlds would become one? Much has happened for our world in the timespan of writing this book. But, perhaps, that was meant to be. Although this year has been hard, I've been reminded again and again just how much I have to be grateful for. In the especially tough days of writing, rewriting, and editing, I could remind myself that no matter how uncertain the future was, I was exactly where I was meant to be and doing exactly what I was meant to do—that is, I suppose, if one believes in that sort of thing. In my life's journey thus far, it's been hard not to.

An attitude of deep-seated appreciation and love has been the fuel for this project, and throughout its many iterations, I would occasionally stop and think, "Man, I can't wait to *finally* be able to write my acknowledgments." Often that thought was accompanied by a smile, and sometimes, I admit, by a furrowed brow. But now, I've made it to the end of this book's journey, and I have the pleasure to share at last just how many people I have to acknowledge. These people have been my much-needed allies, in one way or another—and most often, in many different ways.

First and foremost, I must thank three individuals who have been with me since the early days of creating this book—Eugene Canotal, Chris Stauffer, and Rich Hart. They've each supported me not only by listening to my wild ideas but also by reviewing my early writing drafts and sketched out 'storyboards' for its various features. Without their belief in me and this project, I can't imagine arriving here, at least with as few scars as I have now. Later in this book's development, others entered the scene and provided astute feedback and wholehearted support. Wendy Pots, Gil Woo, Jacey Tramutt, and Evan Sola lent me their hearts and minds, which undoubtedly improved the final product. Although not premeditated on my part, everyone mentioned thus far also comes from diverse ethnocultural and racial backgrounds, philosophical worldviews, and professional career paths. For a book aiming to speak to a wide audience, that's been a meaningful coincidence—or in the words of Jung, an example of synchronicity.

As the journey of writing this book unfolded, I found many new allies. Chief among them have been my own Wise Elders in the world of psychedelic research, scholarship, and practice. From an early stage, Bill Richards' mentorship has helped elevate this passion project into a full-fledged mission. His trust in me to bring it to fruition has been invaluable, and I've been fortunate to call him a friend. Alongside Bill, I'm also deeply grateful for the support of David Presti, Jeff Guss, Mariavittoria Mangini, Françoise Bourzat, Harvey Schwartz, Bob Jesse, Janis Phelps, and Rodney Karr. Our personal conversations have always been enlivening, and each of you have influenced this book and my personal journey in writing it.

Next, I'd like to acknowledge other friends, colleagues, and family who have been supportive at various points. My in-depth conversations with Nicole Wernimont and Daan Keiman about the competing themes and nuances explored in *Beyond the Narrow Life* have been critical, in particular, in 'work-shopping' some of its more subtle messages. In a similar fashion, Alli Feduccia, Tatiana Santini, Valerie Beltrán, Chase Ebert, Addison Kavish, Matt Feldman-Campbell, and Pamela Rhude have acted as sounding boards when I needed to think aloud. Although not a typical part of our everyday family conversations, I must especially thank my parents, Ted and Verna Ortigo, and my brother Kurt for being willing to talk about psychedelics, philosophy, and myth. You supported me at every step and kept me grounded, as only family can do.

Speaking of family, it's been quite a meaningful journey to be the first one in my family to attend college, much less earn an advanced degree. Well before undergoing the trials of advanced education, my roots were firmly planted in rural Arkansas with a loving and hardworking family. Growing up in the country near naturally occurring hot springs underwrote a deep respect and connection with nature. Besides my parents and other extended family, my grandmother Carol Ortigo made sure to foster my intellectual curiosity and academic ambition. Although she passed away before my graduation, I have no doubt she'd be pleased to see how far I've come.

My later years in Atlanta and San Francisco added to the texture of this small-town background. At the University of Arkansas, new worlds opened, and much of this book's themes can be traced to the caring mentorship and support I received from several of my professors. In the Department of Psychology, Dave Schroeder accepted my request to bring personality theory into a social psychology research lab—historically, an unthinkable combination.

My first introduction to Jung and Campbell came from my film studies mentors, Janice Hocker Rushing, who tragically passed away suddenly from cancer soon after we agreed to collaborate, and her husband and colleague Tom Frentz, who took me under his wings as we mourned together and honored her memory. At Emory University, my doctoral work was supported by Drew Westen, Bekh Bradley, Nancy Bliwise, Elizabeth Wilson, and several other professors and supervisors who introduced me to many new vistas of exploration, including the clinical care of survivors of trauma, which became an unexpected but central part of my professional world. On postdoctoral fellowship, mentorship by the late Steve Rao at San Francisco VA and UCSF further supported the role of mindfulness and compassion in my clinical work, which I hope is also demonstrated clearly in this book. In my early career at the National Center for PTSD, Joe Ruzek and Marylene Cloitre continued my professional mentorship in trauma treatment. In fact, if it weren't for Marylene's invitation to coauthor the 2nd edition of *Treating Survivors of Childhood Abuse and Interpersonal Trauma*, I might not have realized how much I enjoy writing in the style offered by books as opposed to research journal articles.

As a culmination of all these experiences and more, this book has been what I describe to my clients as "Capital 'W' Work"—meaning work that represents one's deep-rooted personal values and sense of purpose. Thus, as a creative endeavor, it was critical for me to find the right partners in bringing it to life. From the early days of planning, I set my sights on Synergetic Press because of their overarching mission of raising consciousness, supporting ecological sustainability, and valuing interdisciplinary scholarship. From our first conversation onwards, Doug Reil has been not only very professional and responsive to my inquiries, but also deeply engaged in the unfolding process of the book's development. Once Doug and Deborah Snyder officially welcomed me to the Synergetic team, I was pleased to see that the other staff were just as engaged and enthusiastic about this ambitious project. Chief among them has been Amanda Müller, without whom I couldn't imagine the final product being nearly as expertly executed. Amanda's passion for the subject matter was further supported by her wide-reaching knowledge base. I knew I could trust her in helping midwife *Beyond the Narrow Life*. Furthermore, Amanda served as an ambassador to the talented artists Gustavo Attab,[a] who created

---

[a] To check out Gustavo's work, follow him on Instagram (Gus.Attab) or visit his website at https://gustavoattab.weebly.com/. To learn more about Lysander, visit https://www.ghostkidproductions.com or follow him on Instagram (GhostKidStudio).

this book's original cover, and Lysander Alston-Cramer, who transformed my storyboards into custom interior graphics.[a]

Lastly, I'd like to thank the people who must officially remain nameless—first, the authors of the nine journey reports, and second, my clients. For the writers of the journey reports, thank you for your willingness to share deeply personal experiences for readers to consider as examples of how this book's themes can emerge in non-ordinary states of consciousness. For my clients, I've appreciated learning from each of you and being able to bear witness to the joys and sorrows of this human life, from the distinctive to the shared experiences, and everything in between. I remember all of you, well after therapy has been completed, and I will continue to honor the trust you have placed in me and our work together.

In light of all that precedes, I'd be remiss to leave out the numerous indigenous communities and direct and indirect ancestors, both personal and collective, who have kept the knowledge of psychedelic healing and transformation alive at great risk to themselves. I've been humbled by this opportunity to share my thoughts on psychedelic integration when so many previous generations and communities did not have a voice. Much has been endured by others that I have largely been able to evade due to luck and privilege in living in this day and age. I offer this book with sincerest gratitude for all those who've come before and with heartfelt hope for our future generations.

The Hero's Journey—Stages & Variations

	The Hero with a Thousand Faces—Joseph Campbell (1949/2008)	The Writer's Journey—Christopher Vogler (1990/2020)	The Heroine's Journey—Maureen Murdock (1990/2020)
	World of Common Day	**1. Ordinary World**—limited awareness	**World of Common Day**
Act I Departure	**1. The Call to Adventure**—signs of the vocation of the hero	**2. The Call to Adventure**—inciting incident, increased awareness of problem	**1. Separation from the Feminine**—search for identity
	2. Refusal of the Call—the folly of the flight from the God	**3. Refusal of the Call**—reluctance to change or address the problem	**2a. Identification with the Masculine**—rejection of the feminine
	3. Supernatural Aid—the unsuspected assistance that comes to one who has undertaken their proper adventure	**4. Meeting with the Mentor**—overcoming reluctance	**2b. Gathering Allies**
	4. Crossing the First Threshold	**5. Crossing the First Threshold**—committing to change	**3. The Road of Trials**—meeting ogres and dragons, myths of dependency, female inferiority, & romantic love
	5. Belly of the Whale—passage into the realm of night		**4. Finding the Illusory Boon of Success**—superwoman mystique, myth of never being enough

Box continues on next page

Act II Initiation	6. The Road of Trials—the dangerous aspect of the gods	6. Tests, Allies, Enemies— experimenting with first movement towards change	5. Awakening to Feelings of Spiritual Aridity (Death)— strong women say no, betrayal by the father, the king must die
		7. Approach to the Inmost Cave—preparing for a big change	
	7. The Meeting with the Goddess—the bliss of infancy regained	8. The Supreme Ordeal— attempting the big change, midpoint, death, and rebirth	6. Initiation and Descent to the Goddess—looking for lost pieces of self, meeting the dark mother
	8. Woman as the Temptress— the realization and agony of Oedipus		7. Urgent Yearning to Reconnect with the Feminine—the body/ spirit split, female sexuality, grieving the separation from the feminine, the feminine as preserver and as creator
	9. Atonement with the Father		
	10. Apotheosis		
	11. The Ultimate Boon	9. Reward—seizing the sword, consequences of the attempt (improvements and setbacks)	8. Healing the Mother/ Daughter Split—mother as fate, divine ordinariness, healing in nature and community, woman as mythmaker, reclaiming the power of the feminine

Act III Return	12. **Refusal of the Return**—the world denied	10. **The Road Back**—rededication of efforts to create change	
	13. **The Magic Flight**—escape of Prometheus		
	14. **Rescue from Without**		
	15. **The Crossing of the Return Threshold**—the return to the world of the common day		
	16. **Master of the Two Worlds**	11. **The Resurrection**—climax, final attempt at making the big change	9. **Healing the Wounded Masculine**—finding the inner man with heart, becoming a woman with wisdom and healing powers of the feminine
	17. **Freedom to Live**—the nature and function of the ultimate boon	12. **Return with the Elixir**—denouement, final mastery of the problem	10. **Beyond Duality**—healing the split, integration of masculine and feminine, dual nature of the divine, the circle as a model for living

Note. These stages have been adapted from Campbell (2008, pp. 28-30), Vogler (2020, pp. 6-9, 238-239), and Murdock (2020, pp. vii-x, 5). While introducing the monomyth in *The Hero with a Thousand Faces*, Campbell supplemented the hero's journey with an overview of the Cosmogonic Cycle. This cycle outlines the vision of cosmic creation and destruction that is typically bestowed to the mythic hero (usually during apotheosis). The four overarching stages include (1) *Emanations* (creation out of the void), (2) *The Virgin Birth* (creative and redemptive roles of the divine feminine), (3) *Transformations of the Hero* (variations of the hero across human history), and (4) *Dissolutions* (the eventual return of the manifest world into the void).

Psychedelic Flight Instructions

— William A. Richards, PhD
  Center for Psychedelic and Consciousness Research
  John Hopkins University

The following are edited flight instructions for psychedelic journeys, originally created by Dr. Bill Richards for psilocybin research conducted at John Hopkins University. In partnership with Dr. Richards, I have made minor revisions to these instructions, including replacing 'participant' with 'journeyer.' Note too that these instructions were written for the study co-therapist team to help prepare research volunteers, usually on the day prior to their psilocybin journeys. The italicized script indicates words spoken by therapists to the study volunteers. Thus 'we' refers to the therapist team and 'you' refers to the journeyer.

> *"Please let yourself relax as much as you can. You will never be left alone during your experience. You need not worry about physical safety. We will be here to support you if and when needed and to maintain your physical and psychological safety.*
>
> *You may experience a deep and transcendental experience. You may feel the loss of your usual sense of self and experience a sensation of rebirth or even death. You may experience a feeling that you have ceased to exist as an individual person and are connected with the world or the universe. If you experience the sensation of dying, melting, dissolving, exploding, going crazy, etc.—go ahead.[a] Experience the experience. Remember that the death or transcendence of your ego or your everyday self is always followed by rebirth and return to the familiar world of space and time. The safest way to return to normal is to entrust yourself unconditionally to the emerging experiences."*

Approximately twenty minutes after ingesting psilocybin, journeyers may begin to feel a change in mental state. On occasion, they may feel nausea,

---

[a] Note that these instructions do not apply to acting out or behaving impulsively. This is not stated as explicitly in this script because the context involves two trained therapists and a safe location, in which participants are monitored and supported.

which will typically pass within a short period of time. Should a person experience nausea, encourage them to embrace it or *"Dive into your stomach"* while allowing the music to transport them more deeply within. If the journeyer becomes nauseated and believes they may need to vomit, therapists provide a waste bin and towel already located nearby in the room and then alert the medical staff. Note that journeyers are instructed to avoid eating a large breakfast the morning of psychedelic sessions. Therapists can encourage the journeyer with any of the following, as appropriate:

"Part of your being is discomfort, which shall pass."

"Feel the nausea leaving you, and you will soon return to comfort."

"Nausea is temporary and it will pass, embrace it and then send it on its way."

Therapists may answer any question the journeyer asks. Therapists are free to talk with the journeyer to the extent the journeyer initiates conversation. Or, if the journeyer has been silent for a prolonged period of time, therapists might ask, *"Would you like to describe where you find yourself?"* but without pressure for the journeyer to respond if they choose to remain silent. We encourage therapists, however, to continue to guide the journeyer into progressively deeper experiences using the suggestions below.

Therapists avoid attempting to guide the journeyer down any specific path. Instead, they help the journeyer to enter a deeper experience by encouraging them, as needed, with phrases such as those that follow. Note that many of these phrases and mantras are introduced as part of the preparation session the day before the actual psychedelic experience. By discussing them before the journey, elaborate conversations and Q&A can be avoided during the experience itself, which could distract the journeyer from their internal process.

"There's a mantra that many have found helpful during psilocybin experiences called TLO. It stands for 'Trust, Let Go, and Be Open.' If you have as moment when you wonder how you should respond next, you can silently repeat this mantra to yourself—TLO."

"Trust the trajectory, follow your path"

"If you see a door, what will you do"? (Therapists encourage the journeyer to "walk through it")

"If you see a window, what will you do?" (Therapists encourage the journeyer to "look through it" or "open it")

"Climb staircases, open doors, explore paths, fly over landscapes"

"If you feel like you're dying, melting, dissolving, exploding, going crazy etc.—go ahead, embrace it."

If the journeyer is speaking a lot or trying to explain their experiences, therapists can encourage them to *"go inwards"* and *"collect experiences."* Analyzing their meaning or trying to understand can come later, usually the day after the journey.

"Let your intellect go out and play during the journey. At the end of the day, you can let your intellect revisit each experience to reflect on its meaning."

If the journeyer is feeling fear, therapists can encourage the journeyer to confront the fear respectfully with courage and strength.

"Look the monster in the eye and move towards it...Dig in your heels and ask, 'What are you doing here in my mind?' Or, 'What can I learn from you?' Look for the darkest corner in the basement and shine your light there."

"The same force that takes you deep within will, of its own impetus, return you safely to the everyday world."

If the journeyer is in mild physical pain, therapists can encourage the journeyer to investigate the pain using the phrases below (if confronted with intense or acute pain, therapists immediately notify the medical staff):

"Look into the pain you are experiencing. Focus your attention on it and see what images or memories may arise in your awareness. Where is the source of the pain?"

"Can you visualize the pain? Can you see it clearly for what it is?"

Therapists should be comfortable with silence and willing to step back to let the journeyer's experience unfold naturally. Bearing witness while providing a safe container in which the journeyer can feel at ease and cared for is typically what's most needed. However, over time with more experience, intuition can be honed regarding when and how specific types of support may be beneficial.

Recommended Resources & Other Media

Psychedelic Books

Sacred Knowledge (Richards, 2015)

Consciousness Medicine (Bourzat & Hunter, 2019)

Confrontations with the Unconscious (Hill, 2013)

The Way of the Psychonaut (Grof, 2019)

LSD Psychotherapy (Grof, 2008)

After the Ceremony Ends (Coder, 2017)

Zig Zag Zen (Badiner & Grey, 2015)

The Psychedelic Explorer's Guide (Fadiman, 2011)

The Ketamine Papers (Wolfson & Hartelius, 2016)

Ecstasy: The Complete Guide (Holland, 2001)

Good Chemistry (Holland, 2020)

Psychedelic and Related Online Resources

Psychedelic.Support

Chacruna.net

PsychedelicsToday.com

ExistentialExploration.org

Mythology, Religion, and Spirituality Books

The Hero with a Thousand Faces (Campbell, 2008)

The Writer's Journey (Vogler, 2020)

The Heroine's Journey (Murdock, 2020)

The World's Religions (Smith, 1958/1991)

Tao Te Ching (Lao Tsu, 4th Century BCE)

The Perennial Philosophy (Huxley, 1945/2004)

Personal Growth and Creativity Books

The Artist's Way: A Spiritual Path to Higher Creativity (Cameron, 2016)

Sketch by Sketch: A Creative Path to Emotional Healing and Transformation (Darcey, 2021)

Transcend: The New Science of Self-Actualization (Kaufman, 2020)

Box continues on next page

Film and Television

Visionary Science Fiction, Fantasy, and Drama

The Lord of the Rings (Jackson, 2002-2004)

Star Wars Episodes I-IX (Lucas et al., 1977-2019)

The Matrix Trilogy (Wachowski & Wachowski, 1999-2003)

Contact (Zemeckis, 1997)

Altered States (Russell, 1980)

Enter the Void (Noé, 2009)

Mother! (Aronofsky, 2017)

Us (Peele, 2019)

Arrival (Villeneuve, 2016)

Annihilation (Garland, 2018)

The Dark Crystal (Henson & Oz, 1982)

Prometheus (Scott, 2012)

Blade Runner (Scott, 1985)

Blade Runner 2049 (Villeneuve, 2017)

The Tree of Life (Malick, 2011)

The Last Wave (Weir, 1977)

Existential Comedy

I Heart Huckabees (Russel, 2004)

Burn After Reading (Coen & Coen, 2008)

Rick & Morty (Harmon et al., 2013—present)

Superhero Mythology

Doctor Strange (Derrickson, 2016)

Black Panther (Coogler, 2018)

Captain Marvel (Boden, 2019)

Avengers Infinity War (Russo & Russo, 2018)

Avengers Endgame (Russo & Russo, 2019)

Joker (Phillips, 2019)

The Dark Knight (Nolan, 2008)

Watchmen (Snyder, 2009)

Watchmen (TV Series; Lindelof et al. 2019)

Documentaries	
Cosmos: A Spacetime Odyssey (Druyan et al., 2014)	*Planet Earth* (Fothergill, 2006)
Cosmos: Possible Worlds (Druyan et al., 2020)	*Planet Earth II* (Berlowitz et al., 2016)
One Strange Rock (Aronofsky et al., 2018)	*Blue Planet II* (Honeyborne & Brownlow, 2017)
Joseph Campbell & The Power of Myth (Konner & Perlmutter, 1988)	*Finding Joe* (Solomon, 2011)

Visual Artists	
Michael Divine—TenThousandVisions.com	Andrew (Android) Jones—AndroidJones.com
Peter Mohrbaucher—Angelarium.net	Alex Grey & Allyson Grey—Cosm.org
Gustavo Attab—GustavoAttab.weebly.com	Lysander Alston-Cramer—GhostKidProductions.com

Note. Additional Resources and Recommendations can be found at ExistentialExploration.org

ENDNOTES

PROLOGUE

1 For example reviews of psychedelic research, see Reiff et al., 2020, and Jungaberle et al., 2018.

2 See, for example, Krpan's, 2020, article, "Unburdening the Shoulders of Giants: A Quest for Disconnected Academic Psychology."

3 See Muraresku, 2020, *The Immortality Key: The Secret History of the Religion with No Name*

4 For books about psychedelic history in the West, see Lattin, 2017, and Pollan, 2018.

5 For example, see Labate & Cavnar, 2014. Note that after a landmark Supreme Court decision in 2006 and a few lower court cases, two religious communities, Santo Daime and União do Vegetal, have some protection in the United States for conducting ayahuasca ceremonies for their members.

6 Barker, 2018

7 Strassman, 2001

8 See Holland, 2001, *Ecstasy: The Complete Guide*

9 See Wolfson & Hartelius, 2016, *The Ketamine Papers: Science, Therapy, and Transformation*

10 Letcher, 2007

11 May, 1991, *The Cry for Myth*, p. 15. May goes on to state, "Whether the meaning of existence is only what we put into life by our own individual fortitude, as Sartre would hold, or whether there is a meaning we need to discover, as Kierkegaard would state, the result is the same: myths are our way of finding this meaning and significance. Myths are like the beams in a house: not exposed to outside view, they are the structure which holds the house together so people can live in it."

12 Ibid., p. 27. Note that May was paraphrasing Thomas Mann, a German novelist.

13 Jackson (Director), 2002, *The Lord of the Rings: The Fellowship of the Ring* (Extended Edition). Scene begins at the 2 hr 40 min mark. The original source material comes from Oxford Professor J. R. R. Tolkien's book series written between 1936 and 1949 (prior, during, and after World War II) and originally published in 1954 and 1955 (see Tolkien, 1994).

CHAPTER ONE

1 Campbell & Moyers, 1988/1991, p. 206

2 The word is a combination of Greek roots *psychē* "mind" and *dēloun* "to reveal or manifest" and was coined in a letter by psychiatrist Humphry Osmond when writing to Aldous Huxley. Its first official use was in a publication by Osmond in 1957.

3 Dickens, 1859/1999, p. 1

4 Campbell, 1949/2008, *The Hero with a Thousand Faces*.

5 Campbell, 1949/2008

6 These are the three main 'acts' of Campbell's monomyth, which contains up to 17 stages.

7 To use examples from film, the role of the guide can be seen in the likes of Obi-Wan Kenobi from *Star Wars: Episode IV—A New Hope* (Lucas, 1977), Dumbledore from

the Harry Potter films (especially, Yates, 2007, 2009), Gandalf from *The Lord of the Rings* (Jackson, 2002, 2003, 2004), and Morpheus from *The Matrix* (Wachowski & Wachowski, 1999, 2003a, 2003b).

8 The emphasis on falsifiability, in particular, is attributed to Austrian-born British philosopher Karl Popper's (1935/1959) *The Logic of Scientific Discovery*. His ideas continue to influence scientific inquiry and design across several fields, including psychology. Falsifiability is an exceedingly high bar for many broad-reaching psychological theories and models, but we rely primarily on statistical modeling and probability. Scientific approaches include methods for correcting incorrect assumptions and modifying previously accepted theories based on new data. Social sciences deal with significant complexities that are thornier due to increased problems of sampling, measurement, statistical power, each of which increase error. In addition, most psychological research is based on nomothetic principles, design, and research findings. Nomothetic approaches ask questions about what's true for most people most of the time (within a given population or condition). Idiographic approaches look at individual cases and unique experiences and acknowledge that what's true for the individual isn't necessarily true for everyone else, and vice versa. This book is informed by both approaches, but by emphasizing a personalized journey through self-reflection and experiential activities, I'm encouraging an idiographic exploration of the ideas and themes introduced in this book.

9 His entire response is well worth hearing. 92nd Street Y, 2017, interview of Neil deGrasse Tyson by Robert Krulwich. Timepoint: 1hr:15min.

10 These are symptoms of depression, but only a mental health professional can make this diagnosis after a thorough interview. Many mental health symptoms overlap with other conditions, both psychological and physiological in origin.

11 Vibrant Emotional Health & Substance Abuse and Mental Health Services Administration (SAMSA), n.d., accessed at https://www.SuicidePreventionLifeline.org

THE FIRST ARC

1 From a lecture delivered in 1871 entitled "On the Philosophy of Mythology." See Stone, 2002, p. 150.

2 See Campbell's (1949/2008) *Hero with a Thousand Faces*

3 Fleming (Director), 1939, *The Wizard of Oz*

4 The subject of the original text is translated as 'men,' but I've edited it to be gender neutral. This stanza can be translated in multiple ways, but the usual interpretation often centers around governance. The one who needs to experience awe is the leader of a community or society, for the flip side of awe is fear and respect for the forces outside of one's control. If that leader doesn't show due respect to the people they govern, then eventually the forces of the collective (or perhaps the Tao) will overthrow the leader. I'm taking license by quoting this out of the

governance context, but it's valid still as a warning of the dangers of arrogance and the importance of feeling awe. See Stanza 72 of Lao Tsu's *Tao te Ching* (Feng & English, Trans., 1972/1997).

CHAPTER 2

1 Sagan, 1980/2013, p. 364-365. Emphasis on 'we' is in Sagan's original writing.

2 These shifts in consciousness are usually labeled as *mystical*. In later chapters, we'll review qualities of these states of consciousness as they're measured by validated research and clinical tools, such as the Mystical Experience Questionnaire. For a validation study of the measure, see MacLean et al., 2012.

3 Much of the general scientific findings and estimations of distance are based on common scientific knowledge and are rounded so as not to overwhelm the reader with more precise (and variable) estimates. However, for interested readers who want to explore the numbers discussed here and delve deeper into the material, I recommend several resources including NASA's public website, NASA.gov, and Space.com for easily accessible websites. For key books in the area, I suggest Carl Sagan's *Cosmos* (1980), Brian Greene's (1999) *The Elegant Universe*, and Neil DeGrasse Tyson's (2017) *Astrophysics for People in a Hurry*.

4 Batygin & Brown, 2016. Note that an alternative model is that there's actually a tiny black hole within our solar system.

5 NASA, 2019, "Hypothetical Planet X"

6 Siegel, 2015

7 Sender et al., 2016

8 Rands et al., 2014

9 By 'complete,' I mean a non-ionic hydrogen atom. A complete hydrogen atom has no net charge because the positive charge of its single proton (+) is balanced by the negative charge of its sole electron (−).

10 Frausto da Silva & Williams, 2001, p. 8

11 Hugh Everett first described multiverse theory in 1957 with his "many worlds" hypothesis, but his proposal is one of several others involving a multiverse. See Nomura, 2017.

12 Witten, 1998, p. 1129

13 For a few examples, see Chatwin, 1988, or Bierl et al., 2017

14 Planck Collaboration, 2020

15 World Health Organization, 2020, p. 1. The average lifespan (72 years) is based on data from 2016 (the latest available) across all regions and demographics. Low-income countries have an average lifespan of 62.7 years whereas high-income countries average 80.8 years.

16 Dalrymple, 1991

17 Pearce et al., 2018; Schopf et al., 2018

18 Schlebusch et al., 2017. Note the authors estimate the arrival of homo sapiens to be between 260,000 and 350,000 years ago. My reported number simply splits the difference.

19 Goren-Inbar et al., 2004

20 Note that 'the speed of light' is, here and elsewhere, an abbreviated way to refer to 'the speed of light in a vacuum.'

21 Einstein's theory of relativity has two variations, one based on acceleration (known as special relativity) and the other on gravity (known as general relativity). Special relativity is pertinent when two observers or objects are accelerating at different rates. Its most dramatic effects occur at near-light speeds. Because the speed of light cannot change, time must slow down at higher speeds of travel.

22 Nolan, 2014. Timestamp: 1hr:02min. The scene starts with the crew discussing relativity and gravity, but watch the entire scene for some extra Hollywood dramatic effects.

23 Wittmann & Lehnoff, 2005

24 Adams, 1979, p. 3

25 Sagan, 1980/2013, p. 243-244

26 Yaden et al., 2016.

27 See White's (2014) *The Overview Effect: Space Exploration and Human Evolution* (3rd Edition). Note the original book was first published in 1986. See also, Yaden et al., 2016.

28 According to Dictionary.com's definition of awe. Yaden and colleagues (2019) have also developed the Awe Experience Scale which measures the overall intensity of an awe-inspiring experience as well as six subfacets—(1) *Time* ("I sensed things momentarily slow down."), (2) *Self-Diminishment* ("I felt my sense of self shrink."), (3) *Connectedness* ("I felt a sense of communion with all living things."), (4) *Vastness* ("I felt that I was in the presence of something grand."), (5) *Physical Sensations* ("I felt my jaw drop."), and (6) *Need for Accommodation* ("I felt challenged to mentally process what I was experiencing."). This measure can be taken for free at Kaufman's (2000a) website, SelfActualizationTests.com (see also, Kaufman, 2020b).

29 Dark matter accounts for 26% of known universe whereas 69% is dark energy. That leaves only 5% of the universe being baryonic matter (our everyday material world). See Planck Collaboration, 2016, and Randall, 2018.

30 *Hamlet* Act I, Scene 5, Shakespeare, 1605/1905, p. 34. If interested in philosophy and naturalistic versus metaphysical interpretations of psychedelic experiences, consider Letheby, 2015, 2017, & Sjöstedt-H, 2015.

31 Only grammar, spelling, and potentially identifying details are changed, usually in partnership with the person offering their experience.

32 Druyan et al., 2014

33 Aronofsky et al., 2018

CHAPTER 3

1 Jung, 1957/1990, p. 25

2 As quoted in Stavropoulos, 2003, p. 47

3 Huxley, 1954/2019, p. 8. In summarizing the perspective of philosopher C. D. Broad, Huxley stated, "To make biological survival possible, Mind at Large has to be funneled through the reducing valve of the brain and nervous system. What comes out at the other end is a measly trickle of the kind of consciousness which will help us to stay alive on the surface of this particular planet" (p. 8). Note that Mind at Large is similar to the concept of cosmic consciousness. For a discussion of Huxley and other theorists about the nature of psychedelic effects, see Swanson, 2018.

4 For introductions to Jung, beyond what's provided in this book, I recommend Storr's (1983) *The Essential Jung* and Wilmer's (2015) *Practical Jung*.

5 See Bargh & Morsella, 2008, for a discussion. The quoted phrase comes from p. 73.

6 Defense mechanisms were greatly expanded by Freud's daughter and psychoanalyst Anna Freud, 1937/1993.

7 In clinical research and practice, defense mechanisms are usually organized by their level of development maturity. For example, Vaillant (1994) labeled the four levels of maturity, which correspond to Figure 3.1, as 'psychotic,' 'immature,' 'neurotic,' and 'mature.'

8 See Brenner, 1982, *The Mind in Conflict*

9 Jung, 1963/1989, *Memories, Dreams, Reflections*

10 Jung, 1921/1971, p. 448-450

11 The idea of the *persona* may overlap nicely with other modern psychological concepts that have been researched within non-Jungian frameworks. These alternative but related concepts include the *social self, social self-concept,* or *looking-glass self*. For excellent conceptual reviews of these different terms and models, see Turner & Onorato, 2014, and Oyserman, 2004.

12 Jung was being interviewed by Dr. Richard Evans of the University of Houston. To watch the interview on YouTube, see the video posted by The Introverted Thinker on April 8, 2019. Timestamp: 0-hr:0-min:55-sec

13 Timestamp: 0-hr:1-min:34-sec

14 For thoughtful investigations of such phenomena, see Hogan, 2010; van Dijck, 2013; and Schwartz & Halegoua, 2015

15 For empirical investigations of social media and self-esteem (and personality factors), see Seidman, 2013; Vogel et al., 2014; and Andreassen et al., 2017

16 An alternative framing of personal identity is ego *identity,* which originated from Eric Erickson (1968), whose work has been widely influential. Personal and ego identity has internalized elements of the social self-concept and persona but is broader since it includes the *private self* not shared with others. Although ego identity reflects more of a personality-oriented framework, it can be considered as generally the same as one's personal identity. A personal identity reflects the uniqueness of the individual self, including the collected conscious personality traits, interpersonal styles, goals, beliefs, values and attitudes. Again, for excellent reviews, see Turner & Onorato, 2014, and Oyserman, 2004. We'll revisit some of these different elements of identity and self throughout this book.

17 Early stages of ego identity and self-awareness are accomplished well before adolescence, but because these earlier stages are very basic, this chapter only reviews the later stages of identity formation. If interested in early development, see Rochat, 2003.

18 See Marcia, 1966; Marcia et al., 1993. Note that sometimes, the process of identity development and achievement remains unfinished. If we commit without exploring, we can become stuck in *identity foreclosure*. If we neither explore nor commit, we languish in *identity diffusion*. If we ceaselessly explore but never commit, we suffer from *identity moratorium*.

19 For a meta-analytic review of this research, see Köllner & Schultheiss, 2014. The correlation between implicit and explicit motivations was overall only .13. In specific domains of motivation, implicit-explicit motivations correlated the weakest for power (r = .038), followed by affiliation (r = .116) and finally achievement (r = .139).

20 Jung, 1968, *Man and His Symbols,* p. 72. [sic] is for Jung's use of male pronouns only.

21 Jung, 1948/1970

22 Admittedly, I'm taking some (but not much) license here in interpreting complexes as not inherently negative or pathological. My description of complexes is more neutral and similar to the notion of schema and associational networks. But, Jung himself tied complexes to associational networks. His clinical work and writings about clients who struggled with various complexes impacted the overall negative interpretation of complexes being pathological.

23 For an interesting review of how these implicit associations can work individually and collectively, see Greenwald et al., 2015.

24 Schwartz & Sweezy, 2019; Mithoefer, 2017.

25 For one of Jung's more concise overviews of archetypes and the collective unconscious, see Jung (1937/1980). Since Jung's original work, many writers and theorists have preferred to use the word 'transpersonal' or 'transconsciousness' to refer to these deeper shared realms of the human psyche (see Grof, 1975, and Rushing & Frentz, 1995, respectively).

26 See Campbell & Moyer's, 1991/1988, *The Power of Myth*

27 Star Wars original trilogy films, Episodes IV-VI, consist of *A New Hope* (Lucas, 1977), *The Empire Strikes Back* (Kershner, 1980), and *Return of the Jedi* (Marquand, 1983). The prequel trilogy films, Episodes I-III, include the George Lucas directed *The Phantom Menace* (1999), *Attack of the Clones* (2002), and *Revenge of the Sith* (2005). The sequel trilogy, Episodes VII-IX, refers to *The Force Awakens* (Abrams, 2015), *The Last Jedi* (Johnson, 2017), and *The Rise of Skywalker* (Abrams, 2019).

28 *The Matrix, The Matrix Reloaded, and The Matrix Revolutions* directed by Wachowski and Wachowski (1999, 2003a, 2003b, respectively).

29 Jung described the anima/animus as a key component required to loving the "opposite" sex. I've adjusted this definition to reflect a less rigid, binary view of gender and sexuality

30 Jung referenced the Wise Old Man or Woman, but I think it's fair to update his theory with more gender inclusive language that recognizes the full spectrum of gender expressions and identities outside of a strict binary of man or woman.

31 For one mystical interpretation, see Ponte & Schäfer, 2013. For another analysis, see Mills, 2013.

32 See the work of Stanislav Grof, such as his 1975 book *Realms of the Human Unconscious*. Outside of psychedelics, French paleontologist Pierre Teilhard de Chardin, 1955/1959, also asserted the possibility of universal consciousness.

33 The nature and reason for consciousness itself is mysterious. There are many fundamental but connected debates in philosophy and science, such as the 'hard problem of consciousness' (asking why subjective states exist at all, see Chalmers, 1995) and the mind-body problem, which intersects with the larger debates of monism-vs-dualism and materialism-vs-idealism (in its various formulations, like physicalism-vs-panpsychism). For additional perspectives involving the neuroscience of consciousness, see Koch, 2018, and Koch et al., 2016.

34 As Watts said in a 1961 interview with *Life* magazine, "Eager Exponent of Zen," p. 93

35 For an overview of psychodynamic models of personality, see Westen et al., 2008. If interested in the person-vs-situation and trait-vs-process debates, I recommend Mischel & Shoda, 2008, and Funder, 2008.

36 See Goldberg, 1992; McCrae & John, 1992

37 This idea is known as the lexical hypothesis. For one of the first systematic applications of this hypothesis, see Allport & Odbert, 1936.

38 Kaufman et al., 2016

39 MacLean et al., 2011

40 Wagner et al., 2017

41 I'm referring to the Five Factor Model. See McCrae & Costa, 2008, see Table 5.2, p. 165, for a full description.

42 For discussion of how psychedelics, MDMA, and ketamine affect neuroplasticity, see Ly et al., 2018

43 Validating how different traits interact with one another (and factors like situation, culture, etc.) to impact behavior would require very well-designed studies with incredibly large samples and statistical power, ideally with multiple measures repeated across many points in time.

44 In fact, a meta-analysis by Oh et al. (2011) found observer/other-reported measures of the Five-Factor Model outperformed self- reported versions. That means, on average, other people are better at describing us than we are accurately describing ourselves, a la the Alan Watts quote from earlier in this chapter.

45 See Jung, 1921/1971, *Personality Types.* I've not referred explicitly to Jung's ideas of Extraversion-vs-Introversion, or general attitude/orientation to our outer shared world (Extraversion) or inner world (Introversion) due to confusion with the Big Five conceptualizations of these terms. There is both overlap and distinction, but none of which are particularly enlightening for our current purposes. Some readers might also be wondering why I haven't mentioned the well-known Myers-Briggs Personality Type test (Myers et al., 1998). Note that Myers et al., (1998) added Judging-vs-Perceiving to Jung's original typology. Results from type-based measures can be inconsistent, and interpretations made about types can be exaggerated or too generic to be very useful. Also, consider McCrae's (1994) review of Jung's concepts and Openness to Experience. This review is noteworthy because McCrae is a co-creator of the Five-Factor Model and a popular measure of the Big Five, the NEO-PI-R. For one study looking at the overlap of Myers-Briggs and the Five-Factor Model, see Furnham, 1996.

46 As a bit of film trivia, Neo notices the inscribed Latin version, 'Temet Nosce,' outside the Oracle's door in the first film of The Matrix trilogy (Wachowski & Wachowski, 1999, Timestamp: 1-hr:14-min). The Temple of Delphi was dedicated to Greek god Apollo and was famous in ancient Greece for its own oracle. Note that 'Know Thyself' has multiple meanings, including to know one's place in the world and to show deference to forces greater than oneself (such as Apollo, nature, etc.) and to be self-aware while understanding the risk of self-delusion.

47 The estimate for neurons in the human brain is based on analyses by Azevedo et al., 2009. Only about one in five neurons (19%) are within the cerebral cortex.

48 Koch, 2018, p. S12.

49 Richards, 2015, *Sacred Knowledge: Psychedelics and Religious Experiences,* p. 187

50 The inner healer idea was originally fleshed out by German Jungian Analyst, Adolf Guggenbühl-Craig, 1971/2015. For examples of its use in psychedelic therapy, see the treatment manuals for the MAPS MDMA-assisted psychotherapy trials (Mithoefer, 2017) and Usona's psilocybin-assisted psychotherapy trials (Cooper, 2016). Note that these manuals refer to the *inner healing intelligence,* which is an alternative formulation of the same idea.

51 Truity (n.d.) has several personality tests with a modern interface and feedback system. Their basic feedback is free and sufficient, but they also have paid options. Open-Source Psychometrics Project (n.d.) has test for the Big Five and Jungian Types that are similar to the widely used versions but completely free. SelfActualizationTests.com redirects to a subpage of psychologist and author Scott Barry Kaufman's (2020a) website. His site has several tests of interest and is also free. I have no affiliation with these websites, companies, or other financial interests to disclose.

CHAPTER 4

1 Thich Nhat Hanh, 1975/2016, p. 29-30

2 Dass, 1978

3 This model is a revision and expansion of my previous work with colleagues on Skills Training in Affective and Interpersonal Regulation (STAIR) Narrative Therapy, which includes a model called 'the three channels of emotion.' The current model, however, allows for experiences of thoughts, bodily sensations, and behaviors that occur relatively independent, at least consciously, from direct emotional influences. See Cloitre et al. (2020) for an introduction of the three channels of emotion as described in STAIR Narrative Therapy. Note that many skills included in this chapter are variations of the evidence-based ones we recommend in helping people who suffer from posttraumatic stress, depression, and/or anxiety.

4 *Star Wars: Episode I—The Phantom Menace,* Lucas, 1999. Timestamp: 1-hr:35-min

5 This language of 'fusion' comes from Acceptance and Commitment Therapy (ACT). See, for example, Hayes et al., 2012.

6 This workbook was Julia Cameron's (2016) *The Artist's Way.* To see specific examples from this book, see the creative affirmations on pp. 36-37

7 For a good review of research on optimism, see Sharot, 2011

8 For example, see Jones, 1977, and Jussim, 1986

9 In psychological research, we often prefer the term *affect* partly because emotions affect our subjective experiences, physiological states, and behavioral responses.

10 See, for example, Posner et al., 2005. Note that instead of using activation-vs-deactivation, I refer to intensity because it's more aligned with how we talk about emotions in our everyday language and with common clinical approaches to psychotherapy.

11 Cross-cultural expression is usually studied in terms of nonverbal facial expressions. Work in this area usually focuses on six core emotions: joy, fear, surprise, sadness, disgust, and anger (Ekman & Friesen, 1969, 1971; Ek-

man, 1992). Adaptiveness reflects evolutionary benefits conferred by being able to experience and/or express certain emotions, usually by helping one avoid threats, find a mate (reproductive fitness), and/or connect to a group. The last of which is especially important to social animals like us. At the most basic level, groups provide safety in numbers, and in small tribal life, isolation easily equated to death. The evolutionary work adds emotions of trust and anticipation (Plutchik, 1980, 1994).

12 This is called *emotional granularity* (Barrett, 2004).

13 Multiple definitions exist for primary versus secondary emotions, but my definitions are most aligned with Linehan, 2015

14 Distinctions between guilt and shame are not without controversy and differing opinions. See Miceli & Castelfranchi, 2018.

15 See the 'Feelings Wheel' from STAIR Narrative Therapy (Cloitre et al., 2020, p. 172).

16 In general, emotions are brief and immediate. Moods often involve emotions but span a longer period of time. Attitudes are general feelings about a person, activity, subject, etc. that also tend to be more long-term than emotions.

17 Class psychedelics work predominantly through binding to serotonin's 2A receptors with secondary effects on dopamine and norepinephrine For an excellent and accessible overview of neurochemistry, see David Presti's (2016) *Foundational Concepts in Neuroscience: A Brain-Mind Odyssey.*

18 In the West, Descartes's efforts to divide the mind and body have rippled throughout our cultures and into modern times. Neuroscientists, philosophers, theologians, psychologists, and many others are continuing these eternal debates. For some thoughtful perspectives on issues related to mind-body-brain, see Barret's (2009) article "The Future of Psychology: Connecting Mind to Brain," and David Presti's (2018) edited book *Mind Beyond Brain: Buddhism, Science & the Paranormal.*

19 As phenomenologist Maurice Merleau-Ponty (1962) summarized, "The body is our general medium for having a world" (p. 146).

20 Nietzsche, 1889/2003, *Twilight of the Idols,* p. 44

21 Ibid. Nietzsche asserted that "As long as life is ascending, happiness and instinct are one. (p. 44."

22 You might see a connection in Freud's emphasis on bodily instincts and drives being transformed into more palatable, conscious expressions—for the individual and for society at large. For one examination of these two thinkers, see Waugaman, 1973.

23 This may be especially relevant for people who've experienced trauma. In the book *Walking the Tiger,* Peter Levine (1997) described our body's natural ability to heal in response to various types of trauma: "Because every injury exists within life and life is constantly renewing itself, within every injury is the seed of healing and renewal. At the moment our skin is cut or punctured by a foreign object, a magnificent and precise series of biochemical events is orchestrated through evolutionary wisdom. The body has been designed to renew itself through continuous self-correction. These same principles all apply to the healing of psyche, spirit, and soul" (p. 123).

24 Linehan, 2015

25 Mindfulness-based Stress Reduction was originally developed by Jon Kabat-Zinn (see 2003, 2011). For a workbook, consider Stahl & Goldstein (2010).

26 Cloitre et al., 2020

27 Kurtz, 2007, *Body-centered Psychotherapy: The Hakomi Method* (2nd edition). Reiki, which is Japanese in origin, is another body-oriented approach worth considering (see Rand, 2000). Reiki uses therapeutic touch to 'move energy' in the body to trigger psychophysiological healing while attending to 'chakras' or 'energy centers.' For a scientific review, see Baldwin et al., 2010.

28 Grof & Grof, 2010. Note that although breathwork is 'natural,' people with heart issues or proneness to panic attacks should be cautious.

29 As Ralph Metzner described, vipassana meditation in Buddhism is the "nonanalytical, nonjudgmental observing of the currents of breath…a basic practice, preparatory to the more difficult mindfulness in relation to feelings, sensations, and the stream of thoughts" (Metzner, 2017, p. 357).

30 Developed in the early 1900's by physician Edmund Jacobson; see Jacobson, 1938

31 See Holland's (2020) *Good Chemistry: The Science of Connection from Soul to Psychedelics,* p. xxiii-xxiv.

32 Freezing is another option for when escaping and fighting aren't possible. Psychologically, it can be expressed through dissociation and out-of-body experiences often tied to trauma.

33 Learning by association is classical conditioning. By reward and punishment is operant conditioning. By observation is social learning. Pavlov, Watson, Skinner, and Bandura are the big historical figures in behaviorism, but modern third-wave behavioral approaches share many of the same features. For one thoughtful review, see Hayes, 2012.

34 Rogers, 1951, *Client-Centered Therapy,* p. 485

35 Experiential avoidance is a key concept and target of ACT. Hayes et al., 2012.

36 See, for example, Ram Dass & Rameshwar Das, 2013. For the connection between this metaphor and the individuation process, see Stein, 2015, p. 20.

37 Gopnik, 2009, *The Philosophical Baby*

38 The experiential self is also known as self-as-process. See Hayes et al., 2012, 2020.

39 Self-awareness as explored in the last chapter arises mostly through self-reflection and feedback from others. Gaining self-awareness by reflection involves looking into the past. The experiential self comes from simply being fully present. Expanding contact with the experiential self can involve a form of self-awareness, but this awareness is different in that it doesn't involve interpretations and examinations of personal patterns (which require information across multiple time points—that is, by definition, involving the past and the present).

40 This last point is in line with both Gestalt psychology and the concept of emergent phenomena.

THE SECOND ARC

1 From a lecture given on 23 October 1929. See Jung, 1984, p. 329.

2 George (Trans.), 2003, *The Epic of Gilgamesh.* There are multiple versions of this myth, and within the version I

summarize, Gilgamesh seeks immortality after experiencing the loss of Enkidu, but in the end, he is unsuccessful and must accept and be contented with the life he has and the responsibility to serve his community and humankind.

3 See Walsh, 1994. Note that *shaman* is a generic designator for these roles, and different tribes and traditions have various specific labels for people trained in entering altered states of consciousness to contact a spirit world.

4 Mithoefer, 2017

5 Campbell, 1949/2008

CHAPTER 5

1 Halifax, 2008, p. 48

2 Religions offer a wide range of possibilities for the afterlife, and this statement, of course, collapses across many varieties and nuances. For additional information, see Moreman's (2018) *Beyond the Threshold: Afterlife Beliefs and Experiences in World Religions,* or for religious connections to psychedelic experiences, see Bill Richard's (2015) *Sacred Knowledge: Psychedelics and Religious Experiences.* Another classic text of comparative religion is Houston Smith's (1958/1991) *The World's Religions.*

3 See Dazzi et al. (2014) for a literature review of the risk imposed by asking about suicide.

4 For some interesting scientific and scholarly reviews, see Carter, 2010; Blanke et al., 2016; and Presti, 2018.

5 Some may argue that science defaults to a skeptical rejection of these phenomena. Skepticism is warranted in all scientific pursuits, but to outright reject these phenomena requires at some level an automatic assumption of strict materialism (which itself is as much a philosophical concern of the 'hard problem of consciousness,' as a scientific one).

6 See Sober's, 2015, *Ockham's Razor: A User's Manual,* for a thoughtful review of the concept

7 See Gernert, 2007

8 Daher, Jr., et al. 2017

9 With how frequent 'ego death' is mentioned with DMT, ayahuasca, psilocybin mushrooms, etc., a study by Martial et al., 2019, found subjective descriptions of near-death experiences were most akin to the non-ordinary consciousness elicited by ketamine, not the classic psychedelics.

10 World Health Organization, 2018, average across all regions and sex for year 2016

11 As Welwood (1982) summarizes, existential dread or anxiety "is seen as an ontological anxiety; that is, it arises from our very nature as human beings. And it comes in those moments when we perceive the intrinsic groundlessness of all our personal projects. Anxiety about death is one special case of this....[O]ntological anxiety is distinguished from neurotic anxiety which is self-manufactured and which comes out of our attempts to distract ourselves from this deeper anxiety." (p. 126).

12 *Diagnostic and Statistical Manual* (*DSM-5*), American Psychiatric Association, 2013

13 These statistics come from Kilpatrick et al., 2013, in which 2,953 adults completed an online structured assessment.

14 The 8.3% estimate is based on meeting *DSM-5* criteria when reported symptoms are linked to a single trauma.

When multiple traumas are taken into account, 9.4% of the sample met PTSD criteria at some point in their lifetime.

15 Greenberg et al., 1986

16 See Greenberg & Kosloff, 2008, for a review

17 Or perhaps like writing a book? I cannot deny that possibility.

18 See again, Greenberg & Kosloff, 2008

19 We'll revisit this phenomenon in Chapter 9 when we explore the Shadow.

20 Kesebir & Pyszczynski (2012) summarized the path of denial as such, "Because self-awareness is a prerequisite for existential anxiety, escaping self-awareness can also be an effective way to obviate the problem of existence" (p. 43).

21 See Burke et al., 2010, review, p. 32. For example, increased awareness of our personal death leads to greater attention to and use of positive emotion words in writing (DeWall & Baumeister, 2007; Kashdan et al., 2014).

22 See Wu et al., 2019, for a meta-analytic review of posttraumatic growth. Note that posttraumatic growth and posttraumatic stress can co-occur, and growth can come in the process of posttraumatic healing.

23 Grob et al., 2011; Griffiths et al., 2016; Ross et al., 2016

24 See Chapter 2 "The History of Psychedelic Therapy with the Dying" in Grof & Halifax's (1978) *The Human Encounter with Death*

25 Ross et al., 2016

26 Pahnke & Richards (1966) synthesized the work of William James (1902) and Stace (1960) with the effects of LSD to describe psychedelic-induced mystical experiences. Their core features included: (1) Unity (inner and outer), (2) Objectivity and reality of insights (intuitive knowledge), (3) Transcendence of time and space, (4) Sense of sacredness (numinosity), (5) Deeply-felt positive mood, (6) Paradoxicality, (7) Alleged Ineffability, (8) Transiency of experience, and (9) Positive changes in attitude and/ or behavior. The factors I describe are simplified from the larger conceptual categories based on the analyses of the Mystical Experience Questionnaire by MacLean et al. (2012). To see the 30-item version of the Mystical Experience Questionnaire organized by these factors, visit Trippingly.net (2019, March 1).

27 Foreman, 1990.

28 Griffiths et al., 2019

29 Leary et al., 1964/2007. For the original, see the Baldock's (2009) edited translation by Dawa-Samdup. Stan Grof expanded upon this work by exploring multiple 'books of the dead' across cultures (see Grof, 1973/2013).

30 MacLean et al., 2011; Wagner et al., 2017

31 Noé, 2009

32 For a review and discussion of how life recovered, see Sahney & Benton, 2008

33 Tully, 2012

34 One Buddhist teacher, Shinzen Young, has used the following equation to describe a key predictor of suffering: Suffering = Pain x Resistance (as shared by Neff, 2011, p. 92).

35 For information on the originator of this concept, Motoori Norinaga, see Marra, 2007

36 Coppola, 2003

37 Yalom, 2008

38 Pahnke, 1969, p. 17

39 All I could offer was a suggestion of exploring ketamine-assisted psychotherapy, not because I felt he needed ketamine but because I knew it was legally available and incorporated psychotherapy (which facilitates integration and positive changes induced by ketamine). For more information, see *The Ketamine Papers* (Wolfson & Hartelius, 2016).

40 Freud, 1933/1989, p. 133-134

41 In *LSD and the Mind of the Universe,* religious scholar Chris Bache (2019) describes several beautiful and intense experiences over the course of 73 high-dose LSD sessions (500-600 μg). Beyond the challenges of some particularly harrowing journeys, he also experienced decreased satisfaction and joy with his everyday world. He called this "The Deep Sadness." Bache explained, "I had entered the Divine Expanse so many times, been taken so deeply into its beauty that my wound was particularly deep." Even very positive transformative experiences can be challenging to integrate. Bache didn't regret his journeys, but he recognized the downsides of reaching the psychedelic summit and needing to return to our shared material world.

42 McDowell, 2017

43 This sci-fi film interpretation is sadly not too far askew, given the already high prevalence of suicide in our 'real world.' Interestingly, preliminary research with ayahuasca has suggested that suicidality can be reduced after psychedelic experiences. See Zeifman, et al., 2019.

44 Again, see Martial et al., 2019

45 See Henderson & Oakes, 1963/1990

46 Aronofsky, 2006

47 Aronofsky, 2006. Timestamp: 0-hr:6-min

48 The Doors, 1967

49 Presti, 2019, p. 5

CHAPTER 6

1 Excerpt from Stanza 178 of fourth canto of *Childe Harold's Pilgrimage,* originally written in 1818. See Byron, 1875, p.172.

2 This theme of dialectical relationships and transcending apparent opposites will be most explicitly revisited in our final arc, but it's evident throughout the various tensions explored in this book. It's also a core feature of Jungian individuation and nonduality.

3 Baumeister & Leary, 1995.

4 For example, Csikszentmihalyi (1991) discussed the evolutionary adaptiveness of gregariousness and the survival benefits of culture and knowledge over biological adaptations and instincts (see Chapter 8, p. 166).

5 Hurd et al., 2010-present.

6 See Henderson, 1963/1990, p. 42.

7 DiJulio et al., August 2018. Specific percentages are 22% of US, 23% of UK, and 9% of Japanese adults. These statistics come from a representative sample of people in the US (n = 1003), United Kingdom (n = 1002), and Japan (n = 1000) who completed a phone interview. Although loneliness was over twice as common in the US and UK, Japanese people who felt lonely reported greater severity, on average, and a longer duration of loneliness, often lasting several years. Overall, 4-5% of each population reported severe loneliness.

8 Of note, this survey found that even compared to the UK, another Western individualistic culture, Americans stayed true to their 'pick yourself up by your bootstraps' mentality and emphasized the personal over collective responsibility to address loneliness.

9 See the meta-analysis by Holt-Lunstad et al., 2015, and reviews by Snyder-Mackler et al., 2020, and Hawkley & Cacioppo, 2010.

10 Although major cities are significantly more populated, people in rural areas report more relationships and lower rates of loneliness, on average (Henning-Smith et al., 2019).

11 See Twenge et al., 2018; Primack et al., 2017, 2019.

12 Hunt et al., 2018.

13 Jonze, 2013. The film explores the relationship between human loneliness and artificial intelligence-as-companionship.

14 I'm referring, for example, to in-group/out-group bias, prejudice, group think, etc., and on the other side, primarily selfishness and narcissism.

15 See Mithoefer, 2017, and Cooper, 2016.

16 According to an article in *Science,* the Earth is estimated to have 5 ± 3 million species, but only approximately 1.5 million have been identified. See Costello, May, & Stork, 2013.

17 Hart, 1975, Wesson, 1990

18 If interested, valuable explorations of the Fermi-Hart paradox and related formulations of the search for extraterrestrial intelligence can be found in Ćirković's (2012) *The Astrobiological Landscape,* and Webb's (2015) *If the Universe Is Teeming with Aliens...WHERE IS EVERYBODY?.* For a specific example solution, see Annis's (1999) proposal that gamma-ray bursts, occurring approximately every 100 million years, would wipe out most complex life before it had time to develop consciousness or technology required for interstellar communication and/or travel.

19 For human-centered stories of the search for intelligent life, I recommend *Contact* (Zemeckis, 1997), *Close Encounters of the Third Kind* (Spielberg, 1977), and *Ad Astra* (Gray, 2019).

20 If you're interested in the subatomic or want more details behind the summary provided in this book, I recommend starting with the popular writings of Brian Greene, in this case, *The Fabric of the Cosmos* (2004).

21 Again, see Greene, 2004. To name a few especially important methods of interaction, consider the impact of weak and strong nuclear forces, gravity, chemical reactions and bonding, and quantum entanglement.

22 John Bowlby first outlined modern attachment theory in the 1950's, but his work has spurred decades of innovative research across the entire human lifespan. See Bowlby's (1969/1982, 1973, 1980) original three-volume book series, and Mikulincer & Shaver's (2016) comprehensive scholarly review focused on adult attachment research.

23 Basic Trust versus Mistrust was Erik Erikson's (1959, 1968, 1982) formulation of the first developmental stage, which largely corresponds to Bowlby's attachment theory.

24 Bowlby's colleague Mary Ainsworth established an innovative research program that catapulted attachment theory into less psychoanalytically inclined and more research-ori-

ented audiences (Ainsworth & Wittig, 1969; Ainsworth & Bell, 1970; Ainsworth et al., 1978). Ainsworth's Strange Situation paradigm involves a series of separations and reunions between infants and caregivers, with and without the presence of a stranger. 'Stranger Danger' reactions start around the same time as the attachment system kicks in, around 6-12 months after birth. Ainsworth and colleagues found securely attached infants played and explored when their trusted caregiver was around, and when they left, they became upset. When they returned, these infants were quickly calmed and continued playing again. Insecurely attached infants came in three forms, but only the first two were classified in the original studies. The first was *ambivalent* attachment, in which the infant became upset upon the caregiver leaving and was not consoled when they returned. These infants were anxious throughout. As the second type, the *avoidantly* attached infant acted as if the caregiver wasn't there and had little avert reaction to their leaving and returning. The final insecure attachment style was discovered by Main and Solomon (1986) and is the most heartbreaking—*disorganized* attachment. These infants expressed inconsistent and unusual responses to the caregiver's exit and return. One striking example behavior was an infant who crawled backwards towards the caregiver—a behavioral expression of inner conflict about approach or avoidance for a caregiver who could sooth or harm. Unsurprisingly, disorganized attachment often arises from trauma and intergenerational effects of trauma (see Liotti, 2004).

25 See, especially, Mikulincer & Shaver, 2016.

26 The term internalization is commonly used in object relations theory. Jung's concept of complexes involves internalization of one's experiences of the outside world and relationships as well as connections to the deeper collective unconscious archetypes within an individual.

27 Winnicott, 1960.

28 Types of close relationships most impacted by attachment include but aren't limited to romantic relationships, friendships, familial relationships, mentorships, and therapeutic relationships.

29 See Fraley, 2002; Fraley et al., 2011; Jones et al., 2018.

30 See Fraley & Waller, 1998; Fraley et al., 2003; Mikulincer & Shaver, 2016.

31 Laczkovics et al., 2020; Ciocca et al., 2020.

32 Despite surface-level similarities with Extroversion-vs-Introversion or Agreeableness-vs-Argumentativeness, which reflect a 'normal' range of personality, these descriptions reflect more extreme and rigid defensive strategies. Certainly, extroverts aren't empty vessels and automatons of societal expectations and norms, and introverts aren't rugged anti-conformists who for no one but themselves.

33 Jung, 1957/1990, *The Undiscovered Self,* p. 34

34 Impingement is a term introduced by British psychoanalyst, D. W. Winnicott, to describe how a caregiver can infringe upon an infant or child's ego development and sense of self. See, for example, Winnicott, 1958, 1960.

35 For example, research in attachment, Terror Management Theory, and death salience, see Mikulincer and Florian, 2000, and Florian and Mikulincer, 1998. Secure attachment generally supports healthy management of death

anxiety through symbolic immortality (contributions to society, relationships, etc.) and more connecting, or at least less destructive, worldviews. See Burke et al., 2010, for a systematic review.

36 For one exploration of earned security, see Saunders et al., 2011.

37 See, for example, Norcross & Lambert, 2019. Note that Diener and Monroe's, 2011, meta-analysis found that attachment security/insecurity affects especially the client's perceptions of the therapist-client relationship.

38 As outlined by Rogers, 1963, and connected to attachment security by Fraley & Shaver, 2008, p. 535.

39 Stauffer et al., 2021.

40 Whether psychedelics are taken with the intention for healing or self-exploration, different lessons are possible in the context of others. Authentic shamans and experienced psychonauts may be able to navigate solo journeys, but they're often the exception that proves the rule. The relational context of psychedelic-assisted psychotherapy is understood to be an essential ingredient of psychological transformation. The presence of attentive and caring guides with knowledge of psychedelic states can promote healing and growth while steering journeyers away from spiritual bypass, defensiveness, ego whiplash, and narcissistic fantasies.

41 See Howe, 2007, p. 1.

42 Michael Pollan (2018) offers a similar sentiment in describing platitudes as just truths without the emotion attached and that psychedelics can help attach the emotion (see pp. 70-71, 251, 271).

43 These internalized messages correspond to attachment theory's *internal working models,* which are similar to Jung's notion of a complex (though he used complex primarily to describe pathological patterns). In STAIR Narrative Therapy, we refer to relationship patterns instead of internal working models to use everyday language and avoid jargon (see Cloitre et al., 2020). In STAIR, relationship patterns are translated into "If/when…, then…" statements. For example, "If I tell my partner about my social anxiety, then they'll use it against in the future." Or "When people don't respond to my texts, then I know they don't want to be friends with me."

44 Leary, 1957. See also, Plutchik & Conte, 1997. Note that the interpersonal circumplex represents both a model of personality-based social interaction patterns as well as tool for understanding how specific interactions unfold between two or more people. It supplements but doesn't replace the Five-Factor Model (see, for example, Ghaed & Gallo, 2006).

45 See, for example, Fournier et al., 2011.

46 Determining the relative impact of situational and personality factors is known as the Person-versus-Situation debate. Like many research findings in psychology, the overall evidence supports a 'both/and' conclusion with main (independent) effects and interactions of personality and social factors in predicting behavior. Generally, the clearer and stronger the social expectations are for a given situation (like being quiet in a library), the weaker the effects of personality in determining behavior. The reverse is true for situations with greater ambiguity or perceived freedom, in which personality can be expressed with fewer

direct consequences. When personality overrides the expectations of a strong situation, it may be an indication of problematic personality patterns, socioemotional deficits, or unusual but adaptive responses (such as spontaneous acts of heroism in crisis situations). For an insightful review, see Funder, 2008. For example research, see Judge & Zapata, 2015, and Sherman et al., 2010.

47 See Wilson et al., 2017, and Funder, 2008. Inflexible personality styles interrupt expected patterns of reciprocal and complementary responses. Personality patterns are especially important for the Dominance-vs-Submission axis of the circumplex (see Bluhm et al., 1990). When two dominant people get together a power struggle may ensue, but two people who prefer being submissive may also have problems. Insecure attachment also appears to influence interpersonal circumplex patterns. For example, Haggerty et al. (2009) found both attachment anxiety and avoidance were positively correlated with hostile segments of the interpersonal circumplex.

48 An alternative word for this concept is interdependence, but to avoid reinforcing strict interpretations of causal relationships, I've chosen interconnectedness. For readers interested or familiar with Buddhism, related concepts are dependent origination and the net of Indra. Interconnectedness and systems thinking is relevant as well in internal family systems therapy, which is a foundational approach integrated in MDMA-assisted psychotherapy for PTSD (Mithoefer, 2017; Schwartz and Sweezy, 2020).

49 See Gleick, 2011.

50 Bradbury's (1952/2005) short story "A Sound of Thunder" may or may not have directly inspired the naming of the butterfly effect, which is often traced to Edward Lorenz's rhetorical question about whether a butterfly flapping its wings in Brazil might spark a rippling causal chain that eventually results in a tornado in Tennessee. See, for example, Sinitsyn & Yan, September 21, 2020.

51 Chaos theory and its cousins may not apply in the same way at the quantum level as they appear to at the macro level. See Yan & Sinitsyn, 2020; Sinitsyn & Yan, September 21, 2020.

52 For example applications of chaos theory and nonlinear dynamics in the social sciences, see Rickles et al., 2007, Ayers, 1997.

53 From Camus's, 1955/1991, short story, "The Minotaur, or The Stop in Oran," p. 157. Note that although the first English translation was published in 1955, the original short story in French dates back to 1939.

54 Brown, 2013, *The Power of Vulnerability,* Session 5, Audiobook timestamp 4hr:21min

55 Brown, Timestamp 4hr:23min

56 Brown, Timestamp 4hr:28min

57 Individual therapists, even when trained in couple's therapy, can forget the inherent bias towards a client's point of view. To combat this issue, I remind clients that although I'm going to err on their side, they have far more direct information and experience about what might be the most optimal boundaries for each relationship.

58 Buber, 1923/2012.

59 Note that I-It was Buber's counterpart to I-Thou. Also, of interest, I-Thou extends to relationships with other conscious beings, whether in nature (such as non-human animals) or as part of some divine entity.

60 See, for example, Dass & Bush, 2018.

61 As quoted in Csikszentmihalyi, 1991, p. 173, and cross-referenced with Theophanidis's, August 18, 2014, summary of relevant passages from Aristotle's *Politics* and Francis Bacon's essay, "Of Friendship." Note that Bacon was paraphrasing Aristotle while disagreeing with some of his conclusions. Theophanidis also highlights another relevant quote of Bacon's work, "For a crowd is not company; and faces are but a gallery of pictures; and talk but a tinkling cymbal, where there is no love."

62 Jung was speaking specifically of the therapist-client relationship, but his words apply to any deeper connection. See Jung, 1933/2011, p. 49-50. In a similar sentiment, Csikszentmihalyi (1991) asserts, "The essence of relationship is that in the encounter both persons are changed" (p. 128).

63 A recent meta-analysis of longitudinal data found the mental health benefits of public participation in religious activities and subjective importance of religion were small in overall effect (Garssen et al., 2020). For thorough explorations of the psychology of religion and mental health, see Saroglou, 2020, Rosmarin & Koenig, 2020, & de Rezende-Pinto et al., 2019.

64 See also, Putnam, 2000, *Bowling Alone: The Collapse and Revival of American Community.*

65 James, 1902, p. 525 (postscript) Italicize is in original.

66 Granqvist et al., 2010

67 See Capaldi et al.'s (2014) meta-analysis which found small but positive relationships between nature connectedness and positive emotional experiences, life satisfaction, and well-being.

68 Besides acknowledging human sensory limitations and illusions, I'm also referring to how life on Earth is dependent on several features of our solar system of which we're typically unaware. For example, the gas giant Jupiter, an amazing alien world hostile to life as we know it, is crucial for our very existence. The gravitational pull of Jupiter and the other majestic solar bodies protects us from many dangerous comets that might otherwise collide with Earth and cause another extinction level event.

69 For comparison, Julie Holland's (2020) book *Good Chemistry: The Science of Connection, From Soul to Psychedelics* describes six levels in which people can foster connection: Relationships with oneself, partner, family, community, the Earth, and the Cosmos. Whereas her book ends with the cosmos, our journey began with it so as to loosen our mind's grip on everyday assumptions and perspectives.

70 A similar sentiment was also echoed in Leary's mantra 'Find the others.'

71 Original letter by Jung dated 14 September 1960. Quote in text is from p. 595 of *Letters of C. G. Jung: Vol 2, 1951-1961,* edited by Adler & Jaffé, 1976/2011.

72 Many people can be healed by authentic connection, but this healing takes time, energy, and thoughtfulness. Even healers and trained therapists need to practice health boundary setting and self-care. It's important for everyone to be aware and cautious about feeding a Savior Complex, in which ego-level motivations are pulling the strings.

73 This excerpt of Rilke's *Book of Hours: Love Poems to God,* originally published in German in 1905, is from

Barrows and Macy's (2005) translation with the exception of "else," which I reinserted from Robert Bly's (1980) translation of the final line, "I want to be with those who know secret things or else alone."

74 The Golden Rule is complicated, especially when applying across cultures, but generally, we can interpret it as encouraging us to treat others according to how they want to be treated, just as we'd prefer others to treat us as we'd like. This phrasing addresses misunderstandings that arise when others prefer to be treated differently than we do, for whatever reason. For a thorough exploration of the topic, see philosopher Henry Gensler's (2013) *Ethics and the Golden Rule,* 2013.

75 Brennan et al., 1998

76 John Koenig (n.d.) introduces the word 'sonder' in *The Dictionary of Obscure Sorrows.* His definition is "the realization that each random passerby is living a life as vivid and complex as your own—populated with their own ambitions, friends, routines, worries and inherited craziness—an epic story that continues invisibly around you like an anthill sprawling deep underground, with elaborate passageways to thousands of other lives that you'll never know existed, in which you might appear only once, as an extra sipping coffee in the background, as a blur of traffic passing on the highway, as a lighted window at dusk."

CHAPTER 7

1 Dezelic, 2014, *Meaning-Centered Therapy Workbook,* as quoted in the book's premise.

2 Camus (1955/1991) summarizes the central tension of meaning and meaninglessness (the absurd) as such, "I don't know whether this world has a meaning that transcends it. But I know that I cannot know that meaning and that it is impossible for me just now to know it. What can a meaning outside my condition mean to me? I can understand only in human terms. What I touch, what resists me—that I understand. And these two certainties—my appetite for the absolute and for unity and the impossibility of reducing this world to a rational and reasonable principle — I also know that I cannot reconcile them." (p. 51).

3 Camus was speaking primarily of figurative or philosophical suicide, not literal suicide per se, but the underlying meaning of his question remains largely the same even if taken literally.

4 May, 1991

5 If interested in St. John of the Cross's (1542-1591) related poem, see Starr's (2002) translation of the original Spanish work.

6 For an interesting dialogue on this question, see cosmologist Lawrence Krauss's, 2012, *A Universe from Nothing,* and philosopher David Alpert's, 2012, review and response published by the *New York Times,* "On the Origin of Everything." Diverse viewpoints can also be found in Goldschmidt's, 2014, edited book *The Puzzle of Existence: Why is There Something Rather Than Nothing?*

7 Scientific approaches generally seek to describe and predict. These questions of cosmic meaning and purpose are primarily metaphysical.

8 For some surprising findings, consider that several neuroscience studies have observed preconscious activation of neural pathways prior to a subject expressing conscious intent, but readers should be cautioned about overinterpreting neuroscientific findings (see Saigle et al., 2019; Brass et al., 2019). Another relevant area of research is intrinsic versus extrinsic motivation. See, for example, Donald et al.'s (2020) meta-analysis of the impact of mindfulness interventions on different kinds of motivation. A classic finding is that when our motivation is initially derived independently (intrinsic motivation), being rewarding by someone else for that same behavior (extrinsic motivation) can actually decrease the power of our pre-existing internal motivation. This effect, like other classic findings, is more complicated than summarized, but generally intrinsic motivation is desirable and more sustaining (for a review, see Hendijani et al., 2016).

9 Radical freedom is most central to the philosophy of Sartre, 1943/1992.

10 Common logical fallacies in these discussions include *false equivalencies* (as when conflating the nature-nurture debate with the free will-determinism debate), *strawman arguments* (misrepresenting the opposing side's position or argument), and *false dichotomies* (like the all-or-none variety and the oversimplification of either side as a unitary whole, not a collection of factors within a larger bucket). For related discussion of epigenetics (gene-environment interactions and systems), see Bjorklund, 2018. Critical thinking is a very important but challenging set of skills, even for professionals trained in scientific and philosophical fields of inquiry. For a great resource in the field of psychology, see Sternberg and Halpern, 2020.

11 See Season 3, Episode 6 "Decoherence" (Wrubel et al., 2020, April 19). Scene timestamp: 36min, quote at 39min. Note that this question is a call back to the first season and the entire series' exploration of consciousness and free will with both its human and non-human ('host') characters.

12 In *Being and Nothingness,* Sartre (1943/1992) described the downside of existential freedom and responsibility as being "condemned to be free" (p. 567). Though his statement in this instance was personal, "I'm condemned," his larger argument was that we all are.

13 For instance, see Drew Westen's (2008) *The Political Brain.* It explores the centrality of emotional reasoning in political decision making (over the slower, rationale, information-based processing) and includes relevant research findings and historical examples.

14 For thorough conceptual reviews of motivation, see Forbes, 2011, and Osabiya, 2015.

15 Maslow's (1943) classic hierarchy consisted of the following needs (from lower to highest): physiological, safety, social/belonging/love, esteem, and self-actualization. When a basic need is activated, the underlying motivation manifests primarily in approach or avoidance behavior. If successful, the motivation or need is satisfied. If not, it's frustrated, and we adjust or intensify our efforts in response. For an excellent review and update of Maslow's work, see Kaufman's (2020), *Transcend: The New Science of Self-Actualization.*

16 Alderfer, 1969.

17 These motivations are described as needs for achievement,

affiliation, and power, respectively (see McClelland et al., 1989). Köllner and Schultheiss's (2014) meta-analysis confirmed the correlations between self-reported, explicit/conscious motivations and their implicit, nonconscious/unconscious counterparts are small. Both explicit and implicit motivations influence our behavior. Implicit motivations are more influenced by emotions and usually measured in indirect ways such as differences in reaction times and qualities of a story told based on an ambiguous picture.

18 Frankl, 1992, p. 111.

19 The classic examples are 'just world beliefs' like "People get what they deserve" (karma) and "Everything happens for a reason" (order). Although believing in a just world is helpful and productive in many cases, rigid versions of these beliefs can lead to victim blaming, even in victims themselves. Cognitive Processing Therapy is one evidence-based approach to PTSD that explicitly challenges overly rigid or harmful beliefs, which it calls 'stuck points' through psychoeducation, worksheets, and Socratic questioning (see Resick et al., 2016).

20 Some philosophers and theorists refer to innate existential guilt as *ontological guilt*, but ontological guilt is more conceptual than emotional. Although I agree that responsibility is unavoidable, I prefer taking a less 'hardline' stance and the risk of confusing ontological guilt with emotional guilt and shame. See Khanna's (1969) criticism of existential guilt.

21 See May, 1983; Alderfer, 1969.

22 Kierkegaard, 1843/2019, *Fear and Trembling*.

23 See, for example, Sartre 1943/1992, starting on p. 86

24 Maslow, 1971, p. 34

25 Frankl, 1992. Note that Frankl initially published *Man's Search for Meaning* under a pseudonym in 1946 in German.

26 Frankl, 1992, p. 109. Frankl was paraphrasing Nietzsche's, 1889/2003, *Twilight of the Idols*. His exact words, translated from German, were, "If we have our own 'why' of life we shall get along with almost any 'how.'" Whereas Nietzsche and Freud emphasized motivations for power and pleasure, respectively, Frankl argued the uniquely human desire for meaning superseded these other motivations.

27 Russel, 2004.

28 Favreau, 2019. Scene timestamp: 1hr:06min

29 See Frankl, 1992; Dezelic, 2014, 2017.

30 Psychotherapeutic approaches that emphasize personal meaning, values, or growth are numerous and growing. Logotherapy, sometimes referred to as meaning-centered psychotherapy, is based on Viktor Frankl's work. For example, research, and reviews, see Thir & Batthyány, 2016, Joshi et al., 2014., Vos et al., 2015, and Vos & Vitali, 2018. Acceptance and Commitment Therapy, developed by Steve Hayes and colleagues, is another well researched model that incorporates exploration of personal values and value-directed behavior in its overarching approach. For a transdiagnostic review, see A-tjak et al., 2015, and for a review with anxiety and depression, see Twohig & Levin, 2017. Meaning-centered good, less support for other types of existential.

31 In other words, the Will to Power might be a compromise when the Will to Meaning is unsatisfied. The findings I'm referring to come from Joshi et al.'s (2014) study, which also assessed the Will to Pleasure but primarily as sexual in nature. In a college student population, this motivation may be particularly strong, relatively easy to satisfy, and developmentally appropriate. Questions of meaning can arise at any life stage, but existential crises can be triggered when seeking money, power, and pleasure is frustrated or these desires become over-satiated. These other motivations are not inherently detrimental, but without deeper meaning (that is, in an existential vacuum), they are frequently associated with lower life satisfaction.

32 In myth, common temptations include offerings of comfort, ease, safety, and pleasure, which are delusions, traps, or distractions from the mythic hero's necessary trials. In the end, giving into these temptations will not be fulfilling and/or will have major negative ramifications for the hero or their community. Campbell (2008) described a common component of the middle stage of the monomyth as the "Woman as Temptress." Of course, this is overly gendered. Anyone can act as a figure of temptation, knowingly or otherwise.

33 Maslow offers several definitions in his 1971 book, *The Farther Reaches of Human Nature* (p. 259-269). Transcendence, transcendent meaning, and self-transcendence are recently gaining attention in psychiatry and psychology, outside of psychedelic research. See examples in Kaufman, 2020, Kelley, 2020, and Yaden et al., 2017.

34 Kierkegaard, 1849/2019, *The Sickness unto Death*.

35 Assigning meaning to non-ordinary states of consciousness requires taking leaps of faith, or promoting strict skepticism. Some dismiss mystical experiences as meaningless, as mere hallucinations, which implies that any paradox appearing to be transcended remain, in reality, unchanged. Others argue experiences of transcending paradox reveal a quality of divine reality, the sacred dimension that encapsulates our superficially profane material world with its apparent dualities—none of which are 'real' in the final analysis. Others believe paradox-transcending mystical states provide psychological insights for the individual but not for our human collective. Within psychedelic communities, like all others, tensions exist across several competing interpretations in all the above. For an insightful discussion of the competing interpretations of psychedelic experiences, see Letcher's, 2007, article "Mad Thoughts on Mushrooms," which offers a Foucauldian analysis of the power dynamics involved. Special thanks to Jeff Guss who continuously advocates for reading this paper and contemplating its implications as we navigate all these tensions.

36 As quoted in Yalom, 1980, Existential Psychotherapy, p. 426.

37 See, for example, Labate & Cavnar, 2014.

38 Huxley, 1945/2004, p. 21. The ellipsis removes Huxley's reference to "of Hindu and Christian mystical phraseology" since perennial philosophy integrates other religions besides Hinduism and Christianity. I've also replaced Huxley's use of "man" with "humankind" to be gender neutral and accurate.

39 More recently, Bill Richards has synthesized interdisciplinary scholarship, psychedelic psychotherapy research, and psychospiritual practice in his 2015 book *Sacred Knowl-*

edge. By exploring the psychospiritual dimensions of psychedelic experiences, his book acts as both an excellent introduction and valuable extension of previous work.

40 For research on self-transcendent emotions and well-being, see, for example, Van Cappellen et al., 2013, Haidt & Morris, 2009, & Reker & Woo, 2011.

41 Although similar ideas are found in multiple places, I direct readers interested in the connections to meaning, values, and self-actualization to look first at Maslow's (1971) distinction between being and becoming as two processes highlighted in growth-oriented psychotherapy, see p. 107-108. I separate doing from becoming to distinguish the active goal-directed and passive less intentional aspects of meaningful living. The power of non-action, wu wei in Taoism, and non-attachment to outcome in Buddhism are relevant to these distinctions as well.

42 As people age, perceptions about one's purpose in life can shift to emphasize social integration, quality of relationships, and appreciation of past achievements, which are less reliant on the ability to work and attain greater achievements in the future (see the meta-analysis by Pinquart, 2002). Mindfulness interventions, which focus on present-centered being, have a moderate positive impact on improving one's sense of meaning through decentering the everyday sense of self, increasing authentic self-awareness, and focusing attention on positive experiences (see the meta-analysis by Chu & Mak, 2020).

43 See Ly et al., 2018, for an example of how psilocybin and ketamine facilitate neuroplasticity.

44 Over-assigning meaning might reflect either a narrowly-defined essentialism (a philosophical 'enemy' of existentialism) or what Buddhists call eternalism—the belief that everything and everyone has a single, definite, and immutable meaning, purpose, or 'true' self. Eternalism violates the law of impermanence.

45 From a letter Conrad wrote to John Galsworthy on November 11, 1901, as cited in Said, 2008, p. 37. Conrad was speaking about fictional storytelling and autobiographical characterization which risks ignoring the less noble or more complex layers beyond the public persona and private understanding of oneself or a character.

46 Jung, 1969.

47 To give due credit, this wise question was posed to me by Bob Jesse (personal communication, July 2019).

48 Magical thinking is officially described as a symptom of Schizotypal Personality Disorder in the *DSM-5* (American Psychiatric Association, 2012). If a person's interpretations resonate with their dominant culture or subcultural norms, however, then it's not considered a psychiatric symptom, unless that is, it's causing significant harm. Similar patterns of magical thinking can also be observed in other mental health conditions. If very bizarre or unusual, it may indicate schizophrenia, delusions, or other psychotic disorders. Less bizarre magical thinking may also be observed in people with Obsessive-Compulsive Disorder.

49 The movie to which I'm referring isn't a hypothetical one. It's the 2019 film *Captive State* directed by Rupert Wyatt, which although grim, uses the sci-fi backdrop of an alien invasion to demonstrate how to fight a fascist government using superior technology and comprehensive systems of surveillance and social control.

50 In these examples, the symbolic meaning of being Jesus may be embodying the Self archetype or one's inner qualities of humility, love, and sacredness. The meaning of experiencing a plastic world may be seeing through the shallowness of our material everyday reality. Bourzat (2019) describes five types of psychedelic experiences that relate to our trial of meaning: experiencing meaninglessness (emptiness), reclaiming one's spiritual life (reconnecting to an abandoned faith or finding new faith), encounters with messianic and spiritual archetypes (like various gods), observing the underlying perfection of all things, and experiencing ego dissolution (more colloquially, ego death) (see p. 161-165).

51 See the first stanza of Feng & English's (1973/1997) translation of Lao Tsu's *Tao te Ching.*

52 Frenkel-Brunswick (1949) introduced tolerance for ambiguity as a personality variable that affects cognitive perceptions and emotional reactions to uncertainty. Tolerance of ambiguity is most strongly predicted by openness to experience and extraversion but is negatively correlated with neuroticism (Jach & Smillie, 2019). During stressful situations, higher tolerance for ambiguity may mitigate the tendency towards magical thinking (Keinan, 1994). For a review of research, see Furnham & Marks, 2013.

53 Welwood, 1982, p. 137-138. In this interview, Welwood explains meaning-free-ness as being "free of the struggle to find meaning. The open ground is meaning-free. We create meaning and structure out of it. But these structures can get too dense and thick unless we can let them dissolve back into the meaning-free open ground. Zen *koan* practice is designed to break down our attempts to find meaning. If you struggle to find the meaning of a koan, it doesn't work. Giving up that attempt to find the meaning of the koan opens up another kind of awareness" (p. 138).

54 See, for example, Leong's, 2001, *The Zen Teachings of Jesus,* and his delightfully titled subchapter themes "Seriousness as a sign of the ego," "Humor as a way to truth," and "The 'irreverent' tradition of Zen" (p. 19-31)

55 Not conventionally speaking, but some spiritual thinkers believe our spirit or soul did in fact choose to be born into the exact circumstances to fulfill a specific purpose in life.

56 The Absurd Hero is portrayed as a somewhat tragic hero for Camus, but others like philosopher Rebekka Reinhard offer more optimistic interpretations. Whereas Camus believed absurdity could not be transcended, he believed the Absurd Hero could create meaning through (1) actively revolting against the motivation to reconcile the desire for meaning in the face of meaninglessness, (2) embracing absolute freedom of thought and action, and (3) living life passionately through rich and diverse experiences. For Reinhard's perspective, see her lecture "On the Absurd" posted by TEDx Talks on 27 September 2017. In the posthumously published *Red Book,* Jung spoke of the reciprocal and non-dual nature of meaning and absurdity, "Day does not exist through itself, night does not exist through itself. The reality that exists through itself is day and night. So the reality is meaning and absurdity" (Jung, 2009, p. 242).

57 For a great exploration of fate versus destiny, see Bargdill, 2006. In my use here, fate is what cannot be resisted or changed. Destiny is a meaningful life path that can

be resisted but usually to the detriment of the individual and sometimes to others who would have benefited if the individual did embrace their destiny.

58 In mythic terms, "the utter loss of hope that paradoxically creates a space for renewal" is known as katabasis. See Rushing & Frentz, 1995, p. 214.

59 See, for example, descriptions by philosopher Allen Watts, 1957/1999, *The Way of Zen,* pp. 154-173, and by existential psychologist John Welwood, 1982, pp.137-138.

60 Maslow, 1971, p. 38. Emphasis on 'must' is Maslow's. He attributes his reference of the "worm trying to be god" to Wilson's (1959) *The Stature of Man,* but the question of whether humankind is closer to the gods or lowly worms is an ancient one.

61 See Ridley & Meza-León (2017, August 27), "The Whirly Dirly Conspiracy" (Season 3, Episode 5). Timestamp: 0:17min.

62 The present-day model and research I'm referring to is Acceptance and Commitment Therapy. See Sloshower et al., 2020, and Watts & Luoma, 2020, for its use in current studies of psilocybin-assisted psychotherapy for depression, and for a conceptual overview, see Luoma et al., 2019. The Values Card Sort activity is also being incorporated in a modern adaptation of psilocybin-assisted psychotherapy for alcoholism, a target of the original psychedelic psychotherapy research movement in the 1950's and 60's which also incorporated similar values card sort tasks. See Bogenschutz and Forcehimes, 2016.

63 Based on Kohlberg's stages of moral development. See Kohlberg, 1981, 1984.

64 One caveat might be that the expression of values, virtues, and ethical principles can be evaluated based on their historical, cultural, or evolutionary impact. The criteria used in such evaluations, though, may differ. For example, the evolutionary criteria may define the 'best' values as ones that lead to greater likelihood of procreation and/or survival of the individual, their group, or the entire species, as a collective. A relevant resource to consider in this vein is comparative/primate psychologist Frans de Waal's (2013) *The Bonobo and the Atheist: In Search of Humanism among the Primates.* For Sartre, unethical choices were ones that impeded the freedom of others (or denied one's own freedom or authenticity). were Historically and culturally speaking, the 'best' values might be ones that have survived the 'test of time' and are represented across all modern cultures. Beside perennial philosophy and other already cited sources, consider reading papers by Snarey (1985) and Gibbs et al. (2007), exploring the cross-cultural applicability of Kohlberg's (1981, 1984) moral development model, and the impressively comprehensive handbook *Character Strengths and Virtues* by Peterson and Seligman (2004).

THE FINAL ARC

1 Macy, 1993, p. 51

2 For an archetypal review of the Bodhisattva, see Leighton, 2012

3 Campbell, 2008

4 Hilton, 1933/1990

5 Capra, 1937

6 In his Marvel Cinematic Universe premiere, the young Peter Parker opened up about his motivation to be Spiderman with Tony Stark (aka, Iron Man). Parker paraphrased his now-cliché sentiment with more feeling, "When you can do the things I can, but you don't. And then the bad things happen, they happen because of you." A heavy sense of responsibility is palpable—as is the guilt for past failures. See Russo & Russo, 2016, *Captain America: Civil War*

7 Per the title of Maslow's (1971) posthumously published book, *The Farther Reaches of Human Nature*

8 As defined in Chapter 7, the final trial of meaning, and in the monomyth, apotheosis is the culmination of the middle phase of the hero's journey. In its highest form, apotheosis means attaining a transhuman, transcendent, or godlike state of consciousness or being. Examples are seen in religious allegories of Buddha's enlightenment and Jesus's resurrection, and in fiction, a good example occurs in *The Lord of the Rings* when Gandalf's ascends to the status of White Wizard after his sacrifice in the first film (Jackson, 2002, 2003).

9 Welwood, 2000, especially pp. 11-12.

CHAPTER 8

1 Didion, 1968/2017, p. 139

2 Campbell, *Hero with a Thousand Faces,* p. 163

3 Freud called this motivation the reality principle. See Freud, 1917/1989, p. 444

4 Technically, there's only one correct and logical way to mount toilet paper. For the curious, the answer lies in the original patent—the roll should go over and face outwards.

5 Huxley, 1954/2019, p. 8

6 Terror Management Theory offers an example of how the ego works within our larger multicultural reality. When triggered by existential threats like awareness of mortality, the ego seeks mange distress by reestablishing psychological equilibrium. It uses defense mechanisms to reassert two things: (1) one's culturally-bound worldview remains valid, and (2) one's behavior has met culturally-bound standards of living and worthiness (self-esteem). Both are socially embedded.

7 For information about the default mode network, the effects of psychedelics on it, and related concepts, see Buckner, Andrews-Hanna, & Schacter, 2008; Carhart-Harris & Friston, 2010; Letheby & Gerrans, 2017

8 The modern evidence-based therapy Acceptance and Commitment Therapy (ACT) asserts that efforts to control inner experience are the underlying problem of most psychological disorders. See Hayes, Strosahl, & Wilson, 2012. For its application in psychedelic psychotherapy, see Luoma et al., 2019.

9 This metaphor is commonly used in ACT (for example, Walser & Westrup, 2007, p. 75).

10 Psychological flexibility is the answer to rigid control, according to ACT, but this theme is shared with several other approaches. Flexibility is not just a conscious choice. It has unconscious elements as well. See, for example, Ferguson et al., 2008.

11 Davis et al. (2020) reported this finding based on analyses from a self-report online sample of people who have

had a classic psychedelic experience ('classic' meaning psilocybin mushrooms, LSD, ayahuasca, 5-MeO-DMT, peyote, etc.). For a theoretical overview of the importance of psychological flexibility as a mechanism of psychedelic psychotherapy, see Watts & Luoma, 2020.

12 Stanza 10 of Auden's (1945/1991) "The Maze" (alternative, "The Labyrinth"), p. 303-304

13 See for example, the treatment manuals used for the MAPS MDMA-assisted psychotherapy trials (Mithoefer, 2017) and Usona's psilocybin-assisted psychotherapy trials (Cooper, 2016).

14 See Schwartz, 2013, p. 809. Note too that according to internal family systems therapy, protective parts (managers and firefighters) inadvertently prevent access to the Self by keeping vulnerable parts like exiles outside of conscious awareness. By cultivating the qualities of the Self (the Eight Cs), these different parts are allowed each to have a voice and can become more aligned (versus polarized or domineering).

15 See Jung, 1934/1981, "The Development of Personality," of Vol 17 of *The Collected Works of C. G. Jung*. Matthiessen quotes a heavily edited but relevant section of this work in his chapter, "Shadow Paths," in *Zig Zag Zen* (Badiner & Grey [Ed.], 2015, p. 74).

16 Jung, 1921/1971, p. 448-450

17 Maslow, 1971/1993, p. 34. Maslow would provoke deeper reflection in his students by asking them, "If not you, then who else?" (p. 35). His intention was to encourage greater willingness to undertake the risks of self-actualization and cultivation of one's unique talents and potential.

18 A succinct summary of Jung's psychological interpretation of Christ is found in Segal's, 1998, introduction to *Jung on Mythology*, p. 37-39.

19 For Gandalf's transformation, see *The Fellowship of the Ring and The Two Towers* (Jackson, 2002, 2003). For Neo's full character arc, see *The Matrix, The Matrix Reloaded,* and *The Matrix Revolutions* (Wachowski & Wachowski, 1999, 2003a, 2003b)

20 The atman is also the link to Brahman, the ultimate creator, Godhead, or fabric of all existence. The atman, then, is the connective tissue from the individual self to the cosmic consciousness, that is, if universal consciousness is to be believed. For a succinct summary by a keen scholar and psychonaut, see p. 21, 30-31 of Houston Smith's (1958/1991) *The World's Religions.*

21 See Stein's (2015) *The Principle of Individuation*, p. 5

22 This notion is similar to Kierkegaard's (1849/2019) description of the infinite and finite aspects of human consciousness. "For the [S]elf is a synthesis in which the finite is the limiting factor, and the infinite is the expanding factor" (p. 431)

23 See Rogers's (1961/1995) *On Becoming a Person*, p. 122

24 As a refresher, the Big Five include levels of Extroversion-to-Introversion, Agreeableness-to-Argumentativeness, Conscientiousness-to-Disorganization, Neuroticism-to-Emotional Stability, and Openness to Experience-to-Conventionality. Basic tendencies and characteristic adaptations are concepts from the Five-Factor Model, which we reviewed in Chapter 3. See McCrae & Costa, 2008.

25 The exception might be when an otherwise 'Open' person automatically judges conventional ideas as 'wrong.' For

example research on how psychedelics increase Openness to Experience, see MacLean et al., 2011, and Wagner et al., 2017.

26 Traits here is shorthand for habitual attitudes or psychological proclivities. Jung's model refers to functions, attitudes, and directed libido when describing Extraversion-vs-Introversion, Sensing-vs-Intuiting, and Thinking-vs-Feeling. I'm simplifying language, which risks losing some of the nuances, but for interested readers, I recommend reading Jung's (1921/1971) *Psychological Types,* or Wilmer's (2015) *Practical Jung.* Note that Jung introduced the dominant attitudes of Extraversion and Introversion, which correspond to orientations towards the outer world (or 'shared' reality) or one's inner world, respectively. Jung's distinction of Extroversion-vs-Introversion significantly contributed to the field and our everyday language. However, to avoid confusion with the Big Five domains of the same name (and to streamline this chapter's focus), I only refer to the larger psychological functions in the main text.

27 Jung, 1921/1971, *Psychological Types*, p. 482-483.

28 Jung considered the creation of a new balance or synthesis as the transcendent function of the psyche; see Jung, 1921/1971, *Psychological Types*, p. 480.

29 My use of dialectic is influenced primarily by Hegel's philosophy, which has influenced countless other models, including Jung's. Hegel's work is notoriously dense, but if interested, consider his work, *The Phenomenology of Spirit* (also translated as *Mind;* Hegel, 1807/2018). According to Hill's (2013) summary of Jung's ideas, the transcendent function or integration of the opposing functions can come in two forms—a creative synthesis (largely artistic) or an intellectual understanding (interpretation and meaning dominant) (see p. 140).

30 See Linehan's (2015) DBT *Skills Training Manual (2nd Edition)*

31 Tellegen & Atkinson, 1974

32 Csikszentmihalyi, 1991, *Flow: The Psychology of Optimal Experience,* p. 4

33 Csikszentmihalyi, 1975, p. 43. See also Nakamura & Csikszentmihalyi, 2011, p. 195-196.

34 Abrams, 2019. Scene timestamp: 0-hr:38-min

35 Melfi, 2016. Scene timestamp: 1-hr:43-min

36 This warning aligns with the notion of 'spiritual bypass,' which was previewed in this arc's introduction. See Welwood, 2000, especially p. 11-12.

37 Csikszentmihalyi, 1991, p. 84-85

38 Jacobi, 1968, p. 363.

39 To borrow James Fadiman and Jordan Gruber's (2020) title of their new book, we could also use the metaphor of creating a 'symphony of selves.'

40 This metaphor adapts a commonly used one in ACT to describe the self-as-context idea (see Hayes et al., 2012), but its origins predate ACT. Houston Smith, for example, uses the game of chess to describe atman consciousness in Hinduism. See Smith, 1958/1991, p. 30-31.

41 You might notice having the 'white' pieces be 'bad' is counter to the dominant cultural assumption that dark is bad and white is good. I do so explicitly to counteract this notion which can have, at minimum, implicit racial undertones.

42 ACT refers to three perspectives on the Self: (1) the Self-as-Context (perspective-taking self), (2) the Self-as-Process (experiential self), and (3) Self-as-Content (conceptualized self) (see Hayes et al., 2020). Our typical identity is wrapped up in our Self-as-Content. This chessboard metaphor is similar to Buddhist and Hindu concepts, like the atman referenced earlier in this chapter. As introduced in our trial of death and impermanence, the Buddhist idea of anatta (empty or no-self) is closest to the Self-as-Context.

43 Examples include third-wave behavioral approaches like ACT and Dialectical Behavior therapy.

44 Jung's ideas about the Anima/Animus may benefit from updated language to avoid being misread as over-essentializing gender and/or excluding various non-binary gender representations ('Animo' perhaps?). For strictly heterosexual/straight people, Anima/Animus projections are probably relatively straightforward because the object of desire is a person of another gender. For LGBTQ+ and non-binary folks, these projections are likely multi-layered, potentially involving multifaceted projections. Nevertheless, the Anima/Animus can largely follow the same general pattern of desirable qualities unexpressed in one's outward persona or personal identity. Regardless of any needed technical updates, everyone can benefit from examining their assumptions and expectations about gender and the role gender plays in their lives.

45 If you do want to go full 'Gender Studies,' I recommend Judith Butler's (1990) now-classic book, *Gender Trouble* as well as Eve Sedgwick's (2003) *Touching Feeling*.

46 A good allegory for how memories and emotions impact our self-understanding is seen in Disney Pixar's *Inside Out* (Doctor & Del Carmen [Co-Directors], 2015). The film highlights also how older memories can trigger nostalgia over time, combining happiness with sadness. These more complex emotions reflect the impact of impermanence and is similar to 'mono no aware,' which we discussed in the trial of death and impermanence (Chapter 5).

47 See Csikszentmihalyi, 1991, p. 41-42; cf., Stein, 2015, p. 5

48 Stanza 1 of Lao Tsu's *Tao te Ching* (Feng & English, Trans., 1972/1997)

49 See, for example, Edinger's (1960) concept of the ego-Self axis.

50 As discussed in Chapter 5, re-establishing equilibrium and self-esteem are motivations activated by existential anxiety according to Terror Management Theory. See Greenberg, Pyszczynski, & Solomon, 1986.

51 The loss of internal and external resources is both a potential risk factor and result of trauma, as described by the resource-loss model, one foundation of STAIR Narrative Therapy. See Cloitre et al., 2020.

CHAPTER 9

1 Jung, 1951/1978, "The Shadow," para. 13,   p. 8.

2 Congruent with this idea, religious scholar Elaine Pagels (2003) quotes a particularly relevant segment of the non-canonical Gospel of Thomas. In the Gospel of Thomas, Jesus emphasized the critical nature of one's inner journey and self-awareness, "If you bring forth what is within you, what you bring forth will save you. If you do not bring forth what is within you, what you do not bring forth will destroy you" (p. 53).

3 Jung, 1951/1978, "The Shadow," paras. 13-19, p. 8-9.

4 Schlebusch et al., 2017. Note the authors estimate the arrival of homo sapiens to be between 260,000 and 350,000 years ago. My reported number simply splits the difference.

5 Some important criticisms have been Campbell's ethnocentrism and dismissal of counter perspectives or myths that don't fit the monomythic framework. Unverified rumors have also existed about his antisemitic beliefs.

6 Occasionally, people refer to these positive qualities of the shadow as the Golden Shadow, but Jung, as far as I could find, never used this phrase, nor would it be clear what's 'golden' and what's not. These judgments, in fact, are what separate shadow from ego in the first place.

7 This process might be how people with preoccupied attachment styles (high anxiety, low avoidance) tend to get into relationships with people with dismissing attachment styles (low anxiety, high avoidance).

8 Maslow, 1998, *Toward a Psychology of Being* (3rd ed), p. 90

9 Since the shadow is inherent to being human, the ontological guilt we discussed in Chapter 7's trial of meaninglessness is one way to examine the shadow.

10 An excellent review of sublime, awe, related concepts, and other transcendent emotions can be found in Bethelmy and Corraliza's, 2019, article, "Transcendence and Sublime Experience in Nature." The authors review several historical descriptions of the sublime (including works of Edmund Burke and Immanuel Kant) to modern literary and psychological perspectives. The paper primarily focuses on the creation and validation of a measurement for sublime reactions to nature. The resulting measure had two factors, awe (which, counter to my use of awe vs sublime, emphasized a fearful reaction of powerlessness or insignificance) and *inspiring energy* (a largely positive sense of interconnectedness, harmony, and belonging with nature).

11 Jung refers to the black sun most frequently in his later works exploring the psychological meaning of alchemical concepts and writing. See, for example, Jung, 1970, *Mysterium Coniunctionis* (Vol 14 of the Collected Works).

12 In this passage, Jung was comparing Eastern religious, nondual thinking to Western religious or philosophical frameworks of good-vs-evil (or an understanding of transcendent unity that ignores or dismisses evil). This quote, however, largely captures Jung's emphasis on the shadow as part of a larger whole and necessary for greater psychospiritual development. See p. 265-266, paragraph 335 of Figure 26 caption, 'The Philosophical Tree,' in Jung's, 1954/1983, *Alchemical Studies* (Vol 12 of Collected Works).

13 The Dark Triad was originally introduced by Paulhus & Williams (2002) but much of my conceptual summary here comes from Jones & Paulhus (2011), who connect the Dark Triad with the interpersonal circumplex, and their 2014 measurement development paper.

14 Based on findings of Jones & Paulhus 2014, Kaufman et al., 2019, and Kilmstra et al, 2020. For a critical review of the Dark Triad, see Miller et al., 2019. Also keep in mind these studies are based on majority white partici-

pants from Western samples (like much of psychological research), so these findings may not be entirely representative across cultures.

15 See Kaufman et al., 2019. Interestingly, psychedelic use is correlated with more humanitarian values (Lerner & Lyvers, 2006), but this association may be due to other factors and not as a direct cause of the psychedelic experience itself. More controlled research is needed to explore cause-and-effect.

16 Malcolm Gladwell's (2019) book *Talking to Strangers* makes the case that when a person behaves as expected in a situation we're more trusting, even when they're actually lying. In the reverse, the more incongruent a person is with our expectations of how they should behave (or how we think we'd behave in the same situation), the more distrusting we are. One important conclusion is that people who're very good at manipulation, deceit, and wielding power (the successful psychopath, CEO, lawyer, politician) are harder to catch based on first impressions or social skills. See also Linlienfeld et al.'s, 2015, review of scientific research on the notion of a 'successful psychopathy.'

17 Stated in first paragraph of Kaufman et al.'s, 2019, discussion section.

18 'Protect-and-connect' is Julie Holland's (2020) preferred description for the parasympathetic nervous system. Alternatives include 'rest and digest' and 'tend and befriend' (see *Good Chemistry*, p. xxii).

19 Lucas, 1999, *Star Wars: The Phantom Menace*. Scene starts at timestamp 1-hr:30-min.

20 From the sixth chapter of Hesse's (1919) novel *Demian*. As quoted in Knowles, 2007, *Oxford Dictionary of Modern Quotations*, p. 152.

21 Social psychology has introduced concepts like group think, the bystander effect (or diffusion of responsibility), and Pygmalion effect (expectancy effects), but on-going research, as expected, has shown many nuances and complexities. For a general review and reconsideration of many of these classic findings, see Smith and Haslam's (2017) edited collection, *Social Psychology: Revisiting the Classic Studies* (2nd Edition). Personality, social, and situational factors generally interact to determine an individual's behavior at any given point in time.

22 Admittedly, this question is inspired by The Cranberries' (1993) debut album, *Everybody Else is Doing It, so Why Can't We?*

23 For an overview of psychological mechanisms of radicalization, see Trip et a., 2019.

24 Although splitting the difference for every complex issue is a logical fallacy (since each issue is different and multifaceted), polarized black-and-white views are unproductive and often dangerous. Jonathan Haidt's work is worth exploring if you're willing to challenge any personal convictions in the political realm. See Haidt, 2012, *The Righteous Mind*.

25 Nolan, 2008.

26 Ibid, Scene Timestamp: 0-hr:19-min

27 Phillips, 2019.

28 Stan Grof coined this phrase (see for example, Grof, 1980/2008, p. 11). For an extensive, in-depth exploration of the shadow side of psychedelics from a Jungian per-

spective, see Scott Hill's, 2013, excellent book *Confrontation with the Unconscious,* in which Hill is candid about his own "hellish" psychedelic experiences and how his work in psychedelics have been part of his own journey of integration (and healing).

29 For some reviews of the current psychedelic research, see Reiff et al., 2020, and Jungaberle et al., 2018.

30 Jung wrote this letter in English on 10 April 1954, and its contents were reproduced in Adler & Jaffé's (Eds.), 1976/2011, *C. G. Jung Letters* (Vol 2, 1951-1961), pp. 163-174 (this excerpt comes from pp. 172-173). Jung was speaking of mescaline primarily, but he also knew vaguely of LSD. Jung wrote other letters with similar sentiments but in a generally more detached and professional tone to a well-known psychedelic advocate Al Hubbard (15 February 1955, pp. 222-224) and Los Angeles psychologist Betty Eisner (12 August 1957, pp. 382-383). To Hubbard, he asserted that psychedelic experiences would give only psychological insights, at best, and not metaphysical ones. To Eisner, he warned that psychedelics would trigger, "a regrettable regression for a cultivated individual, a dangerously simple 'Ersatz' [artificial or inferior imitation] and substitute for true religion" (p. 383).

31 Charles Manson, a textbook psychopath, appeared more successful when he employed LSD as a tool for manipulation, but because of their ability to find vulnerable people to manipulate, I'd argue that predators like Manson are the problem, not psychedelics. Some of the stories about MK-ULTRA and Manson have reached the status of legend and may not be entirely true (see O'Neill, 2019). Still, Carhart-Harris et al. (2015) found that LSD does increased suggestibility.

32 The post-World War II historical context also played no small part in Jung's cautions about our underdeveloped sense of ethical responsibility, and he directed alluded to the lingering effects of nuclear weaponry.

33 Smith, 1963, as cited by Hill, 2013, p. 115. Note that Smith used the word 'religious,' not spiritual, but the sentiment, I believe, remains intact while avoiding misinterpretations of the word 'religious' as pertaining only to orthodox, traditional, or institutionalized forms of spirituality.

34 Leary, 1995, p. 257, as also quoted and commented on by Hill, 2013, p. 78.

35 Bill Richards has offered a measured perspective on Leary based on his experiences as a psychologist involved in both the original period of Western research and during our current psychedelic renaissance. See, in particular, pp. 120-123 of his book *Sacred Knowledge,* 2015.

36 See Smith et al., 2004, p. 137. After offering his alternative to Leary's 'Turn On, Tune In, Drop Out,' Smith proceeded to add several qualifiers and cautions.

37 Developing 'above ground' training programs allows the creation of accreditation and certification processes that hold both the programs and trained providers accountable for boundary violations (e.g., sexual contact between guide and journeyer, including sexual assaults). Ideally, training in basic competencies and ethical principles will prevent most violations, but even recent history has shown that violations can occur despite training and oversight. For a description of one early training program (CIIS), see Phelps, 2017. For the MAPS MDMA-assisted psychother-

apy code of ethics, see Carlin & Scheld, 2019.

38 By describing her experiences within the Mazatec tradition in Mexico, Françoise Bourzat has offered a worthy model for respectful cross-cultural exchange, as described in her 2019 book, *Consciousness Medicine*. In addition to her training in Western models of psychotherapy, Bourzat has experienced traditional ceremonies from several indigenous cultures. Most prominently, she's fostered an ongoing relationship with the Mazatec tribe in Mexico's Sierra Madre Mountains. Under the guidance of tribal elder Julieta Casimiro, her training has spanned decades. Keenly aware of the harm done by many Westerners entering indigenous communities, Bourzat has demonstrated a genuine cultural humility while asking how we might learn from and adapt these practices for our modern culture, not how we can take their power for our own use, devested of our responsibility to nature or the communities who have kept these traditions alive. The tension between appropriation and respectful adaptation is a central concern when traversing multiple worlds where one holds disproportionate socioeconomic power and is too often assumed to be intellectually and morally superior.

39 See Nielson & Guss, 2018, for a thoughtful exploration of the impact of psychedelic therapists having their own psychedelic experience or being psychedelic naïve.

40 As Michael Mithoefer stated during a week-long MAPS-sponsored MDMA psychotherapy training retreat, there can be about "20 years of transference in 8 hours" (personal communication, June 24th, 2019). The heights and depths of transference (idealization and devaluation) can be on steroids when non-ordinary states of consciousness are involved, so understanding that and knowing how to deal with such transferences is a core competency for psychedelic psychotherapists.

41 Leary, 1995, p. 28

42 I was introduced to the phrase 'intention without expectation' by psilocybin and MDMA-assisted therapy researcher and therapist, Chris Stauffer (personal communication, October 2020), but it's commonly used by therapists and guides when helping people in the preparation phase of psychedelic therapy.

43 Insights regarding these manifestations come from a variety of personal and informal sources. Special thanks to Evan Sola (personal communication, August 2020). See also Hill, pp. 13, 71-81, 123-125.

44 See Campbell & Moyers, 1988, p. 222, and Vogel, 2020, p. 55-58

45 Keiman, personal communication, October and November 2020

46 Interestingly, the Western secularized use of meditation has risks similar to psychedelics—cultural appropriation, dilution of the transformative aspects of a practice, and co-optation by institutional, financial, and political power structures (see Huntington, Jr, 2015).

47 Hill, 2013, p. 47.

48 Examples of different types of love include romantic (eros), friendly-platonic (philia), familial (storge), hospitable (xenia), and divine (agape).

49 I'm referring specifically to Sternberg's, 1986, triangular theory of (romantic) love. For a study of cross-cultural support, see Sorokowski et al., 2020.

50 Bill Richards (2015) describes agape as "the love of God… that not only heals those who experience it, but also demands expression in and through their lives in interaction with other people and the world" (p. 55). If interested in cross-cultural explorations of agape, consider Sir John Templeton's (1999) *Agape Love: A Tradition Found in Eight World Religions*.

51 For alternative and complementary perspectives, I recommend Hofmann, Grossman, and Hinton's, 2011, review of compassion and loving-kindness, and Stanford University's The Center for Compassion and Altruism Research and Education (C-CARE) webpage (http://ccare.standford.edu), specifically their Education FAQ subpage. One short yet comprehensive definition I found described compassion as "an orientation of mind that recognizes pain and the universality of pain in human experience and the capacity to meet that pain with kindness, empathy, equanimity and patience. While self-compassion orients to our own experience, compassion extends this orientation to others' experience," Feldman & Kuyken, 2011/2013, p. 145. Note this citation refers to a reproduction, in book form, of the 2011 special issue of *Contemporary Buddhism An Interdisciplinary Journal* (Vol 12, Issue 1).

52 I'm borrowing the phrase "moral force" from DeSteno's PsychologyToday online article from 11 March 2011.

53 The concept of the panopticon dates back to Bentham's architectural prison design of the 18th century, but it was used by Foucault as a metaphor for social and institutional power. For a more recent examination of the panopticon in light of digital surveillance (socially and by governmental and corporate entities), see Galič, Timan, & Koops, 2017. For unaware readers, Sauron is the name of the Dark Lord from *The Lord of the Rings*.

54 One specific source of shame bears mentioning—sex and pleasure. In modern therapy, healing from shame is a critical component for people who've learned that sex and sensual pleasure are bad, dangerous, or meaningless. Some people undergoing psychedelic journeys experience a reawakening of sexual energy and interests. Others confront the harm done by certain religious or societal taboos involving sexuality, which is especially relevant to LGBTQ+ communities. Sexism can also play a significant role in programming these unrealistic and harmful (double) standards.

55 Campbell, 2008, described "Atonement with the Father" as part of the second act of the hero's journey and thus before the hero's return. The father could be a parental figure or divine creator, but regardless, atonement as a concept is not gender-specific (either for the giver or receiver).

56 I'm referring especially to the work on moral injury and clinical interventions to support recover from moral injury. For recent conceptual and research reviews, see Griffin et al., 2019, and Wortmann et al., 2017.

57 Research on religious beliefs, mental health, and social justice beliefs is nuanced and fascinating. As way of a few examples (in US samples), one study found that religiously inclined people who believed in a more punitive God (versus a more benevolent and forgiving one) had a greater likelihood of social anxiety, paranoia, obsession, and compulsion (Stilton et al., 2014). Another study found beliefs in more transcendent forms of evil (like the Devil

and demonic figures) and punishment (like Hell or karma) increased support for harsher punishments for criminal behavior, but in an interesting twist, greater participation in religious practice (reading sacred texts, attending regular services, praying, etc.) was linked to less punitive attitudes. Based on the overall data, the authors concluded that beliefs about evil were more influential than beliefs about God's nature on a person's opinions about crime and punishment (Baker & Booth, 2016).

58 To disentangle personal motivations and blind spots from 'purer' forms of justice, Harvard philosopher John Rawls (1999) has posed the following thought experiment: How would you design a justice system (or society) to be fair if you knew at the conclusion of doing so, you'd randomly be assigned your socioeconomic, ethnic, racial, gender, and other demographics? This thought experiment is sometimes referred to as the veil of ignorance.

59 When describing the interplay of vulnerability, compassion, and spiritual development (from a Buddhist perspective), Welwood, 1982, summarized that an innate "tender heart" when fully cultivated would transform into an "awakened heart" (p. 137).

60 Summarizing 70 studies with an overall participant pool of 6,949 people, the meta-analysis by Campbell and Sedikides, 1999, found consistent support for self-serving biases (e.g., attributing success of others to situational or chance factors but one's own successes to innate talents or effort). The effect was found to be stronger when people subjectively felt more threatened.

61 Unconscious, implicit bias can have a small effect on average (when compared to explicit beliefs and emotions) (see, for example, Oswald et al., 2013). However, as Greenwald et al., 2015, argue collectively and over time, small effects have much larger impacts.

62 See, for example, Haidt, 2012

63 Kornfield, 1993, *A Path with Heart*, p. 50. Kornfield was paraphrasing an early Buddhist saying from the Pali canon (Magandiya Suta in the Sutta Nipata).

64 Despite opposing this outcome, many existential thinkers have been criticized for not offering a clear ethical framework for social relationships. Simone de Beauvoir accepted the challenge, and advocated for an ethics of maximizing freedom, not just for the individual (meaning oneself) but for all others. de Beauvoir's work on existential ethics is outlined in her 1948 book, *The Ethics of Ambiguity*. To humanize these philosophers, it's interesting to note that Sartre was both her colleague and her partner. The two are buried with a shared tombstone in Paris.

65 Jung, 1921/1971, p. 449, paragraph 761 in "Definitions" section of *Psychological Types* (Collected Works of C. G. Jung, Vol 6).

66 Jackson, 2002. Scene Timestamp: 2-hr:40-min

67 Jung, 1963/1989, p. 189, *Memories, Dreams, Reflections*

68 Waheed, 2019, Salt, p. 220

69 Although this saying is frequently attributed online to ancient Chinese wisdom (see, for example, Hornaday, September 23, 2019), I could not verify an original source. In lieu of that, I discussed the proverb with two friends of Chinese heritage, Gil Woo and Valerie Chueh, who both agreed it was consistent with traditional Chinese values but neither had ever heard it (personal communication,

August 2020).

70 I was taught this lesson in Taekwondo when I was trained as a child by GrandMaster JeeHo Lee. Before sparring, we learned to bow respectfully, but to keep our eyes on the opponent, in case they lacked honor and might attack preemptively.

CHAPTER 10

1 Coogler, 2018. Scene timestamp: 2-hr:05 min

2 According to second definition of adjective 'narrow' from OxfordLanguages, n.d., available by Google search.

3 See, for example, Jung, 1951/1978, "Gnostic Symbols of the Self," para. 304, p. 195

4 Matthew 7:14 (King James Version)

5 Campbell & Moyers, 1988, p. 193

6 Lama Surya Das, 2015, "The Zen Commandments," *Zig Zag Zen*, p. 193.

7 I say ideally because various forms of child abuse are far too common.

8 Season 1, Episode 4, "Trial," Guercio & McTeigue, January 1, 2020. Timestamp: 0-hr:13-min

9 Richards, 2015, p. 212, part of the book's "Epilogue: A Concise Report of Insights from the Frontier Where Science and Spirituality are Meeting." Emphasis on the second 'is' is found in the original statement.

10 Personal communication, January 2020. See also, Bourzat & Hunter, 2019.

11 Whereas Buddhism generally emphasizes emptying the contents of our individual ego-self, Western approaches have typically emphasized organizing and containing the psyche within a larger whole or contacting a unified transcendent self. Of course, there are many exceptions to this distinction. For some relevant discussion from Western psychological viewpoints, see Peoples, 2000, and Fadiman & Gruber, 2020.

12 See von Franz, 1968, p. 249

13 Achebe, 1959/1994. For the entire poem, see Yeats, 2008, "The Second Coming," p. 200.

14 See Davies, Farrell, & Matthews, 1982, and Rushing & Frentz, 1995, *Projecting the Shadow: The Cyborg Hero in American Film*.

15 Recently, communication scholars have become interested again in meaningful films and media that evoke self-transcendent experiences, characterized by being in touch with our interconnectedness, spirituality, and moral/ethical virtues (like altruism). See Oliver et al., 2018.

16 I'm referring specifically to Finn whose moral intuition led him to abandon the New Order in *The Force Awakens* (Abrams, 2015) and the anonymous slave child with force sensitivity in *The Last Jedi* (Johnson, 2017). Rey's supposed lack of special lineage in *The Last Jedi* was revised to be an even darker genetic heritage in *The Rise of Skywalker* (Abrams, 2019). She was actually the granddaughter of the ultimate evil, Emperor Palpatine. Many of us needed to hear the message that anyone can fight for the greater good, whether a 'nobody' or a descendant of 'evil' ancestors.

17 Kraehenmann, 2017, compared and contrasted the neurological and phenomenological aspects of dream states and psychedelic experiences. His conclusion was that psyche-

delic states were closest to lucid dreaming.

18 Jung called these dreams "big dreams" because they possessed a "'numinous' quality," meaning a powerful spiritual, religious, or mythic undertone (see Jung, 1939/1982, para. 528).

19 See Stein, 2015, pp. 25-27.

20 For an example review, consider Hartogsohn, 2018. Following popular reports, researchers have begun investigating the potential of microdosing to enhance cognitive abilities and creativity, but controlled research is still needed to confirm preliminary findings and safety. See, for example, Prochazkova et al., 2018, and Rifkin et al., 2020.

21 This quote comes from a postscript Frankl added in 1984 to his book *Man's Search for Meaning,* originally published in German in 1946. Frankl's statement was part of a call to be alert while remaining "tragically optimistic" (Frankl, 1992, p. 154).

22 For a scientific review of this 'law,' see Diamond, 2005. When tasks are simple, the relationship between performance and arousal is linear and positive (high arousal equals better performance). It's only when tasks are complex that the sweet spot is in the middle.

23 For a nice review of the positive impact of worry, see Ro, August 26, 2020.

24 Respectively, Spielberg, 1977; Zemeckis, 1997; Emmerich, 1996; Scott, 1979.

25 My work at the National Center for PTSD focused on developing and evaluating apps and web-based mental health programs (for example, Mindfulness Coach, STAIR Emotion Coach, webSTAIR). Outside the VA, I've provided consultation on augmented and virtual reality projects to support mental health and personal growth. For a full suite of free programs that also protect confidentiality of users, see the National Center for PTSD's VA Mobile Apps web page: https://www.ptsd.va.gov/appvid/mobile/index.asp

26 For example, Orlowski's (2020) *The Social Dilemma* is a thought-provoking documentary about the shadow side of social media. Social media is so engrained in most modern cultures, it's unclear how to dial back its influence. But we do need to sound the alarm and work on mitigating its negative psychological and societal impact.

27 See, for example, Eden et al., 2012, *Singularity Hypotheses: A Scientific and Philosophical Assessment.* Eden et al. define the technological singularity as "an event or phase that will radically change human civilization, and perhaps even human nature itself, [likely] before the middle of the 21st century" (p. 1).

28 *Godzilla* (Honda, 1954; Edwards, 2014), *The Circle* (Ponsoldt, 2017), *A Scanner Darkly* (Linklater, 2006), *Inception* (Nolan, 2010), *2001: A Space Odyssey* (Kubrick, 1968), *The Matrix trilogy* (Wachowski & Wachowski, 1999, 2003a, 2003b), *Ex Machina* (Garland, 2014), *Interstellar* (Nolan, 2014), *Contagion* (Soderbergh, 2011), and *2012* (Emmerich, 2009).

29 Toffler, 1970, especially p. 12, 343, 428. See also, Schroeter's (Ed), 2020, *After Shock.*

30 For especially psychedelic-inspired *Star Trek,* see *Star Trek: The Motion Picture* (Wise, 1979) and *Star Trek Discovery* (Fuller et al., 2017-present).

31 *The Terminator* (Cameron, 1984), *Terminator 2: Judgment Day* (Cameron, 1991), *Terminator 3: Rise of the Machines* (Mostow, 2003), *Terminator Salvation* (McG, 2009), *Terminator Genisys* (Taylor, 2015), and *Terminator: Dark Fate* (Miller, 2019).

32 This adage predates Maslow, but the closest approximation (minus the inclusion of modern-day technology, of course) was Maslow (1966).

33 May, 1975/1994, p. 20

34 See Houston Smith, 2003, *Beyond the Postmodern Mind: The Place of Meaning in a Global Civilization* (3rd edition).

35 To be more precise, the Dunning-Kruger effect describes a pattern where people higher in competence, skill, or knowledge are better able to assess their own abilities whereas people lower in competence, skill, or knowledge are not only worse but also significantly overestimate their abilities (see Kruger & Dunning, 1999; Dunning, 2011). This effect has been observed, for example, in politics, especially when a person's political identity is made salient (Anson, 2018), and with anti-vaccination attitudes (Motta et al., 2018). The ability to observe and think about one's own thinking (metacognition or self-reflective abilities) is a partial contributor to the Dunning-Kruger effect (see McIntosh et al., 2019). The effect is a specific example of self-serving biases such as the better-than-average effect, also known as illusory superiority (for a review and meta-analysis, see Zell et al., 2020). For a conceptual review of intellectual humility, in particular, see Du & Cai, 2020.

36 I'm influenced in particular by Eve Sedgewick's call for reparative approaches to critical theory and the overzealous problematizing within the humanities. Sedgewick uses psychoanalyst Melanie Klein's theory of the depressive and schizoid (paranoid) positions to good effect in her 2003 book *Touching Feeling: Affect, Pedagogy, Performativity* (see Chapter 4).

37 Although this formulation is my own, I'm influenced primarily by Janice Hocker Rushing and Tom Frentz who served as my film studies mentors. Their 1995 book *Projecting the Shadow* asserts the need for a transmodern mythological framework that supplants the dominant postmodern deconstruction of mythology and meta-narratives. Since their book, other terms have come and gone to describe very similar sentiments as transmodernism, including metamodernism which has gained some traction in the last five years. To avoid confusion and distracting academic sidebars, I've settled on 'meta' as a simple enough moniker for this multifaceted synthesis. For discussions of metamodernism, see Abramson (January 9, 2017), Dember (April 17, 2018), and Henriques & Görtz (April 17, 2020).

38 For the most comprehensive definition of 'meta,' see the entry within Dictionary.com's (n.d.) *Pop Culture Dictionary.* I suppose we shouldn't forget 'meta' also echoes the field of metaphysics, the study of the fundamental nature of reality or "the first principles of things." For a thoughtful exploration of psychedelics and metaphysics from a Western philosophical perspective, see Peter Sjöstedt-H's (2015) *Neumenautics: Metaphysics–Meta-Ethics–Psychedelics.*

39 I first played with this idea of hybridization and metahuman in my mythic film analysis of the hybrid human-alien Ripley clone and her double-sided initiation and individuation journey in Alien Resurrection (Jeunet, 1997; Ortigo, 2007).

40 Jung, 1921/1976, *Psychological Types,* para. 93, p. 63. Emphasis on 'play' is in the original text.

41 See, for example, Richards, 2015, pp. 51, 169.

42 Of note, compassion and appreciative joy are two core attitudes encouraged in Buddhism, with the latter being an "empathic response to good fortune," one's own and others' (Olendzki, 2013, p. 62).

43 Speaking of ambiguity, tolerance of ambiguity (as introduced in our trial of meaning and meaninglessness) is positively correlated with creativity (Zenasni et al., 2008).

44 Although Jung described the Trickster archetype in negative terms, some scholars have argued for its positive and productive aspects. For example, the Trickster can be helpful in cross-cultural and multicultural education settings (see de Bruijn, 2019). African American and Native American scholarship has also described the importance of trickster qualities and perspectives in fostering resilience while needing to exist and function in multiple spaces as part of marginalized communities (see, for example, Ballinger, 2004; Roberts, 1982). For an insightful critique of anti-coyote sentiments, see also Otessa Moshfegh's (2016, July 6) *The New Yorker* article, "Coyotes, The Ultimate American Tricksters."

45 See, for example, Leong's (2001) discussion of irreverence in *The Zen Teachings of Jesus* (pp. 19-31).

46 See Verse 8 and 78 of Lao Tzu's (1972/1997) *Tao te Ching.*

47 Derrickson, 2016. Scene timestamp: 1-hr:23-min [normalize throughout book]

48 Abrams, 2019. Scene timestamp: 1-hr:53-min [normalize throughout book]

49 Campbell, 2008, pp. 153, 155, 186; see also, Vogler, 2020, pp. 255-257.

50 As research has demonstrated, intellectual abilities and personality traits, especially Openness to Experience, influence creative achievements (see Kaufman et al., 2016), but like creativity itself, these variables are themselves multifaceted. If interested in cultivating creativity, I highly recommend Julia Cameron's (2016) now-classic workbook, *The Artist's Way.* For an academically inclined but still accessible overview of creativity, see Puccio's (2014) *The Creative Thinker's Toolkit.*

51 As part of existential psychotherapy, van Deurzen (2012) has outlined an approach for "taking stock" of one's underlying assumptions, personal values, and existing talents. Reflecting on these elements may help pinpoint a direction of focus. The second suggestion in Box 10.3 adapts this approach to include perceived needs of society in place of one's basic assumptions, though gaining clarity about one's assumptions is undoubtedly crucial to living more successfully in the world.

52 Campbell & Moyers, 1988, p. 118-121, 229-230

53 Richards, 2015, p. 211

54 After writing this metaphor, a friend reminded me that Shakespeare too, in his play *As You Like It,* compares life to a play, though in an abbreviated form and ultimately with a different purpose. His purpose was to highlight the changes in each stage of life that ultimately end in death. The most eloquent and related quote for us comes from the character Jaques: "All the world's a stage, And all the men and women merely players. They have their exits and their entrances, And one man in his time plays many parts." For the complete speech, visit Poetry Foundation: https://www.poetryfoundation.org/poems/56966/speech-all-the-worlds-a-stage

EPILOGUE

1 Campbell, 2008, p. 196-204

2 While advocating for a similar attitude, Campbell (2008) references the words of Catholic priest and theologian Saint Thomas Aquinas as well as a line from Hinduism's Kena Upanishad, which Campbell translates as "To know is not to know; not to know is to know" (p. 202).

3 Quoted from Jung's letter to Michael Serrano dated 14 September 1960. See Adler & Jaffé's (1976/2011) *C. G. Jung Letters,* Vol 2, p. 595. The entire letter can be found on pp. 590-597.

4 Ibid., p. 595

5 Campbell, 2008, p. 205-210

6 Although Ram Dass shared this mantra elsewhere too, I suggest watching the short 2017 documentary *Ram Dass, Going Home* by Derek Peck. This film captures some of Dass's final reflections on film leading up to his eventual passing on 22 December 2019.

7 This verse of Lao Tsu's *Tao te Ching* is from Feng & English's (1972/1997) translation in the 25th Anniversary Edition.

8 See lecture transcript dated 22 June 1932 in Jung's (1997) *Visions, Vol. 2: Notes of the Seminar Given in 1930-1934,* p. 759-760.

92nd Street Y. (2017, May 10). A mind-expanding tour of the cosmos with Neil deGrasse Tyson and Robert Krulwich [Video]. https://www.youtube.com/watch?v=AyAK3QBn-MGQ

A-tjak, J. G., Davis, M. L., Morina, N., Powers, M. B., Smits, J. A., & Emmelkamp, P. M. (2015). A meta-analysis of the efficacy of Acceptance and Commitment Therapy for clinically relevant mental and physical health problems. *Psychotherapy and psychosomatics, 84*(1), 30-36.

Abrams, J. J. (Director). (2015). *Star wars: Episode VII–The force awakens* [Film]. Lucasfilm Ltd.

Abrams, J. J. (Director). (2019). *Star wars: Episode IX–The rise of Skywalker* [Film]. Lucasfilm Ltd.

Abramson, S. (2017, January 9). *What is metamodernism?* Huffpost. https://www.huffpost.com/entry/what-is-metamodernism_b_586e7075e4b0a5e600a788cd?guccounter=1

Achebe, C. (1994). *Things fall apart*. Anchor Books. (Original work published 1959)

Adams, D. (1979). *The hitchhiker's guide to the galaxy*. Pocket Books.

Adler, G., & Jaffé, A. (Eds.) (2011). *C. G. Jung Letters, Vol 2: 1951-1961* (R. F. C. Hull, Trans.). Routledge. (Original work published 1976)

Ainsworth, M. D. S., & Bell, S. M. (1970). Attachment, separation, and exploration: Illustrated by the behavior of one-year-olds in a strange situation. *Child Development, 41*, 49–67.

Ainsworth, M. D. S., Blehar, M. C., Waters, E., & Wall, S. (1978). *Patterns of attachment: A psychological study of the strange situation*. Lawrence Erlbaum Associates.

Ainsworth, M. D. S., & Wittig, B. A. (1969). Attachment and exploratory behavior of one-year-old children in a strange situation. *Determinants of Infant Behavior, 4*, 111-136.

Alderfer, C. P. (1969). An empirical test of a new theory of human needs. *Organizational Behavior and Human Performance, 4*(2), 142-175.

Allport, G. W., & Odbert, H. S. (1936). *Trait-names: A psycho-lexical study*. Psychological Review Company.

Alpert, D. (2012, March 23). On the origin of everything. *New York Times*. https://www.nytimes.com/2012/03/25/books/review/a-universe-from-nothing-by-lawrence-m-krauss.html?auth=login-facebook

American Psychiatric Association. (2013). *Diagnostic and statistical manual of mental disorders* (5th ed.). American Psychiatric Publishing.

Andreassen, C. S., Pallesen, S., & Griffiths, M. D. (2017). The relationship between addictive use of media, narcissism, and self-esteem: Findings from a large national survey. *Addictive Behaviors, 64*, 287-293.

Annis, J. (1999). An astrophysical explanation for the great silence. *Journal of the British Interplanetary Society, 52*, 19–22.

Anson, I. G. (2018). Partisanship, political knowledge, and the dunning-kruger effect. *Political Psychology, 39*(5), 1173-1192.

Antony, M. M., & Roemer, L. (2011). *Behavior therapy*. American Psychological Association.

Aronofsky, D. (Director). (2006). *The fountain* [Film]. Warner Bros.

Aronofsky, D. (Director). (2017). *Mother!* [Film]. Protozoa Pictures.

Aronofsky, D., Root, J., Lovering, P., Franklin, S., Pastore, T., & Renner, M. (Executive Producers). (2018). *One strange rock* [TV series]. Nutopia.

Aster, A. (Director). (2018). *Hereditary* [Film]. A24.

Atherton, O. E., Grijalva, E., Roberts, B. W., & Robins, R. W. (2020). Stability and change in personality traits and major life goals from college to midlife. *Personality and Social Psychology Bulletin*, 0146167220949362.

Auden, H. W. (1991). The maze. In E. Mendelson (Ed.), *Collected poems* (p. 303-305). Vintage Books. (Original work published in 1945)

Ayers, S. (1997). The application of chaos theory to psychology. *Theory & Psychology, 7*(3), 373-398.

Azevedo, F. A., Carvalho, L. R. B., Grinberg, L. T., Farfel, J. M., Ferretti, R. E. L., Leite, R. E. P., Filho, W. J., Lent, R., & Herculano-Houzel, S. (2009). Equal numbers of neuronal and nonneuronal cells make the human brain an isometrically scaled-up primate brain. *Journal of Comparative Neurology, 513*(5), 532-541.

Badiner, A. & Grey, A. (Eds.). (2015). *Zig zag Zen: Buddhism and psychedelics* (New ed.). Synergetic Press.

Baker, J. O., & Booth, A. L. (2016). Hell to pay: Religion and punitive ideology among the American public. *Punishment & society, 18*(7), 151-176.

Baldock, J. (Ed.). (2009). *The Tibetan book of the dead: The manuscript of the Bardo Thödol* (L. K. Dawa-Samdup, Trans.). Chartwell Books.

Baldwin, A. L., Vitale, A., Brownell, E., Scicinski, J., Kearns, M., & Rand, W. (2010). The touchstone process: An ongoing critical evaluation of Reiki in the scientific literature. *Holistic Nursing Practice, 24*(5), 260-276.

Ballinger, F. (2006). *Living sideways: Tricksters in American Indian oral traditions*. University of Oklahoma Press.

Baron-Reid, C., & DellaGrottaglia, J. (2018). *The spirit animal oracle*. Hay House, Inc.

Bargdill, R. W. (2006). Fate and destiny: Some historical distinctions between the concepts. *Journal of Theoretical and Philosophical Psychology, 26*(1-2), 205-220.

Bargh, J. A., & Morsella, E. (2008). The unconscious mind. *Perspectives on Psychological Science, 3*(1), 73–79.

Barker, S. A. (2018). N, N-Dimethyltryptamine (DMT), an endogenous hallucinogen: Past, present, and future research to determine its role and function. *Frontiers in Neuroscience, 12*, 536.

Bethelmy, L. C., & Corraliza, J. A. (2019). Transcendence and sublime experience in nature: Awe and inspiring energy. *Frontiers in Psychology, 10*, 509.

Barrett, L. F. (2004). Feelings or words? Understanding the content in self-report ratings of experienced emotion. *Journal of Personality and Social Psychology, 87*, 266–281.

Barrett L. F. (2009). The future of psychology: Connecting mind to brain. *Perspectives on Psychological Science, 4*(4), 326–339.

Batygin, K., & Brown, M. E. (2016). Evidence for a distant giant planet in the solar system. *The Astronomical Journal*, *151*(2), 22-33.

Baumeister, R. F., & Leary, M. R. (1995). The need to belong: Desire for interpersonal attachments as a fundamental human motivation. *Psychological Bulletin, 117*, 497–529.

Berlowitz, V., Gunton, M., Brickell, J., & Hugh-Jones, T. (Executive Producers). (2016). *Planet Earth II* [TV series]. BBC.

Besler, A. (2019, October 17). *10 calls to action: Toward an LGBTQ-affirmative psychedelic therapy*. Chacruna. https://chacruna.net/10-calls-to -action-toward-an-lgbtq-affirmative-psychedelic-therapy/#fn-12302-8

Bierl, A., Christopoulos, M., & Papachrysostomou, A. (Eds.) (2017). *Time and space in anciety myth, religion, and culture*. de Gruyter.

Bjorklund, D. F. (2018). Behavioral epigenetics: The last nail in the coffin of genetic determinism. *Human Development, 61*(1), 54-59.

Blanke, O., Faivre, N., & Dieguez, S. (2016). Leaving body and life behind: Out-of-body and near-death experience. In S. Laureys, O. Gosseries, & G. Tononi (Eds.), *The neurology of consciousness: Cognitive neuroscience and neuropathology* (2nd ed.) (p. 323-347). Elsevier Academic Press.

Bluhm, C., Widiger, T. A., & Miele, G. M. (1990). Interpersonal complementarity and individual differences. *Journal of Personality and Social Psychology, 58*(3), 464–471.

Boden, A. (Director). (2019). *Captain Marvel* [Film]. Marvel Studios.

Bogenschutz, M. P., & Forcehimes, A. A. (2017). Development of a psychotherapeutic model for psilocybin-assisted treatment of alcoholism. *Journal of Humanistic Psychology, 57*(4), 389-414.

Bourzat, F., & Hunter, C. (2019). *Consciousness medicine: Indigenous wisdom, entheogens, and expanded states of consciousness for healing and growth*. North Atlantic Books.

Bovend'Eerdt, T. J. H., Botell, R. E., & Wade, D. T. (2009). Writing SMART rehabilitation goals and achieving goal attainment scaling: A practical guide. *Clinical Rehabilitation, 23*(4), 352-361.

Bowlby, J. (1973). *Attachment and loss, Vol. 2: Separation: Anxiety and anger*. Hogarth Press.

Bowlby, J. (1980). *Attachment and loss, Vol. 3: Loss: Sadness and depression*. Hogarth Press.

Bowlby, J. (1982). *Attachment and loss, Vol. 1: Attachment* (2nd ed.). Basic Books. (Original work published 1969)

Bradbury, R. (2005). *Bradbury stories: 100 of his most celebrated tales*. William Morrow. (Original short story *A sound of thunder* published 1952)

Brass, M., Furstenberg, A., & Mele, A. R. (2019). Why neuroscience does not disprove free will. *Neuroscience & Biobehavioral Reviews, 102*, 251-263.

Brenner, C. (1982). *The mind in conflict*. New York, NY: International Universities Press.

Brennan, K. A., Clark, C. L., & Shaver, P. R. (1998). Self-report measures of adult romantic attachment: An integrative overview. In J. A. Simpson and W. S. Rholes (Eds.), *Attachment theory and close relationships* (pp. 46-76). Guilford Press.

Brown, B. (2013). *The power of vulnerability: Teachings on authenticity, connection, and courage* [Audiobook]. Sounds True.

Buber, M. (2012). *I and Thou: A translation with a prologue "I and You" and notes by Walter Kaufmann* (W. Kaufmann, Trans.). eBookIt.com. (Original German work published 1923)

Buckner, R. L., Andrews-Hanna, J. R., & Schacter, D. L. (2008). The brain's default network: Anatomy, function, and relevance to disease. In A. Kingstone & M. B. Miller (Eds.), *Annals of the New York Academy of Sciences, Vol. 1124: The year in cognitive neuroscience* (p. 1–38). Blackwell Publishing.

Burke, B. L., Martens, A., & Faucher, E. H. (2010). Two decades of Terror Management Theory: A meta-analysis of mortality salience research. *Personality and Social Psychology Review, 14*(2), 155-195.

Butler, J. (1990). *Gender trouble: Feminism and the subversion of identity*. Routledge.

Byron, G. G. B. B. (1875). Childe Harold's Pilgrimage. In *The poetical works of Lord Byron: With memoir, explanatory notes, etc.* (pp. 122-173). Frederick Warne & Company.

Cameron, J. (2016). *The artist's way: A spiritual path to higher creativity* (25th anniversary ed.). Penguin Random House.

Cameron, J. F. (Director). (1984). *The terminator* [Film]. Hemdale.

Cameron, J. F. (Director). (1991). *Terminator 2: Judgment day* [Film]. Carolco Pictures.

Campbell, J. (2008). *The hero with a thousand faces* (3rd ed.). New World Library. (Original work published 1949)

Campbell, J., & Moyers, B. (1991). *The power of myth* (B. S. Flowers, Ed.). Anchor Books.

Campbell, W. K., & Sedikides, C. (1999). Self-threat magnifies the self-serving bias: A meta-analytic integration. *Review of General Psychology, 3*(1), 23-43.

Camus, A. (1991). *The myth of Sisyphus, and other essays* (J. O'Brien, Trans.). Vintage Books. (Original work published 1942 [French] and 1955 [English trans.])

Capaldi, C. A., Dopko, R. L., & Zelenski, J. M. (2014). The relationship between nature connectedness and happiness: A meta-analysis. *Frontiers in Psychology, 5*, 976.

Capra, F. (Director). (1937). *Lost horizon* [Film]. Columbia.

Carbon Based Lifeforms, & Nanmark, E. (2017). Derelicts [Song]. On *Derelicts* [Album]. Leftfield Records.

Carhart-Harris, R. L., Kaelen, M., Whalley, M. G., Bolstridge, M., Feilding, A., & Nutt, D. J. (2015). LSD enhances suggestibility in healthy volunteers. *Psychopharmacology, 232*(4), 785-794.

Carhart-Harris, R. L., & Friston, K. J. (2010). The default-mode, ego-functions and free-energy: A neurobiological account of Freudian ideas. *Brain, 133*(4), 1265-1283.

Carlin, S. C., & Scheld, S. (2019). MAPS MDMA-assisted psychotherapy code of ethics. *MAPS Bulletin, 29*(1), 24-27.

Carter, C. (2010). *Science and the near-death experience: How consciousness survives death*. Inner Traditions.

Chalmers, D. J. (1995). Facing up to the problem of consciousness. *Journal of Consciousness Studies, 2*(3), 200-219.

Chatwin, B. (1988). *The songlines*. Penguin Books.

Cheremisinov, S. (2017). Seven lights [Song]. On *The signals* [Album]. Sergey Cheremisinov.

Chu, S. T-W., & Mak, W. W. S. (2020). How mindfulness enhances meaning in life: A meta-analysis of correlational studies and randomized controlled trials. *Mindfulness, 11*, 177-193.

Ciocca, G., Rossi, R., Collazzoni, A., Gorea, F., Vallaj, B., Stratta, P., Longo, L., Limoncin, E., Mollaioli, D., Gibertoni, D., Santarnecchi, E., Pacitti, F., Niolu, C., Siracusano, A., Jannini, E. A., & Di Lorenzo, G. (2020). The impact of attachment styles and defense mechanisms on psychological distress in a non-clinical young adult sample: A path analysis. *Journal of Affective Disorders, 273*, 384–390.

Ćirković, M. M. (2012). *The astrobiological landscape: Philosophical foundations of the study of cosmic life.* Cambridge University Press.

Cloitre, M., Cohen, L. R., Ortigo, K. M., Jackson, C. L., & Koenen, K. C. (2020). *Treating survivors of childhood abuse and interpersonal trauma: STAIR Narrative Therapy* (2nd edition). Guilford Press.

Coder, K. E. (2017). *After the ceremony ends: A companion guide to help you integrate visionary plant medicine experiences.* Shine Mojo, LLC.

Coen, E., & Coen, J. (2008). *Burn after reading* [Film]. Relativity Media.

Coogler, R. (Director). (2018). *Black Panther* [Film]. Marvel Studios.

Cooper, K. M. (2016). *Guide manual: Psilocybin-assisted therapy in the research setting.* Usona Institute.

Coppola, S. (Director). (2003). *Lost in translation* [Film]. American Zoetrope.

Costa, P. T., Jr., & McCrae, R. R. (1992). *NEO PI-R professional manual.* Psychological Assessment Resources.

Costello, M. J., May, R. M., & Stork, N. E. (2013). Can we name Earth's species before they go extinct?. *Science, 339*(6118), 413-416.

Csikszentmihalyi, M. (1975). Play and intrinsic rewards. *Journal of Humanistic Psychology, 15*(3), 41-63.

Csikszentmihalyi, M. (1991). *Flow: The psychology of optimal experience.* HarperPerennial.

Daher, Jr., J. C., Damiano, R. F., Lucchetti, A. L. G., Moreira-Almeida, A., & Lucchetti, G. (2017). Research on experiences related to the possibility of consciousness beyond the brain: A bibliometric analysis of global scientific output. *The Journal of Nervous and Mental Disease, 205*(1), 37-47.

Dalrymple, G. B. (1991). *Ancient Earth, ancient skies: The age of the earth and its cosmic surroundings.* Stanford University Press.

Darcey, S. (2021). *Sketch by sketch: A creative path to emotional healing and transformation.* St. Martin's Essentials.

Das, L. S. (2015). The Zen commandments. In A. Badiner & A. Grey (Eds.), *Zig zag Zen: Buddhism and psychedelics* (New ed., pp. 184-193). SynergeticPress.

Dass, R. (1971). *Be here now.* Lama Foundation.

Dass, R., & Bush, M. (2018). *Walking each other home: Conversations on loving and dying.* SoundsTrue.

Dass, R. & Das, R. (2013) *Polishing the mirror: How to live from your spiritual heart.* Sounds True, Inc.

Davies, R. A., Farrell, J. M., & Matthews, S. S. (1982). The dream world of film: A Jungian perspective on cinematic communication. *The Western Journal of Speech Communication, 46*(4), 326-343.

Davis, A. K., Barrett, F. S., & Griffiths, R. R. (2020). Psychological flexibility mediates the relations between acute psychedelic effects and subjective decreases in depression and anxiety. *Journal of Contextual Behavioral Science, 15*, 39-45.

Dazzi, T., Gribble, R., Wessely, S., & Fear, N. T. (2014). Does asking about suicide and related behaviours induce suicidal ideation? What is the evidence?. *Psychological Medicine, 44*(16), 3361–3363.

De Beauvoir, S. (1948). *The ethics of ambiguity* (B. Frechtman, Trans.). Citadel Press.

de Bruijn, A. (2019). From representation to participation: Rethinking the intercultural educational approach to folktales. *Children's Literature in Education, 50*, 315–332.

de Rezende-Pinto, A., Schumann, C. S. C., & Moreira-Almeida, A. (2019). Spirituality, religiousness and mental health: Scientific evidence. In G. Lucchetti, M. Fernando, & R. F. Damiano (Eds.), *Spirituality, Religiousness and Health: From research to clinical practice* (pp. 69-86). Springer.

de Waal, F. (2013). *The bonobo and the atheist: In search of humanism among the primates.* W. W. Norton & Company.

Dezelic, M. (2014). *Meaning-centered therapy workbook: Based on Viktor Frankl's logotherapy and existential analysis.* Presence Press International.

Dezelic, M. (2017). Meaning constructs and meaning-oriented techniques: Clinical applications of meaning and existential exploration. *Journal of Constructivist Psychology, 30*(1), 32-41.

Dember, G. (2018, April 17). *After postmodernism: Metamodern methods in the arts.* Medium.https://medium.com/what-is-metamodern/after-postmodernism-eleven-metamodern-methods-in-the-arts-767f7b646cae

Derrickson, S. (Director). (2016). *Doctor Strange* [Film]. Marvel Studios.

DeSteno, D. (2011, March 11). *The power of compassion as a moral force: Can compassion extinguish punishment?* Psychology Today. https://www.psychologytoday.com/us/blog/out-character/201103/the-power-compassion-moral-force

DeWall, C. N., & Baumeister, R. F. (2007). From terror to joy: Automatic tuning to positive affective information following mortality salience. *Psychological Science, 18*(11), 984-990.

Diamond, D. M. (2005). Cognitive, endocrine and mechanistic perspectives on non-linear relationships between arousal and brain function. *Nonlinearity in Biology, Toxicology, Medicine, 3*(1), 1–7.

Dickens, C. (1999). *A tale of two cities.* Dover Publications. (Original work published 1859)

Dictionary.com (n.d.). Awe. In *Dictionary.com online dictionary.* Retrieved October 13, 2020, from https://www.dictionary.com/browse/awe

Dictionary.com (n.d.). Meta. In *Dictionary.com pop culture dictionary.* Retrieved September 16, 2020, from https://www.dictionary.com/e/pop-culture/meta/

Didion, J. (2017). *Slouching towards Bethlehem: Essays.* Open Road Integrated Media. (Original work published 1968)

Diener, M. J., & Monroe, J. M. (2011). The relationship between adult attachment style and therapeutic alliance in individual psychotherapy: A meta-analytic review. *Psychotherapy, 48*(3), 237-248.

DiJulio, B., Hamel, L., Muñana, C., & Brodie, M. (2018, August). Loneliness and social isolation in the United States, the United Kingdom, and Japan: An international survey. *Kaiser Family Foundation.* http://files.kff.org/attachment/Report-Loneliness-and-Social-Isolation-in-the-United-States-the-United-Kingdom-and-Japan-An-International-Survey

Docter, P., (Director) & Del Carmen, R. (Co-Director). (2015). *Inside out* [Film]. Disney Pixar.

Donald, J. N., Bradshaw, E. L., Ryan, R. M., Basarkod, G., Ciarrochi, J., Duineveld, J. J., Guo, J., & Sahdra, B. K. (2020). Mindfulness and its association with varied types of motivation: A systematic review and meta-analysis using self-determination theory. *Personality and Social Psychology Bulletin, 46*(7), 1121-1138.

Druyan, A., McFarlane, S., Braga, B., & Cannold, M. (Executive Producers). (2014). *Cosmos: A spacetime odyssey* [TV series]. 21st Century Fox.

Druyan, A., McFarlane, S., Braga, B., & Clark, J. (Executive Producers). (2020). *Cosmos: Possible worlds* [TV series]. Cosmos Studios; Fuzzy Door Productions.

Du, J., & Cai, Y. (2020). Owning one's intellectual limitations: A review of intellectual humility. *Psychology, 11*(7), 1009-1020.

Dunning, D. (2011). The Dunning-Kruger effect: On being ignorant of one's own ignorance. In *Advances in experimental social psychology* (Vol. 44, pp. 247-296). Academic Press.

Eager exponent of Zen: Ex-Anglican priest spreads an Eastern philosophy in the U.S. (1961, April 21). *Life, 50*(16), 88-93.

Eden, A. H., Moor, J. H., Søraker, J. H., & Steinhart, E. (2012). *Singularity hypotheses: A scientific and philosophical assessment.* Springer.

Edinger, E. (1960). The ego-Self paradox. *Journal of Analytic Psychology, 5,* 3-18.

Edwards, G. (Director). (2014). *Godzilla* [Film]. Legendary Pictures; Warner Bros.

Ekman, P., & Friesen, W. V. (1969). The repertoire of nonverbal behavior—Categories, origins, usage and coding. *Semiotica, 1,* 49-98.

Ekman, P., & Friesen, W. (1971). Constants across cultures in the face and emotion. *Journal of Personality and Social Psychology, 17*(2), 124-129.

Emmerich, R. (Director). (1996). *Independence day* [Film]. Centropolis Entertainment.

Emmerich, R. (Director). (2009). *2012* [Film]. Centropolis Entertainment.

Erikson, E. H. (1968). *Identity: Youth and crisis.* W. W. Norton & Co.

Erikson, E. H. (1959). *Identity and the life cycle.* W. W. Norton & Co.

Erikson, E. H. (1982). *The life cycle completed.* W. W. Norton & Co.

Fadiman, J. (Ed.). (2011). *The psychedelic explorer's guide: Safe, therapeutic, sacred journeys.* Park Street Press.

Fadiman, J., & Gruber, J. (2020). *Your symphony of selves: Discover and understand more of who we are.* Park Street Press.

Favreau, J. (Director). (2019). *The Lion King.* Disney.

Feldman, C., & Kuyken, W. (2013). Compassion in the landscape of suffering. In J. M. G. Williams & J. Kabat-Zinn (Eds.), *Mindfulness: Diverse perspectives on its meaning, origins and applications* (pp. 143-155). Routledge. (Original work published 2011)

Ferguson, M. J., Hassin, R., & Bargh, J. A. (2008). Implicit motivation: Past, present, and future. In J. Y. Shah & W. L. Gardner (Eds.), *Handbook of motivation science* (p. 150–166). Guilford Press.

Fleming, V. (Director). (1939). *The wizard of oz* [Film]. Metro-Goldwyn-Mayer.

Florian, V., & Mikulincer, M. (1998). Symbolic immortality and the management of the terror of death. *Journal of Personality and Social Psychology, 74,* 725-734.

Forbes, D. L. (2011). Toward a unified model of human motivation. *Review of General Psychology, 15*(2), 85-98.

Foreman, R. K. C. (Ed.)(1990). *The problem of pure consciousness: Mysticism and philosophy.* Oxford University Press.

Fournier, M. A., Moskowitz, D. S., & Zuroff, D. C. (2011). Origins and applications of the interpersonal circumplex. In L. M. Horowitz & S. Strack (Eds.), *Handbook of interpersonal psychology: Theory, research, assessment and therapeutic interventions* (pp. 57-74). John Wiley & Sons.

Fothergill, A. (Producer). (2006). *Planet Earth* [TV series]. BBC.

Frankl, V. (1992). *Man's search for meaning: An introduction to logotherapy* (4th ed., I. Lasch, Trans.). Beacon Press.

Frausto da Silva, J. J. R., & Williams, R. J. P. (2001). The chemical elements in biology. *The biological chemistry of the elements: The inorganic chemistry of life* (2nd ed., pp. 7-28). Oxford University Press.

Fraley, R. C. (2002). Attachment stability from infancy to adulthood: Meta-analysis and dynamic modeling of developmental mechanisms. *Personality and Social Psychology Review, 6*(2), 123-151.

Fraley, R. C., & Shaver, P. R. (2008). Attachment theory and its place in contemporary personality theory and research. In O. P. John, R. W. Robins, & L. A. Pervin (Eds.), *Handbook of personality: Theory and research* (3rd ed.; pp. 518-541). Guilford Press.

Fraley, R. C., Spieker, S. J., Cummings, E. M., Cassidy, J., Sroufe, L. A., Waters, E., & Beauchaine, T. P. (2003). Are infant attachment patterns continuously or categorically distributed? A taxometric analysis of strange situation behavior. *Developmental Psychology, 39*(3), 387-404.

Fraley, R. C., Vicary, A. M., Brumbaugh, C. C., & Roisman, G. I. (2011). Patterns of stability in adult attachment: An empirical test of two models of continuity and change. *Journal of Personality and Social Psychology, 101*(5), 974-992.

Fraley, R. C., & Waller, N. G. (1998). Adult attachment patterns: A test of the typological model. In J. A. Simpson & W. S. Rholes (Eds.), *Attachment theory and close relationships* (pp. 77–114). Guilford Press.

Frenkel-Brunswik, F. (1949). Intolerance of ambiguity as an emotional and perceptual personality variable. *Journal of Personality, 18,* 108–143.

Freud, A. (1993). *The ego and the mechanisms of defence* (C. Baines, Trans.). Karnac Books. (Original German work published 1937)

Freud, S. (1989). *Introductory lectures on psycho- analysis* (Standard ed.; J. Strachey, Trans., Ed.). W. W. Norton & Company. (Original German work published 1917)

Freud, S. (1989). *New introductory lectures on psycho-analysis* (J. Strachey, Trans., Ed.). (Standard ed.). W. W. Norton & Company. (Original German work published 1933)

Fuller, B., Semel, D., Roddenberry, R., Roth, T., Goldsman, A., Kadin, H., Berg, G. J., Harberts, A., & Kurtzman, A. (Executive Producers). (2017-present). *Star trek discovery* [TV series]. Secret Hideout; Roddenberry Entertainment; Living Dead Guy Productions; CBS Television Studios.

Funder, D. C. (2008). Persons, situations, and person-situation interactions. In O. P. John, R. W. Robins, & L. A. Pervin (Eds.), *Handbook of personality: Theory and research* (3rd ed.; pp. 568-580). Guilford Press.

Furnham, A. (1996). The big five versus the big four: the relationship between the Myers-Briggs Type Indicator (MBTI) and NEO-PI five factor model of personality. *Personality and Individual Differences, 21*(2), 303-307.

Furnham, A., & Marks, J. (2013). Tolerance of ambiguity: A review of the recent literature. *Psychology, 4*(9), 717-728.

Future Problem Solving Program International. (n.d.). Retrieved September 15, 2020, from https: //www.fpspi.org

Galič, M., Timan, T., & Koops, B. J. (2017). Bentham, Deleuze and beyond: An overview of surveillance theories from the panopticon to participation. *Philosophy & Technology, 30*(1), 9-37.

Garland, A. (Director). (2014). *Ex machina* [Film]. Film4.

Garland, A. (Director). (2018). *Annihilation* [Film]. Skydance Media.

Garssen, B., Visser, A., & Pool, G. (2020). Does spirituality or religion positively affect mental health? Meta-analysis of longitudinal studies. *The International Journal for the Psychology of Religion*, 1-17.

Gensler, H. J. (2013). *Ethics and the golden rule*. Routledge

George, A. (Trans.). (2003). *The epic of Gilgamesh*. Penguin Classics.

Gernert, D. (2009). Ockham's razor and its improper use. *Cognitive Systems, 7*(2), 133-138.

Ghaed, S. G., & Gallo, L. C. (2006). Distinctions among agency, communion, and unmitigated agency and communion according to the interpersonal circumplex, five-factor model, and social-emotional correlates. *Journal of Personality Assessment, 86*(1), 77-88.

Gibbs, J. C., Basinger, K. S., Grime, R. L., & Snarey, J. R. (2007). Moral judgment development across cultures: Revisiting Kohlberg's universality claims. *Developmental Review, 27*(4), 443-500.

Gladwell, M. (2019). *Talking to strangers: What we should know about the people we don't know*. Little, Brown and Company.

Gleick, J. (2011). *Chaos: Making a new science* (Expanded ed.). Open Road Integrated Media.

Goldberg, L. R. (1992). The development of markers for the Big-Five factor structure. *Psychological Assessment, 4*(1), 26-42.

Goldschmidt, T. (Ed.). (2014). *The puzzle of existence: Why is there something rather than nothing?* Routledge.

Goldsmith, J. (1999). The cloud [Song]. On *Star trek: The motion picture–20th anniversary collector's edition soundtrack* [Album]. Columbia Records. (Original album 1979).

Gopnik, A. (2009). *The philosophical baby: What children's minds tell us about truth, love and the meaning of life*. Random House.

Goren-Inbar, N., Alperson, N., Kislev, M. E., Simchoni, O., Melamed, Y., Ben-Nun, A., & Werker, E. (2004). Evidence of hominin control of fire at Gesher Benot Ya'aqov, Israel. *Science, 304*, 725-727.

Granqvist, P., Mikulincer, M., & Shaver, P. R. (2010). Religion as attachment: Normative processes and individual differences. *Personality and Social Psychology Review, 14*(1), 49-59.

Gray, J. (Director). (2019). *Ad astra* [Film]. Regency Enterprises.

Greenberg, J., & Kosloff, S. (2008). Terror management theory: Implications for understanding prejudice, stereotyping, intergroup conflict, and political attitudes. *Social and Personality Psychology Compass, 2*(5), 1881-1894

Greenberg, J., Pyszczynski, T., & Solomon, S. (1986). The causes and consequences of a need for self-esteem: A terror management theory. In R. F. Baumeister (Ed.), *Public self and private self* (pp. 189-212). Springer-Verlag.

Greenberger, D., & Padesky, C. A. (2016). *Mind over mood: Change how you feel by changing the way you think* (2nd ed). Guildford Press.

Greene, B. (1999). *The elegant universe: Superstrings, hidden dimensions, and the quest for the ultimate theory*. W. W. Norton & Company.

Greene, B. (2005). *The fabric of the universe: Space, time, and the texture of reality*. Vintage Books.

Greenwald, A. G., Banaji, M. R., & Nosek, B. A. (2015). Statistically small effects of the Implicit Association Test can have societally large effects. *Journal of Personality and Social Psychology, 108*(4), 553–561.

Griffin, B. J., Purcell, N., Burkman, K., Litz, B. T., Bryan, C. J., Schmitz, M., Villierme, C., Walsh, J., & Maguen, S. (2019). Moral injury: An integrative review. *Journal of Traumatic Stress, 32*(3), 350-362.

Griffin, D. W., & Bartholomew, K. (1994). Models of the self and other: Fundamental dimensions underlying measures of adult attachment. *Journal of Personality and Social Psychology, 67*, 430–445

Griffiths, R. R., Hurwitz, E. S., Davis, A. K., Johnson, M W., & Jesse, B. (2019). Survey of subjective "God encounter experiences": Comparisons among naturally occurring experiences and those occasioned by the classic psychedelics psilocybin, LSD, ayahuasca, or DMT. *PLoS ONE, 14*(4), e0214377.

Griffiths, R. R., Johnson, M W., Carducci, M. A., Umbricht, A., Richards, W. A., Richards, B. D., Cosimano, M. P., & Klinedinst, M. A., (2016). Psilocybin produces substantial and sustained decreases in depression and anxiety in patients with life-threatening cancer: A randomized double-blind trial. *Journal of Psychopharmacology, 30*(12), 1181-1197.

Grob, C. S., Danforth, A. L., Chopra, G. S., Hagerty, M., McKay, C. R., Halberstadt, A. L., & Greer, G. R. (2011). Pilot study of psilocybin treatment for anxiety in patients with advanced-stage cancer. *Archives of General Psychiatry, 68*(1), 71-78.

Grof, S. (1975). *Realms of the human unconscious: Observations from LSD research*. The Viking Press.

Grof, S. (2008). *LSD psychotherapy*. MAPS. (Original work published 1980)

Grof, S. (2013). *Books of the dead: Manuals for living and dying* (J. Purce, Ed.). Thames & Hudson. (Original work published 1973)

Grof, S. (2019). *The way of the psychonaut: Encyclopedia for inner journeys* (Volumes 1 & 2). MAPS.

Grof, S., & Grof, C. (2010). *Holotropic breathwork: A new approach to self-exploration and therapy*. SUNY Press.

Grof, S., & Halifax, J. (1978). *The human encounter with death*. E. P. Dutton.

Guercio, M. B. (Writer), & McTeigue, J. (Director & Executive Producer). (2020, January 1). Trial (Season 1, Episode 4) [TV series episode]. In M. Petroni, M. Burnett, R. Downey, J. McTeigue, & A. Deane, (Executive Producers), *Messiah*. Think Pictures, Inc.; Industry Entertainment Partners; MGM Television.

Guggenbühl-Craig, A. (2015). *Power in the helping professions*

(M. Grubitz, Trans.). Spring Publications. (Original German work published 1971)

Haggerty, G., Hilsenroth, M. J. and Vala-Stewart, R. (2009). Attachment and interpersonal distress: Examining the relationship between attachment styles and interpersonal problems in a clinical population. *Clinical Psychology Psychotherapy*, 16(1), 1-9.

Hahn, T. N. (2016). *The miracle of mindfulness: An introduction to the practice of meditation* (M. Ho, Trans.). Beacon Press. (Original work published 1975)

Haidt, J. (2012). *The righteous mind: Why good people are divided by politics and religion*. Pantheon.

Haidt, J., & Morris, J. P. (2009). Finding the self in self-transcendent emotions. *Proceedings of the National Academy of Sciences*, 106(19), 7687-7688.

Halifax, J. (2008). *Being with dying: Cultivating compassion and fearlessness in the presence of death*. Shambhala.

Harmon, D., Roiland, J., Fino, J. A., Russo II, Jo., & McMahan, M. (Executive Producers). (2013- present). *Rick and Morty* [TV series]. Williams Street; Harmonious Claptrap; Starburns Industries; Justin Roiland's Solo Vanity Card Productions!; Rick and Morty, LLC.; Green Portal Productions.

Hart, M. H. (1975). An explanation for the absence of extraterrestrials on Earth. *The Quarterly Journal of the Royal Astronomical Society*, 16, 128–135

Hartogsohn, I. (2018). The meaning-enhancing properties of psychedelics and their mediator role in psychedelic therapy, spirituality, and creativity. *Frontiers in Neuroscience*, 12,129.

Hawkley, L., & Cacioppo, J. (2010). Loneliness matters: A theoretical and empirical review of consequences and mechanisms. *Annals of Behavioral Medicine*, 40, 218–227.

Hayes, S. C. (2012). Humanistic psychology and contextual behavioral perspectives. *Psychotherapy*, 49(4), 455-460.

Hayes, S. C., Law, S., Malady, M., Zhu, Z., & Bai, X. (2020). The centrality of sense of self in psychological flexibility processes: What the neurobiological and psychological correlates of psychedelics suggest. *Journal of Contextual Behavioral Science*, 15, 30-38.

Hayes, S. C., Strosahl, K. D., & Wilson, K. G. (2012). *Acceptance and Commitment Therapy: The process and practice of mindful change* (2nd ed). Guilford Press.

Hegel, G. W. F. (2018). *The phenomenology of spirit (The phenomenology of mind)* (J. B. Baillie, Trans.). LULU Press. (Original German work published 1807)

Henderson, J. L. (1990). Initiation as spiritual education. In J. L. Henderson & M. Oakes, *The wisdom of the serpent: The myths of death, rebirth, and resurrection* (pp. 41-59). Princeton University Press. (Original work published 1963)

Henderson, J. L., & M. Oakes (1990). *The wisdom of the serpent: The myths of death, rebirth, and resurrection*. Princeton University Press. (Original work published 1963)

Hendijani, R., Bischak, D. P., Arvai, J., & Dugar, S. (2016). Intrinsic motivation, external reward, and their effect on overall motivation and performance. *Human Performance*, 29(4), 251-274.

Henning-Smith, C., Moscovice I., & Kozhimannil, K. (2019). Differences in social isolation and its relationship to health by rurality. *The Journal of Rural Health*, 35(4), 540-549.

Henriques, G., & Görtz, D. (2020, April 17). *What is metamodernism? Metamodernism is the cultural code that comes after postmodernism*. PsychologyToday. https://www.psychologytoday.com/us/blog/theory-knowledge/202004/what-is-metamodernism

Henson, J., & Oz, F. (Directors). (1982). *The dark crystal* [Film]. Henson Associates.

Herzberg, G., Conour, K., Butler, J., Emerson, A., Gillooly, L. S., Gold, V., Hayes, M., Mix, L., & Sienknecht, E. (2019, December 18). *Towards an Ethos of Equity and Inclusion in the Psychedelic Movement*. Chacruna. https://chacruna.net/towards-an-ethos-of-equity-and-inclusion-in-the-psychedelic-movement/

Hill, S. J. (2013). *Confrontation with the unconscious: Jungian depth psychology and psychedelic experience*. Muswell Hill Press.

Hilton, J. (1990). *Lost horizon*. Reader's Digest Association. (Original work published 1933)

Hofmann, S. G., Grossman, P., & Hinton, D. E. (2011). Loving-kindness and compassion meditation: Potential for psychological interventions. *Clinical Psychology Review*, 31(7), 1126-1132.

Hogan, B. (2010). The presentation of self in the age of social media: Distinguishing performances and exhibitions online. *Bulletin of Science, Technology, & Society*, 30(6), 377-386.

Holland, J. (2001). *Ecstasy: The complete guide: A comprehensive look at the risk and benefits of MDMA*. Park Street Press.

Holland, J. (2020). *Good medicine: The science of connection, from soul to psychedelics*. HarperCollins.

Holt-Lunstad, J., Smith, T. B., Baker, M., Harris, T., & Stephenson, D. (2015). Loneliness and social isolation as risk factors for mortality: A meta-analytic review. *Perspectives on Psychological Science*, 10 (2), 227-237.

Honda, I. (Director). (1954). *Godzilla* [Film]. Toho.

Honeyborne, J., & Brownlow, M. (Executive Producers). (2017). *Blue planet II* [TV series]. BBC.

Hornaday, F. (2019, September 23). *Bamboo proverbs: 9 great quotes about bamboo*. Bambu Batu: The House of Bambu. https://bambubatu.com/bamboo-proverbs-great-quotes-about-bamboo/

Howe, D. W. (2007). *What hath God wrought: The transformation of America, 1815-1848*. Oxford University Press.

Hunt, M. G., Marx, R., Lipson, C., & Young, J. (2018). No more FOMO: Limiting social media decreases loneliness and depression. *Journal of Social and Clinical Psychology*, 37(10), 751-768.

Huntington Jr, C. W. (2015). The triumph of narcissism: Theravāda Buddhist meditation in the marketplace. *Journal of the American Academy of Religion*, 83(3), 624-648.

Hurd, G. A., Alpert, D., Kirkman, R., Eglee, C. H., Mazzara, G., Gimple, S. M., Nicotero, G., Luse, T., Incaprera, J., & Darabont, F. (Executive Producers). (2010-present). *The walking dead* [TV series]. AMC Studios; Idiot Box; Circle of Confusion; Skybound; Valhalla.

Huxley, A. (2004). *The perennial philosophy: An interpretation of the great mystics, East and West*. HarperCollins. (Original work published 1945)

Huxley, A. (2019). *Doors of perception* [eBook edition]. OTB eBook Publishing. (Original work published 1954)

Jach, H. K., & Smillie, L. D. (2019). To fear or fly to the unknown: Tolerance for ambiguity and Big Five personality traits. Journal of Research in Personality, 79, 67-78.

Jackson, P. (2002). *The lord of the rings: The fellowship of the ring* (Extended Ed.) [Film]. New Line Cinema.

Jackson, P. (2003). *The lord of the rings: The two towers* (Extended Ed.) [Film]. New Line Cinema.

Jackson, P. (2004). *The lord of the rings: The return of the king* (Extended Ed.) [Film]. New Line Cinema.

Jacobi, J. (1968). Symbols in an individual analysis. In C. G. Jung and A. Jaffé's (Eds.) *Man and his symbols* (pp. 323-374). Dell Publishing.

Jacobson, E. (1938). *Progressive relaxation: A physiological and clinical investigation of muscular states and their significance in psychology and medical practice* (2nd ed.). University of Chicago Press.

James, W. (1902). *The varieties of religious experience: A study in human nature.* Longmans, Green, and Co.

Jeunet, J. (Director). (1997). *Alien resurrection* [Film]. 20th Century Fox.

John, O. P., & Srivastava, S. (1999). The Big Five trait taxonomy: History, measurement, and theoretical perspectives. In L. A. Pervin & O. P. John (Eds.), *Handbook of personality: Theory and research* (2nd ed.; pp. 102-138). Guilford Press.

Johnson, R. (Director). (2017). *Star wars: Episode VIII–The last Jedi* [Film]. Lucasfilm Ltd.

Jones, D. N., & Paulhus, D. L. (2011). Differentiating the Dark Triad within the interpersonal circumplex. In L. M. Horowitz & S. Stack (Eds.), *Handbook of interpersonal psychology: Theory, research, assessment, and therapeutic interventions* (pp. 249-269). Wiley & Sons.

Jones, D. N., and Paulhus, D. L. (2014). Introducing the short Dark Triad (SD3): a brief measure of dark personality traits. *Assessment, 21,* 28–41.

Jones, J. D., Fraley, R. C., Ehrlich, K. B., Stern, J. A., Lejuez, C. W., Shaver, P. R., & Cassidy, J. (2018). Stability of attachment style in adolescence: An empiral test of alternative developmental processes. *Child Development, 89*(3), 871-880.

Jones, R. A. (1977). *Self-fulfilling prophecies: Social, psychological, and physiological effects of expectancies.* Lawrence Erlbaum Associates.

Jonze, S. (2013). *Her* [Film]. Annapurna Pictures.

Joshi, C., Marszalek, J. M., Berkel, L. A., & Hinshaw, A. B. (2014). An empirical investigation of Viktor Frankl's logotherapeutic model. *Journal of Humanistic Psychology, 54*(2), 227-253.

Judge, T. A., & Zapata, C. P. (2015). The person-situation debate revisited: Effect of situation strength and trait activation on the validity of the Big Five personality traits in predicting job performance. *Academy of Management Journal, 58*(4), 1149-1179.

Jung, C. G. (1967). The philosophical tree. In *Alchemical studies* (Collected works of C. G. Jung, Volume 13; H. Read, M. Fordham, G. Adler, & W. McGuire, Eds..; R.F.C. Hull, Trans.) (pp. 251-350). Princeton University Press. (Original German work published 1954)

Jung, C. G., & Jaffé, A. (Eds.). (1968). *Man and his symbols.* Dell Publishing.

Jung, C. G. (1968). Approaching the unconscious. In C. G. Jung and A. Jaffé's (Eds.) *Man and his symbols* (pp. 1-94). Dell Publishing.

Jung, C. G. (1969). *Synchronicity: An acausal connecting principle* (2nd ed.; R. F. C. Hull, Trans.). Princeton University Press.

Jung, C. G. (1970). *Mysterium coniunctionis: An inquiry into the separation and synthesis of psychic opposites in alchemy* (Collected works of C. G. Jung, Volume 14, 2nd ed.; G. Ad-

ler, Ed., & R. F. C. Hull, Trans.). Princeton University Press.

Jung, C. G. (1970). A review of the complex theory. In *The structure and dynamics of the psyche* (Collected works of C. G. Jung, Volume 8, 2nd ed.; G. Adler, Ed., & R.F.C. Hull, Trans.) (pp. 92-106). Princeton University Press. (Original German work published 1948)

Jung, C. G. (1976). *Psychological types* (Collected works of C. G. Jung, Volume 6, 3rd ed.; H. Read, M. Fordham, G. Adler, & W. McGuire, Eds.; R.F.C. Hull & H. G. Baynes, Trans.). Princeton University Press. (Original German work published 1921)

Jung, C. G. (1978). *Aion: Researches into the phenomenology of the Self* (Collected works of C. G. Jung, Volume 9, Part II, 2nd ed.; H. Read, M. Fordham, G. Adler, & W. McGuire, Eds.; R. F. C. Hull, Trans.). Princeton University Press. (Original German work published 1951).

Jung, C. G. (1980). A review of the complex theory. In *The archetypes and the collective unconscious* (Collected works of C. G. Jung, Volume 9, Part 1, 2nd ed; H. Read, M. Fordham, G. Adler, & W. McGuire, Eds..; R.F.C. Hull, Trans.) (pp. 42-53). Princeton University Press. (Original German work published 1937)

Jung, C. G. (1982). On the psychogenesis of Schizophrenia. In *The psychogenesis of mental disease* (Collected works of C. G. Jung, Volume 3; H. Read, M. Fordham, G. Adler, & W. McGuire, Eds..; R.F.C. Hull, Trans.) (pp. 42-53). Princeton University Press. (Original work published 1939)

Jung, C. G. (1984). *Dream analysis, Vol 1: Notes on the seminar given in 1928-1930* (W. McGuire, Ed.) Routledge.

Jung, C. G. (1989). *Memories, dreams, reflections* (A. Jaffe, Ed.; R. & C. Winston, Trans.). Random House, Inc. (Original German work published 1963)

Jung, C. G. (1990). The undiscovered self. In *The undiscovered self* with *Symbols and the interpretation of dreams* (Collected works of C. G. Jung, Volumes 10 & 18; R.F.C. Hull, Trans.) (pp. 1-61). Princeton University Press. (Original German work published 1957)

Jung, C. G. (1997). *Visions, Vol. 2: Notes of the Seminar Given in 1930-1934* (C. Douglas, Ed.). Princeton University Press.

Jung, C. G. (2009). *The red book: Liber novus* (S. Shamdasani, Ed., Trans., M. Kyburz, Trans., J. Peck, Trans.). W. W. Norton & Company.

Jung, C. G. (2014). *Modern man in search of a soul* (W. S. Dell & C. F. Baynes, Trans.). Routledge. (Original work published 1933)

Jung, C. G. (1981). The development of personality. In *Development of personality* (Collected works of C. G. Jung, Volume 17, 3rd ed.; R. F. C. Hull, Trans.) Princeton University Press. (Original German work published 1934)

Jungaberle, H., Thal, S., Zeuch, A., Rougemont-Bücking, A., von Heyden, M., Aicher, H., & Scheidegger, M. (2018). Positive psychology in the investigation of psychedelics and entactogens: A critical review. *Neuropharmacology, 142,* 179-199.

Jussim, L. (1986). Self-fulfilling prophecies: A theoretical and integrative review. *Psychological Review, 93*(4), 429.

Kabat-Zinn, J. (2003). Mindfulness-based interventions in context: Past, present, and future. *Clinical Psychology: Science and Practice, 10*(2), 144-156.

Kabat-Zinn, J. (2011). Some reflections on the origins of MBSR, skillful means, and the trouble with maps. *Contemporary Buddhism, 12*(1), 281-306.

Kashdan, T. B., DeWall, C. N., Schurtz, D. R., Deckman, T., Lykins, E. L. B., Evans, D. R., McKenzie, J., Segerstrom, S. C., Gailliot, M. T., & Brown, K. W. (2014). More than words: Contemplating death enhances positive emotional word use. *Personality and Individual Differences, 71*, 171-175.

Kaufman, S. B. (2020a). *Self-actualization tests*. Scott Barry Kaufman (SBK). https://scottbarry kaufman.com/selfactualizationtests/

Kaufman, S. B. (2020b). *Transcend: The new science of self-actualization*. TarcherPerigee.

Kaufman, S. B., Quilty, L. C., Grazioplene, R. G., Hirsh, J. B., Gray, J. R., Peterson, J. B., & DeYoung, C. G. (2016). Openness to experience and intellect differentially predict creative achievement in the arts and sciences. *Journal of Personality, 84*(2), 248-258.

Kaufman, S. B., Yaden, D. B., Hyde, E., & Tsukayama, E. (2019). The light vs. dark triad of personality: Contrasting two very different profiles of human nature. *Frontiers in Psychology, 10*, 467.

Keinan, G. (1994). Effects of stress and tolerance of ambiguity on magical thinking. *Journal of Personality and Social Psychology, 67*(1), 48–55.

Kelley, J. L. (2020). Outline for a future psychiatry: the transcendent meaning model (TMM). *International Review of Psychiatry*, 1-10.

Kershner, P. (Director). (1980). *Star wars: Episode V–The empire strikes back* [Film]. Lucasfilm Ltd.

Kesebir, P., & Pyszczynski, T. (2012). The role of death in life: Existential aspects of human motivation. In R. M. Ryan (Ed.), *The Oxford handbook of human motivation* (p. 43–64). Oxford University Press.

Khanna, P. (1969). A critique of existential guilt. *Psychotherapy: Theory, Research & Practice, 6*(3), 209-211.

Kierkegaard, S. (2019). Fear and trembling. In *The Kierkegaard collection* (p.10-128) [ebook edition]. Blackmore Dennette. (Original Danish work published 1843)

Kierkegaard, S. (2019). The sickness unto death. In *The Kierkegaard collection* (p. 408-536) [ebook edition]. Blackmore Dennette. (Original Danish work published 1849)

Kilpatrick, D. G., Resnick, H. S., Milanak, M. E., Miller, M. W., Keyes, K. M., & Friedman, M. J. (2013). National estimates of exposure to traumatic events and PTSD prevalence using *DSM-IV* and *DSM-5* criteria. *Journal of Traumatic Stress, 26*(5), 537-547.

Kim, A. (Writer), & Kelly, B. J. (Director). (2020, August 27). Moist vessel (Season 1, Episode 4) [TV series episode]. In A. Kurtzman, H. Kadin, R. Roddenberry, T. Roth, K. Krentz, & M. McMahan (Executive Producers), *Star trek: Lower Decks*. CBS Eye Animation Productions; Secret Hideout; Important Science; Roddenberry Entertainment; Titmouse, Inc.

Klimstra, T. Jeronimus, B. F., Sijtsema, J. J., & Denissen, J. J. A. (2020). The unfolding dark side: Age trends in dark personality features. *Journal of Research in Personality, 85*, 103915.

Knowles, E. (Ed.)(2007). *Oxford dictionary of modern quotations* (3rd ed.). Oxford University Press.

Koch, C. (2018). What is consciousness? Scientists are beginning to unravel a mystery that has long vexed philosophers. *Nature, 557*, S8-S12.

Koch, C., Massimini, M., Boly, M., & Tononi, G. (2016). Neural correlates of consciousness: Progress and problems. *Nature Reviews Neuroscience, 17*, 307–321.

Kohlberg, L. (1981). *The philosophy of moral development: Moral stages and the idea of justice (Essays on moral development, Vol1)*. Harper & Row.

Kohlberg, L. (1984). *The psychology of moral development: The nature and validity of moral stages (Essays on moral development, Vol 2)*. Harper & Row.

Köllner, M. G., & Schultheiss, O.C. (2014). Meta- analytic evidence of low convergence between implicit and explicit measures of the needs for achievement, affiliation, and power. *Frontiers in Psychology, 5*(826), 1-20.

Koenig, J. (n.d.). Sonder. In *The dictionary of obscure sorrows*. https://www.dictionaryofobscuresorrows.com/post/23536922667/sonder

Konner, J., & Perlmutter, A. H. (Producers). (1988). *Joseph Campbell and the power of myth* [TV series]. Apostrophe S.

Kornfield, J. (1993). *A path with heart: A guide through the perils and promises of spiritual life*. Bantham.

Kraehenmann R. (2017). Dreams and psychedelics: Neurophenomenological comparison and therapeutic implications. *Current Neuropharmacology, 15*(7), 1032–1042.

Krauss, L. M. (2012). A universe from nothing: Why there is something rather than nothing. Free Press.

Krpan, D. (2020). Unburdening the shoulders of giants: A quest for disconnected academic psychology. *Perspectives on Psychological Science, 15*(4), 1042-1053.

Kruger, J., & Dunning, D. (1999). Unskilled and unaware of it: how difficulties in recognizing one's own incompetence lead to inflated self-assessments. *Journal of Personality and Social Psychology, 77*(6), 1121-1134.

Kubrick, S. (Director). (1968). *2001: A space odyssey* [Film]. Stanley Kubrick Productions.

Kurtz, R. (2007). *Body-centered psychotherapy: The Hakomi method: The integrated use of mindfulness, nonviolence, and the body* (2nd ed.). LifeRhythm.

Kurtzman, A., Kadin, H., Roddenberry, R., Roth, T., Krentz, K., & McMahan, M. (Executive Producers). (2020-present). *Star trek: Lower decks* [TV series]. CBS Eye Animation Productions; Secret Hideout; Important Science; Roddenberry Entertainment; Titmouse, Inc.

Labate, B. C., & Cavnar, C. (Eds.). (2014). *Ayahuasca shamanism in the Amazon and beyond*. Oxford University Press.

Laczkovics, C., Fonzo, G., Bendixsen, B., Shpigel, E., Lee, I., Skala, K., Prunas, A., Gross, J., Steiner, H., & Huemer, J.(2020). Defense mechanism is predicted by attachment and mediates the maladaptive influence of insecure attachment on adolescent mental health. *Current Psychology, 39*, 1388-1396.

Lao Tsu. (1997). *The Tao te Ching: 25th Anniversary Edition* (G. Feng & J. English, Trans.). Vintage Books. (Original translation published in 1972)

Lattin, D. (2017). *Changing our minds: Psychedelic sacraments and the new psychotherapy*. SynergeticPress.

Leary, T. (1957). *Interpersonal diagnosis of personality: A functional theory and methodology for personality evaluation*. Ronald Press.

Leary, T. (1995). *High priest* (New ed.). Ronin.

Leary, T., Metzner, R., & Alpert, R. (2007). *The psychedelic experience: A manual based on the Tibetan book of the dead*. Citadel Press. (Original work published 1964)

Leighton, T. D. (2012). *Faces of compassion: Classic Bodhisattva* archetypes and their modern expression: An introduction to Mahayana Buddhism (Revised ed.). Wisdom Publications.

Leong, K. S. (2001). *The Zen teachings of Jesus (Revised and Expanded Ed.)*. Crossroad.

Lerner, M., & Lyvers, M. (2006). Values and beliefs of psychedelic drug users: A cross-cultural study. *Journal of Psychoactive Drugs*, 38(2), 143-147.

Letcher, A. (2007). Mad thoughts on mushrooms: Discourse and power in the study of psychedelic consciousness. *Anthropology of Consciousness*, 18(2), 74-97.

Letheby, C. (2015). The philosophy of psychedelic transformation. *Journal of Consciousness Studies*, 22(9-10), 170-193.

Letheby, C. (2017). Naturalizing psychedelic spirituality. *Zygon*, 52(3), 623-642.

Letheby, C., & Gerrans, P. (2017). Self unbound: Ego dissolution in psychedelic experience. *Neuroscience of Consciousness*, 3(1), 1-11.

Levine, P. A., & Frederick, A. (1997). *Walking the tiger: Traumatic healing*. North Atlantic Books.

Lilienfeld, S. O., Watts, A. L., & Smith, S. F. (2015). Successful psychopathy: A scientific status report. *Current Directions in Psychological Science*, 24(4), 298-303.

Lindelof, D., Spezialy, T., Kassell, N., Williams, S., & Iberti, J. E. (Executive Producers). (2009). *Watchmen* [TV series]. White Rabbit; Paramount; DC Entertainment; Warner Bros.

Linehan, M. M. (2015). *DBT skills training manual* (2nd ed). Guilford Press.

Linklater, R. (Director). (2006). *A scanner darkly* [Film]. Thousand Words.

Liotti, G. (2004). Trauma, dissociation, and disorganized attachment: Three strands of a single braid. *Psychotherapy: Theory, Research, Practice, Training*, 11(4), 472-486.

Lucas, G. (Director). (1977). *Star wars: Episode IV–A new hope* [Film]. Lucasfilm Ltd.

Lucas, G. (Director). (1999). *Star wars: Episode I–The phantom menace* [Film]. Lucasfilm Ltd.

Lucas, G. (Director). (2002). *Star wars: Episode II–Attack of the clones* [Film]. Lucasfilm Ltd.

Lucas, G. (Director). (2005). *Star wars: Episode III–Revenge of the Sith* [Film]. Lucasfilm Ltd.

Luoma, J. B., Sabucedo, P., Eriksson, J., Gates, N., & Pilecki, B. C. (2019). Toward a contextual psychedelic-assisted therapy: perspectives from acceptance and commitment therapy and contextual behavioral science. *Journal of Contextual Behavioral Science*, 14, 136-145.

Ly, C., Greb, A. C., Cameron, L. P., Wong, J. M., Barragan, E. V., Wilson, P. C., ...& Duim, W. C. (2018). Psychedelics promote structural and functional neural plasticity. *Cell Reports*, 23(11), 3170-3182.

Machine Elf 1735. (2011). *Plutchik's wheel of emotions*. From Wikipedia.org https://en.wikipedia.org/wiki/Robert_Plutchik#/media/File:Plutchik-wheel.svg

MacLean, K. A., Johnson, M. W., & Griffiths, R. R. (2011). Mystical experiences occasioned by the hallucinogen psilocybin lead to increases in the personality domain of openness. *Journal of Psychopharmacology*, 25(11), 1453-1461.

MacLean, K. A., Leoutsakos, J. S., Johnson, M. W., & Griffiths, R. R. (2012). Factor analysis of the Mystical Experience Questionnaire: A study of experiences occasioned by the hallucinogen psilocybin. *Journal for the Scientific Study of Religion*, 51(4), 721-737.

Macy, J. (1993). Schooling our intention: A talk by Joanna Macy. *Tricycle: The Buddhist Review*, 3(2), 48-51.

Main, M., & Solomon, J. (1986). Discovery of an insecure-disorganized/disoriented attachment pattern. In T. B. Brazelton & M. W. Yogman (Eds.), *Affective development in infancy* (pp. 95-124). Ablex Publishing.

Malick, T. (Director). (2011). *The tree of life* [Film]. River Road Entertainment.

Marcia, J. E. (1966). Development and validation of ego identity status. *Journal of Personality and Social Psychology*, 3, 551–558.

Marcia, J. E., Waterman, A. S., Matteson, D. R., Archer, S. L., & Orlofsky, J. L. (1993). *Ego identity: A handbook for psychosocial research*. Springer-Verlag.

Marquand, R. (Director). (1983). *Star wars: Episode VI–Return of the Jedi* [Film]. Lucasfilm Ltd.

Marra, M. F. (Ed., Trans.). (2007). *The poetics of Motoori Norinanga: A hermeneutical journey*. University of Hawai'i Press.

Martial, C., Cassol, H., Charland-Verville, V., Pallavicini, C., Sanz, C., Zamberlan, F., Vivot, R. M., Erowid, F., Erowid, E., Laureys, S., Greyson, B., & Tagliazucchi, E. (2019). Neurochemical models of near-death experiences: A large-scale study based on the semantic similarity of written reports. *Consciousness and Cognition*, 69, 52-69.

Maslow A. H. (1943). A theory of human motivation. *Psychological Review*, 50(4), 370-396.

Maslow, A. H. (1966). *The psychology of science: A reconnaissance*. Harper & Row.

Maslow, A. H. (1993). *The farther reaches of human nature*. Arkana. (Original work published 1971)

Maslow, A. (1998). *Toward a psychology of being* (3rd ed.). Wiley.

Matthiessen, P. (2015). Shadow paths. In A. Badiner & A. Grey (Eds.), *Zig zag Zen: Buddhism and psychedelics* (New ed., pp. 73-76). Synergetic Press.

May, R. (1983). *The discovery of being*. W. W. Norton & Company.

May, R. (1991). *The cry for myth*. W. W. Norton & Company.

May, R. (1994). *The courage to create*. W. W. Norton & Company. (Original work published 1975)

McClelland, D. C., Koestner, R., and Weinberger, J. (1989). How do self-attributed and implicit motives differ? *Psychological Review*, 96, 690–702

McCrae, R. R., & Costa, Jr, P. T. (2008). The five- factor theory of personality. In O. P. John, R. W. Robins, & L. A. Pervin, *Handbook of personality: Theory and research* (3rd ed.) (pp. 159-181). Guilford Press.

McCrae, R. R., & John, O. P. (1992). An introduction to the Five-Factor Model and its applications. *Journal of Personality*, 60(2), 175-215.

McDowell, C. (Director). (2017). *The discovery* [Film]. Endgame Entertainment.

McG. (Director). (2009). *Terminator salvation* [Film]. Columbia Pictures.

McIntosh, R. D., Fowler, E. A., Lyu, T., & Della Sala, S. (2019). Wise up: Clarifying the role of metacognition in the Dunning-Kruger effect. *Journal of Experimental Psychology: General*, 148(11), 1882–1897.

McKenna, T. (1992). *Food of the gods: The search for the original tree of knowledge: A radical history of plants, drugs and human evolution*. Bantam.

Melfi, T. (Director). (2016). *Hidden figures* [Film]. Levantine Films.

Merleau-Ponty, M. (1962). *Phenomenology of perception* (C. Smith, Trans.). Routledge & Kegan Paul.

Metzner, R. (2015). A new look at the psychedelic *Tibetan book of the dead*. In A. Badiner & A. Grey (Eds.), *Zig zag Zen: Buddhism and psychedelics* (New ed., pp. 9-18). Synergetic Press.

Metzner, R. (2017). *Ecology of consciousness: The alchemy of personal, collective, and planetary transformation*. Reveal Press.

Miceli, M., & Castelfranchi, C. (2018). Reconsidering the differences between shame and guilt. *Europe's Journal of Psychology, 14*(3), 710-733.

Mikulincer, M., & Florian, V. (2000). Exploring individual differences in reactions to mortality salience: Does attachment style regulate terror management mechanisms? *Journal of Personality and Social Psychology, 79*, 260-273.

Mikulincer, M., & Shaver, P. R. (2016). *Attachment in adulthood: Structure, dynamics, and change* (2nd ed.). Guilford Press.

Miller, J. D., Vize, C., Crowe, M. L., & Lynam, D. R. (2019). A critical appraisal of the dark-triad literature and suggestions for moving forward. *Current Directions in Psychological Science, 28*(4), 353-360.

Miller, T. (Director). (2019). *Terminator: Dark fate* [Film]. Paramount Pictures.

Mills, J. (2013). Jung's metaphysics. *International Journal of Jungian Studies, 5*(1), 19-43.

Mischel, W., & Shoda, Y. (2008). Toward a unified theory of personality: Integrating dispositions and processing dynamics within the cognitive-affective processing system. In O. P. John, R. W. Robins, & L. A. Pervin (Eds.), *Handbook of personality: Theory and research* (3rd ed.; pp. 208-241). Guilford Press.

Mithoefer, M. (2017). *A manual for MDMA-assisted psychotherapy in the treatment of posttraumatic stress disorder* (Vers. 8.1). Multidisciplinary Association for Psychedelic Studies.

Moreman, C. M. (2018) *Beyond the threshold: Afterlife beliefs and experiences in world religions*. Rowman & Littlefield.

Moshfegh, O. (2016, July 6). *Coyotes, the ultimate American tricksters*. The New Yorker. https://www.newyorker.com/culture/culture-desk/coyotes-the-ultimate-american-tricksters/amp

Mostow, J. (Director). (1991). *Terminator 3: Rise of the machines* [Film]. Columbia Pictures.

Motta, M., Callaghan, T., & Sylvester, S. (2018). Knowing less but presuming more: Dunning- Kruger effects and the endorsement of anti-vaccine policy attitudes. *Social Science & Medicine, 211*, 274-281.

Muraresku, B. C. (2020). *The immortality key: The secret history of the religion with no name*. St. Marti"s Publishing Group.

Murdock, M. (2020). *The heroine's journey: Woman's quest for wholeness* (30th Anniversary ed.). Shambhala.

Muschietti, A. (Director). (2017). *It: Chapter one* [Film]. New Line Cinema.

Myers, I. B., McCaulley, M. H., Quenk, N. L., & Hammer, A. L. (1998). *MBTI manual: A guide to the development and use of the Myers-Briggs Type Indicator* (3rd ed.). Consulting Psychologists Press.

Nakamura, J., & Csikszentmihalyi, M. (2011). Flow theory and research. In S. J. Lopez & C. R. Snyder (Eds.), *The Oxford handbook of positive psychology* (pp. 195-206). Oxford University Press.

National Aeronautics and Space Administration (NASA). (n.d.). *NASA.gov*. https://www.nasa.gov

National Aeronautics and Space Administration (NASA). (2019, January 16). *Hypothetical Planet X*. https://solarsystem.nasa.gov/planets/hypothetical-planet-x/in-depth/

National Center for PTSD. (n.d.). *VA Mobile Apps*. National Center for PTSD. Retrieved November 30, 2020, from https://www.ptsd.va.gov/appvid/mobile/index.asp

Neff, Kristin, Ph.D. (2011). *Self-compassion: The proven power of being kind to yourself*. William Morrow.

Nielson, E. M., & Guss, J. (2018). The influence of therapists' first-hand experience with psychedelics on psychedelic-assisted psychotherapy research and therapist training. *Journal of Psychedelic Studies, 2*(2), 64-73.

Nietzsche, F. (2003). *The twilight of the idols* and *The Anti-Christ* (R. J. Hollingdale, Trans.). Penguin Books. (Original German work published 1889 & 1895)

Noé, G. (Director). (2009). *Enter the void* [Film]. Fidélité Productions.

Nolan, C. (Director). (2008). *The dark knight* [Film]. Warner Bros.

Nolan, C. (Director). (2010). *Inception* [Film]. Legendary Pictures.

Nolan, C. (Director). (2014). *Interstellar* [Film]. Legendary Pictures.

Nomura, Y. (2017). The quantum multiverse. *Scientific American, 316*(6), 28-35.

Norcross, J. C., & Lambert, M. J. (Eds.). (2019). *Psychotherapy relationships that work, Volume 1: Evidence-based therapist contributions* (3rd ed.). Oxford University Press.

Nour, M. M., Evans, L., & Carhart-Harris, R. L. (2017). Psychedelics, personality and political perspectives. *Journal of Psychoactive Drugs, 49*(3), 182-191.

Oh, I.-S., Wang, G., & Mount, M. K. (2011). Validity of observer ratings of the Five-Factor Model of personality traits: A meta-analysis. *Journal of Applied Psychology, 96*(4), 762–773.

Olendzki, A. (2013). The construction of mindfulness. In J. M. G. Williams & J. Kabat-Zinn (Eds.), *Mindfulness: Diverse perspectives on its meaning, origins and applications* (pp. 55-70). Routledge. (Original work published 2011)

Oliver, M. B., Raney, A. A., Slaxter, M. D., Appel, M., Hartmann, T., Bartsch, A., ... & Vorderer, P. (2018). Self-transcendent media experiences: Taking meaningful media to a higher level. *Journal of Communication, 68*(2), 380-389.

O'Neill, T. (2019). *Chaos: Charles Manson, the CIA, and the secret history of the sixties*. Little, Brown and Company.

Open-Source Psychometrics Project. (n.d.). *Open-source psychometrics project*. https://openpsychometrics.org

Orlowski, J. (Director). (2020). *The social dilemma* [Film]. Exposure Labs; Argent Pictures; The Space Program; Netflix.

Ortigo, K. M. (2007). "I'm a stranger here myself:" Forced individuation in *Alien Resurrection. Journal of Religion and Popular Culture, 17*, para. 1-67.

Ortigo, K. M., Westen, D., DeFife, J., & Bradley, B. (2013). Attachment, social cognition, and posttraumatic stress symptoms in a traumatized, urban population: Evidence for the mediating role of object relations. *Journal of Traumatic Stress, 26*, 361–368.

Osabiya, B. J. (2015). The effect of employees' motivation on organizational performance. *Journal of Public Administration and Policy Research, 7*(4), 62–75.

Osmond, H. (1957). A review of the clinical effects of psychotomimetic agents. *Annals of the New York Academy of Science, 66*(3), 418–434.

Oswald, F. L., Mitchell, G., Blanton, H., Jaccard, J., & Tetlock, P. E. (2013). Predicting ethnic and racial discrimination: A meta-analysis of IAT criterion studies. *Journal of Personality and Social Psychology, 105*(2), 171–192.

Ott. (2003). Smoked glass and chrome [Song]. In *Blumenkraft* [Album]. Ottsonic.

OxfordLanguages. (n.d.). Narrow. In *OxfordLanguages.com English dictionary*. Retrieved September 14, 2020 from https://languages.oup.com/google-dictionary-en/

Oyserman, D. (2004). Self-concept and identity. In M. B. Brewer & M. Hewstone (Eds.), *Perspectives on social psychology: Self and social identity* (p. 5–24). Blackwell Publishing.

Pagels, E. (2003). *Beyond belief: The secret Gospel of Thomas*. Vintage Books.

Pahnke, W. (1969). The psychedelic mystical experience in the human encounter with death. *Harvard Theological Review, 62*(1), 1-21.

Pahnke, W. N., & Richards, W. A. (1966). Implications of LSD and experimental mysticism. *Journal of Religion and Health, 5*(3), 175-208.

Paulhus, D. L., & Williams, K. M. (2002). The dark triad of personality: Narcissism, Machiavellianism, and psychopathy. *Journal of Research in Personality, 36*, 556-563.

Pearce, B. K. D., Tupper, A. S., Pudritz, R. E., & Higgs, P. G. (2018). Constraining the time interval for the origin of life on earth. *Astrobiology, 18*(3), 343-364.

Peck, D. (Director). (2017). *Ram Dass, Going home* [Film]. Further Pictures.

Peele, J. (2019). *Us* [Film]. Monkeypaw.

Peoples, K. M. (2000). Why the self is, and is not, empty: Trauma and transcendence in the postmodern psyche. In E. Spezzano & C. Spezzano (Eds.), *Psychoanalysis at its limits: Navigating the postmodern turn* (pp 239-269). Free Association Books.

Peterson, C., & Seligman, M. E. (2004). *Character strengths and virtues: A handbook and classification* (Vol. 1). Oxford University Press.

Phelps, J. (2017). Developing guidelines and competencies for the training of psychedelic therapists. *Journal of Humanistic Psychology, 57*(5), 450-487.

Phillips, T. (Director). (2019). *Joker* [Film]. Warner Bros.

Pink Floyd. (2014). *The endless river* [Album]. Columbia Records.

Pink Floyd. (2016). *The dark side of the moon* [Album]. Pink Floyd Music Ltd. (Original album 1973)

Pink Floyd. (2016). *Wish you were here* [Album]. Pink Floyd Music Ltd. (Original album 1975)

Pink Floyd. (2016). *The wall* [Album]. Pink Floyd Music Ltd. (Original album 1979)

Pinquart, M. (2002). Creating and maintaining purpose in life in old age: A meta-analysis. *Ageing International, 27*(2), 90-114.

Planck Collaboration. (2016). Planck 2015 results: XIV. Dark energy and modified gravity. *Astronomy & Astrophysics, 594*(A14), 1-31.

Planck Collaboration. (2020). Planck 2018 results: VI. Cosmological parameters. *Astronomy & Astrophysics, 641*(A6), 1-67.

Plutchik, R. (1980). *Emotion: A psychoevolutionary synthesis*. Harper & Row.

Plutchik, R. (1994). *The psychology and biology of emotion*. HarperCollins.

Plutchik, R. E., & Conte, H. R. (Eds.). (1997). *Circumplex models of personality and emotions*. American Psychological Association.

Pollan, M. (2018). *How to change your mind: What the new science of psychedelics teaches us about consciousness, dying, addiction, depression, and transcendence*. Penguin Books.

Ponsoldt, J. (Director). (2017). *The circle* [Film]. Image Nation Abu Dhabi.

Pont, D. V., & Schäfer, L. (2013). Carl Gustav Jung, quantum physics and the spiritual mind: A mystical vision of the twenty-first century. *Behavioral Science, 3*, 601-618.

Popper, K. (1959). *The logic of scientific discovery*. Hutchinson & Co. (Original German work published 1934)

Posner, J., Russell, J. A., & Peterson, B. S. (2005). The circumplex model of affect: An integrated approach to affective neuroscience, cognitive development, and psychopathology. *Developmental Psychopathology, 17*(3), 715-734.

Presti, D. E. (2016). *Foundational concepts in neuroscience: A brain-mind odyssey*. W.W. Norton & Company.

Presti, D. E. (Ed.) (2018). *Mind beyond brain: Buddhism, science, and the paranormal*. Columbia University Press.

Presti, D. E. (2019). A memorial tribute to Ralph Metzner: Scholar, teacher, shaman (18 May 1936 to 14 March 2019). *The Journal of Transpersonal Psychology, 51*(1), 1-5.

Primack, B. A., Karim, S. A., Shensa, A., Bowman, N., Knight, J., & Sidani, J. E. (2019). Positive and negative experiences on social media and perceived social isolation. *American Journal of Health Promotion, 33*(6), 859-868.

Primack, B. A., Shensa, A., Sidani, J. E., Whaite, E. O., yi Lin, L., Rosen, D., Colditz, J. B., Radovic, A., & Miller, E. (2017). Social media use and perceived social isolation among young adults in the US. *American Journal of Preventive Medicine, 53*(1), 1-8.

Prochazkova, L., Lippelt, D. P., Colzato, L. S., Kuchar, M., Sjoerds, Z., & Hommel, B. (2018). Exploring the effect of microdosing psychedelics on creativity in an open-label natural setting. *Psychopharmacology, 235*(12), 3401-3413.

Puccio, G. J. (2014). *The creative thinker's toolkit* [Audiobook]. Teaching Company.

Putnam, R. D. (2000). *Bowling alone: The collapse and revival of American community*. Simon and Schuster.

Randall, L. (2018). What is dark matter? An elusive substance that permeates the universe exerts many detectable gravitational influences yet eludes direct detection. *Nature, 557*, S6-S7.

Rands, C. M., Meader, S., Ponting, C. P., & Lunter, G. (2014). 8.2% of the human genome Is constrained: Variation in rates of turnover across functional element classes in the human lineage. *PLOS Genetics, 10*(7): e1004525.

Rawls, J. (1999). *A theory of justice* (Revised ed.). Harvard University Press.

Reiff, C. M., Richman, E. E., Nemeroff, C. B., Carpenter, L.,

Widge, A. S., Rodriguez, C. I., Kalin, N. H., & McDonald, W. M. (2020). Psychedelics and psychedelic-assisted psychotherapy: Clinical implications. *American Journal of Psychiatry, 177*(5), 391-410.

Reker, G. T., & Woo, L. C. (2011). Personal meaning orientations and psychosocial adaptation in older adults. *Sage Open, 1*(1), 1-10.

Resick, P. A., Monson, C. M., & Chard, K. M. (2017). *Cognitive processing therapy for PTSD: A comprehensive manual.* Guildford Press.

Richards, B. (2015). *Sacred knowledge: Psychedelics and religious experiences.* Columbia University Press.

Rickles, D., Hawe, P., & Shiell, A. (2007). A simple guide to chaos and complexity. *Journal of Epidemiology & Community Health, 61*(11), 933-937.

Ridley, R. (Writer), & Meza-León, J. (Director). (2017, August 27). "The Whirly Dirly Conspiracy" (Season 3, Episode 5) [TV series episode]. In D. Harmon & J. Roiland (Executive Producers), *Rick and Morty* [TV series]. Williams Street; Harmonious Claptrap; Justin Roiland's Solo Vanity Card Productions!; Rick and Morty, LLC.

Rifkin, B. D., Maraver, M. J., & Colzato, L. S. (2020). Microdosing psychedelics as cognitive and emotional enhancers. *Psychology of Consciousness: Theory, Research, and Practice, 7*(3), 316–329.

Rilke, R. M. (1980). *I am too alone in the world: Ten poems* (R. Bly, Trans.). Silver Hands Press. (Original German work published 1905)

Rilke, R. M. (2005). *Rilke's Book of hours: Love poems to God* (A. Barrows & M. Macy, Trans.). Penguin. (Original German work published 1905)

Ro, C. (2020, August 26). *The surprising upsides of worrying.* BBC. https://www.bbc.com/future/article/20200824-why-worrying-isnt-as-bad-as-you-think

Roberts, J. W. (1982). Strategy, morality, and worldview of the Afroamerican spirituals and trickster tales. *The Western Journal of Black Studies, 6*(2), 101-107.

Rochat, P. (2003). Five levels of self-awareness as they unfold early in life. *Consciousness and Cognition, 12*, 717-731.

Rogers, C. R. (1951). *Client-centered therapy: Its current practice, implications and theory.* Boston: Houghton Mifflin.

Rogers, C. R. (1963). The concept of the fully functioning person. *Psychotherapy: Theory, Research & Practice, 1*(1), 17–26

Rogers, C. R. (1995). *On becoming a person: A therapist's view of psychotherapy.* Houghton Mifflin. (Original work published in 1961)

Rose, S. & Noel, D. (2019). *A yogic path oracle card deck and guidebook.* Alpha

Rosmarin, D. H., & Koenig, H. G. (Eds.). (2020). *Handbook of spirituality, religion, and mental health.* Academic Press.

Ross, S., Bossis, A., Guss, J., Agin-Liebes, G., Malone, T., Cohen, B., Mennenga, S. E., Belser, A., Kalliontzi, K., Babb, J., Su, Z., Corby, P., & Schmidt, B. L. (2016). Rapid and sustained symptom reduction following psilocybin treatment for anxiety and depression in patients with life-threatening cancer: A randomized controlled trial. *Journal of Psychopharmacology, 30*(12), 1165-1180.

Rushing, J. H., & Frentz, T. S. (1995). *Projecting the shadow: The cyborg hero in American film.* The University of Chicago Press.

Russel, D. O. (Director). (2004). *I heart Huckabees* [Film]. Fox Searchlight.

Russell, K. (Director). (1980). *Altered states* [Film]. Warner Bros.

Russo, A., & Russo, J. (Directors). (2016). *Captain America: Civil war* [Film]. Marvel Studios.

Russo, A., & Russo, J. (Directors). (2018). *Avengers: Infinity wars* [Film]. Marvel Studios.

Russo, A., & Russo, J. (Directors). (2019). *Avengers: Endgame* [Film]. Marvel Studios.

Sagan, C. (2013). *smos: With a new foreword by Neil deGrasse Tyson & introduction by Ann Druyan.* Ballantine Books. (Original work published 1980)

Sahney, S., & Benton, M. J. (2008). Recovery from the most profound mass extinction of all time. *Proceedings of the Royal Society: Biological Sciences, 275*(1636), 759–765.

Said, E. W. (2008). *Joseph Conrad and the fiction of autobiography.* Columbia University Press.

Saigle, V., Dubljević, V., & Racine, E. (2018). The impact of a landmark neuroscience study on free will: A qualitative analysis of articles using Libet and colleagues' methods. *AJOB Neuroscience, 9*(1), 29-41.

Sartre, J. P. (1992). *Being and nothingness: A phenomenological essay on ontology* (H. E. Barnes, Trans.). Washington Square Press. (Original published in French 1943)

Saroglou, V. (2020). *The psychology of religion.* Routledge.

Saunders, R., Jacobvitz, D., Zaccagnino, M., Beverung, L. M., & Hazen, N. (2011). Pathways to earned-security: The role of alternative support figures. *Attachment & Human Development, 13*(4), 403-420.

Schlebusch, C. M., Malmström, H., Günther, T., Sjödin, P., Coutinho, A., Edlund, H., Munters, A. R., Vicente, M., Steyn, M., Soodyall, H., Lombard, M., & Jakobsson, M. (2017). Southern African ancient genomes estimate modern human divergence to 350,000 to 260,000 years ago. *Science, 358*, 652-655.

Schopf, J. W., Kitajima, K., Spicuzza, M. J., Kudryavtsev, A. B., & Valley, J. W. (2018). SIMS analyses of the oldest known assemblage of microfossils document their taxon-correlated carbon isotope compositions. *Proceedings of the National Academy of Sciences of the United States of America, 115*(1), 53-58.

Schroeter, J. (Ed.). *After shock: The world's foremost futurists reflect on 50 years of future shock—and look ahead to the next 50.* John August Media.

Schwartz, R. C. (2013). Moving from acceptance toward transformation with internal family systems (IFS). *Journal of Clinical Psychology: In Session, 69*(8), 805-816.

Schwartz, R., & Halegoua, G. R. (2015). The spatial self: Location-based identity performance on social media. *New Media & Society, 17*(10), 1643-1660.

Schwartz, R. C., & Sweezy, M. (2020). Internal Family Systems Therapy (2nd ed.). Guilford Press.

Scott, R. (Director). (1979). *Alien* [Film]. 20th Century Fox.

Scott, R. (Director). (2012). *Prometheus* [Film]. Scott Free Productions.

Scott, R. (Director). (1985). *Blade runner* [Film]. The Ladd Company.

Sherman, R. A., Nave, C. S., & Funder, D. C. (2010). Situational similarity and personality predict behavioral consistency. *Journal of Personality and Social Psychology, 99*(2), 330–343.

Sedgwick, E. K. (2003). *Touching feeling: Affect, pedagogy, performativity.* Duke University Press.

Segal, R. A. (Ed.). (1998). *Jung on mythology.* Princeton University Press.

Seidman, G. (2013). Self-presentation and belonging on Facebook: How personality influences social media use and motivations. *Personality and Individual Differences, 54*(3), 402-407.

Sender, R., Fuchs, S., & Milo, R. (2016). Revised estimates for the number of human and bacteria cells in the body. *PLOS Biology, 14*(8), e1002533

Shakespeare, W. (n.d.). Speech: "All the world's a stage." *Poetry Foundation.* https://www.poetry foundation.org/poems/56966/speech-all-the-worlds-a-stage

Shakespeare, W. (1905). *Hamlet.* E. P. Dutton & Company. (Original work 1609)

Sharot, T. (2011). The optimism bias. *Current Biology, 21*(23), R941-R945.

Siegel, E. (2015). *Beyond the galaxy: How humanity looked beyond our Milky Way and discovered the entire universe.* World Scientific Publishing.

Silton, N. R., Flannelly, K. J., Galek, K., & Ellison, C. G. (2014). Beliefs about God and mental health among American adults. *Journal of Religion and Health, 53,* 1285-1296.

Sinitsyn, N. A., & Yan, B. (2020, September 21). *The quantum butterfly noneffect: A familiar concept from chaos theory turns out to work differently in the quantum world.* Scientific American. https://www.scientificamerican.com/article/the-quantum-butterfly-noneffect/

Sjöstedt-H, P. (2015). *Neumenautics: Metaphysics–Meta-Ethics–Psychedelics.* Psychedelic Press.

Sloshower, J., Guss, J., Krause, R., Wallace, R. M., Williams, M. T., Reed, S., & Skinta, M. D. (2020). Psilocybin-assisted therapy of major depressive disorder using Acceptance and Commitment Therapy as a therapeutic frame. *Journal of Contextual Behavioral Science, 15,* 12-19.

Smith, H. (1963). Do drugs have religious import? *The Journal of Philosophy, 61,* 517-539.

Smith, H. (1991). *The world's religions: Our great wisdom traditions.* HarperCollins. (Original work published in 1958)

Smith, H. (2003). *Beyond the postmodern mind: The place of meaning in a global civilization* (3rd ed.). Quest Books.

Smith, H., Grob, C., Jesse, R., Bravo, G., Agar, A., & Walsh, R. (2004). Do drugs have religious import? A 40 year retrospective. *Journal of Humanistic Psychology, 44*(2), 120-140.

Smith, J. R., & Haslam, A. (Eds.). (2017). *Social psychology: Revisiting the classic studies.* Sage.

Snarey, J.R. (1985). Cross-cultural universality of social-moral development: A critical review of Kohlbergian research. *Psychological bulletin, 97*(2), 202-232.

Snyder, Z. (Director). (2009). *Watchmen* [Film]. Warner Bros.

Snyder-Mackler, N., Burger, J. R., Gaydosh, L., Belsky, D. W., Noppert, G. A., Campos, F. A., Bartolomucci, A., Yang, Y. C., Aiello, A. E., O'Rand, A., Harris, K. M., Shively, C. A., Alberts, S. C. & Tung, J. (2020). Social determinants of health and survival in humans and other animals. *Science, 368*(6493), 1-12.

Sober, E. (2015). *Ockham's razor: A user's manual.* Cambridge University Press.

Soderbergh, S. (2011). *Contagion* [Film]. Participant Media.

Solomon, P. T. (2011). *Finding Joe* [Film]. Pat & Pat Productions.

Soriah, & Sain, A. (2011). Ximehua [Song]. On *Eztica* [Album]. Sain/Ugalde.

Sorokowski, P., Sorokowska, A., Karwowski, M., Groyecka, A., Aavik, T., Akello, G., ... & Atama, C. S. (2020). Universality of the triangular theory of love: Adaptation and psychometric properties of the Triangular Love Scale in 25 countries. *The Journal of Sex Research,* 1-10.

Space.com. (n.d.). https://www.space.com

Spielberg, S. (Director). (1977). *Close encounters of the third kind* [Film]. EMI Films.

St. John of the Cross. (2002). *Dark night of the soul* (M. Starr, Trans.). Riverhead Books.

Stahl, B., & Goldstein, E. (2010). *A mindfulness- based stress reduction workbook.* New Harbinger.

Stamets, P. (2005). *Mycelium running: How mushrooms can help save the world.* Ten Speed Press.

Stauffer, C. S., Anderson, B. A, Ortigo, K. M., & Woolley, J. D. (2021, in press). Psilocybin-assisted group therapy and attachment: Observed reduction in attachment anxiety and influences of attachment insecurity on the psilocybin experience. *ACS Pharmacology & Translational Science.* https://doi.org/10.1021/acsptsci.0c00169

Stavropoulos, S. (2003). *The beginning of all wisdom: Timeless advice from the ancient Greeks.* Marlowe & Company.

Stein, M. (2015). *The principle of individuation: Toward the development of human consciousness.* Chiron Publications.

Sternberg, R. J. (1986). A triangular theory of love. *Psychological Review, 93*(2), 119-135.

Sternberg, R. J., & Halpern, D. F. (Eds.). (2020). *Critical thinking in psychology* (2nd ed.). Cambridge University Press.

Stoker, B. (2001). *Dracula* (Modern Library Paperback Ed.). Random House, Inc. (Original work published 1897)

Stone, J. R. (Ed.). (2002). *The essential Max Müller: On language, mythology, and religion.* Palgrave.

Storr, A. (Ed.). (1999). *The essential Jung: Selected and introduced by Anthony Storr* (R.F.C. Hull, Trans). Princeton University Press.

Strassman, R. (2001). *DMT: The spirit molecule: A doctor's revolutionary research into the biology of near-death and mystical experiences.* Park Street Press.

Swanson, L. R. (2018). Unifying theories of psychedelic drug effects. *Frontiers in Pharmacology, 9*(172), 1-23.

Taylor, A. (Director). (2015). *Terminator genisys* [Film]. Skydance Productions.

TEDx Talks. (2017, September 27). *On the absurd–Rebekka Reinhard–TEDxUniHeidelberg* [Video]. https://www.youtube.com/watch?v=_QFpB0ZXBkk&feature=youtu.be

Teilhard de Chardin, P. (1959). *The phenomenon of man* (B. Wall, Trans.). William Collins Sons. (Original French work published 1955)

Tellegen, A., & Atkinson, G. (1974). Openness to absorbing and self-altering experiences ("absorption"), a trait related to hypnotic susceptibility. *Journal of Abnormal Psychology, 83*(3), 268-277.

Templeton, J. (1999). *Agape love: A tradition in eight world religions.* Templeton Foundation Press.

The Center for Compassion and Altruism Research and Education. (n.d.). *Compassion.* http://ccare.stanford.edu/research/wiki/compassion-definitions/compassion/ http://ccare.stanford.edu

The Cranberries. (1993). *Everybody else is doing it, so why* aren't we? [Album]. Windmill Lane Studios.

The Doors. (1967). Break on through (to the other side) [Song]. On *The Doors* [Album]. Elektra.

The Introverted Thinker. (2019, April 8). *Interview with Dr Carl Jung 1957* [Video]. https://www.youtube.com/watch?v=_QFpB0ZXBkk&feature=youtu.be

Theophanidis, P. (2014, August 18). *"Whosoever is delighted in solitude…" Francis Bacon*. Aphelis. https://aphelis.net/whosoever-delighted-solitude-bacon/

Thir, M., & Batthyány, A. (2016). The state of empirical research on logotherapy and existential analysis. In A. Batthyány (Ed.), *Logotherapy and existential analysis: Proceedings of the Viktor Frankl Institute Vienna, Volume 1* (pp. 53-74). Springer.

Toffler, A. (1970). *Future shock*. Bantam Books.

Tolkien, J. R. R. (1994). *The lord of the rings* (One- Volume Ed.). Houghton Mifflin. (Original work published 1954 and 1955)

Trip, S., Bora, C. H., Marian, M., Halmajan, A., and Drugas, M. I. (2019) Psychological mechanisms involved in radicalization and extremism. A rational emotive behavioral conceptualization. *Frontiers in Psychology*, 10(437), 1-8.

Trippingly Peak Experiences. (2019, March 1). *The Mystical Experience Questionnaire (30 Questions)*. Trippingly Peak Experiences. https://www.trippingly.net/lsd-studies/2018/5/22/the-mystical-experience-questionnaire-30-questions

Truity. (n.d.). *Truity*. https://truity.com

Tully, R. (2012). Collision course. *Nature*, 488, 600–601.

Turner, J. C., & Onorato, R. S. (1999). Social identity, personality, and the self-concept: A self-categorization perspective. In T. R. Tyler, R. M. Kramer, & O. P. John (Eds.), *The psychology of the social self* (pp. 11-46). Psychology Press.

Twenge, J. M., Joiner, T. E., Rogers, M. L., & Martin, G. N. (2018). Increases in depressive symptoms, suicide-related outcomes, and suicide rates among US adolescents after 2010 and links to increased new media screen time. *Clinical Psychological Science*, 6(1), 3-17.

Twohig, M. P., & Levin, M. E. (2017). Acceptance and Commitment Therapy as a treatment for anxiety and depression: A review. *Psychiatric Clinics*, 40(4), 751-770.

Tyson, N. d. (2017). *Astrophysics for people in a hurry*. W. W. Norton & Company.

Vaillant, G. E. (1994). Ego mechanisms of defense and personality psychopathology. *Journal of Abnormal Psychology*, 103(1), 44-50.

Van Cappellen, P., Saroglou, V., Iweins, C., Piovesana, M., & Fredrickson, B. L. (2013). Self-transcendent positive emotions increase spirituality through basic world assumptions. *Cognition & Emotion*, 27(8), 1378-1394

van Deurzen, E. (2012). *Existential counseling and psychotherapy in practice* (3rd ed.). Sage.

van Dijck, J. (2013). 'You have one identity': Performing the self on Facebook and LinkedIn. *Media, Culture & Society*, 35(2), 199-215.

Vibrant Emotional Health & Substance Abuse and Mental Health Services Administration (SAMSA). (n.d.). *National Suicide Prevention Lifeline*. Retried from https://www.SuicidePreventionLifeline.org

Villeneuve, D. (Director). (2016). *Arrival* [Film]. FilmNation Entertainment.

Villeneuve, D. (Director). (2017). *Blade runner 2049* [Film]. Alcon Entertainment.

Villoldo, A., Baron-Reid, C., Lobos, M., & DellaGrottaglia, J. (2018). *Mystical shaman oracle deck and guidebook*. Hay House, Inc.

Vogel, E. A., Rose, J. P., Roberts, L. R. & Eckles, K. (2015). Social comparison, social media, and self- esteem. *Psychology of Popular Media Culture*, 3(4), 206-222.

Vogler, C. (2020). *The writer's journey: Mythic structure for writers* (M. Montez, Illus.; 25th anniversary / 4th ed). Michael Wiese Productions.

Vos, J., Craig, M., & Cooper, M. (2015). Existential therapies: A meta-analysis of their effects on psychological outcomes. *Journal of Consulting and Clinical Psychology*, 83(1), 115-128.

Vos, J., & Vitali, D. (2018). The effects of psychological meaning-centered therapies on quality of life and psychological stress: A metaanalysis. *Palliative & Supportive Care*, 16(5), 608-632.

von Franz, M.-L. (1968). The process of individuation. In C. G. Jung and A. Jaffé's (Eds.) *Man and his symbols* (pp. 157-254). Dell Publishing.

Wachowski, La., & Wachowski, Li. (Directors). (1999). *The matrix* [Film]. Warner Bros.

Wachowski, La., & Wachowski, Li. (Directors). (2003a). *The matrix reloaded* [Film]. Warner Bros.

Wachowski, La., & Wachowski, Li. (Directors). (2003b). *The matrix revolutions* [Film]. Warner Bros.

Wagner, M. T., Mithoefer, M. C., Mithoefer, A. T., MacAulay, R. K., Jerome, L., Yazar-Klosinski, B., & Doblin, R. (2017). Therapeutic effect of increased openness: Investigating mechanism of action in MDMA-assisted psychotherapy. *Journal of Psychopharmacology*, 31(8), 967-974.

Waheed, N. (2019). *Salt* [eBook edition]. CreateSpace.

Walle, E. A., Reschke, P. J., & Knothe, J. M. (2017). Social referencing: Defining and delineating a basic process of emotion. *Emotion Review*, 9(3), 245-252.

Walser, R. D., & Westrup, D. (2007). *Acceptance and Commitment Therapy for the treatment of post-traumatic stress disorder and trauma-related problems: A practitioner's guide to using mindfulness and acceptance strategies*. New Harbinger.

Walsh, R. (1994). The making of a shaman: Calling, training, and culmination. *Journal of Humanistic Psychology*, 34(3), 7-30.

Watts, A. (1999). *The way of zen*. Vintage Spiritual Classics. (Original work published 1957)

Watts, R., & Luoma, J. B. (2020). The use of the psychological flexibility model to support psychedelic assisted therapy. *Journal of Contextual Behavioral Science*, 15, 92-102.

Waugaman, R. (1973). The intellectual relationship between Nietzsche and Freud. *Psychiatry*, 36(4), 458-467.

Webb, M. (Director). (2009). *(500) days of summer* [Film]. Dune Entertainment.

Webb, S. (2015). *If the universe is teeming with aliens...Where is everybody?: Seventy-five solutions to the fermi paradox and the problem of extraterrestrial life* (2nd Ed). Springer.

Weir, P. (1977). *The last wave* [Film]. McElroy & McElroy.

Welwood, J. (1982). Vulnerability and power in the therapeutic process: Existential and Buddhist perspectives. *The Journal of Transpersonal Psychology*, 14(2), 125-139.

Welwood, J. (2000). *Toward a psychology of awakening: Buddhism, psychotherapy, and the path of personal and spiritual transformation*. Shambhala Publications.

Wesson, P. S. (1990). Cosmology, extraterrestrial intelligence, and a resolution of the Fermi-Hart paradox. *Quarterly Journal of the Royal Astronomical Society, 31*, 161-170.

Westen, D. (2008). *The political brain: The role of emotion in deciding the fate of the nation.* PublicAffairs.

Westen, D., Gabbard, G. O., & Ortigo, K. M. (2008). Psychoanalytic approaches to personality. In O. P. John, R. W. Robins, & L. A. Pervin, *Handbook of personality: Theory and research* (3rd Edition) (pp. 61-113). Guilford Press.

Wilmer, H. A. (2015). *Practical Jung: Nuts and bolts of Jungian psychotherapy (2nd ed.).* Chiron Publications.

Wilson, C. (1959). *The stature of man.* Houghton Mifflin.

Wilson, S., Stroud, C. B., & Durbin, C. E. (2017). Interpersonal dysfunction in personality disorders: Meta-analytic review. *Psychological Bulletin, 143*(7), 677-734.

Winnicott, D. W. (1958). The capacity to be alone. *International Journal of Psycho-Analysis, 39*, 416-420.

Winnicott, D. W. (1960). The theory of the parent-infant relationship. *International Journal of Psycho-analysis, 41*, 585-595.

Wise, R. (Director). (1979). *Star trek: The motion picture* [Film]. Paramount.

Witten, E. (1998). Magic, mystery, and matrix. *Notices of the AMS, 45*(9), 1124-1129.

Wittmann, M., & Lehnhoff, S. (2005). Age effects in perception of time. *Psychological Reports, 97*(3), 921-935.

Wolfson, P., & Hartelius, G. (Eds.). (2016). *The ketamine papers: Science, therapy, and transformation.* MAPS.

World Health Organization. (2020). *World health statistics 2020: Monitoring health for the sustainable development goals (SDG).* https://apps.who.int/iris/bitstream/handle/10665/332070/9789240005105-eng.pdf

Wortmann, J. H., Eisen, E., Hundert, C., Jordan, A. H., Smith, M. W., Nash, W. P., & Litz, B. T. (2017). Spiritual features of war-related moral injury: A primer for clinicians. *Spirituality in Clinical Practice, 4*(4), 249-261.

Wrubel, S. (Writer), Joy, L. (Writer), & Getzinger, J. (Director). (2020, April 19). Decoherence (Season 3, Episode 6) [TV series episode]. In J. J. Abrams, J. Nolan, L. Joy, R. J. Lewis, A. Wickham, B. Stephenson, & D. Thé (Executive Producers), *Westworld.* HBO Entertainment; Kilter Films; Bad Robot Productions; Warner Bros. Television.

Walden, K. S., & Rassouli. (2018). *The hero's journey dream oracle.* Llewellyn Publications.

White, F. (2014). *The overview effect: Space exploration and human evolution* (3rd ed.). American Institute of Aeronautics and Astronautics.

Wu, X., Kaminga, A. C., Dai, W., Deng, J., Wang, Z., Pan, X., & Liu, A. (2019). The prevalence of moderate-to-high posttraumatic growth: A systematic review and meta-analysis. *Journal of Affective Disorders, 243*, 408-415.

Wyatt, R. (Director). *Captive state* [Film]. Participant

Yaden, D. B., Haidt, J., Hood Jr, R. W., Vago, D. R., & Newberg, A. B. (2017). The varieties of self-transcendent experience. *Review of General Psychology, 21*(2), 143-160.

Yaden, D. B., Iwry, J., Slack, K. J., Eichstaedt, J. C., Zhao, Y., Vaillant, G. E., & Newberg, A. B. (2016). The overview effect: awe and self-transcendent experience in space flight. *Psychology of Consciousness: Theory, Research, and Practice, 3*(1), 1-11.

Yaden, D. B., Kaufman, S. B., Hyde, E., Chirico, A., Gaggioli, A., Zhang, J. W., & Keltner, D. (2019). The development of the Awe Experience Scale (AWE-S): A multifactorial measure for a complex emotion. *The Journal of Positive Psychology, 14*(4), 474-488.

Yalom, I. D. (1980). *Existential psychotherapy.* Basic Books.

Yalom, I. D. (2008). *Staring at the sun: Overcoming the terror of death.* Jossey-Bass (Wiley).

Yan, B., & Sinitsyn, N. A. (2020). Recovery of damaged information and the out-of-time-ordered correlators. *Physical Review Letters, 125*, 040605.

Yates, D. (Director). (2007). *Harry Potter and the order of the phoenix* [Film]. Warner Bros.

Yates, D. (Director). (2009). *Harry Potter and the half-blood prince* [Film]. Warner Bros.

Yeats, W. B. (2008). *Collected poems of W. B. Yeats* (R. J Finneran, Ed.; New ed.). Collier Books.

Younger Brother. (2007). Psychic gibbon [Song]. On *The last days of gravity* [Album]. Twisted.

Zeifman, R. J., Palhano-Fontes, F., Hallak, J., Arcoverde, E., Maia-Oliveira, J. P., & Araujo, D. B. (2019). The impact of ayahuasca on suicidality: Results from a randomized controlled trial. *Frontiers in Pharmacology, 10*, 1325.

Zell, E., Strickhouser, J. E., Sedikides, C., & Alicke, M. D. (2020). The better-than-average effect in comparative self-evaluation: A comprehensive review and meta-analysis. *Psychological Bulletin, 146*(2), 118–149.

Zemeckis, R. (Director). (1997). *Contact* [Film]. South Side Amusement Company.

Zenasni, F., Besancon, M., & Lubart, T. (2008). Creativity and tolerance of ambiguity: An empirical study. *The Journal of Creative Behavior, 42*(1), 61-73.

Interpersonal Circumplex 164, 165, 290
Interstellar 31, 39
Intimacy 159, 169, 177, 202, 293, 305,
Introversion 253, 254
Intuition or Intuiting 255, 256, 258,
   301, 345, 371
Isolation 158, 286

James, William 174
Jedi 84
Jesus 211, 252, 327
Joker 296
Journey Waypoint 27, 51, 81, 119, 149,
   187, 241, 279, 325
Jung, Carl Gustav 53, 56, 57, 59, 63,
   159, 172, 176, 210, 249, 250, 260,
   290, 293, 298, 305, 310, 332, 343,
   368

Ketamine 265, 270, 271
Kierkegaard, Søren 193, 197, 203
King T'challa 325
Knowledge 127, 227, 328
Koans 214

Leary, Timothy 127-129, 164, 299, 300,
   347
Libido 14
Light Triad 291, 292
Loneliness 196
Lord Byron 149
Loss 123, 128, 196
Lost in Translation 132
Love 171, 227, 286, 287, 305, 341
LSD (Lycergic acid diethylamide) 99,
   109, 299, 300

Magical Thinking 210, 211
Man's Search for Meaning 199
Mandala 356, 362

Mantra 86
Marvel 6, 73, 346
MDMA (3,4-Methylenedioxymetham-
   phetamine) 60, 69, 114
Meaning 97, 114, 187, 189, 190, 191,
   198, 199, 208, 212, 216, 219, 223,
   231, 236, 286
Meaninglessness 196, 223
Meditation 17, 45, 49, 75, 79, 91, 107,
   111, 142, 146, 180, 184, 219, 223,
   268, 272, 316, 320, 356, 360
Memory 261
Meta 340, 341, 347, 357
Metaphysical 42, 64, 204, 207
Metzner, Ralph 127, 128, 139
Microdosing 303, 304
Middle Way 327
Mind-body connection 91
Mindfulness 81, 103
Mitwelt 196
Mono no aware 131, 132, 173
Monomyth 5-7, 61, 113, 328, 338
   See also: Hero's Journey
Mood 4, 14, 57, 91, 119, 126, 335
Motivations 54, 196, 202
Mysteries 36, 40, 52, 65
Mythology 1, 61, 63, 113, 151, 167,
   187, 189, 204, 284, 296, 297, 327,
   330, 342, 346, 351, 352

Nature 122, 149
Neuroplasticity 69, 210
Neuroticism 291, 293
Non-human 7-9, 38, 52, 154, 172, 310

Observed 285
Observer 27, 285
OCEAN 67
Ockham's Razor 121

BEYOND
THE NARROW LIFE